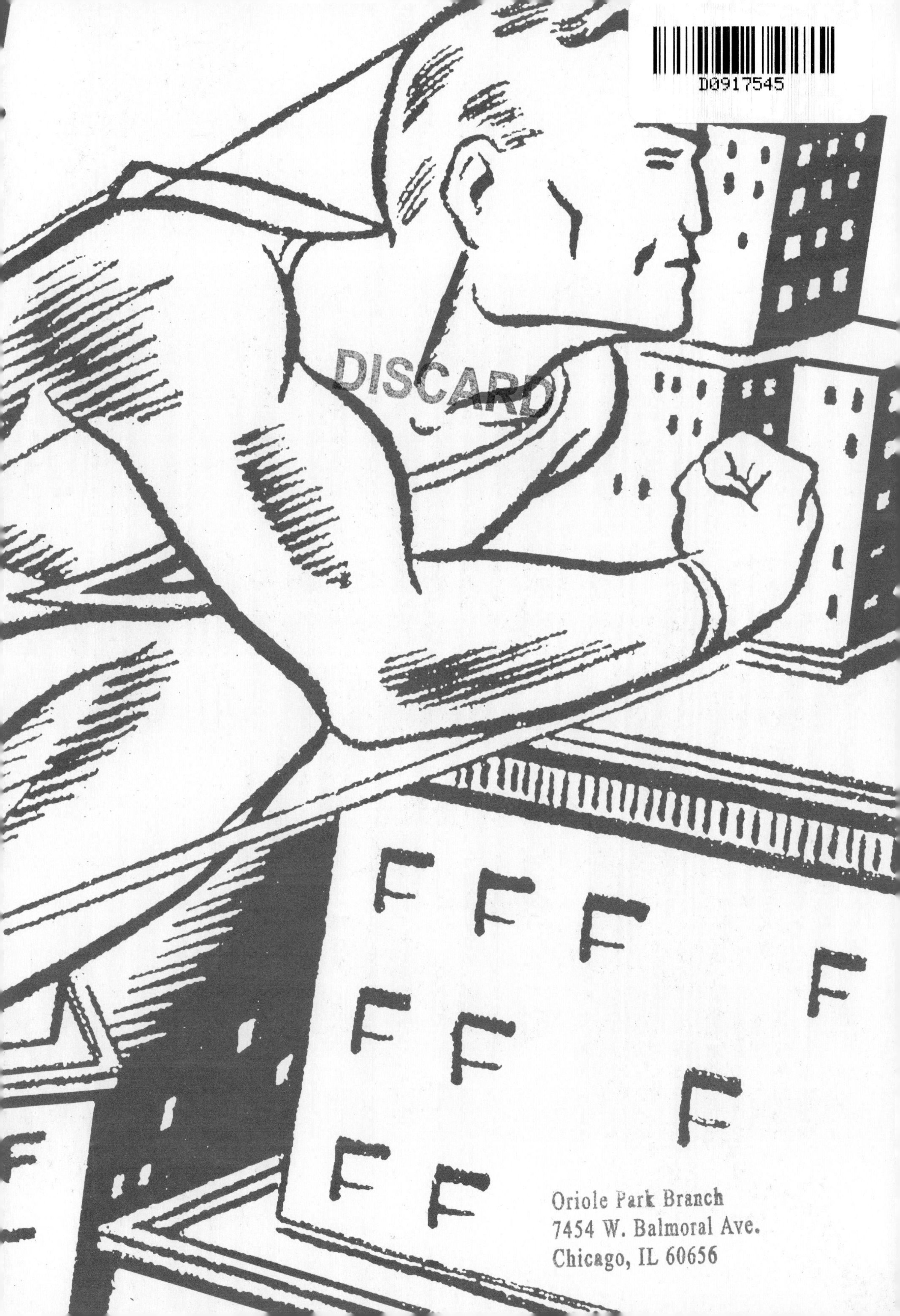

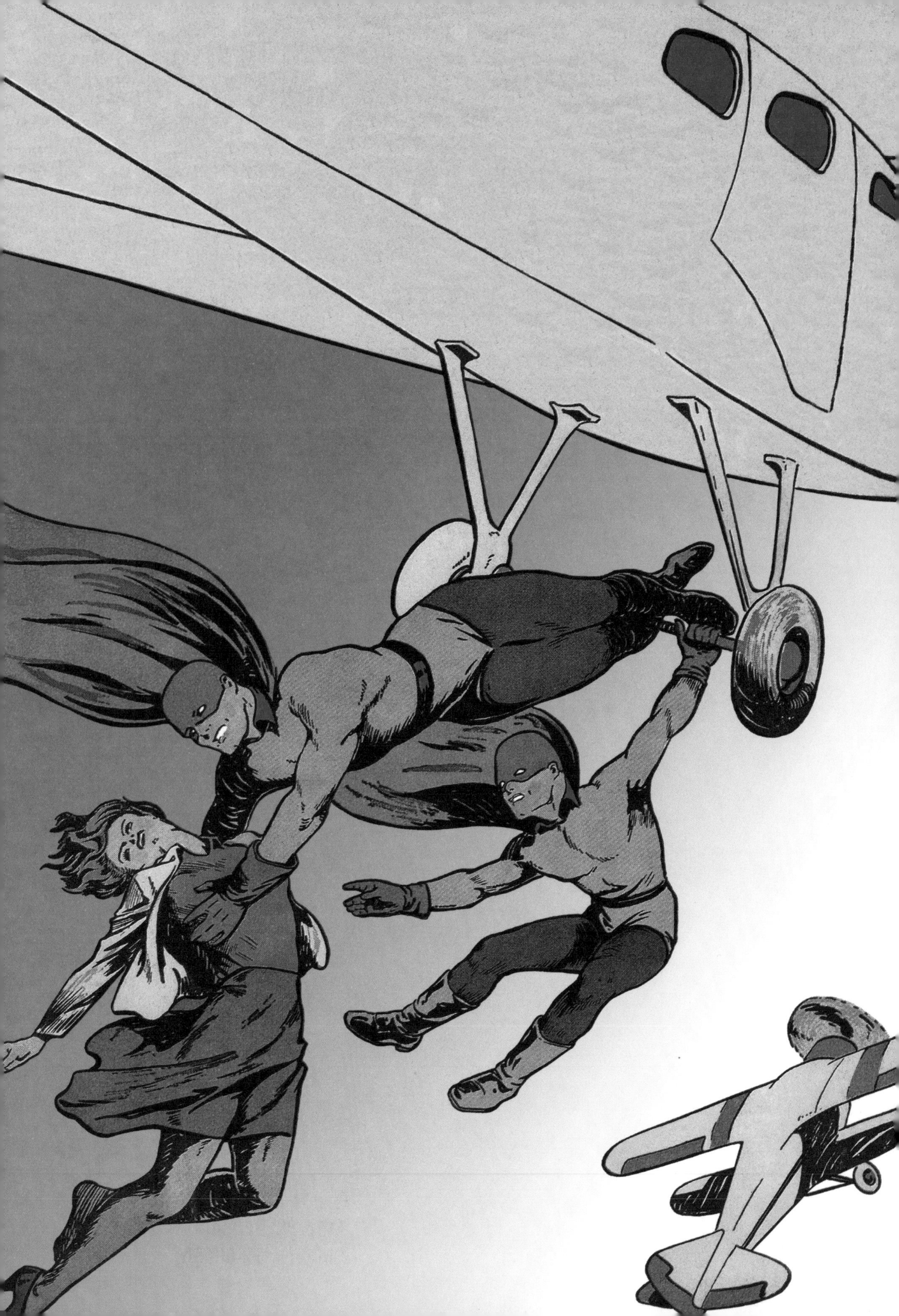

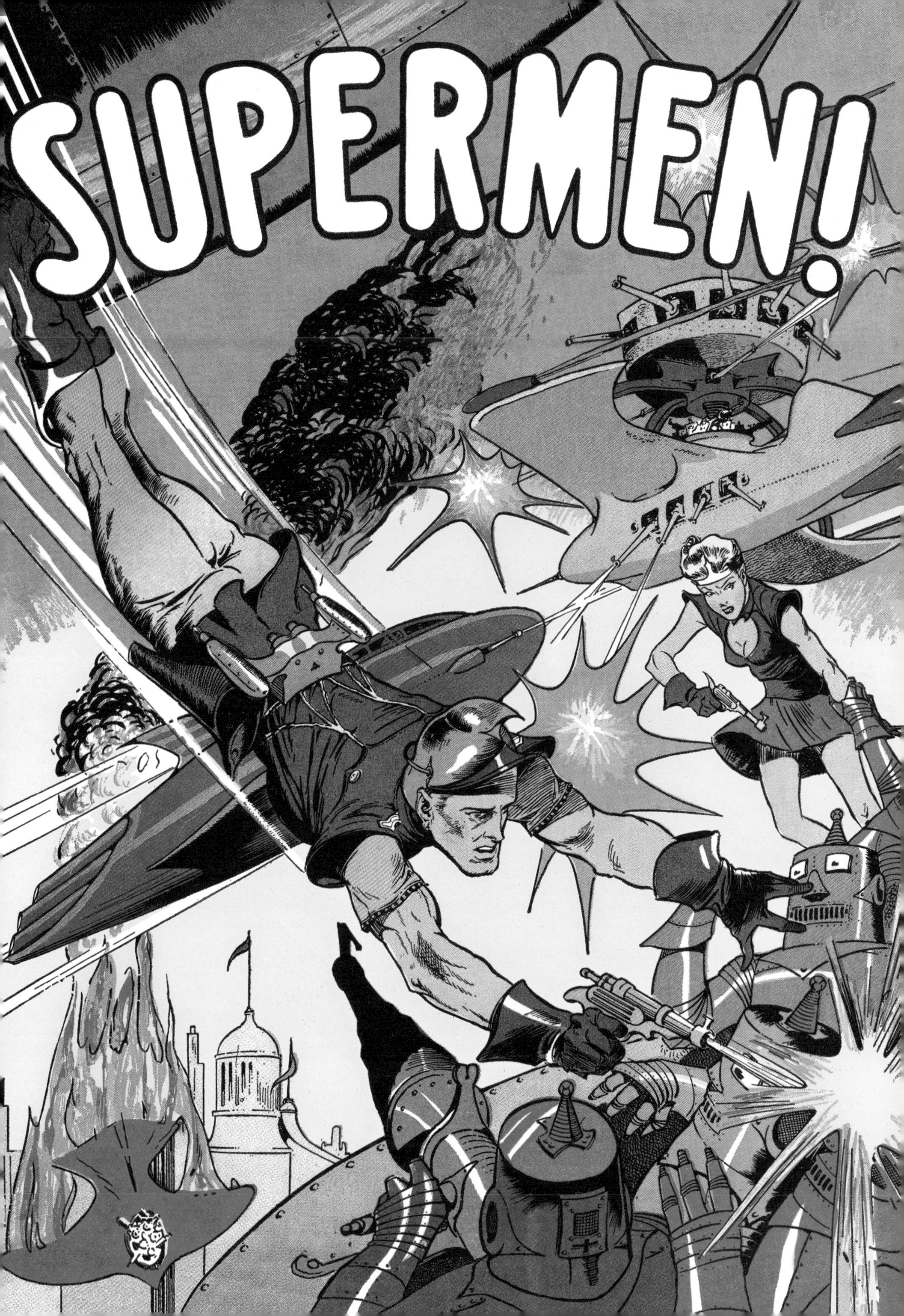
SUPERMEN!

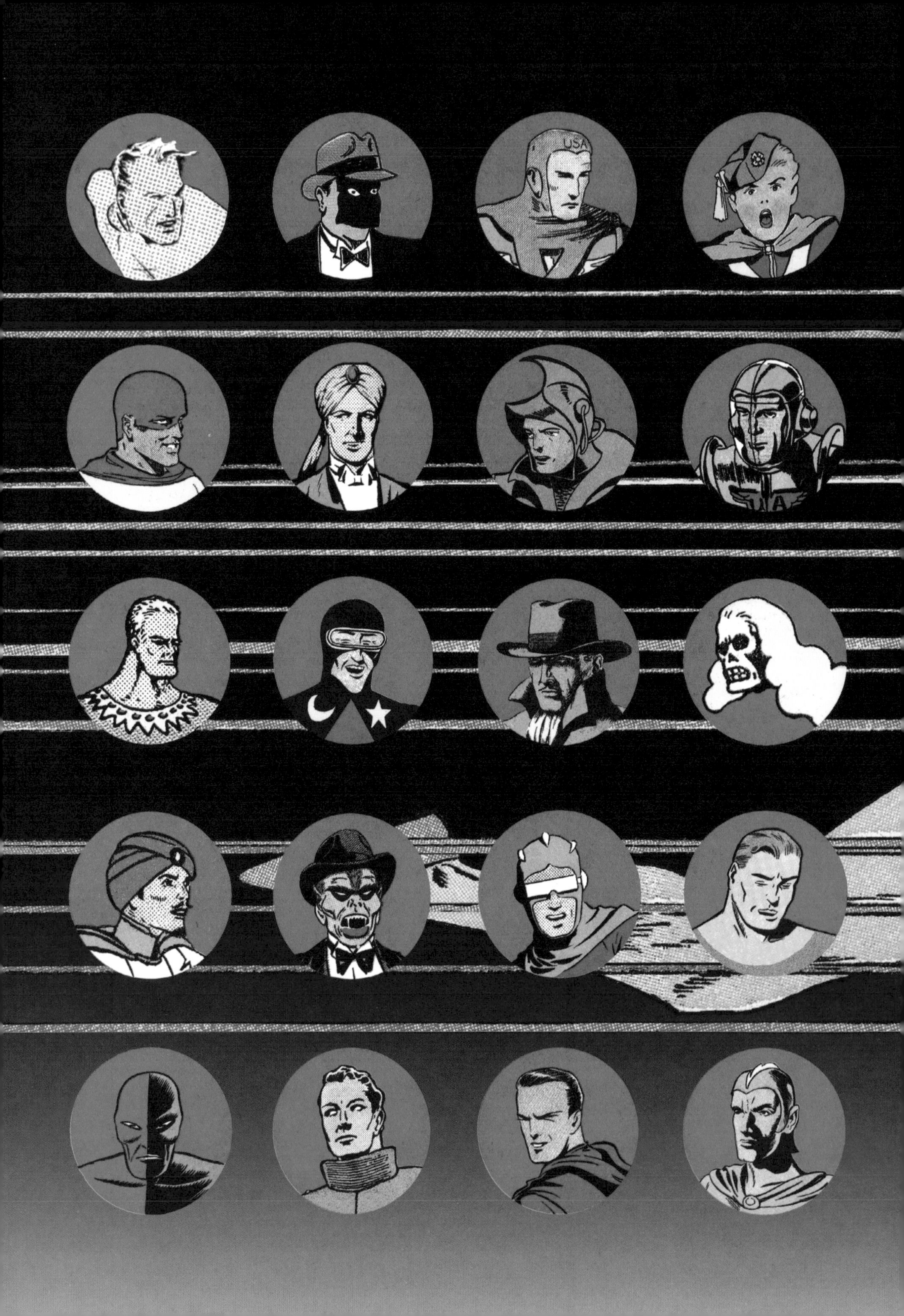

# SUPERMEN!

## THE FIRST WAVE OF COMIC BOOK HEROES 1936-41

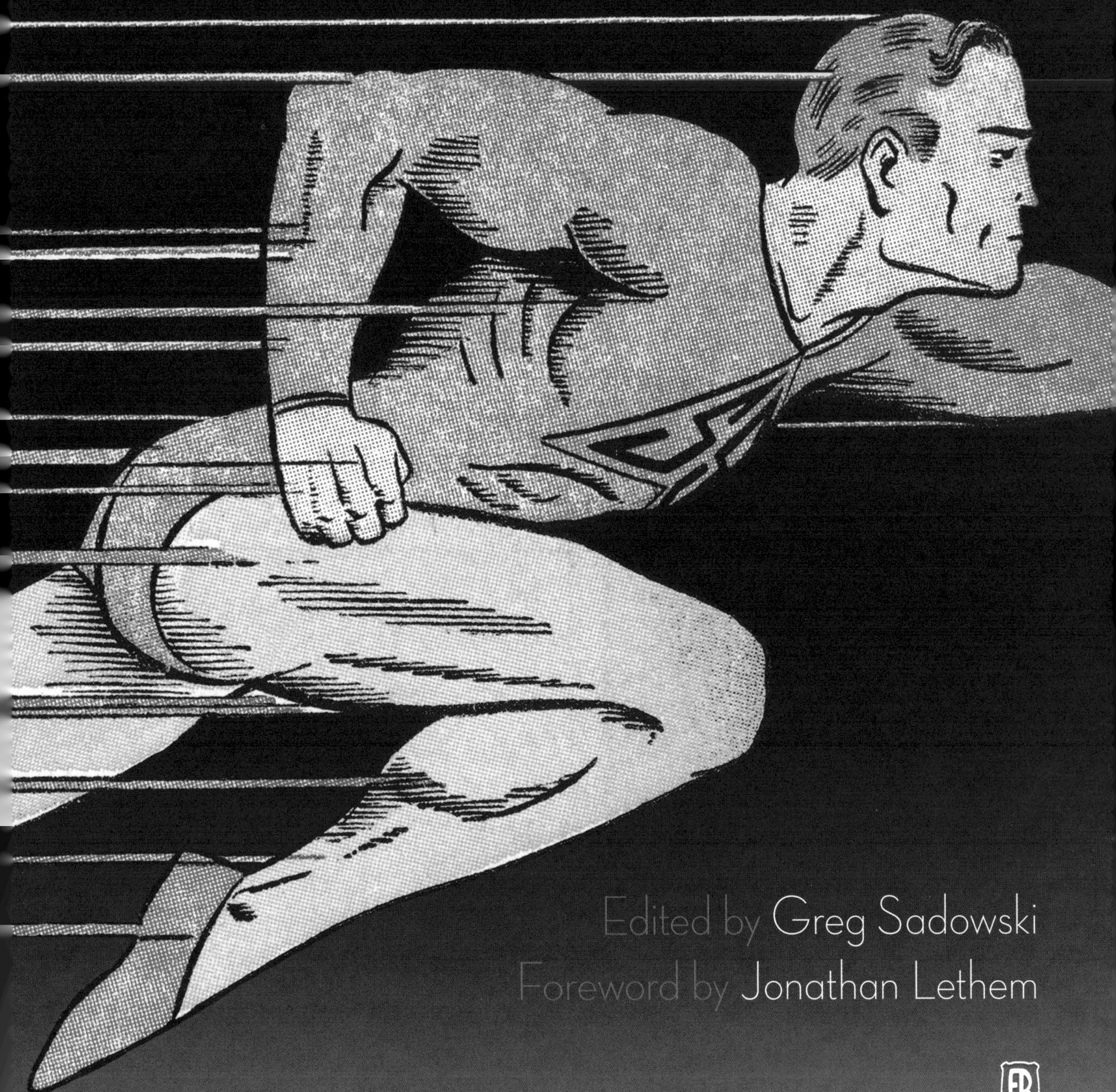

Edited by Greg Sadowski

Foreword by Jonathan Lethem

FANTAGRAPHICS BOOKS

Seattle, Washington

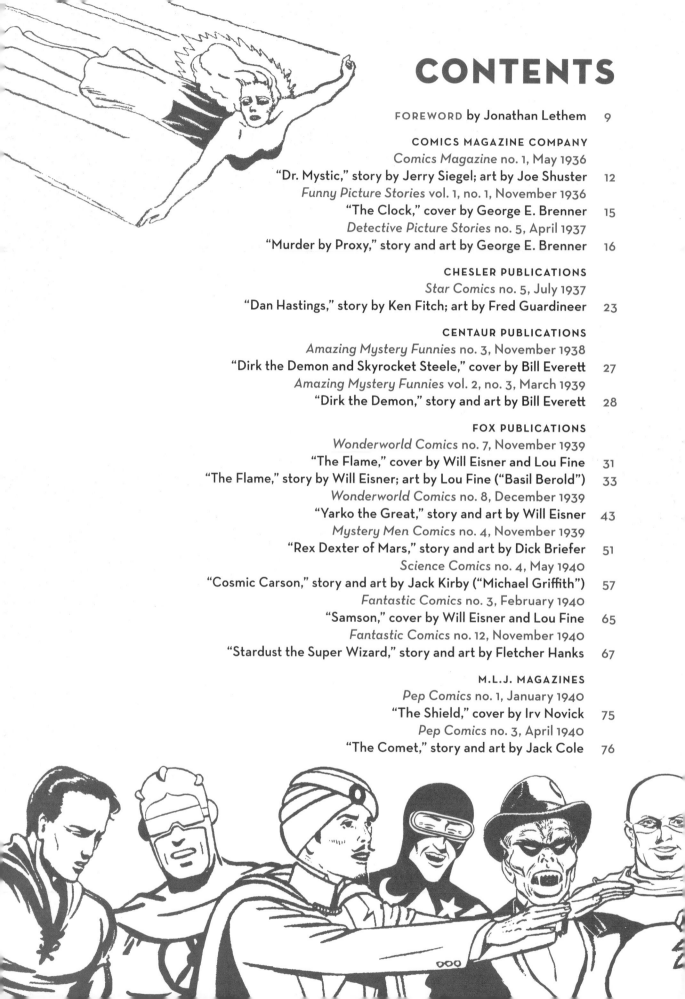

# CONTENTS

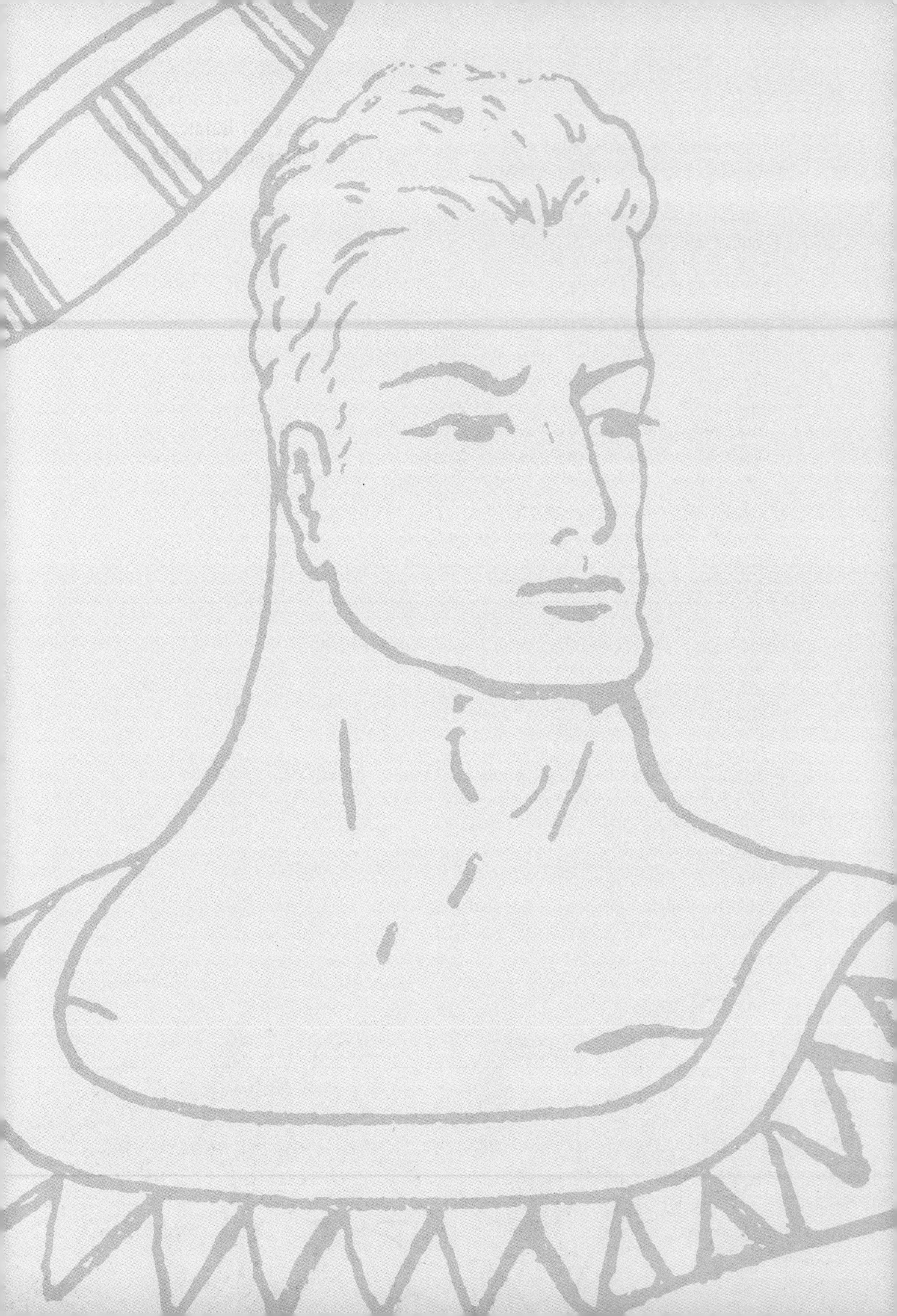

# Foreword
## by Jonathan Lethem

SO, ANSWER THE QUESTION, EVEN IF ONLY IN THE PRIVACY OF YOUR MIND:
Who was your first? No, go further back even than your 'official' first —
recollect, if you can, not the first superhero with whom you consummated
your curiosities, but the first who gave you an inkling, the first to stir the
curiosities you hadn't know you possessed, the first human outline in a
cape flashing through your dawning gaze. Was it Adam West's Batman?
A tattered five-year-old issue of *The Silver Surfer*, in some godlike prodigal
older brother's dorm? A *Mad Magazine* parody? Underdog? Some kid on
your summer beach who clutched a towel to either side of his neck and
leaped yelping off a dune and then looked at you like you were stupid for
not getting the reference that burned so powerfully in his mind?

If you're approximately of my generation, things untangled themselves
pretty quickly, after that first disordered flush of infatuation. Superheroes,
when you looked into the subject, appeared to spring from a few stolid
figures and then to degenerate into a fractious and enthralling rabble. That's
to say, I'm forty-five years old, and for me, Superman and Batman were
pretty much like my parents. The anchor DC characters were heartening to
have around, and good in a crunch, and sometimes, with their long histories,
still surprising when you dug their old photographs out of the trunk — you
hung out with people who looked like that? You dated him? But, increasingly,
dull, and taken for granted. (Wonder Woman, Flash, and Aquaman were
your aunts and uncles, familiar without being vivid.) Marvel's first-order
characters were pretty established too, but they still had the alluring scent of
their fresh invention over them. They were something like cool kids who'd
lived on your block in the decade before you started playing on the street,
and now were off at college or in the army, but their legend persisted. I'd
put Thor and the other Avengers in that range, and the Fantastic Four, and
Hulk, and Dr. Strange. Spider-Man was your older brother, of course — a
great guy, an idol, but he didn't belong to you. What was wholly yours were
your contemporaries, the oddities launching themselves before your eyes:
Ghost Rider and Warlock and Luke Cage and Kobra and Ragman and

Omega the Unknown, or nutty gangs like The Guardians of the Galaxy and The Defenders. These were as thrilling and unreliable as new friends in the schoolyard, and they lived in a world your parents, or Superman, would never even begin to understand. Beyond them lie even more anti-heroic antiheroes, The Watchmen and Invisibles needed to gratify our recomplicating appetites.

It may be latent in human psychology to model the world on a fall-from-innocence, since we each go through one. I can't know, because I speak as an American, and I do know that as a culture we're disastrously addicted to easy fantasies of a halcyon past, one always just fading from view, a land where things were more orderly and simple. (The model is doubly useful, equally open to our patronizing dismissals of the past and to our maudlin comparisons to a corrupted present.) For that reason, so many really smashing cultural investigations open up a window onto the truly disordered and frequently degenerate origins of things we've sentimentalized as pure and whole and pat.

A collection like *Supermen!* works like a reverse-neutron bomb to assumptions about the birth of the superhero image: it tears down the orderly structures of theory and history and leaves the figures standing in full view, staring back at us in all their defiant disorienting particularity, their blazing strangeness. Like Luc Sante's *Low Life*, or Michael Lesy's *Wisconsin Death Trip*, in the place of generalizations about the vanished past it offers a revelatory nightmare of anecdote and evidence that the place we came from is as deep and strange as any place we might have been ourselves, or might imagine we are on the way to going. Just as the drug slang and hippie argot or jive talk that struck me as so characteristic of the 1970s when I came of age so often turned out to be rooted in '20s and '30s jazz-hipster vernacular, just as Pre-Code Hollywood film can so often seem shockingly advanced, so many motifs and gestures we might have claimed as typical of our own postmodern comics-era turn out to be rooted in earlier explorations.

That's not to say this isn't primitive stuff (or that much of the pleasure it imparts is in its crudity and naïveté), only that the primitive stuff, when you turn your eyes to it, turns out to be so rich and singular, so jam-packed with curdled or mangled sophistications borrowed from other mediums and forms, and so verging on precognitive sight in its total blindness. And, that the primitive stuff can force your suspicion of how primitive the sophisticated stuff of the present might be, too, in ways we can barely know. Beyond that, my own generalizations turn useless: one can only turn to the catalogue of marvels within, the oblique id on display in the tendency of these artists to instinctively side with their sneering, cackling villains, so much more like cartoonists than the heroes, thus displaying a howling self-loathing; the Flame, being flogged in silhouette, and his seeming readiness to undress in the long panel in which he contemplates his seductive rescuer ("Only one thing can stop them," she teases him: "Fire!"); the Basil Wolverton science fiction Spacehawk story, each panel like some uncanny rebus, all surfaces stirring from beneath with some incompletely disclosed or acknowledged emotional disquiet, a barely-sublimated mystical Freudian dream;  Sub-Zero's absurd masochistic fracas with Professor X, who in his lumpen brown armor comes as near as any comics villain ever did to embodying SHITMAN (Sub-Zero even punishes him with a shower at the finish, adding "make it hot!"); the insane verbal and visual poetry of Fletcher Hanks, who can smash your mind merely with the force of his unexpected hyphenization ("IF I CAN DOMINATE THOSE VULTURES UP THERE, I'LL BE ABLE TO CON-QUER THE EARTH!"); Rex Dexter's rocketships and robots plainly cribbed from the pulp science fiction magazine covers of Frank R. Paul; Jack Cole's hysterical and frenzied battle between the intrepid proto-Plastic-Man Daredevil and the towering racist monstrosity The Claw; even these comics' side-matter, the revealingly insecure declarations that these vastly forgettable Supermen are permanent institutions, on-going concerns ("'Marvelo' Monarch of Magicians will appear in each and every issue of *Big-Shot Comics*/Reserve Your Copy NOW!"), elsewhere begging for some confirming echo in the void in which their creators labored ("Do You Like The Skyman? Why Not Write In And Tell Us So? Explain Why And What You Like About The Skyman — and What You'd Like To See Him Do!"). To give yourself to the pages in which these Supermen appear is to helplessly rediscover the magnetic force of a totally opaque and infinitely awkward and versatile iconography, to recover the seed of mystery at the heart of superhero love to begin with — like learning a foreign language that turns out to be the only tongue you've ever spoken.

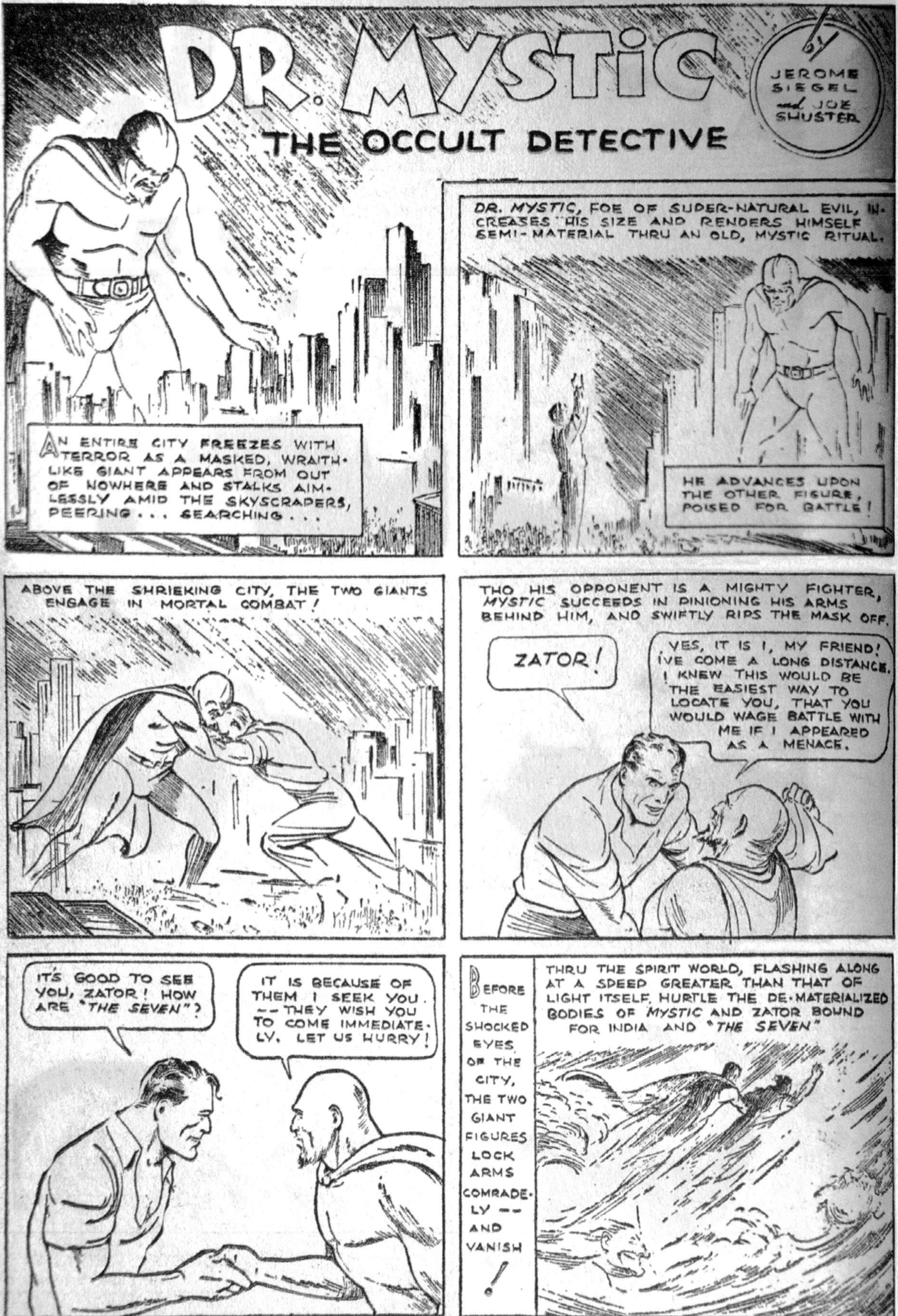
DR. MYSTIC
THE OCCULT DETECTIVE
by JEROME SIEGEL and JOE SHUSTER
AN ENTIRE CITY FREEZES WITH TERROR AS A MASKED, WRAITH-LIKE GIANT APPEARS FROM OUT OF NOWHERE AND STALKS AIMLESSLY AMID THE SKYSCRAPERS, PEERING . . . SEARCHING . . .
DR. MYSTIC, FOE OF SUPER-NATURAL EVIL, INCREASES HIS SIZE AND RENDERS HIMSELF SEMI-MATERIAL THRU AN OLD, MYSTIC RITUAL.
HE ADVANCES UPON THE OTHER FIGURE, POISED FOR BATTLE!
ABOVE THE SHRIEKING CITY, THE TWO GIANTS ENGAGE IN MORTAL COMBAT!
THO HIS OPPONENT IS A MIGHTY FIGHTER, MYSTIC SUCCEEDS IN PINIONING HIS ARMS BEHIND HIM, AND SWIFTLY RIPS THE MASK OFF.
ZATOR!
YES, IT IS I, MY FRIEND! I'VE COME A LONG DISTANCE. I KNEW THIS WOULD BE THE EASIEST WAY TO LOCATE YOU, THAT YOU WOULD WAGE BATTLE WITH ME IF I APPEARED AS A MENACE.
IT'S GOOD TO SEE YOU, ZATOR! HOW ARE "THE SEVEN"?
IT IS BECAUSE OF THEM I SEEK YOU. -- THEY WISH YOU TO COME IMMEDIATELY. LET US HURRY!
BEFORE THE SHOCKED EYES OF THE CITY, THE TWO GIANT FIGURES LOCK ARMS COMRADELY -- AND VANISH!
THRU THE SPIRIT WORLD, FLASHING ALONG AT A SPEED GREATER THAN THAT OF LIGHT ITSELF, HURTLE THE DE-MATERIALIZED BODIES OF MYSTIC AND ZATOR BOUND FOR INDIA AND "THE SEVEN"

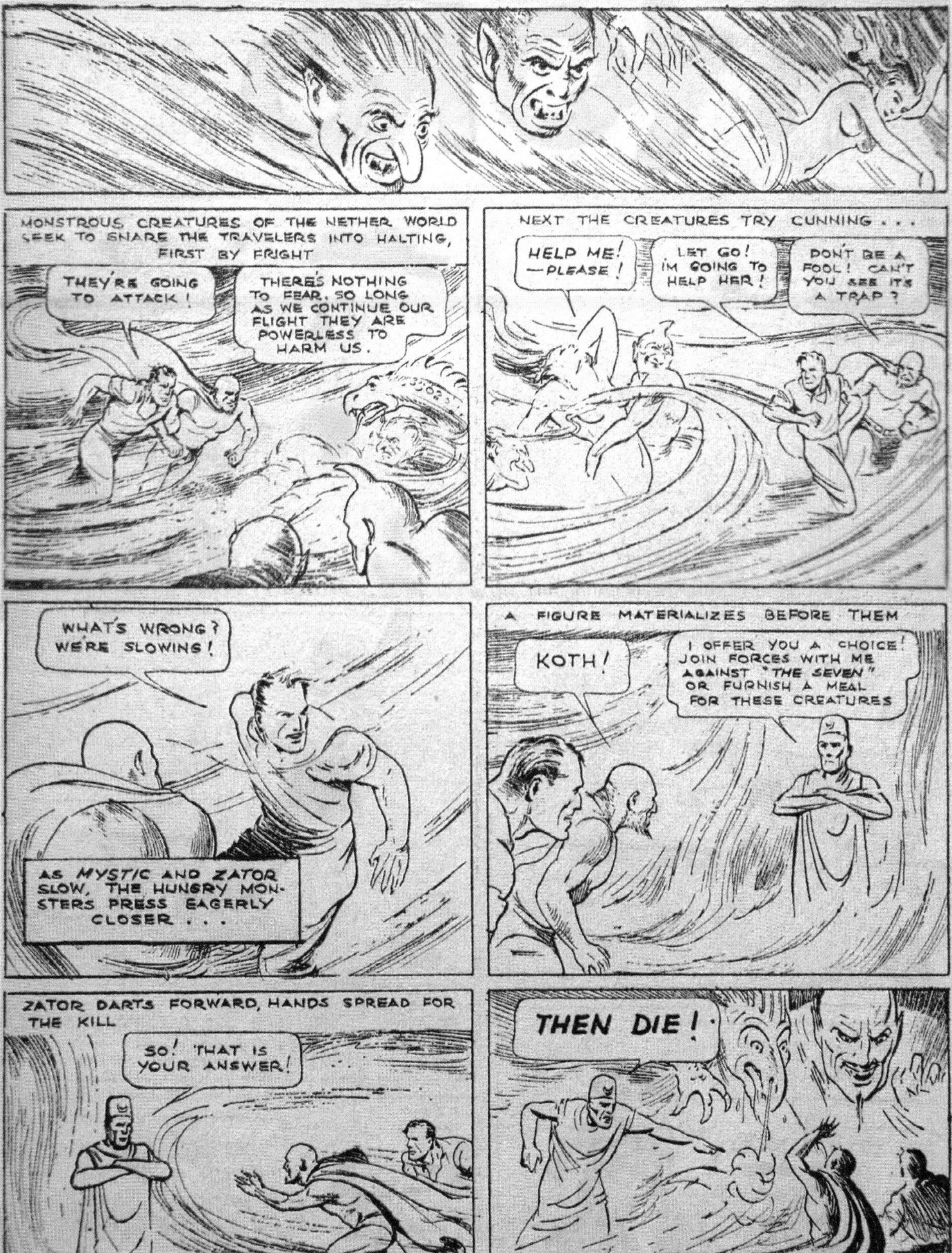
MONSTROUS CREATURES OF THE NETHER WORLD SEEK TO SNARE THE TRAVELERS INTO HALTING, FIRST BY FRIGHT
THEY'RE GOING TO ATTACK!
THERE'S NOTHING TO FEAR. SO LONG AS WE CONTINUE OUR FLIGHT THEY ARE POWERLESS TO HARM US.
NEXT THE CREATURES TRY CUNNING . . .
HELP ME! —PLEASE!
LET GO! I'M GOING TO HELP HER!
DON'T BE A FOOL! CAN'T YOU SEE IT'S A TRAP?
WHAT'S WRONG? WE'RE SLOWING!
AS MYSTIC AND ZATOR SLOW, THE HUNGRY MONSTERS PRESS EAGERLY CLOSER . . .
A FIGURE MATERIALIZES BEFORE THEM
KOTH!
I OFFER YOU A CHOICE! JOIN FORCES WITH ME AGAINST "THE SEVEN" OR FURNISH A MEAL FOR THESE CREATURES
ZATOR DARTS FORWARD, HANDS SPREAD FOR THE KILL
SO! THAT IS YOUR ANSWER!
THEN DIE!
THE MONSTROSITIES CLOSE IN WITH A TRIUMPHANT RUSH!
TO BE CONTINUED —

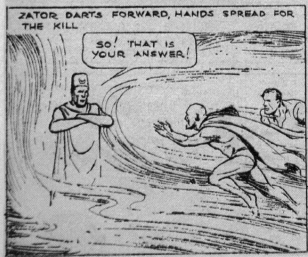

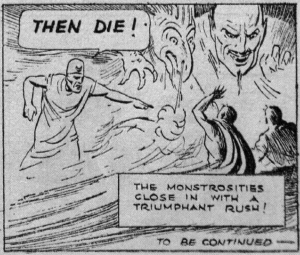

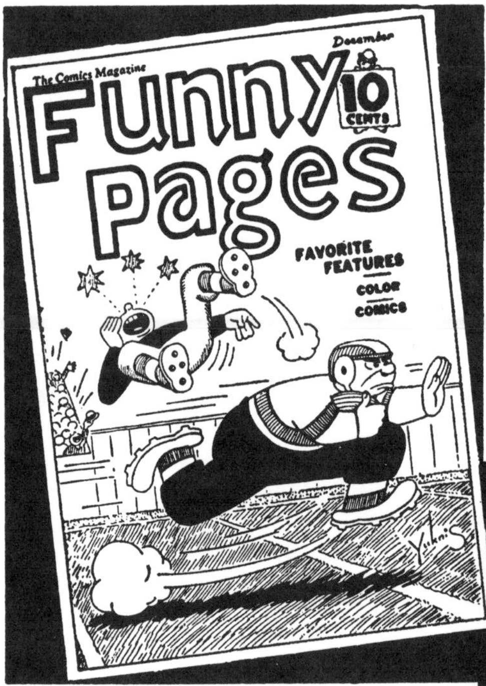
The Comics Magazine
December
Funny Pages
10 CENTS
FAVORITE FEATURES
COLOR COMICS

## ALL THE WORLD JOINED HANDS AROUND "FUNNY PAGES" IT HAS WHAT IT TAKES

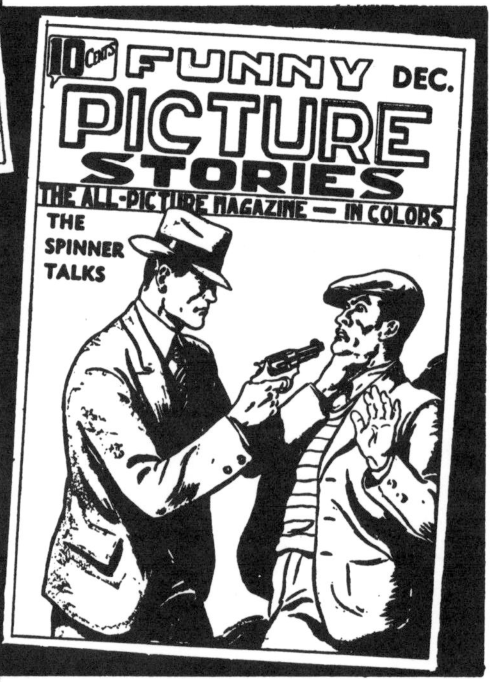
10 CENTS
FUNNY
DEC.
PICTURE
STORIES
THE ALL-PICTURE MAGAZINE — IN COLORS
THE SPINNER TALKS

## NEXT CAME THE BIG RAVE ABOUT FUNNY "PICTURE STORIES"

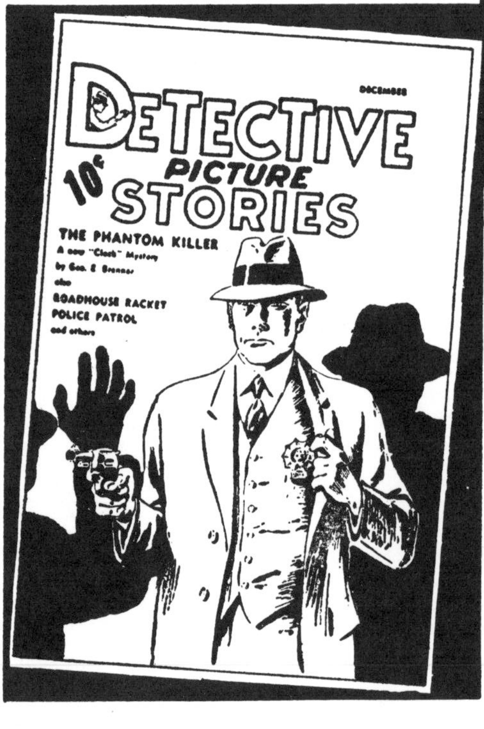
DECEMBER
DETECTIVE
PICTURE
STORIES
10¢
THE PHANTOM KILLER
also
ROADHOUSE RACKET
POLICE PATROL
and others

## AND NOW EVERY ONE IS A FAN FOR DETECTIVE PICTURE STORIES

**It gives you Action in pictures—thrills that are new—vivid colors that make the stories live. Have you bought your copy?**

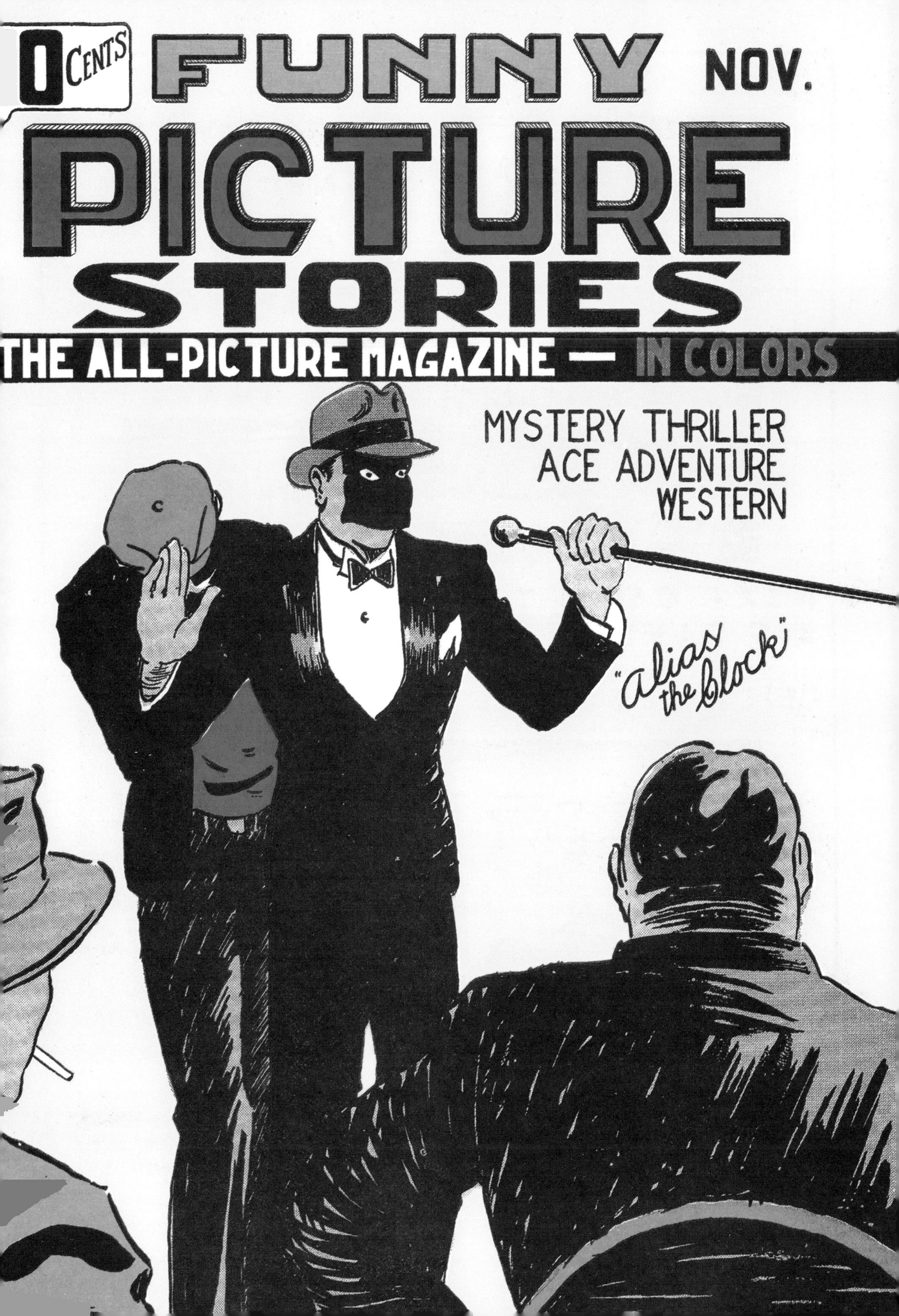
0 CENTS
FUNNY
NOV.
PICTURE
STORIES
THE ALL-PICTURE MAGAZINE — IN COLORS
MYSTERY THRILLER
ACE ADVENTURE
WESTERN
"Alias the Clock"

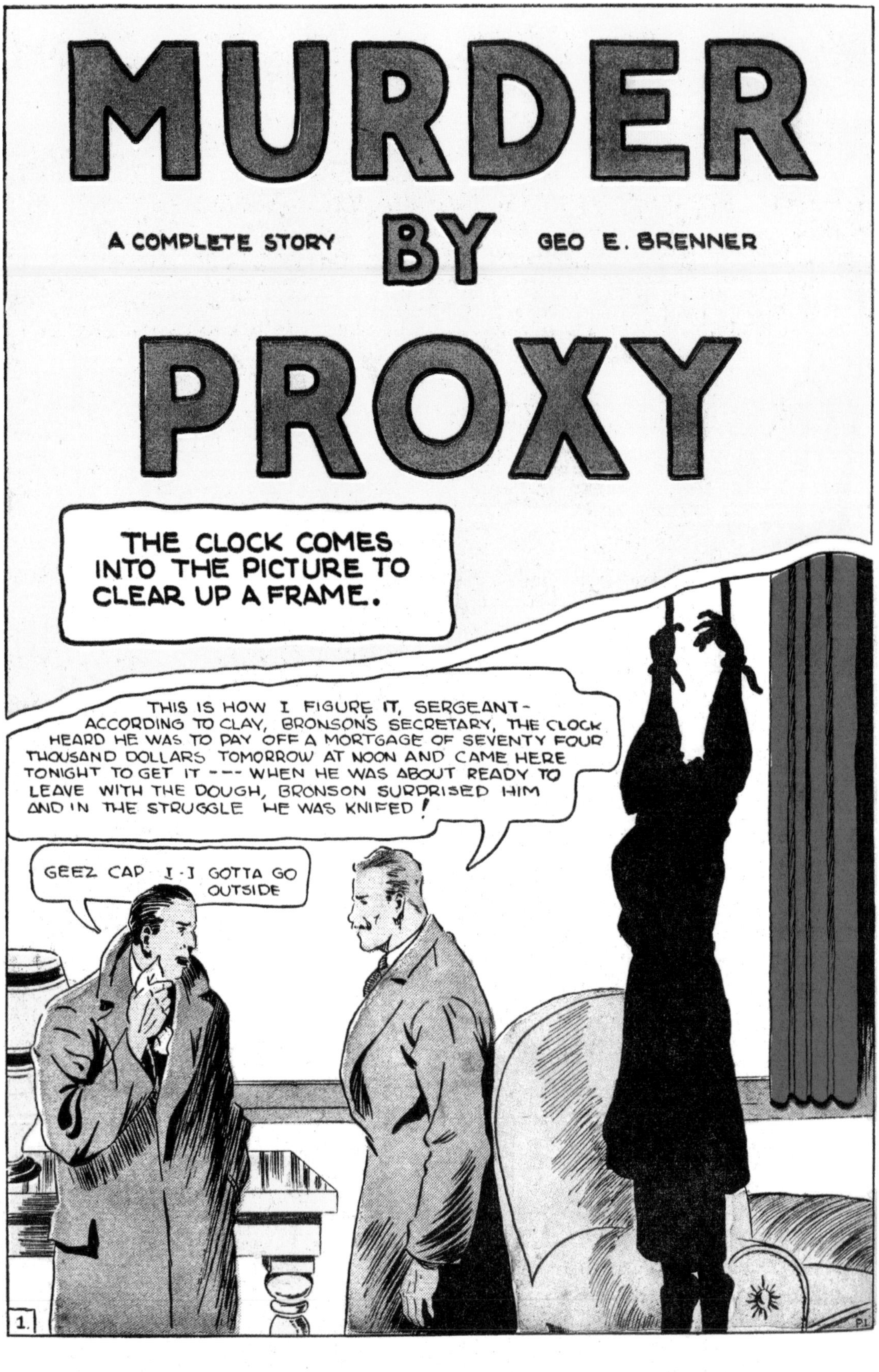
MURDER BY PROXY
A COMPLETE STORY
GEO E. BRENNER
THE CLOCK COMES INTO THE PICTURE TO CLEAR UP A FRAME.
THIS IS HOW I FIGURE IT, SERGEANT- ACCORDING TO CLAY, BRONSON'S SECRETARY, THE CLOCK HEARD HE WAS TO PAY OFF A MORTGAGE OF SEVENTY FOUR THOUSAND DOLLARS TOMORROW AT NOON AND CAME HERE TONIGHT TO GET IT --- WHEN HE WAS ABOUT READY TO LEAVE WITH THE DOUGH, BRONSON SURPRISED HIM AND IN THE STRUGGLE HE WAS KNIFED!
GEEZ CAP I-I GOTTA GO OUTSIDE
1.

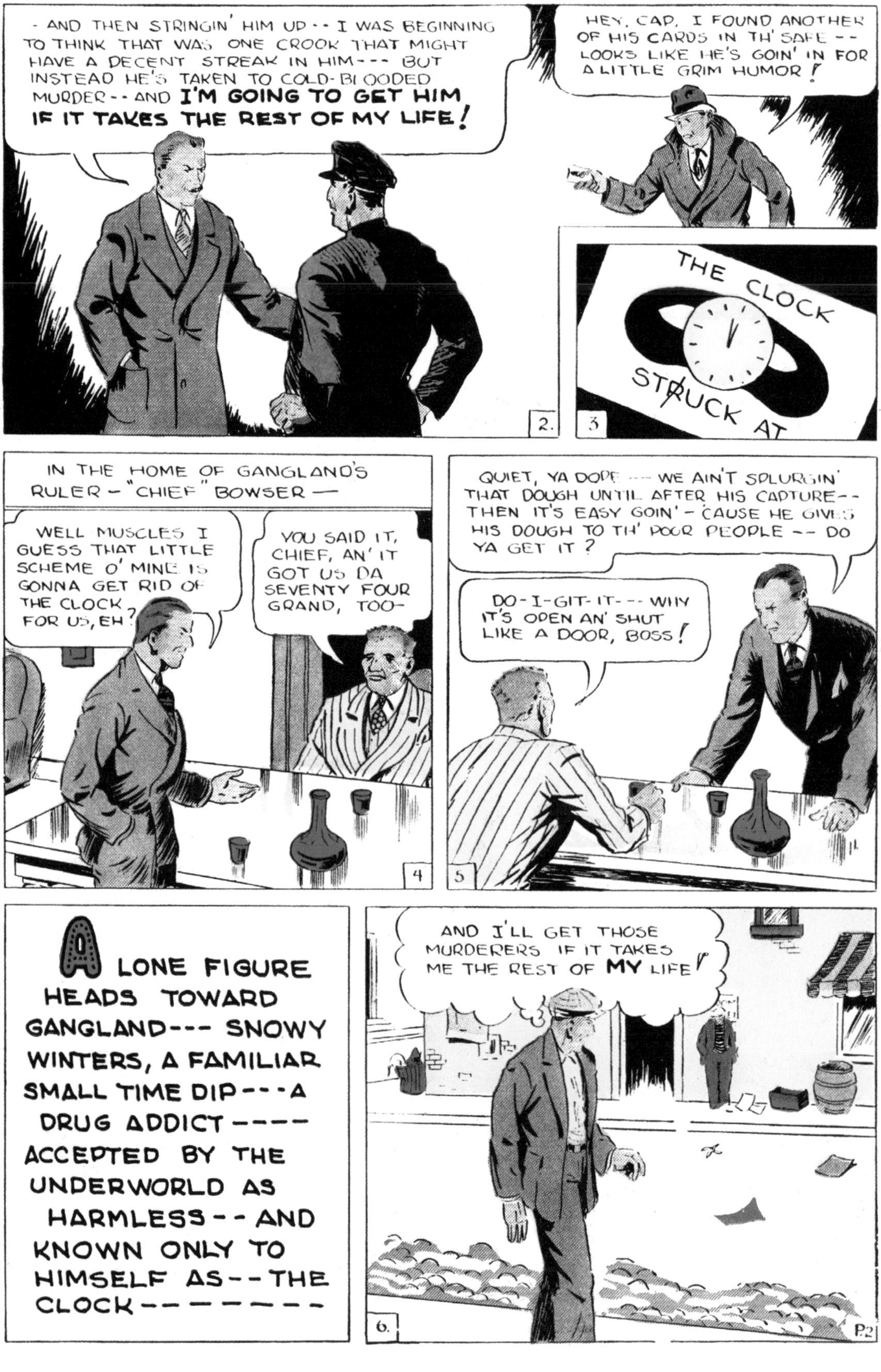
- AND THEN STRINGIN' HIM UP - - I WAS BEGINNING TO THINK THAT WAS ONE CROOK THAT MIGHT HAVE A DECENT STREAK IN HIM - - - BUT INSTEAD HE'S TAKEN TO COLD-BLOODED MURDER - - AND I'M GOING TO GET HIM IF IT TAKES THE REST OF MY LIFE!
HEY, CAP, I FOUND ANOTHER OF HIS CARDS IN TH' SAFE - - LOOKS LIKE HE'S GOIN' IN FOR A LITTLE GRIM HUMOR!
THE CLOCK
STRUCK AT
IN THE HOME OF GANGLAND'S RULER - "CHIEF" BOWSER -
WELL MUSCLES I GUESS THAT LITTLE SCHEME O' MINE IS GONNA GET RID OF THE CLOCK FOR US, EH?
YOU SAID IT, CHIEF, AN' IT GOT US DA SEVENTY FOUR GRAND, TOO-
QUIET, YA DOPE --- WE AIN'T SPLURGIN' THAT DOUGH UNTIL AFTER HIS CAPTURE - - THEN IT'S EASY GOIN' - 'CAUSE HE GIVES HIS DOUGH TO TH' POOR PEOPLE -- DO YA GET IT ?
DO - I - GIT - IT - - - WHY IT'S OPEN AN' SHUT LIKE A DOOR, BOSS!
A LONE FIGURE HEADS TOWARD GANGLAND --- SNOWY WINTERS, A FAMILIAR SMALL TIME DIP - - - A DRUG ADDICT ---- ACCEPTED BY THE UNDERWORLD AS HARMLESS - - AND KNOWN ONLY TO HIMSELF AS - - THE CLOCK --------
AND I'LL GET THOSE MURDERERS IF IT TAKES ME THE REST OF MY LIFE!

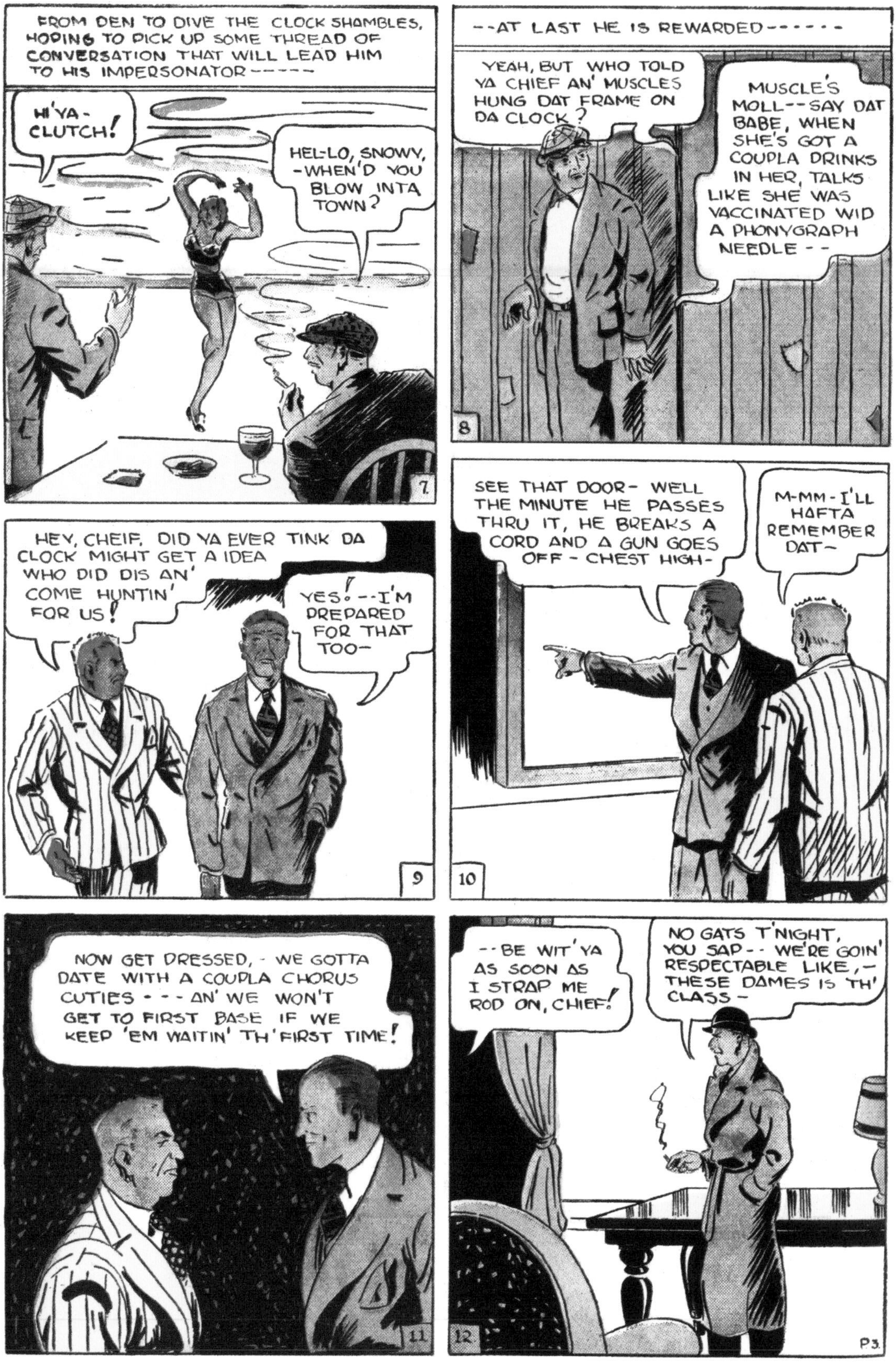
FROM DEN TO DIVE THE CLOCK SHAMBLES, HOPING TO PICK UP SOME THREAD OF CONVERSATION THAT WILL LEAD HIM TO HIS IMPERSONATOR -----
HI'YA-CLUTCH!
HEL-LO, SNOWY, -WHEN'D YOU BLOW INTA TOWN?
7
--AT LAST HE IS REWARDED------
YEAH, BUT WHO TOLD YA CHIEF AN' MUSCLES HUNG DAT FRAME ON DA CLOCK?
MUSCLE'S MOLL--SAY DAT BABE, WHEN SHE'S GOT A COUPLA DRINKS IN HER, TALKS LIKE SHE WAS VACCINATED WID A PHONYGRAPH NEEDLE--
8
HEY, CHEIF, DID YA EVER TINK DA CLOCK MIGHT GET A IDEA WHO DID DIS AN' COME HUNTIN' FOR US!
YES!--I'M PREPARED FOR THAT TOO-
9
SEE THAT DOOR- WELL THE MINUTE HE PASSES THRU IT, HE BREAKS A CORD AND A GUN GOES OFF - CHEST HIGH-
M-MM-I'LL HAFTA REMEMBER DAT-
10
NOW GET DRESSED, - WE GOTTA DATE WITH A COUPLA CHORUS CUTIES --- AN' WE WON'T GET TO FIRST BASE IF WE KEEP 'EM WAITIN' TH' FIRST TIME!
11
--BE WIT'YA AS SOON AS I STRAP ME ROD ON, CHIEF!
NO GATS T'NIGHT, YOU SAP-- WE'RE GOIN' RESPECTABLE LIKE,- THESE DAMES IS TH' CLASS-
12
P3.

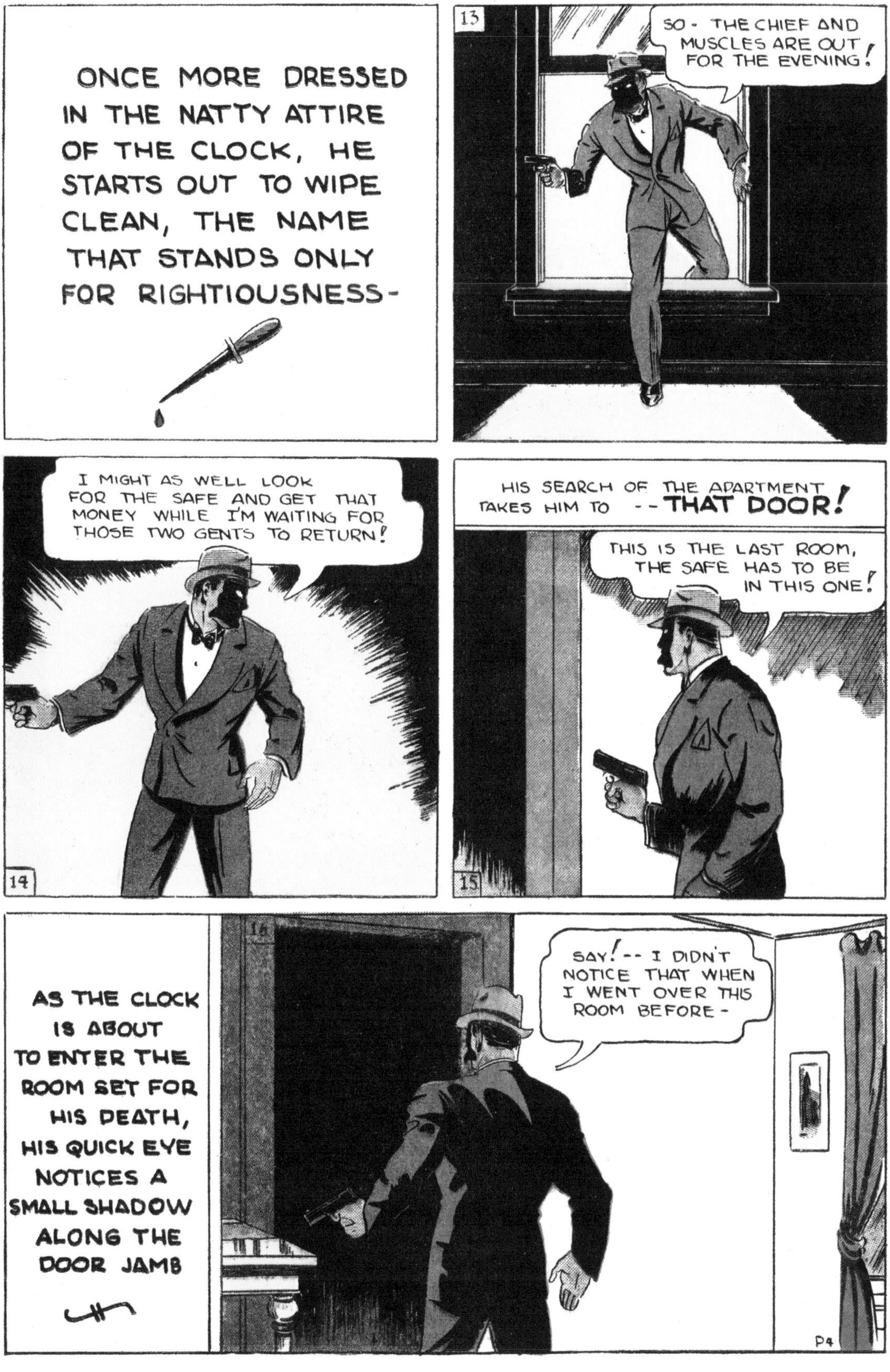
ONCE MORE DRESSED IN THE NATTY ATTIRE OF THE CLOCK, HE STARTS OUT TO WIPE CLEAN, THE NAME THAT STANDS ONLY FOR RIGHTIOUSNESS-
13
SO - THE CHIEF AND MUSCLES ARE OUT FOR THE EVENING!
I MIGHT AS WELL LOOK FOR THE SAFE AND GET THAT MONEY WHILE I'M WAITING FOR THOSE TWO GENTS TO RETURN!
14
HIS SEARCH OF THE APARTMENT TAKES HIM TO --THAT DOOR!
THIS IS THE LAST ROOM, THE SAFE HAS TO BE IN THIS ONE!
15
AS THE CLOCK IS ABOUT TO ENTER THE ROOM SET FOR HIS DEATH, HIS QUICK EYE NOTICES A SMALL SHADOW ALONG THE DOOR JAMB
16
SAY! -- I DIDN'T NOTICE THAT WHEN I WENT OVER THIS ROOM BEFORE -
P4

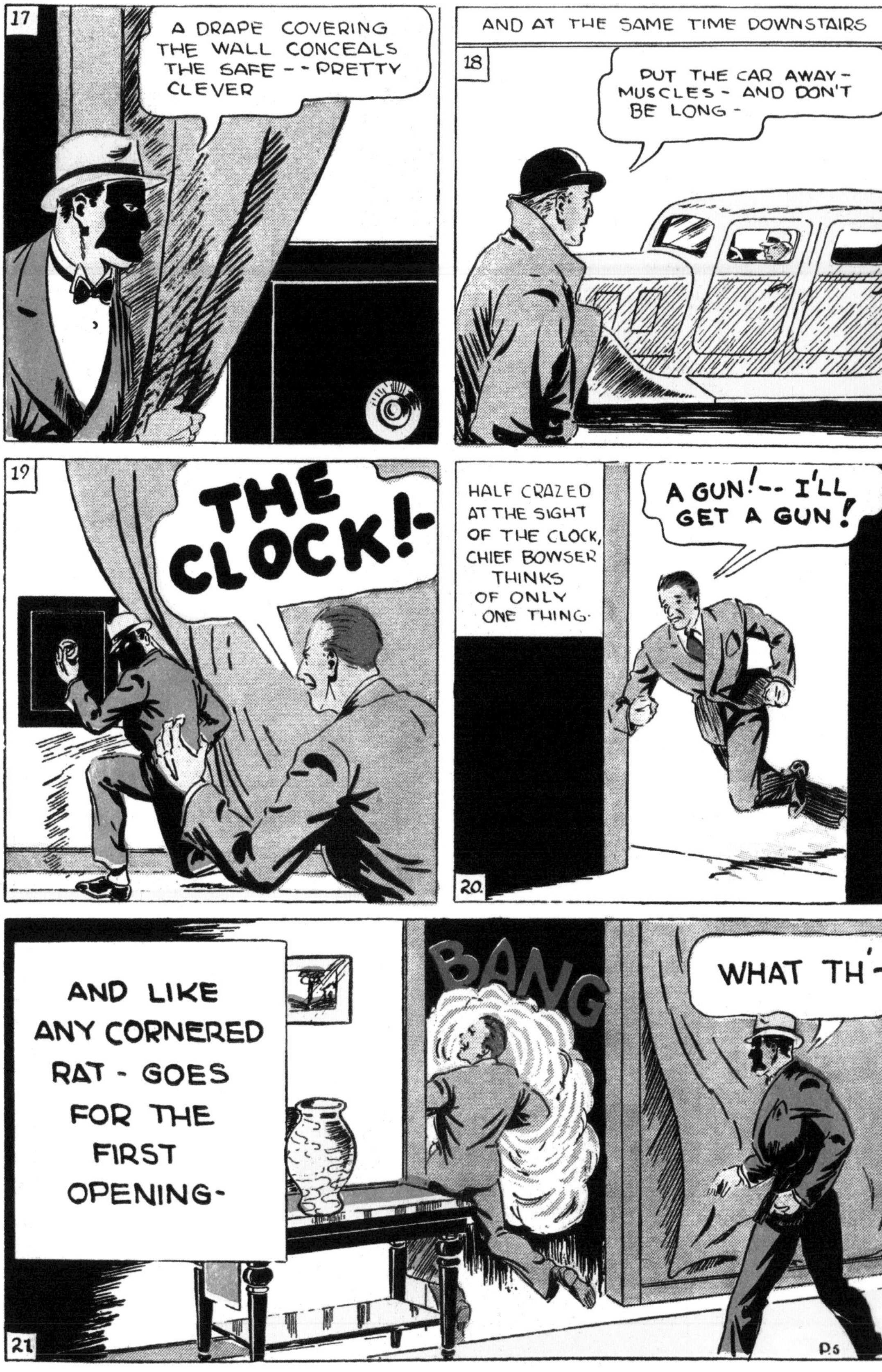
17
A DRAPE COVERING THE WALL CONCEALS THE SAFE - - PRETTY CLEVER
AND AT THE SAME TIME DOWNSTAIRS
18
PUT THE CAR AWAY - MUSCLES - AND DON'T BE LONG -
19
THE CLOCK! -
HALF CRAZED AT THE SIGHT OF THE CLOCK, CHIEF BOWSER THINKS OF ONLY ONE THING.
A GUN! -- I'LL GET A GUN!
20.
AND LIKE ANY CORNERED RAT - GOES FOR THE FIRST OPENING -
BANG
WHAT TH' -
21
P.S

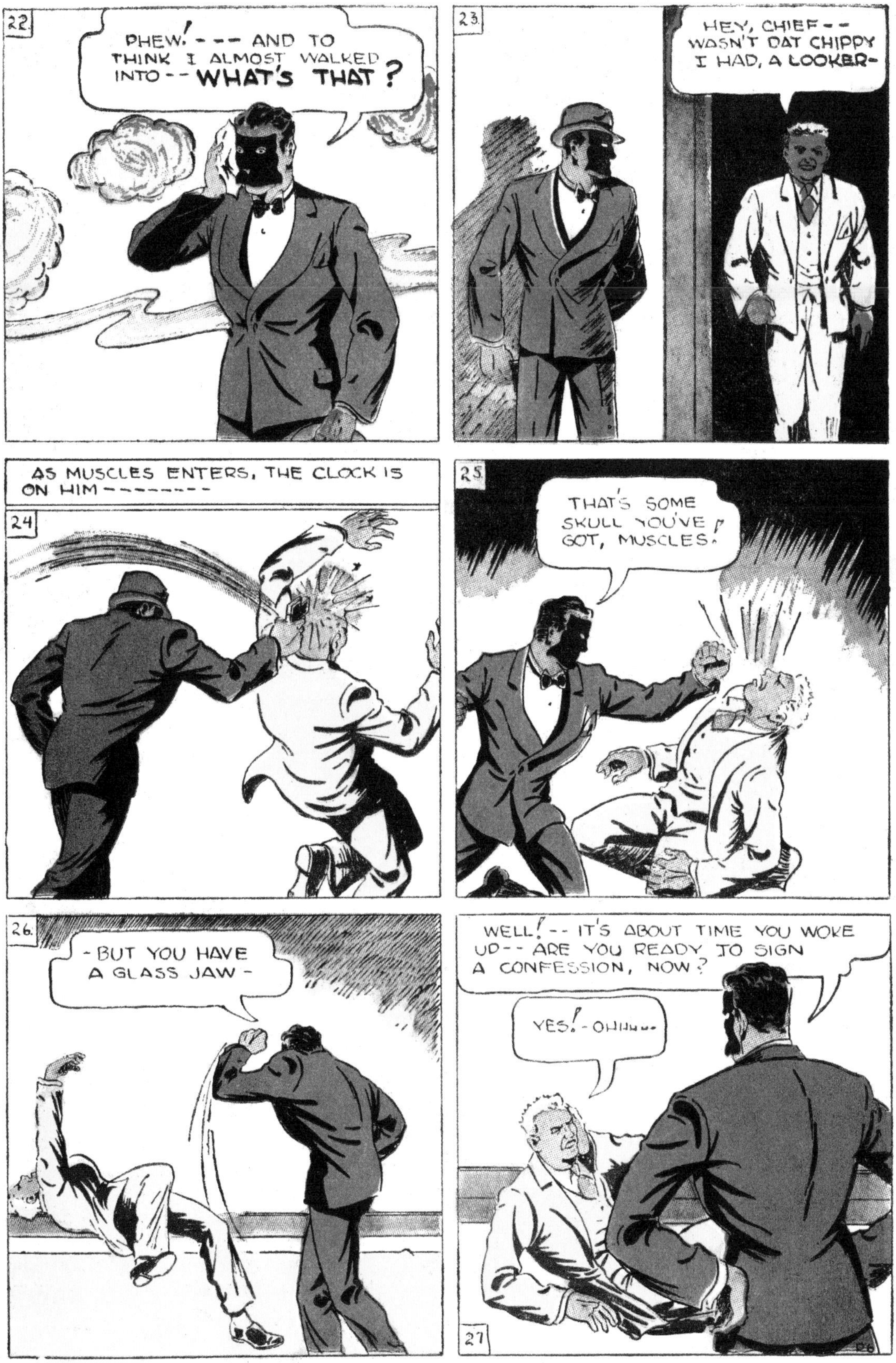
22.
PHEW! --- AND TO THINK I ALMOST WALKED INTO -- WHAT'S THAT?
23.
HEY, CHIEF -- WASN'T DAT CHIPPY I HAD, A LOOKER-
AS MUSCLES ENTERS, THE CLOCK IS ON HIM --------
24
25
THAT'S SOME SKULL YOU'VE GOT, MUSCLES!
26.
-BUT YOU HAVE A GLASS JAW-
WELL! -- IT'S ABOUT TIME YOU WOKE UP -- ARE YOU READY TO SIGN A CONFESSION, NOW?
YES! -OHHHH..
27

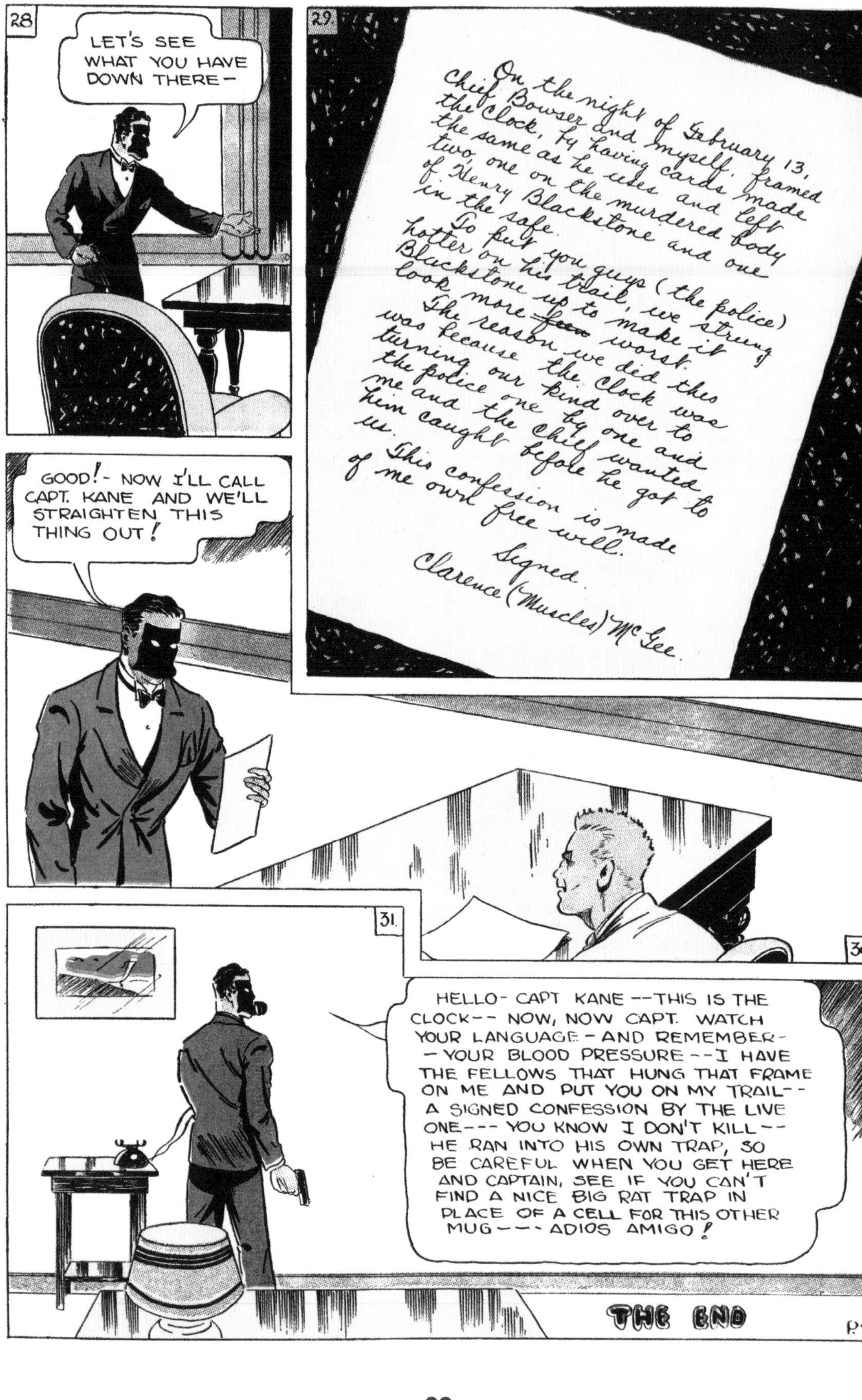
28
LET'S SEE WHAT YOU HAVE DOWN THERE—
29.
On the night of February 13,
Chief Bowser and myself, framed
the Clock, by having cards made
the same as he uses and left
two, one on the murdered body
of Henry Blackstone and one
in the safe.
To put you guys (the police)
hotter on his trail, we strung
Blackstone up to make it
look more worst.
The reason we did this
was because the Clock was
turning our kind over to
the police one by one and
me and the Chief wanted
him caught before he got to
us.
This confession is made
of me own free will.
Signed.
Clarence (Muscles) McGee.
GOOD!— NOW I'LL CALL CAPT. KANE AND WE'LL STRAIGHTEN THIS THING OUT!
30
31.
HELLO- CAPT KANE --THIS IS THE CLOCK-- NOW, NOW CAPT. WATCH YOUR LANGUAGE - AND REMEMBER - - YOUR BLOOD PRESSURE --I HAVE THE FELLOWS THAT HUNG THAT FRAME ON ME AND PUT YOU ON MY TRAIL-- A SIGNED CONFESSION BY THE LIVE ONE--- YOU KNOW I DON'T KILL-- HE RAN INTO HIS OWN TRAP, SO BE CAREFUL WHEN YOU GET HERE AND CAPTAIN, SEE IF YOU CAN'T FIND A NICE BIG RAT TRAP IN PLACE OF A CELL FOR THIS OTHER MUG--- ADIOS AMIGO!
THE END

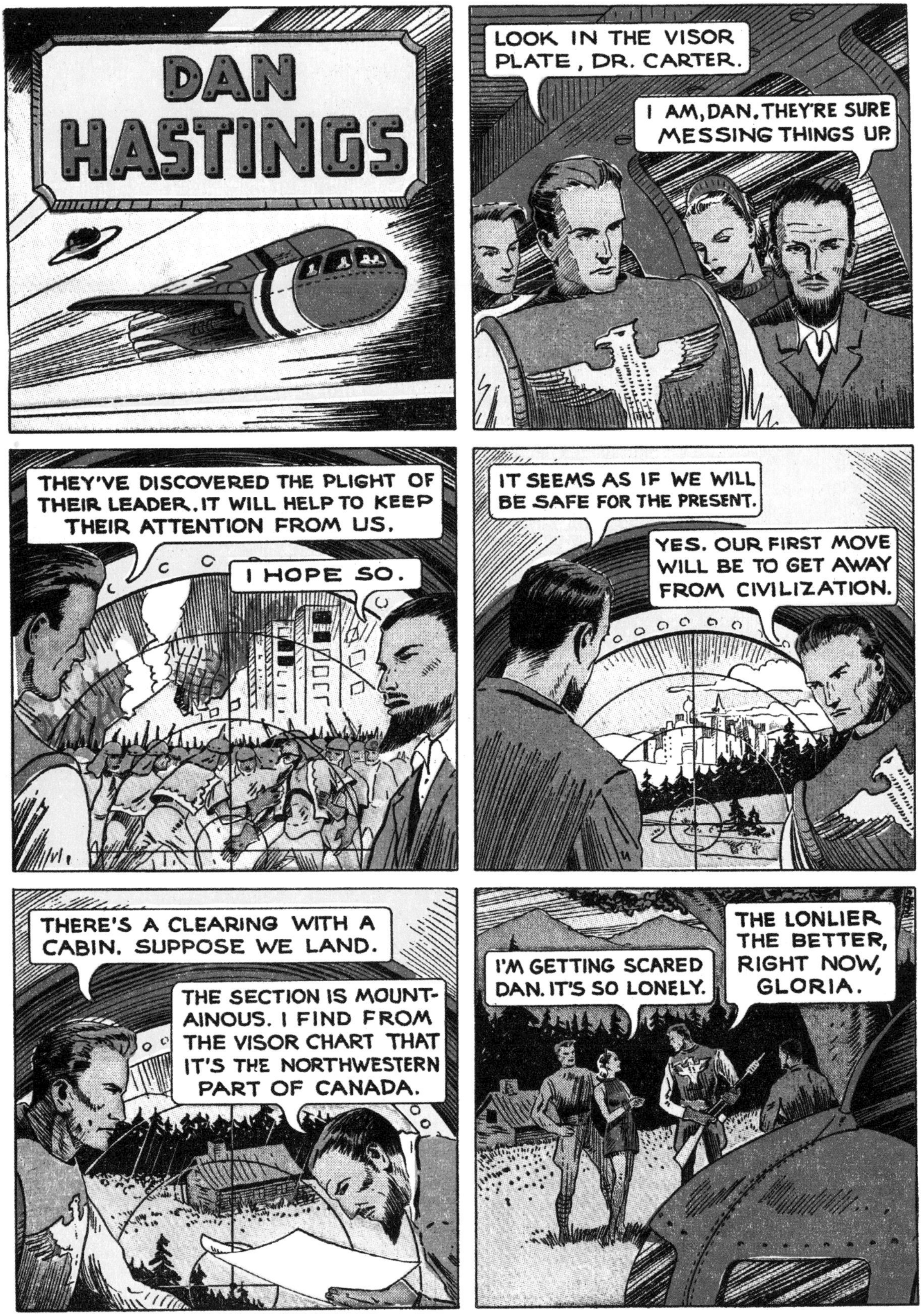
DAN HASTINGS
LOOK IN THE VISOR PLATE, DR. CARTER.
I AM, DAN. THEY'RE SURE MESSING THINGS UP.
THEY'VE DISCOVERED THE PLIGHT OF THEIR LEADER. IT WILL HELP TO KEEP THEIR ATTENTION FROM US.
I HOPE SO.
IT SEEMS AS IF WE WILL BE SAFE FOR THE PRESENT.
YES. OUR FIRST MOVE WILL BE TO GET AWAY FROM CIVILIZATION.
THERE'S A CLEARING WITH A CABIN. SUPPOSE WE LAND.
THE SECTION IS MOUNTAINOUS. I FIND FROM THE VISOR CHART THAT IT'S THE NORTHWESTERN PART OF CANADA.
I'M GETTING SCARED DAN. IT'S SO LONELY.
THE LONLIER THE BETTER, RIGHT NOW, GLORIA.

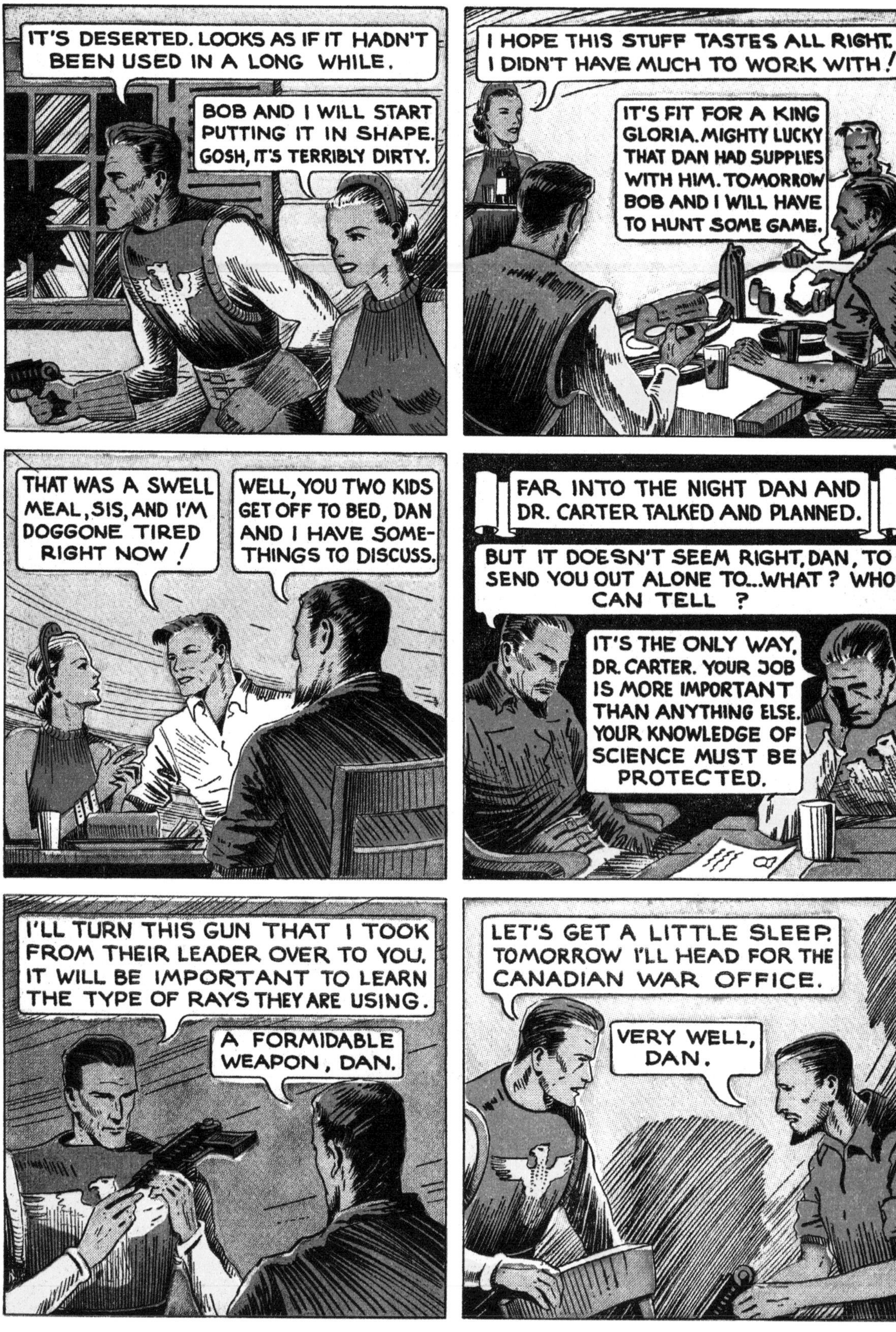
IT'S DESERTED. LOOKS AS IF IT HADN'T BEEN USED IN A LONG WHILE.
BOB AND I WILL START PUTTING IT IN SHAPE. GOSH, IT'S TERRIBLY DIRTY.
I HOPE THIS STUFF TASTES ALL RIGHT. I DIDN'T HAVE MUCH TO WORK WITH!
IT'S FIT FOR A KING GLORIA. MIGHTY LUCKY THAT DAN HAD SUPPLIES WITH HIM. TOMORROW BOB AND I WILL HAVE TO HUNT SOME GAME.
THAT WAS A SWELL MEAL, SIS, AND I'M DOGGONE TIRED RIGHT NOW!
WELL, YOU TWO KIDS GET OFF TO BED, DAN AND I HAVE SOME-THINGS TO DISCUSS.
FAR INTO THE NIGHT DAN AND DR. CARTER TALKED AND PLANNED.
BUT IT DOESN'T SEEM RIGHT, DAN, TO SEND YOU OUT ALONE TO...WHAT? WHO CAN TELL ?
IT'S THE ONLY WAY, DR. CARTER. YOUR JOB IS MORE IMPORTANT THAN ANYTHING ELSE. YOUR KNOWLEDGE OF SCIENCE MUST BE PROTECTED.
I'LL TURN THIS GUN THAT I TOOK FROM THEIR LEADER OVER TO YOU. IT WILL BE IMPORTANT TO LEARN THE TYPE OF RAYS THEY ARE USING.
A FORMIDABLE WEAPON, DAN.
LET'S GET A LITTLE SLEEP. TOMORROW I'LL HEAD FOR THE CANADIAN WAR OFFICE.
VERY WELL, DAN.

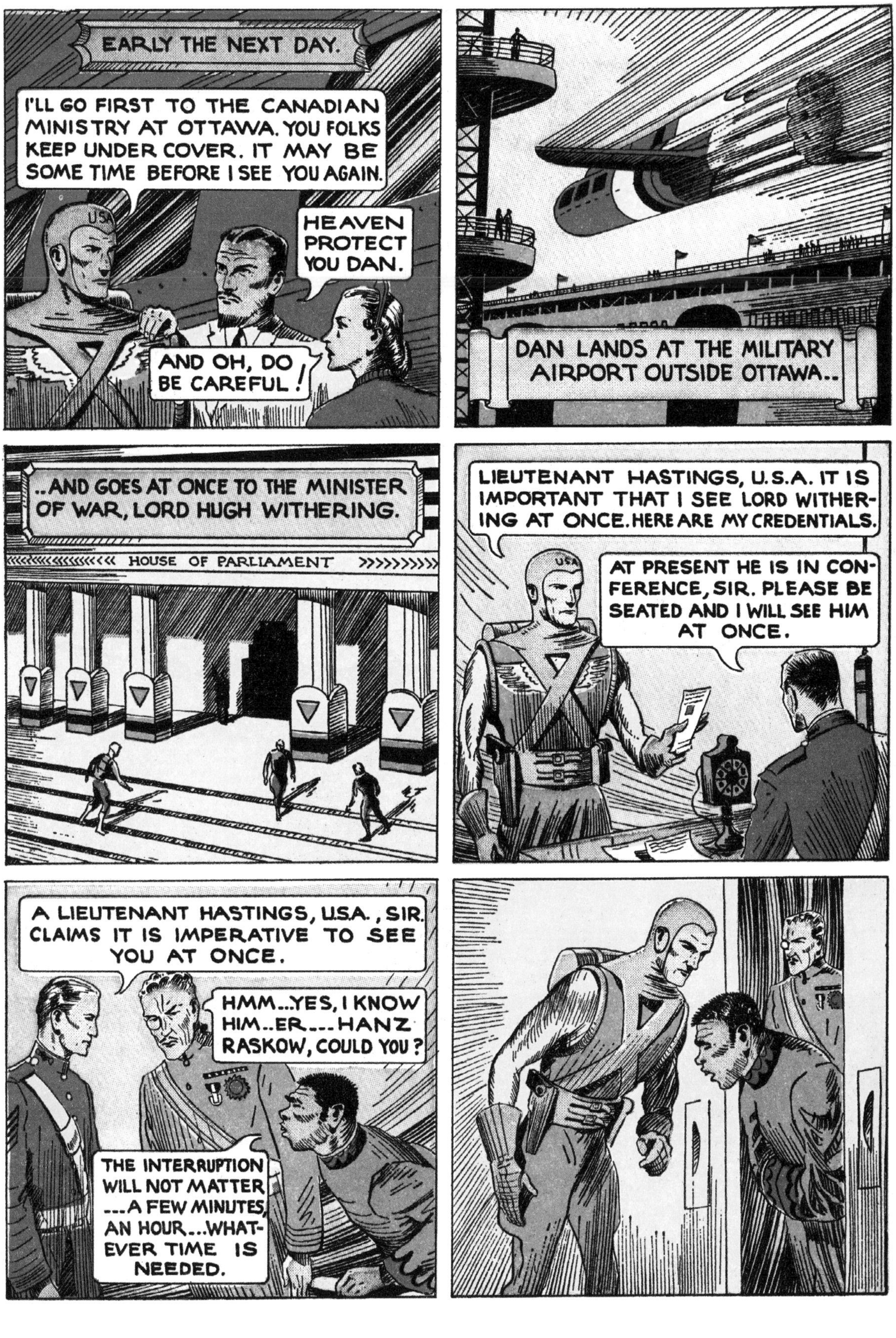
EARLY THE NEXT DAY.
I'LL GO FIRST TO THE CANADIAN MINISTRY AT OTTAWA. YOU FOLKS KEEP UNDER COVER. IT MAY BE SOME TIME BEFORE I SEE YOU AGAIN.
HEAVEN PROTECT YOU DAN.
AND OH, DO BE CAREFUL!
USA
DAN LANDS AT THE MILITARY AIRPORT OUTSIDE OTTAWA..
..AND GOES AT ONCE TO THE MINISTER OF WAR, LORD HUGH WITHERING.
HOUSE OF PARLIAMENT
LIEUTENANT HASTINGS, U.S.A. IT IS IMPORTANT THAT I SEE LORD WITHERING AT ONCE. HERE ARE MY CREDENTIALS.
AT PRESENT HE IS IN CONFERENCE, SIR. PLEASE BE SEATED AND I WILL SEE HIM AT ONCE.
A LIEUTENANT HASTINGS, U.S.A., SIR. CLAIMS IT IS IMPERATIVE TO SEE YOU AT ONCE.
HMM...YES, I KNOW HIM..ER...HANZ RASKOW, COULD YOU?
THE INTERRUPTION WILL NOT MATTER ...A FEW MINUTES, AN HOUR...WHATEVER TIME IS NEEDED.

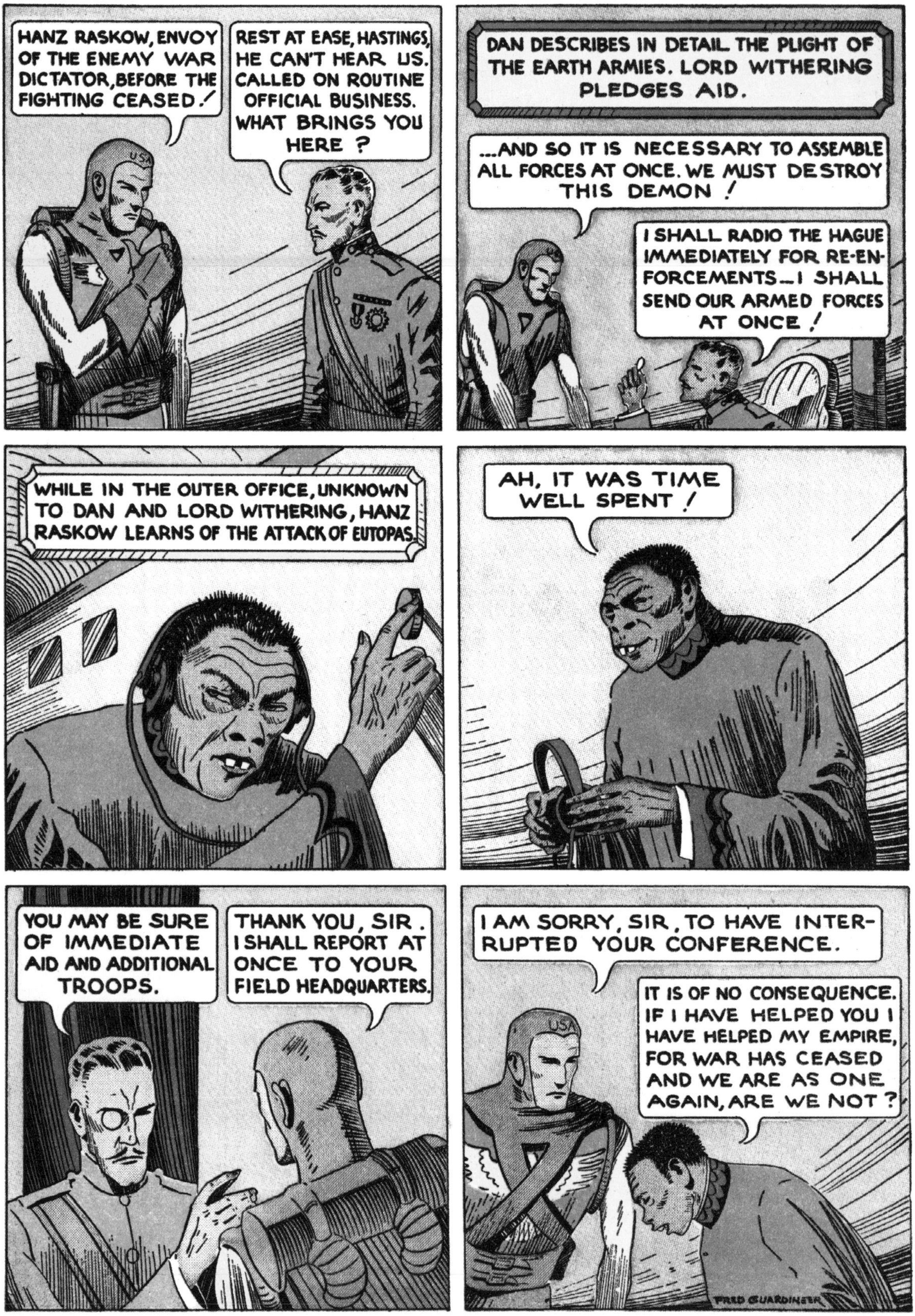
HANZ RASKOW, ENVOY OF THE ENEMY WAR DICTATOR, BEFORE THE FIGHTING CEASED!
REST AT EASE, HASTINGS, HE CAN'T HEAR US. CALLED ON ROUTINE OFFICIAL BUSINESS. WHAT BRINGS YOU HERE ?
DAN DESCRIBES IN DETAIL THE PLIGHT OF THE EARTH ARMIES. LORD WITHERING PLEDGES AID.
...AND SO IT IS NECESSARY TO ASSEMBLE ALL FORCES AT ONCE. WE MUST DESTROY THIS DEMON !
I SHALL RADIO THE HAGUE IMMEDIATELY FOR RE-ENFORCEMENTS—I SHALL SEND OUR ARMED FORCES AT ONCE !
WHILE IN THE OUTER OFFICE, UNKNOWN TO DAN AND LORD WITHERING, HANZ RASKOW LEARNS OF THE ATTACK OF EUTOPAS.
AH, IT WAS TIME WELL SPENT !
YOU MAY BE SURE OF IMMEDIATE AID AND ADDITIONAL TROOPS.
THANK YOU, SIR. I SHALL REPORT AT ONCE TO YOUR FIELD HEADQUARTERS.
I AM SORRY, SIR, TO HAVE INTERRUPTED YOUR CONFERENCE.
IT IS OF NO CONSEQUENCE. IF I HAVE HELPED YOU I HAVE HELPED MY EMPIRE, FOR WAR HAS CEASED AND WE ARE AS ONE AGAIN, ARE WE NOT ?
FRED GUARDINEER

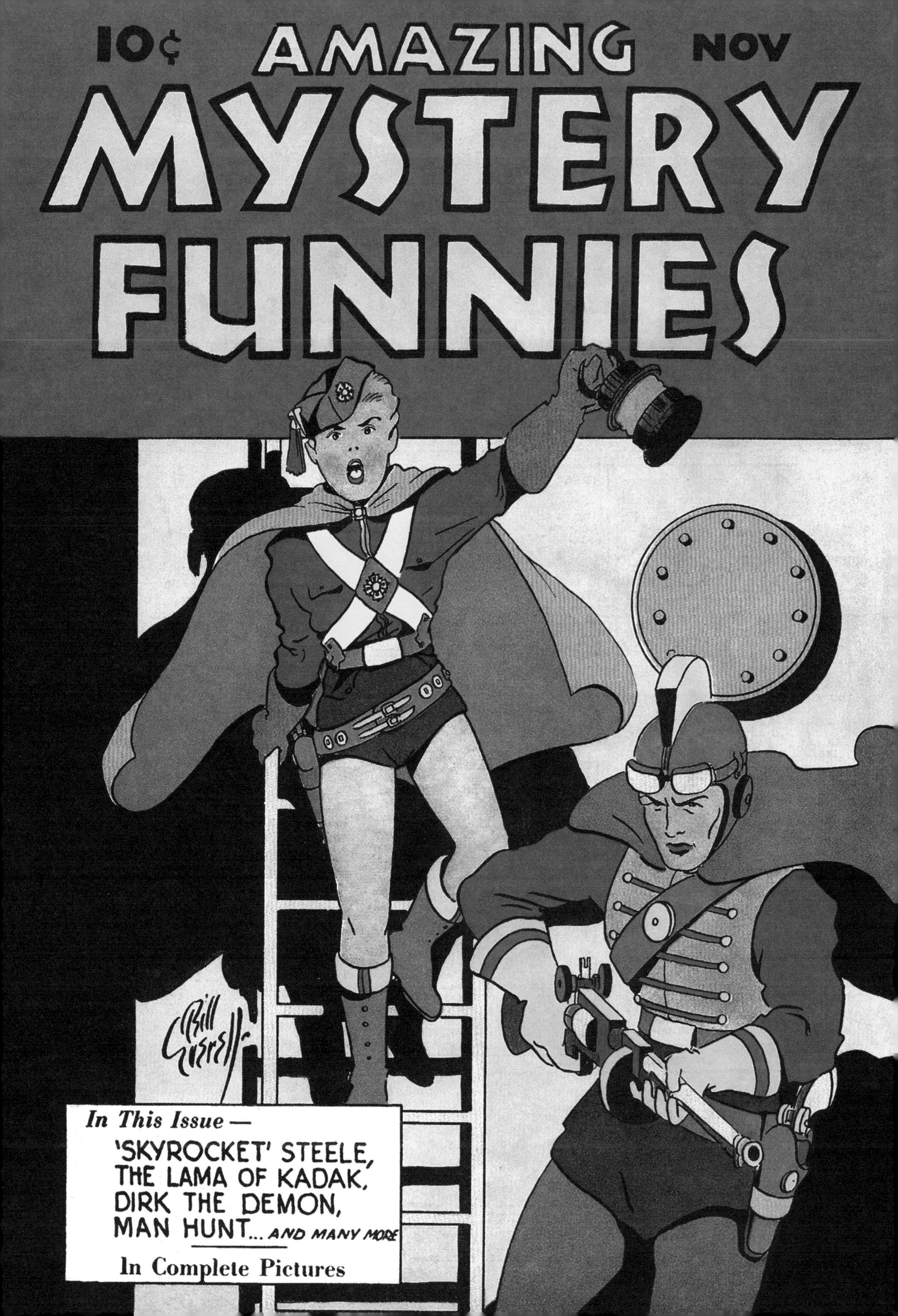
10¢
AMAZING
NOV
MYSTERY
FUNNIES
Bill Everett
In This Issue —
'SKYROCKET' STEELE,
THE LAMA OF KADAK,
DIRK THE DEMON,
MAN HUNT... AND MANY MORE
In Complete Pictures

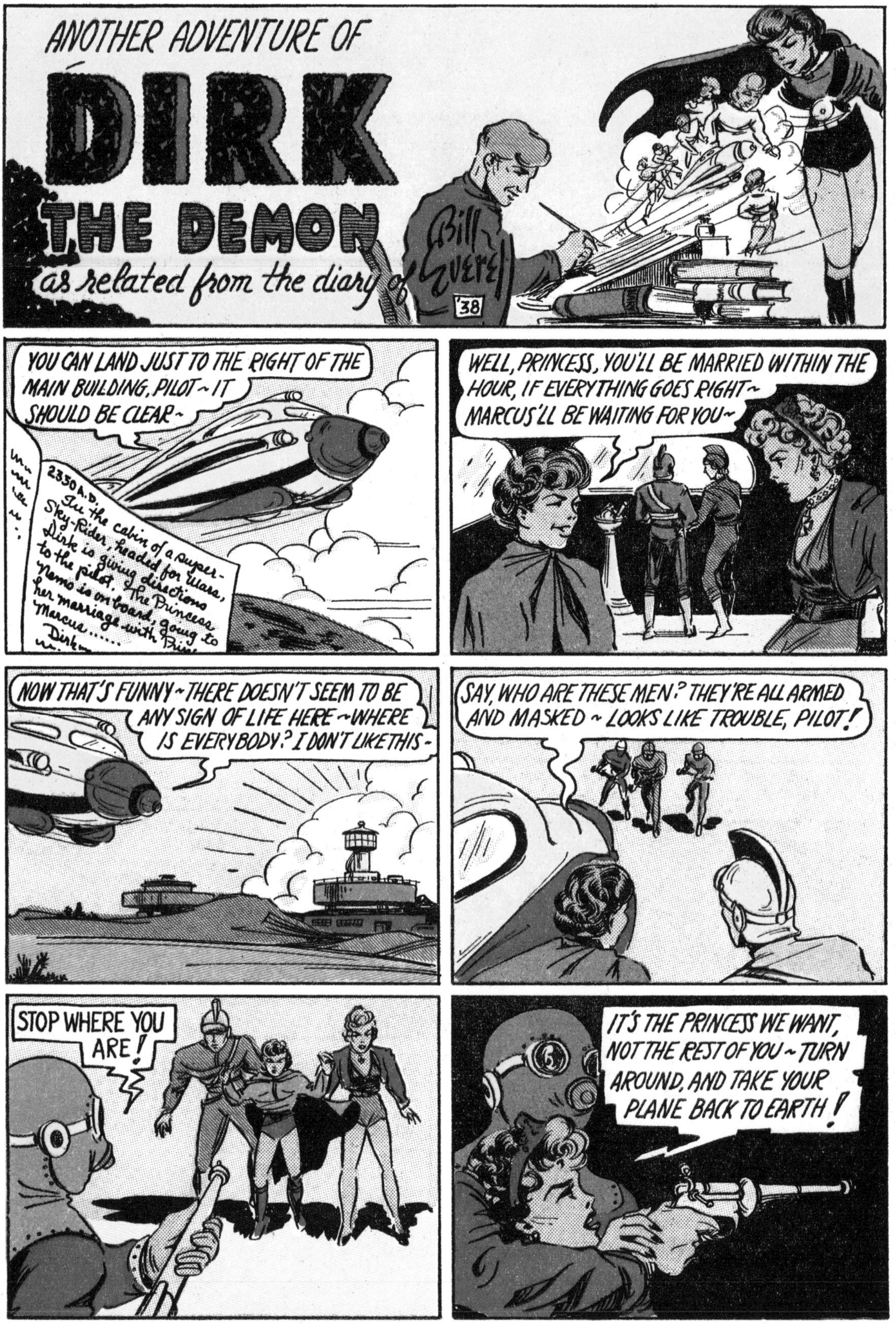

ANOTHER ADVENTURE OF
DIRK THE DEMON
as related from the diary of Bill Everett '38
YOU CAN LAND JUST TO THE RIGHT OF THE MAIN BUILDING, PILOT ~ IT SHOULD BE CLEAR ~
2350 A.D. In the cabin of a super-Sky-Rider, headed for Mars, Dirk is giving directions to the pilot. The Princess Nemo is on board, going to her marriage with Prince Marcus......
WELL, PRINCESS, YOU'LL BE MARRIED WITHIN THE HOUR, IF EVERYTHING GOES RIGHT ~ MARCUS'LL BE WAITING FOR YOU ~
NOW THAT'S FUNNY ~ THERE DOESN'T SEEM TO BE ANY SIGN OF LIFE HERE ~ WHERE IS EVERYBODY? I DON'T LIKE THIS ~
SAY, WHO ARE THESE MEN? THEY'RE ALL ARMED AND MASKED ~ LOOKS LIKE TROUBLE, PILOT!
STOP WHERE YOU ARE!
IT'S THE PRINCESS WE WANT, NOT THE REST OF YOU ~ TURN AROUND, AND TAKE YOUR PLANE BACK TO EARTH!

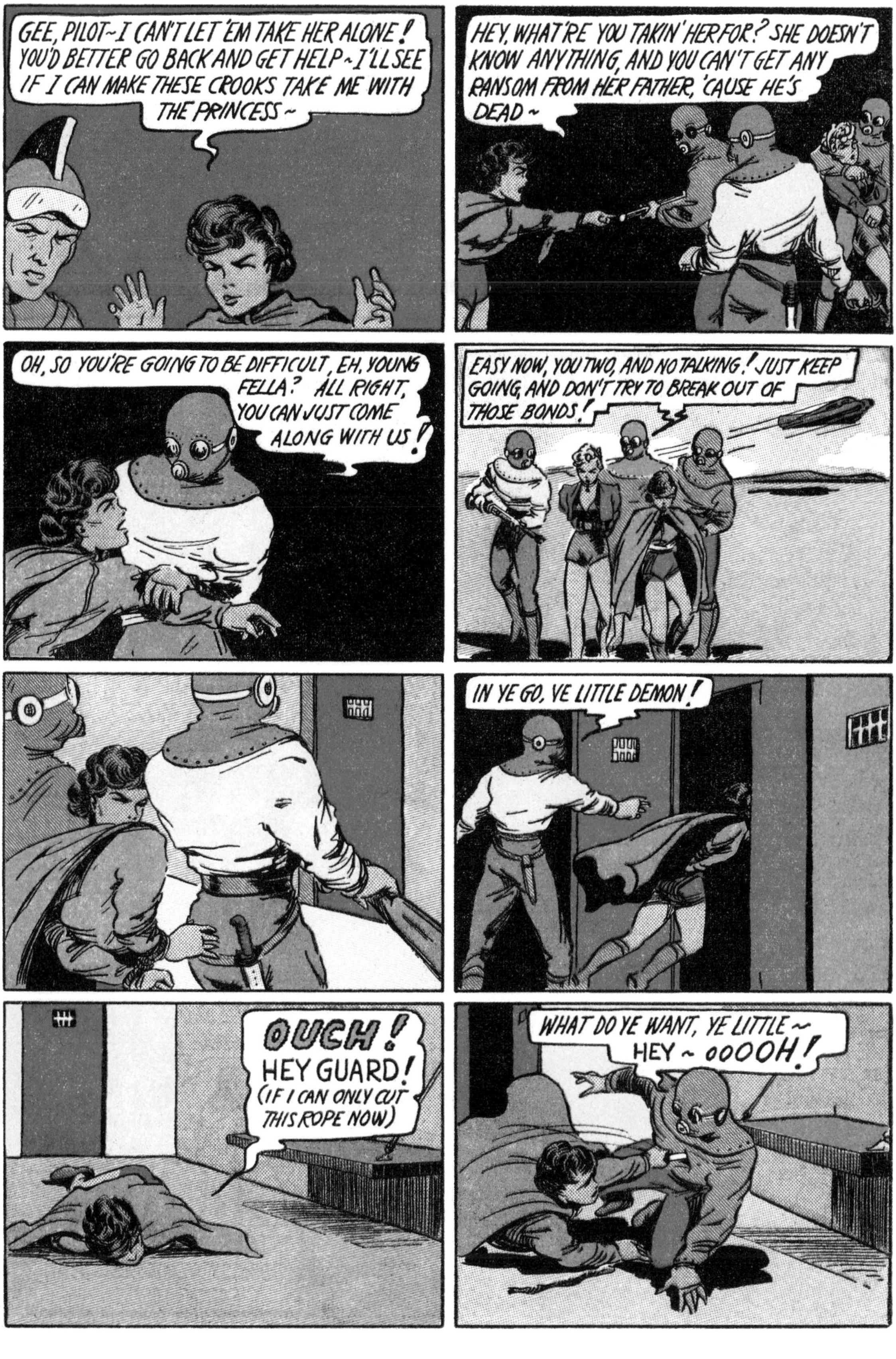
GEE, PILOT~I CAN'T LET 'EM TAKE HER ALONE! YOU'D BETTER GO BACK AND GET HELP~I'LL SEE IF I CAN MAKE THESE CROOKS TAKE ME WITH THE PRINCESS~
HEY, WHAT'RE YOU TAKIN' HER FOR? SHE DOESN'T KNOW ANYTHING, AND YOU CAN'T GET ANY RANSOM FROM HER FATHER, 'CAUSE HE'S DEAD~
OH, SO YOU'RE GOING TO BE DIFFICULT, EH, YOUNG FELLA? ALL RIGHT, YOU CAN JUST COME ALONG WITH US!
EASY NOW, YOU TWO, AND NO TALKING! JUST KEEP GOING, AND DON'T TRY TO BREAK OUT OF THOSE BONDS!
IN YE GO, YE LITTLE DEMON!
OUCH! HEY GUARD! (IF I CAN ONLY CUT THIS ROPE NOW)
WHAT DO YE WANT, YE LITTLE~ HEY~ OOOOH!

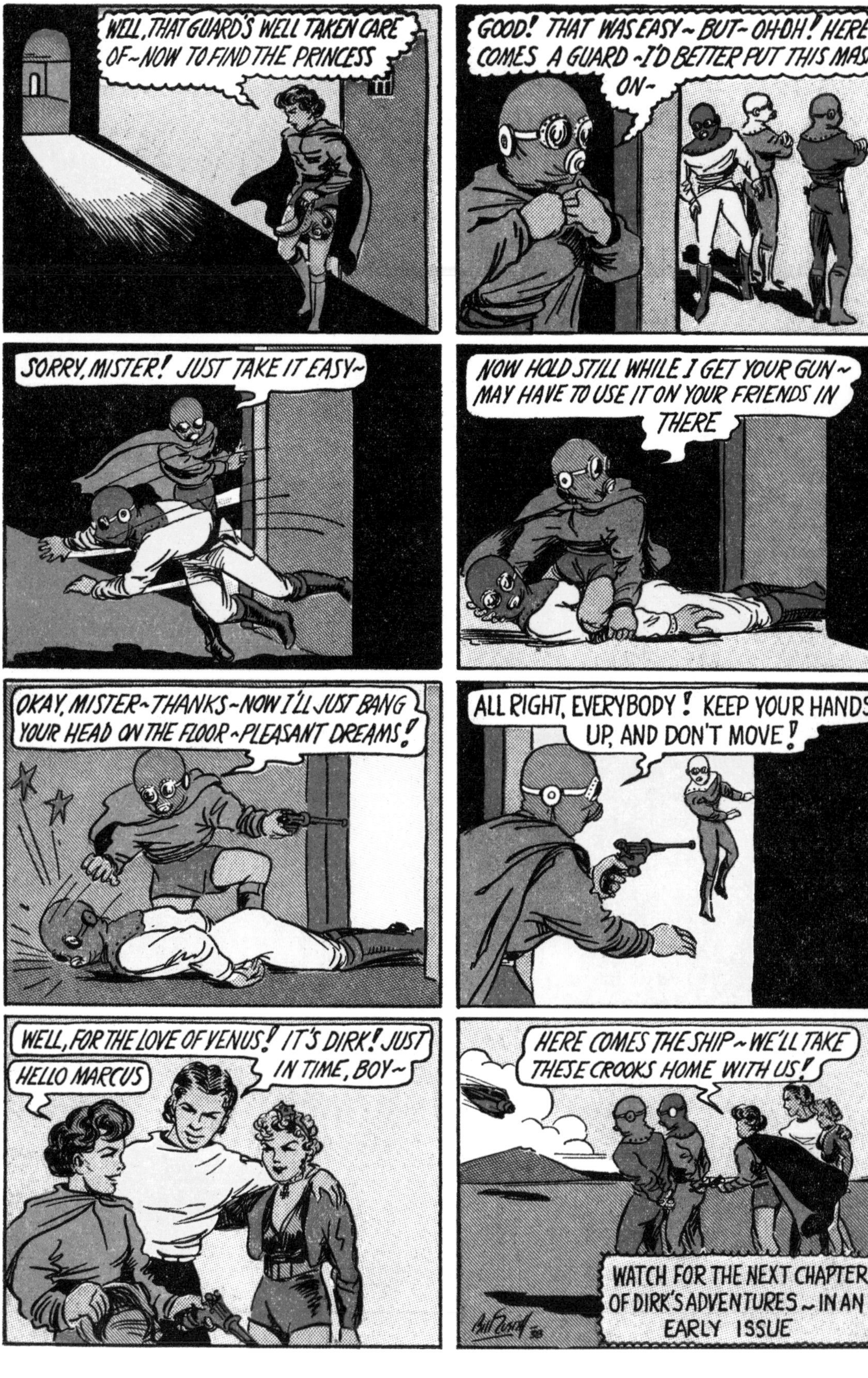
WELL, THAT GUARD'S WELL TAKEN CARE OF~NOW TO FIND THE PRINCESS
GOOD! THAT WAS EASY~BUT~OH-OH! HERE COMES A GUARD~I'D BETTER PUT THIS MASK ON~
SORRY, MISTER! JUST TAKE IT EASY~
NOW HOLD STILL WHILE I GET YOUR GUN~ MAY HAVE TO USE IT ON YOUR FRIENDS IN THERE
OKAY, MISTER~THANKS~NOW I'LL JUST BANG YOUR HEAD ON THE FLOOR~PLEASANT DREAMS!
ALL RIGHT, EVERYBODY! KEEP YOUR HANDS UP, AND DON'T MOVE!
WELL, FOR THE LOVE OF VENUS! IT'S DIRK! JUST IN TIME, BOY~
HELLO MARCUS
HERE COMES THE SHIP~WE'LL TAKE THESE CROOKS HOME WITH US!
WATCH FOR THE NEXT CHAPTER OF DIRK'S ADVENTURES~IN AN EARLY ISSUE

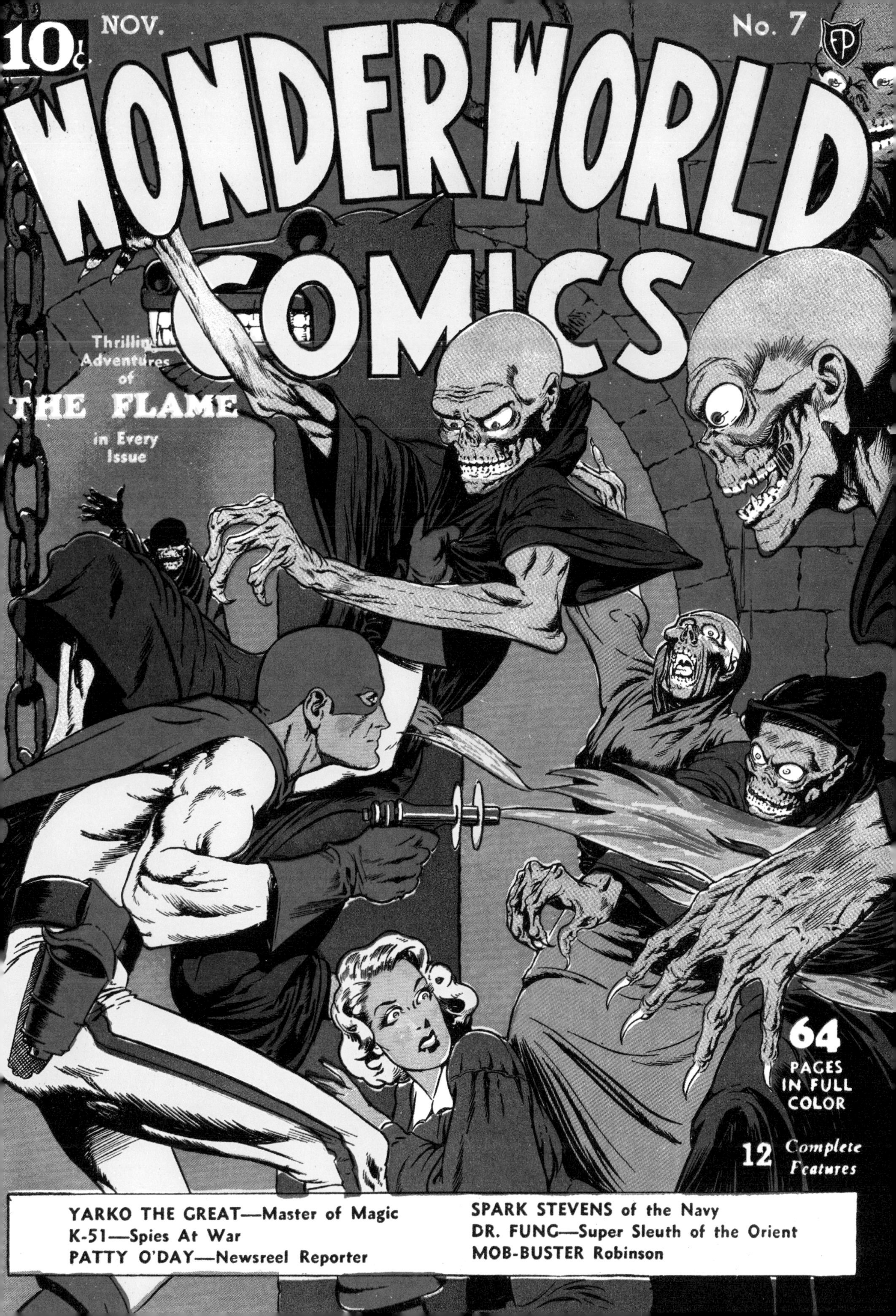
10¢
NOV.
No. 7
FP
WONDERWORLD COMICS
Thrilling Adventures of THE FLAME in Every Issue
64 PAGES IN FULL COLOR
12 Complete Features
YARKO THE GREAT—Master of Magic
K-51—Spies At War
PATTY O'DAY—Newsreel Reporter
SPARK STEVENS of the Navy
DR. FUNG—Super Sleuth of the Orient
MOB-BUSTER Robinson

# BE SURE TO GET THE NEW

## *MYSTERYMEN* COMICS

*On Sale About the 15th of Every Month*

**IT'S PACKED WITH ACTION, THRILLS AND FUN AND CHOCK FULL OF SUCH NEW FEATURES AS:**

---

**The BLUE BEETLE**

---

**BANCROFT OF SCOTLAND YARD**

---

**LIEUT. DRAKE OF THE UNITED STATES NAVY**

---

**REX DEXTER OF MARS**

Rex returns to Earth in time to save it from destruction at the hands of the invading Moonmen.

---

**The MYSTERY MAN**

A startling new character who will become the greatest figure in comics.

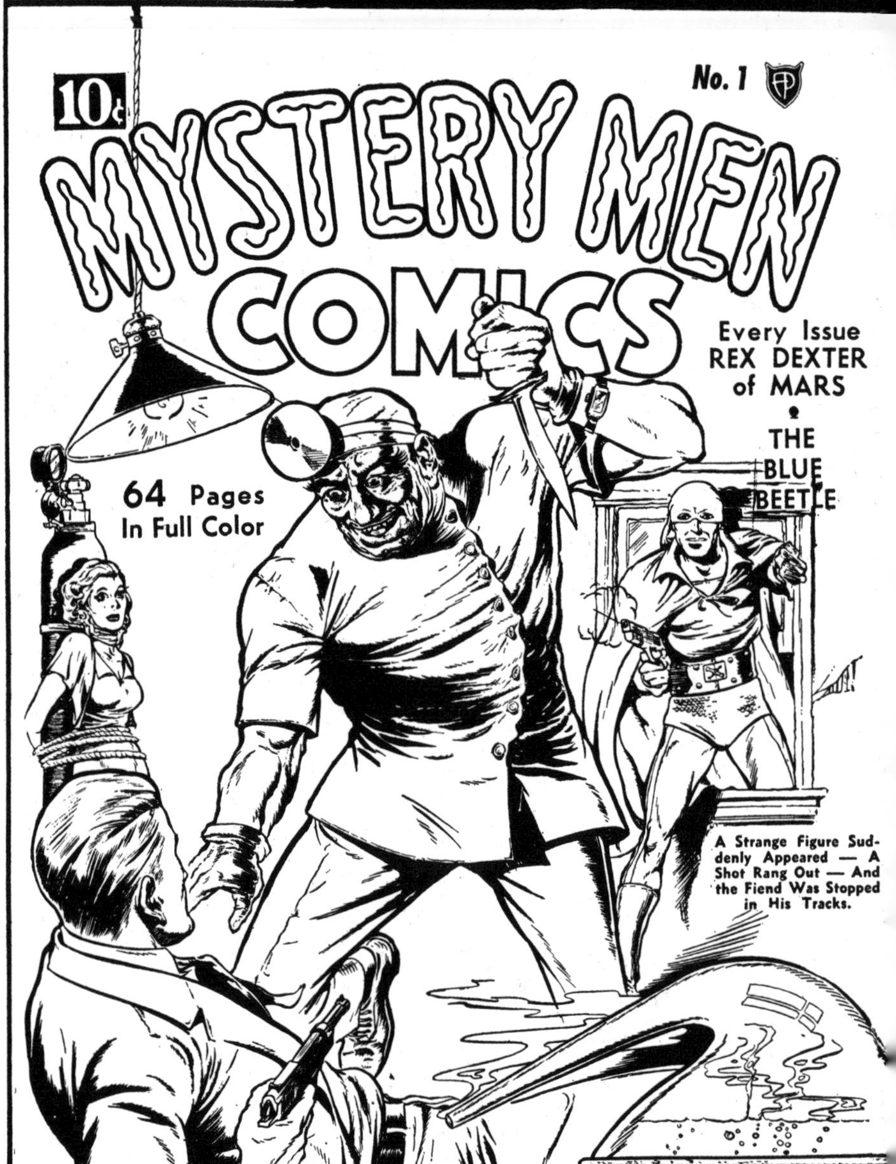

10¢
No. 1
MYSTERY MEN COMICS
Every Issue REX DEXTER of MARS • THE BLUE BEETLE
64 Pages In Full Color
A Strange Figure Suddenly Appeared — A Shot Rang Out — And the Fiend Was Stopped in His Tracks.
THRILLS • FUN • MYSTERY • EXCITING EXPLOITS


# 64 PAGES ALL IN FULL COLOR

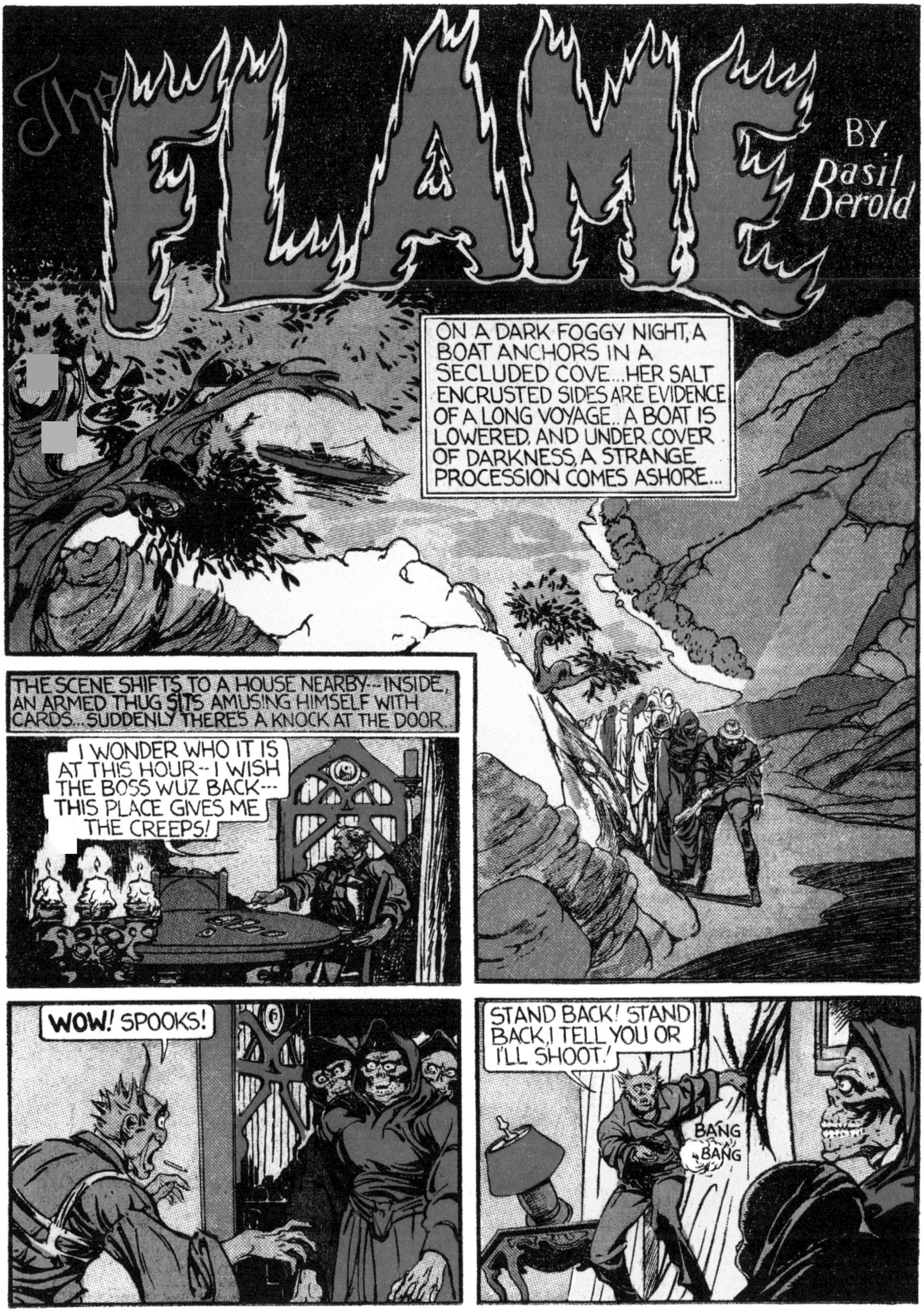
The FLAME
BY Basil Berold
ON A DARK FOGGY NIGHT, A BOAT ANCHORS IN A SECLUDED COVE...HER SALT ENCRUSTED SIDES ARE EVIDENCE OF A LONG VOYAGE.. A BOAT IS LOWERED, AND UNDER COVER OF DARKNESS, A STRANGE PROCESSION COMES ASHORE...
THE SCENE SHIFTS TO A HOUSE NEARBY--INSIDE, AN ARMED THUG SITS AMUSING HIMSELF WITH CARDS...SUDDENLY THERE'S A KNOCK AT THE DOOR.
I WONDER WHO IT IS AT THIS HOUR--I WISH THE BOSS WUZ BACK--- THIS PLACE GIVES ME THE CREEPS!
WOW! SPOOKS!
STAND BACK! STAND BACK, I TELL YOU OR I'LL SHOOT!
BANG
BANG

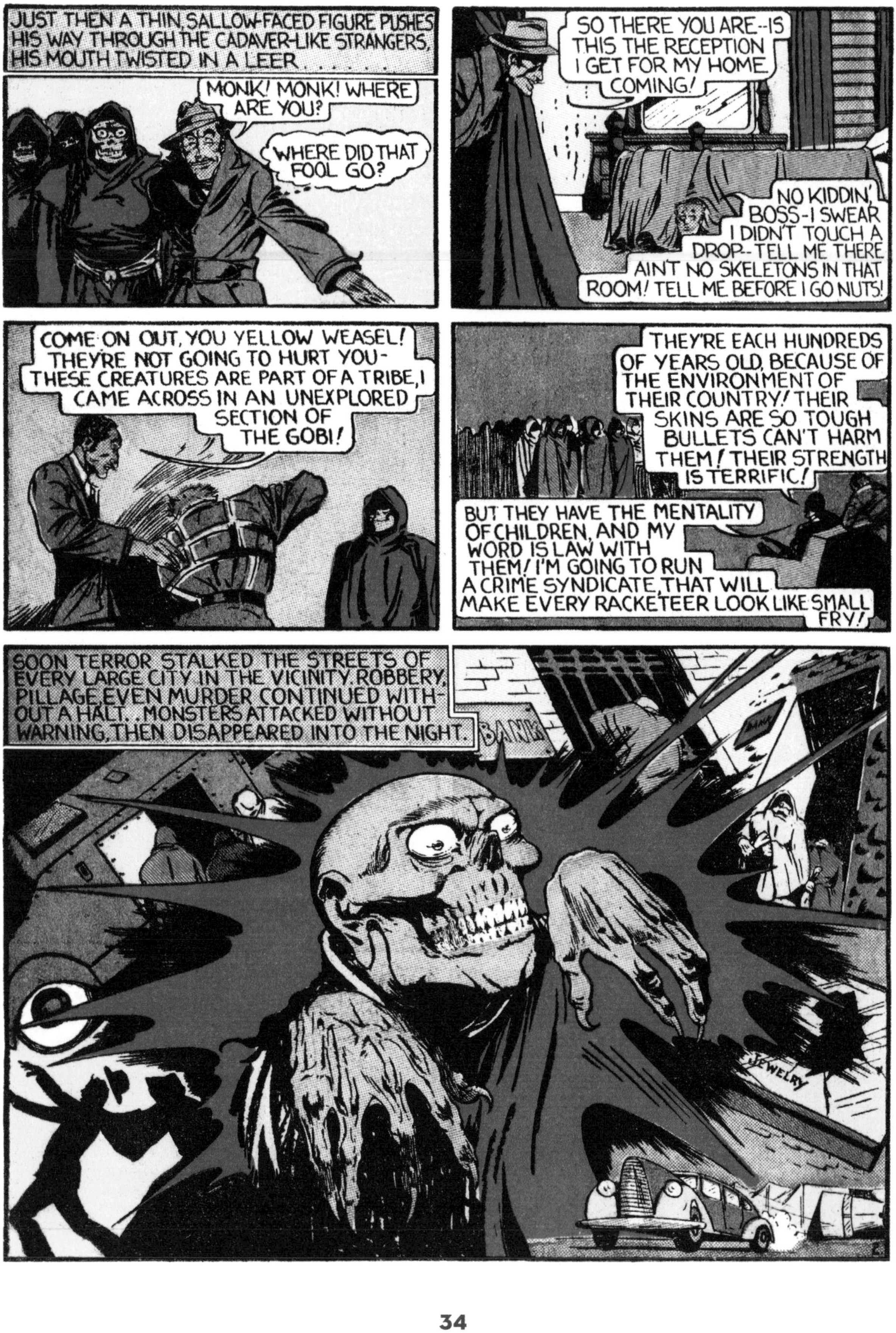
JUST THEN A THIN, SALLOW-FACED FIGURE PUSHES HIS WAY THROUGH THE CADAVER-LIKE STRANGERS, HIS MOUTH TWISTED IN A LEER . . . . . .
MONK! MONK! WHERE ARE YOU?
WHERE DID THAT FOOL GO?
SO THERE YOU ARE--IS THIS THE RECEPTION I GET FOR MY HOME COMING!
NO KIDDIN', BOSS-I SWEAR I DIDN'T TOUCH A DROP--TELL ME THERE AIN'T NO SKELETONS IN THAT ROOM! TELL ME BEFORE I GO NUTS!
COME ON OUT, YOU YELLOW WEASEL! THEY'RE NOT GOING TO HURT YOU- THESE CREATURES ARE PART OF A TRIBE, I CAME ACROSS IN AN UNEXPLORED SECTION OF THE GOBI!
THEY'RE EACH HUNDREDS OF YEARS OLD, BECAUSE OF THE ENVIRONMENT OF THEIR COUNTRY! THEIR SKINS ARE SO TOUGH BULLETS CAN'T HARM THEM! THEIR STRENGTH IS TERRIFIC!
BUT THEY HAVE THE MENTALITY OF CHILDREN, AND MY WORD IS LAW WITH THEM! I'M GOING TO RUN A CRIME SYNDICATE, THAT WILL MAKE EVERY RACKETEER LOOK LIKE SMALL FRY!
SOON TERROR STALKED THE STREETS OF EVERY LARGE CITY IN THE VICINITY. ROBBERY, PILLAGE, EVEN MURDER CONTINUED WITHOUT A HALT. . MONSTERS ATTACKED WITHOUT WARNING, THEN DISAPPEARED INTO THE NIGHT.
BANK
JEWELRY

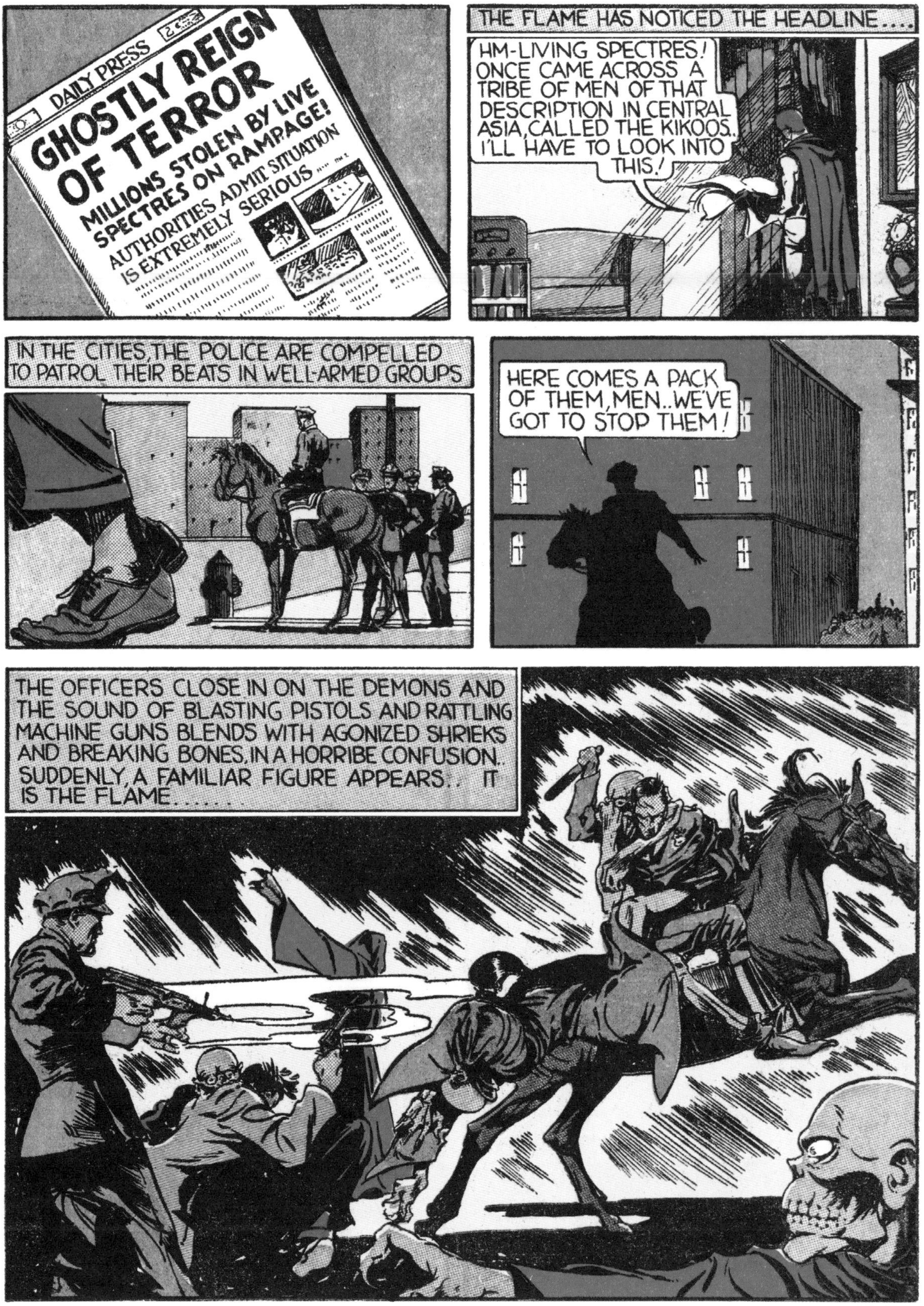
DAILY PRESS
GHOSTLY REIGN OF TERROR
MILLIONS STOLEN BY LIVE SPECTRES ON RAMPAGE!
AUTHORITIES ADMIT SITUATION IS EXTREMELY SERIOUS
THE FLAME HAS NOTICED THE HEADLINE....
HM-LIVING SPECTRES! ONCE CAME ACROSS A TRIBE OF MEN OF THAT DESCRIPTION IN CENTRAL ASIA, CALLED THE KIKOOS. I'LL HAVE TO LOOK INTO THIS!
IN THE CITIES, THE POLICE ARE COMPELLED TO PATROL THEIR BEATS IN WELL-ARMED GROUPS
HERE COMES A PACK OF THEM, MEN.. WE'VE GOT TO STOP THEM!
THE OFFICERS CLOSE IN ON THE DEMONS AND THE SOUND OF BLASTING PISTOLS AND RATTLING MACHINE GUNS BLENDS WITH AGONIZED SHRIEKS AND BREAKING BONES, IN A HORRIBE CONFUSION. SUDDENLY, A FAMILIAR FIGURE APPEARS.. IT IS THE FLAME.....

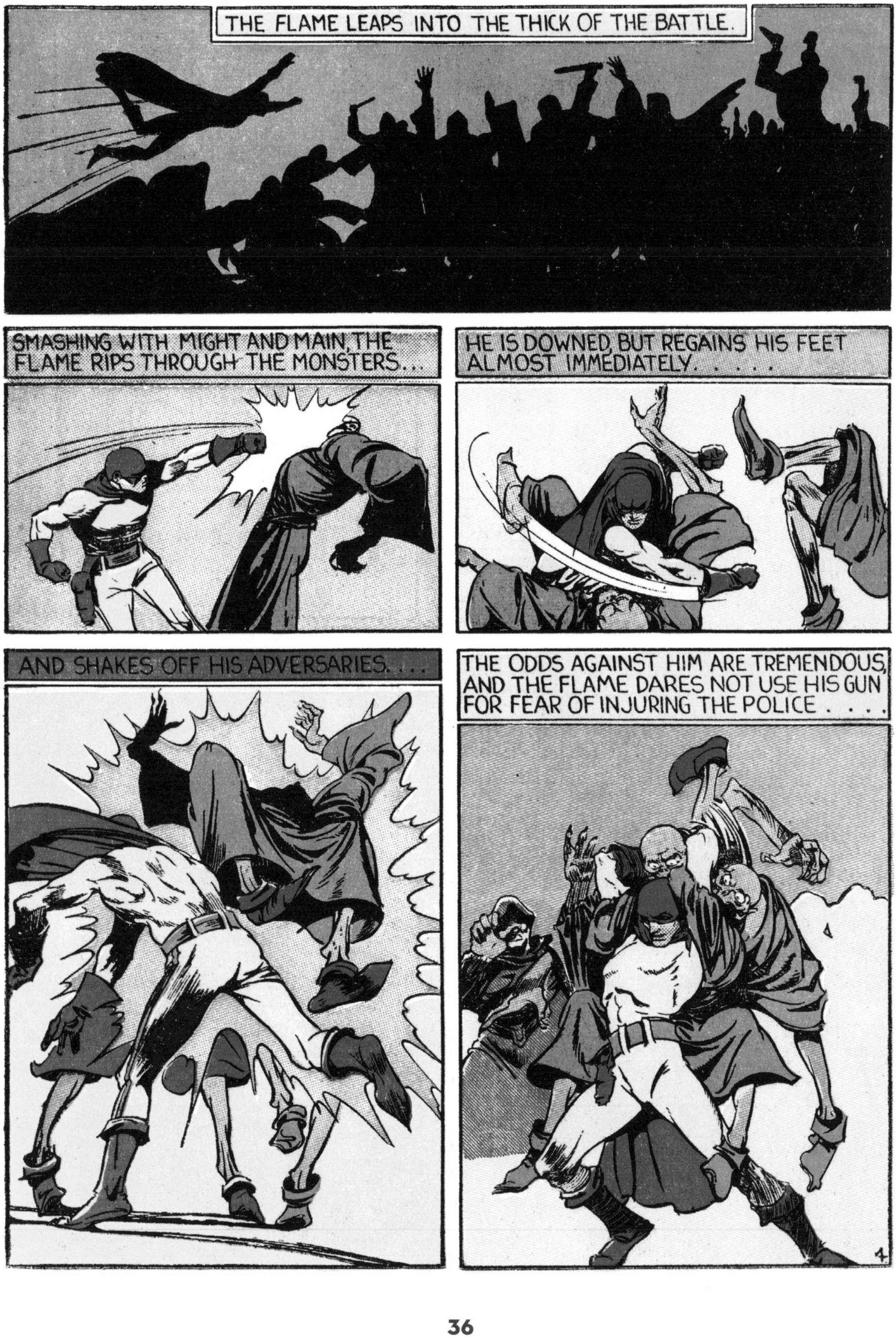
THE FLAME LEAPS INTO THE THICK OF THE BATTLE.
SMASHING WITH MIGHT AND MAIN, THE FLAME RIPS THROUGH THE MONSTERS...
HE IS DOWNED, BUT REGAINS HIS FEET ALMOST IMMEDIATELY. . . .
AND SHAKES OFF HIS ADVERSARIES. . . .
THE ODDS AGAINST HIM ARE TREMENDOUS, AND THE FLAME DARES NOT USE HIS GUN FOR FEAR OF INJURING THE POLICE . . . .
4

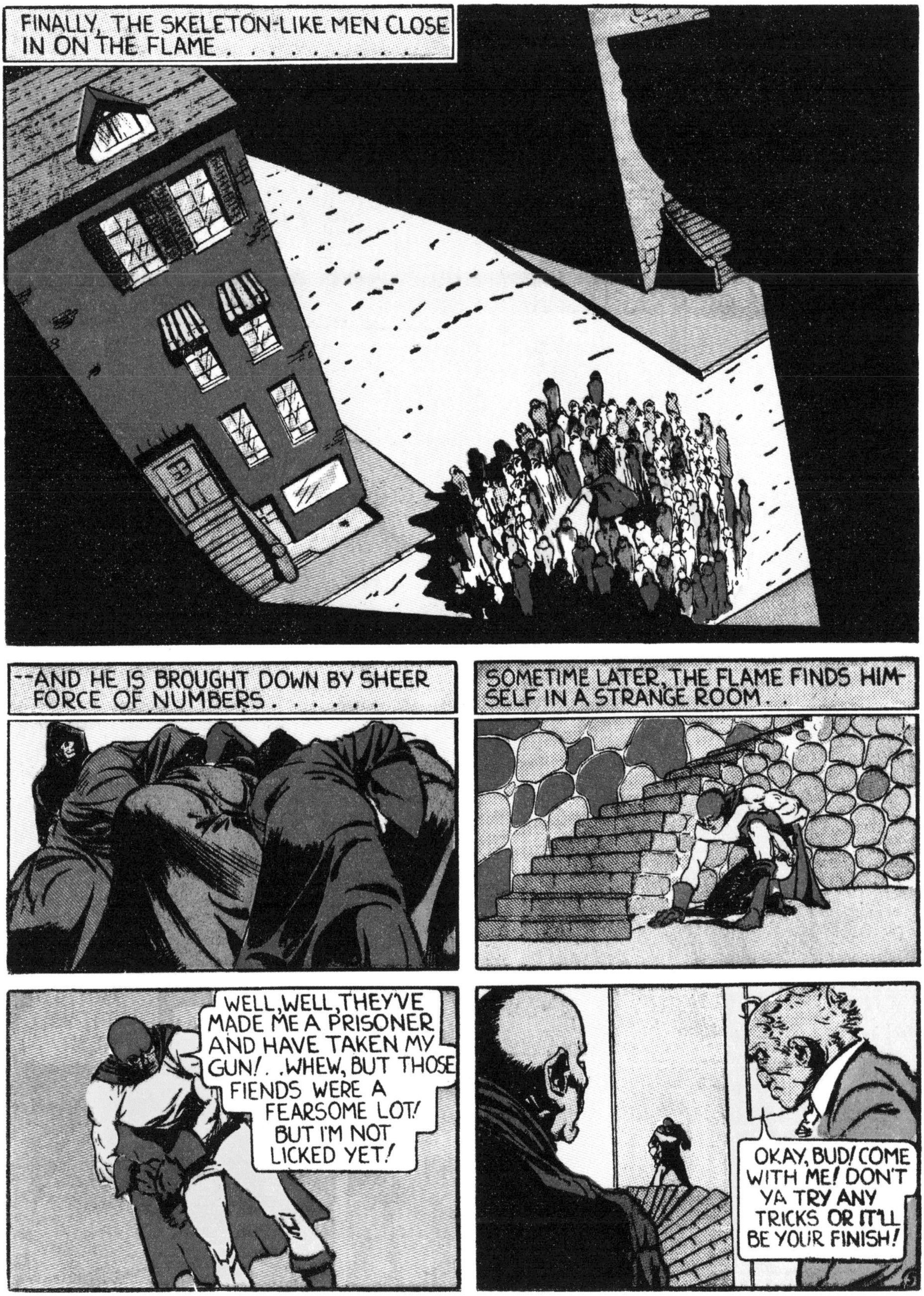
FINALLY, THE SKELETON-LIKE MEN CLOSE IN ON THE FLAME . . . . . . . . . .
--AND HE IS BROUGHT DOWN BY SHEER FORCE OF NUMBERS . . . . . .
SOMETIME LATER, THE FLAME FINDS HIMSELF IN A STRANGE ROOM . .
WELL, WELL, THEY'VE MADE ME A PRISONER AND HAVE TAKEN MY GUN! . .WHEW, BUT THOSE FIENDS WERE A FEARSOME LOT! BUT I'M NOT LICKED YET!
OKAY, BUD! COME WITH ME! DON'T YA TRY ANY TRICKS OR IT'LL BE YOUR FINISH!

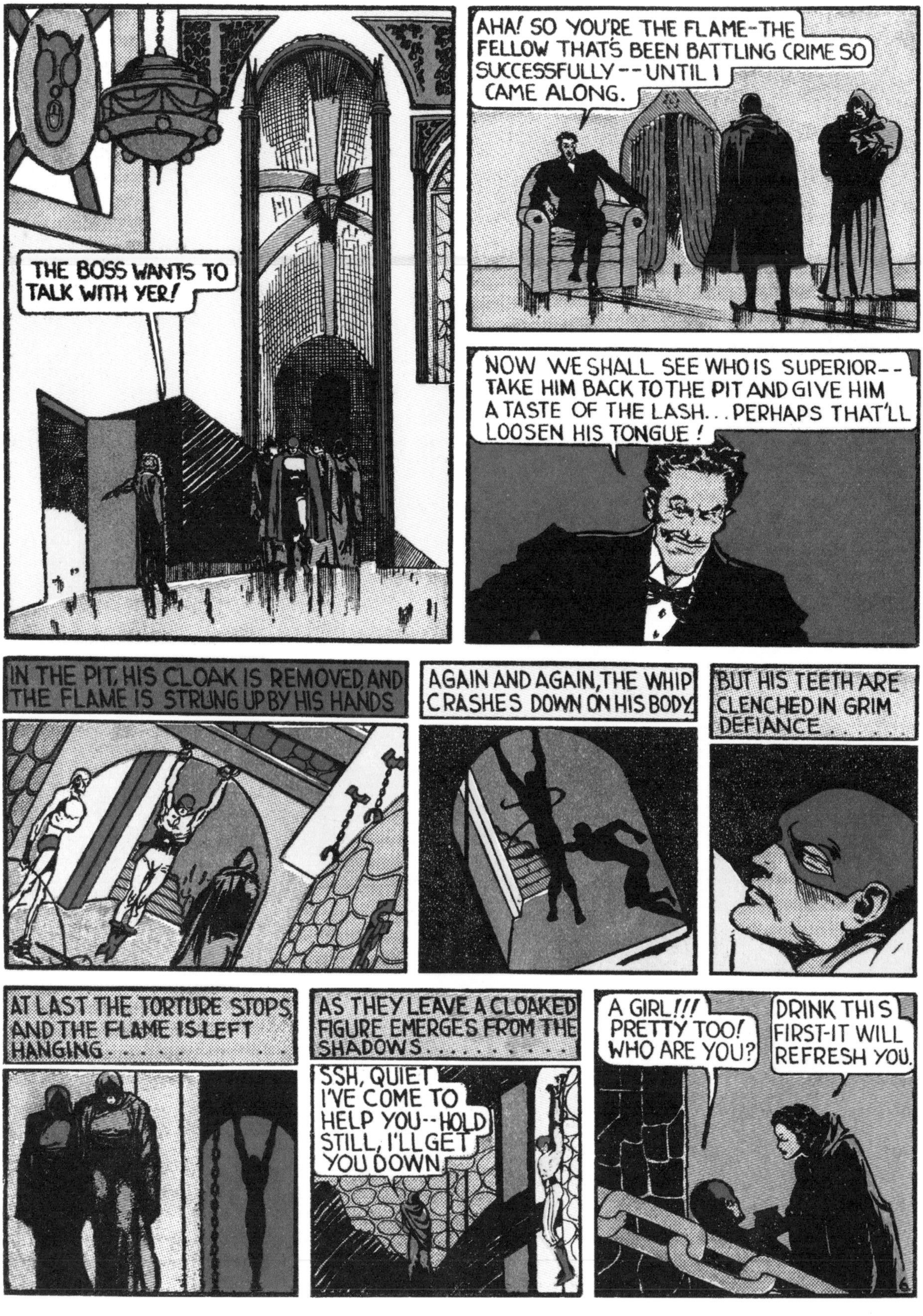
THE BOSS WANTS TO TALK WITH YER!
AHA! SO YOU'RE THE FLAME-THE FELLOW THAT'S BEEN BATTLING CRIME SO SUCCESSFULLY--UNTIL I CAME ALONG.
NOW WE SHALL SEE WHO IS SUPERIOR--TAKE HIM BACK TO THE PIT AND GIVE HIM A TASTE OF THE LASH... PERHAPS THAT'LL LOOSEN HIS TONGUE!
IN THE PIT, HIS CLOAK IS REMOVED, AND THE FLAME IS STRUNG UP BY HIS HANDS
AGAIN AND AGAIN, THE WHIP CRASHES DOWN ON HIS BODY
BUT HIS TEETH ARE CLENCHED IN GRIM DEFIANCE......
AT LAST THE TORTURE STOPS, AND THE FLAME IS LEFT HANGING.........
AS THEY LEAVE A CLOAKED FIGURE EMERGES FROM THE SHADOWS..........
SSH, QUIET I'VE COME TO HELP YOU--HOLD STILL, I'LL GET YOU DOWN.
A GIRL!!! PRETTY TOO! WHO ARE YOU?
DRINK THIS FIRST-IT WILL REFRESH YOU.
6

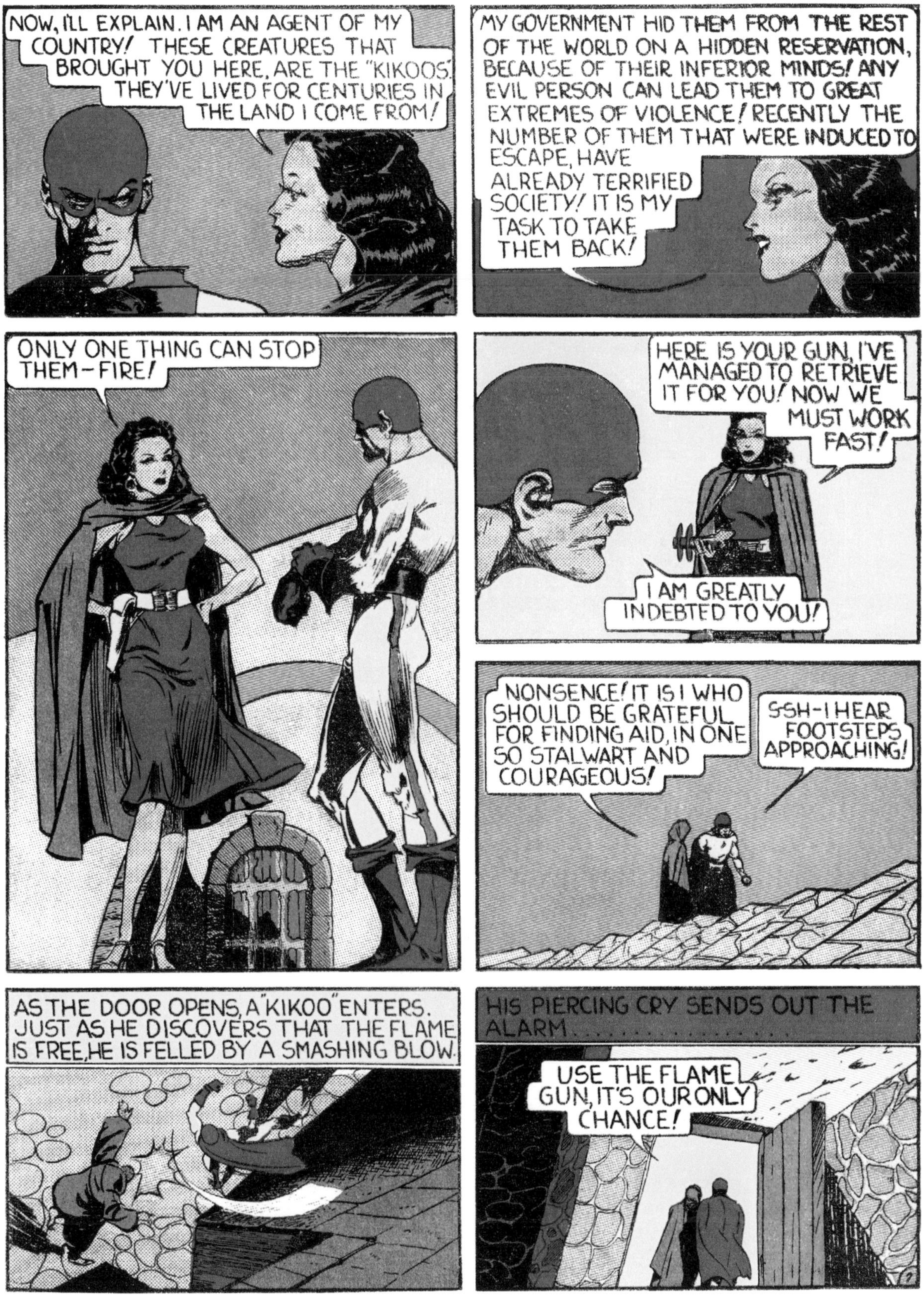
NOW, I'LL EXPLAIN. I AM AN AGENT OF MY COUNTRY! THESE CREATURES THAT BROUGHT YOU HERE, ARE THE "KIKOOS" THEY'VE LIVED FOR CENTURIES IN THE LAND I COME FROM!
MY GOVERNMENT HID THEM FROM THE REST OF THE WORLD ON A HIDDEN RESERVATION, BECAUSE OF THEIR INFERIOR MINDS! ANY EVIL PERSON CAN LEAD THEM TO GREAT EXTREMES OF VIOLENCE! RECENTLY THE NUMBER OF THEM THAT WERE INDUCED TO ESCAPE, HAVE ALREADY TERRIFIED SOCIETY! IT IS MY TASK TO TAKE THEM BACK!
ONLY ONE THING CAN STOP THEM—FIRE!
HERE IS YOUR GUN, I'VE MANAGED TO RETRIEVE IT FOR YOU! NOW WE MUST WORK FAST!
I AM GREATLY INDEBTED TO YOU!
NONSENCE! IT IS I WHO SHOULD BE GRATEFUL FOR FINDING AID, IN ONE SO STALWART AND COURAGEOUS!
S-SH—I HEAR FOOTSTEPS APPROACHING!
AS THE DOOR OPENS, A "KIKOO" ENTERS. JUST AS HE DISCOVERS THAT THE FLAME IS FREE, HE IS FELLED BY A SMASHING BLOW.
HIS PIERCING CRY SENDS OUT THE ALARM..............
USE THE FLAME GUN, IT'S OUR ONLY CHANCE!

AFTER HIM DON'T LET HIM ESCAPE! TEAR HIM TO SHREDS!

A WOMAN,TOO? HO! DON'T TOUCH THE WOMAN!! I'LL TEND TO HER IN MY OWN WAY!

THE FLAME SHAKES OFF THE FIRST ATTACKERS.............

THE GUN--USE THE GUN!

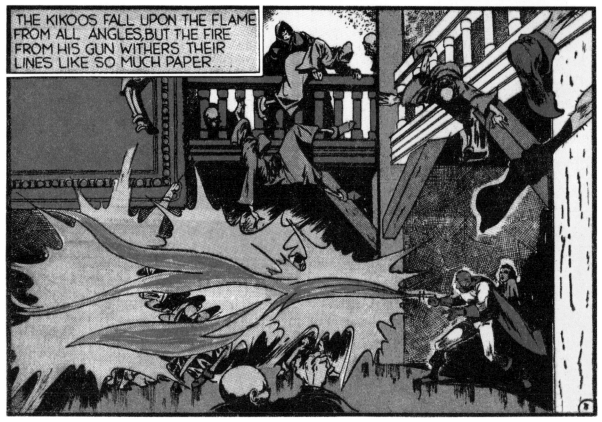

THE KIKOOS FALL UPON THE FLAME FROM ALL ANGLES, BUT THE FIRE FROM HIS GUN WITHERS THEIR LINES LIKE SO MUCH PAPER

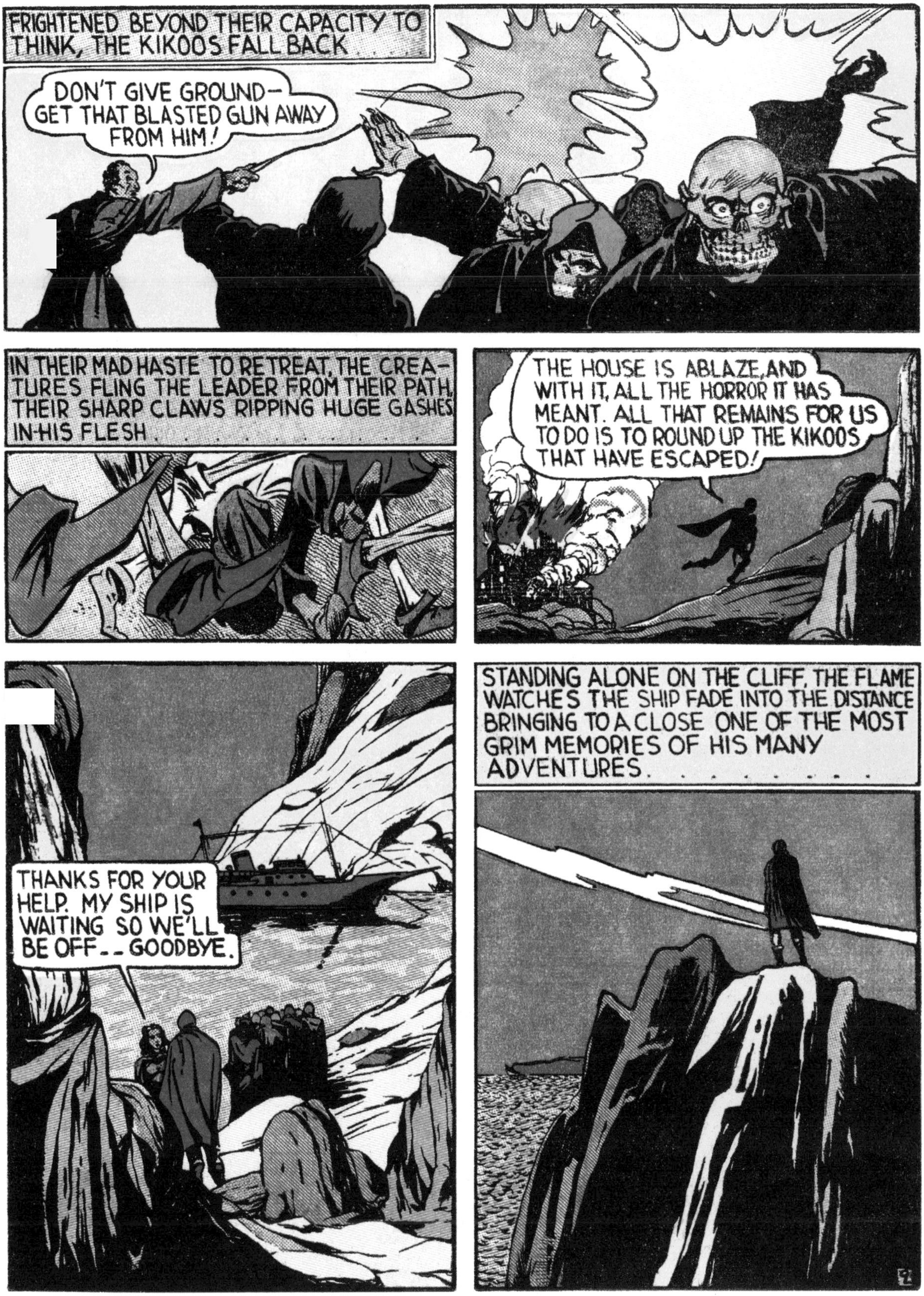
FRIGHTENED BEYOND THEIR CAPACITY TO THINK, THE KIKOOS FALL BACK . . . .
DON'T GIVE GROUND— GET THAT BLASTED GUN AWAY FROM HIM!
IN THEIR MAD HASTE TO RETREAT, THE CREATURES FLING THE LEADER FROM THEIR PATH, THEIR SHARP CLAWS RIPPING HUGE GASHES IN HIS FLESH . . . . . . .
THE HOUSE IS ABLAZE, AND WITH IT, ALL THE HORROR IT HAS MEANT. ALL THAT REMAINS FOR US TO DO IS TO ROUND UP THE KIKOOS THAT HAVE ESCAPED!
THANKS FOR YOUR HELP. MY SHIP IS WAITING SO WE'LL BE OFF - - GOODBYE.
STANDING ALONE ON THE CLIFF, THE FLAME WATCHES THE SHIP FADE INTO THE DISTANCE BRINGING TO A CLOSE ONE OF THE MOST GRIM MEMORIES OF HIS MANY ADVENTURES. . . . . . .

WATCH

FOR

THIS

COVER

•

***THE***

***GREATEST***

***10c***

***WORTH***

***ON***

***THE***

***NEWSSTANDS***

•

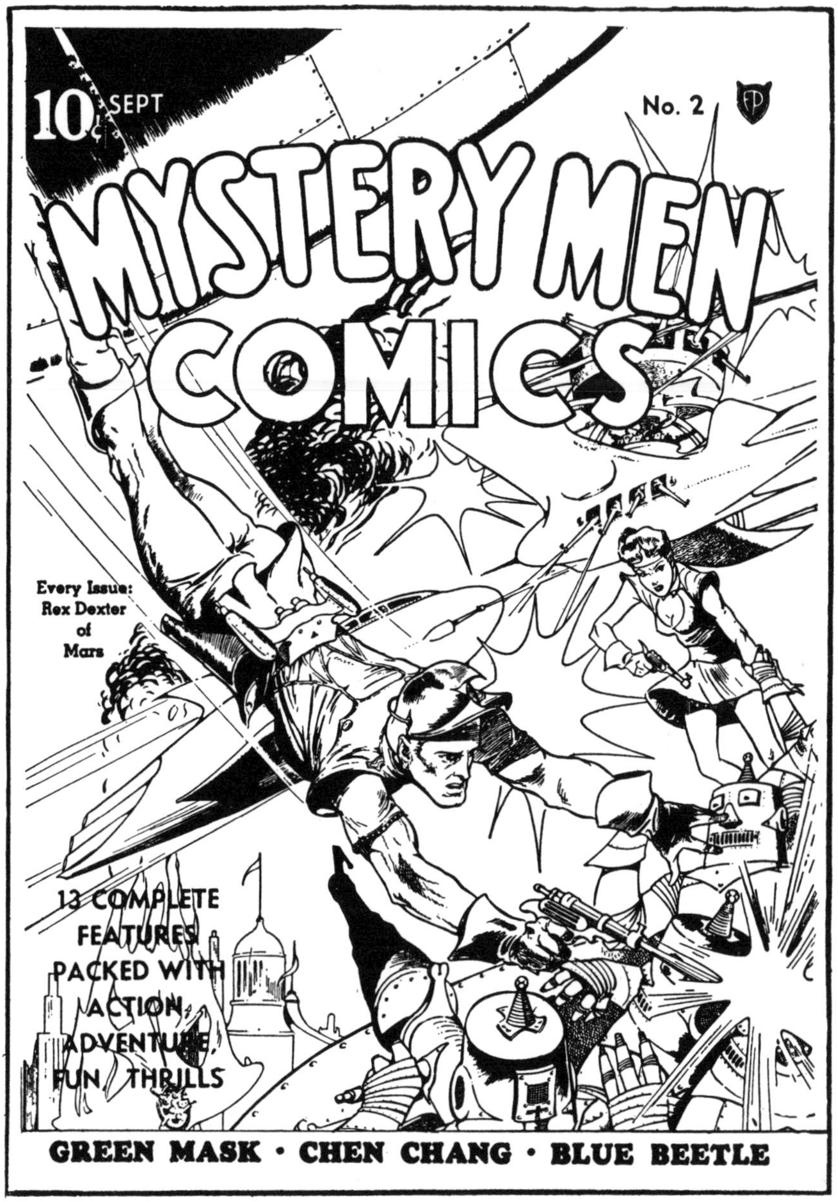
10¢
SEPT
No. 2
MYSTERY MEN
COMICS
Every Issue: Rex Dexter of Mars
13 COMPLETE FEATURES PACKED WITH ACTION ADVENTURE FUN THRILLS
GREEN MASK · CHEN CHANG · BLUE BEETLE

**On Sale About the 15th of Every Month**

THOUSANDS OF KIDS ARE FOLLOWING: THE GREEN MASK, THE BLUE BEETLE, ZANZIBAR, DENNY SCOTT OF THE BENGAL LANCERS, D-13 SECRET AGENT AND A HOST OF OTHERS . . . . . . DON'T MISS IT!

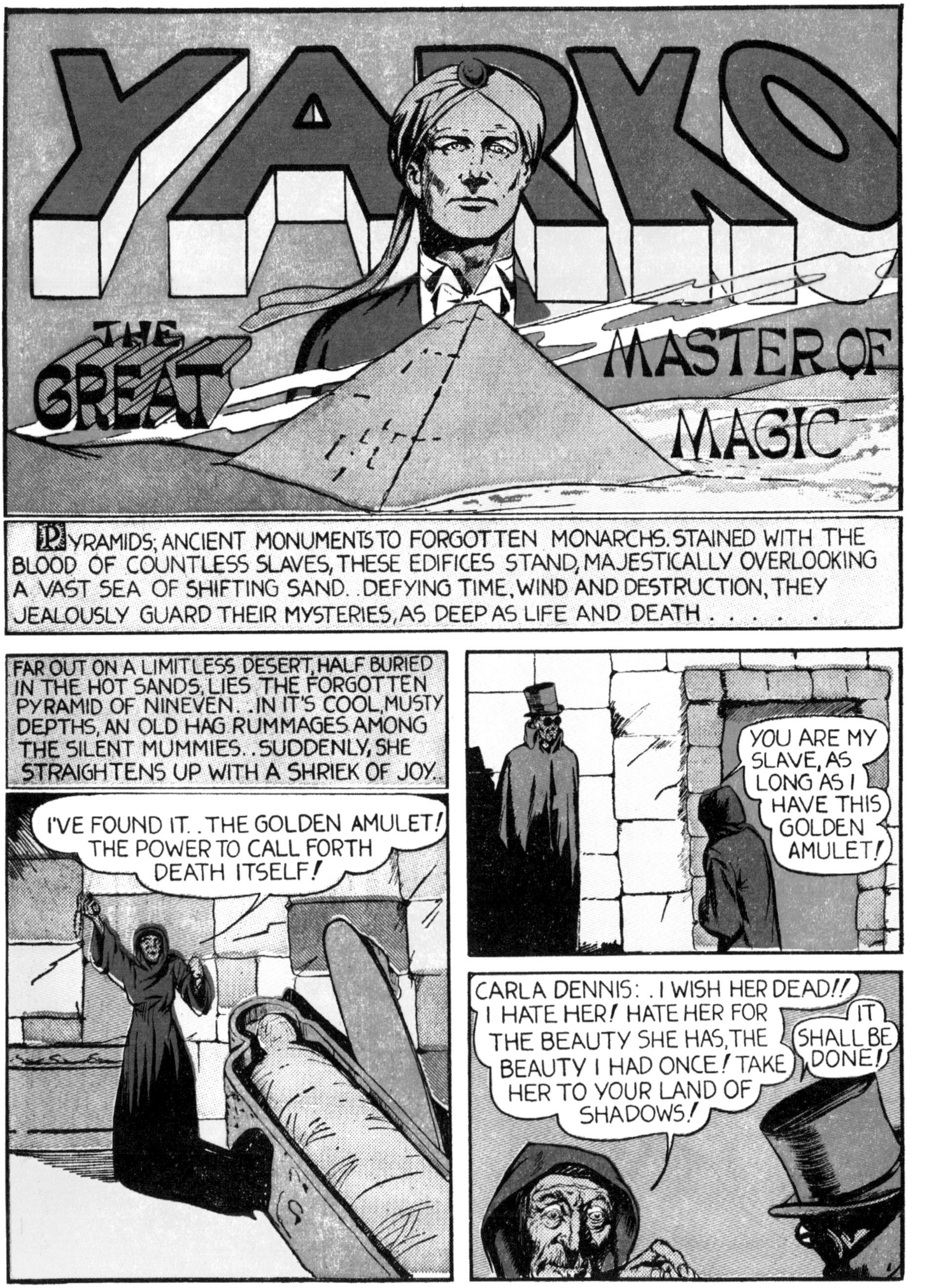
YARKO
THE GREAT
MASTER OF MAGIC
PYRAMIDS; ANCIENT MONUMENTS TO FORGOTTEN MONARCHS. STAINED WITH THE BLOOD OF COUNTLESS SLAVES, THESE EDIFICES STAND, MAJESTICALLY OVERLOOKING A VAST SEA OF SHIFTING SAND. . DEFYING TIME, WIND AND DESTRUCTION, THEY JEALOUSLY GUARD THEIR MYSTERIES, AS DEEP AS LIFE AND DEATH . . . .
FAR OUT ON A LIMITLESS DESERT, HALF BURIED IN THE HOT SANDS, LIES THE FORGOTTEN PYRAMID OF NINEVEN. . IN IT'S COOL, MUSTY DEPTHS, AN OLD HAG RUMMAGES AMONG THE SILENT MUMMIES. . SUDDENLY, SHE STRAIGHTENS UP WITH A SHRIEK OF JOY.
I'VE FOUND IT. . THE GOLDEN AMULET! THE POWER TO CALL FORTH DEATH ITSELF!
YOU ARE MY SLAVE, AS LONG AS I HAVE THIS GOLDEN AMULET!
CARLA DENNIS: . I WISH HER DEAD!! I HATE HER! HATE HER FOR THE BEAUTY SHE HAS, THE BEAUTY I HAD ONCE! TAKE HER TO YOUR LAND OF SHADOWS!
IT SHALL BE DONE!

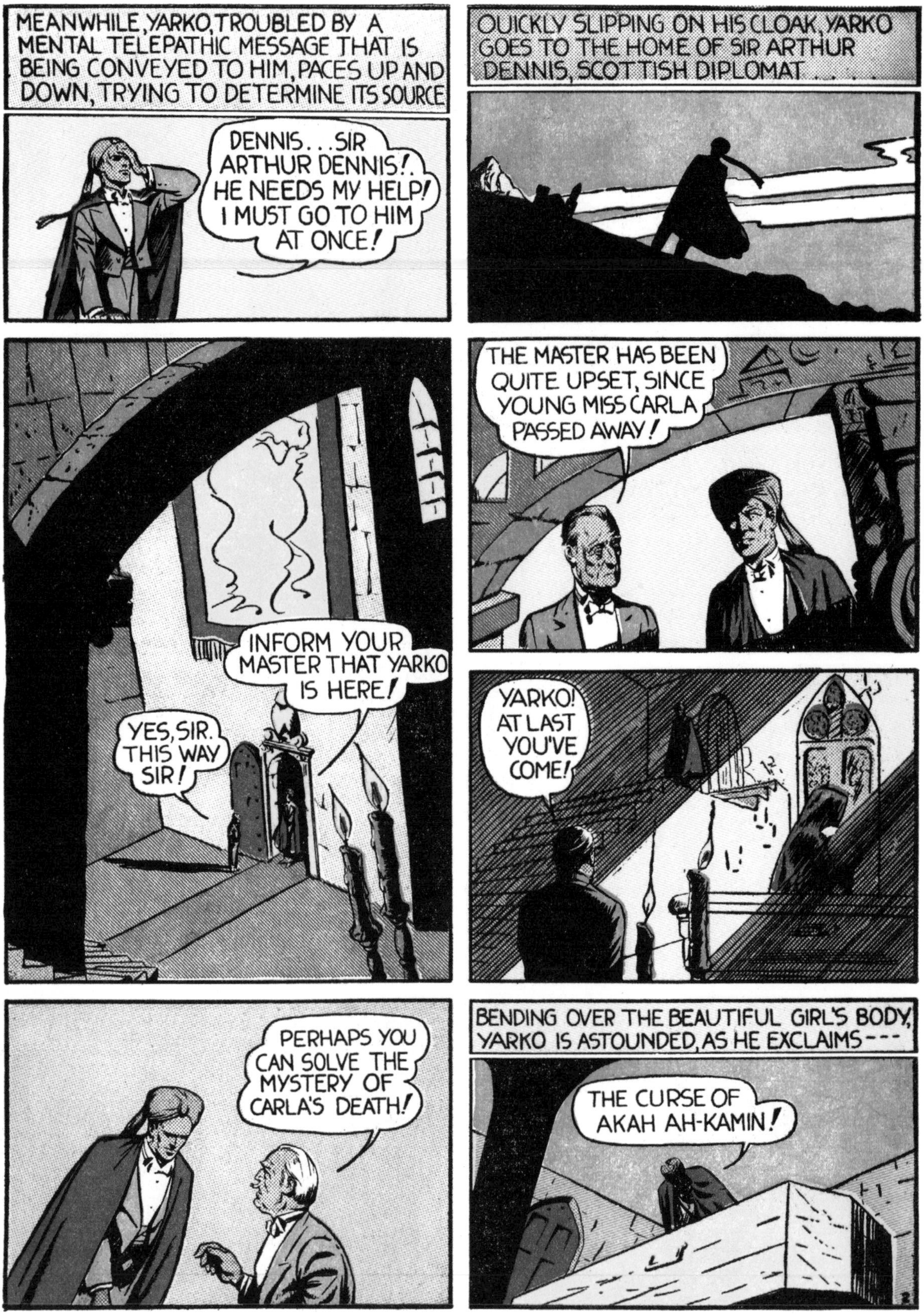
MEANWHILE, YARKO, TROUBLED BY A MENTAL TELEPATHIC MESSAGE THAT IS BEING CONVEYED TO HIM, PACES UP AND DOWN, TRYING TO DETERMINE ITS SOURCE
DENNIS...SIR ARTHUR DENNIS!. HE NEEDS MY HELP! I MUST GO TO HIM AT ONCE!
QUICKLY SLIPPING ON HIS CLOAK, YARKO GOES TO THE HOME OF SIR ARTHUR DENNIS, SCOTTISH DIPLOMAT . . . .
INFORM YOUR MASTER THAT YARKO IS HERE!
YES, SIR. THIS WAY SIR!
THE MASTER HAS BEEN QUITE UPSET, SINCE YOUNG MISS CARLA PASSED AWAY!
YARKO! AT LAST YOU'VE COME!
PERHAPS YOU CAN SOLVE THE MYSTERY OF CARLA'S DEATH!
BENDING OVER THE BEAUTIFUL GIRL'S BODY, YARKO IS ASTOUNDED, AS HE EXCLAIMS---
THE CURSE OF AKAH AH-KAMIN!

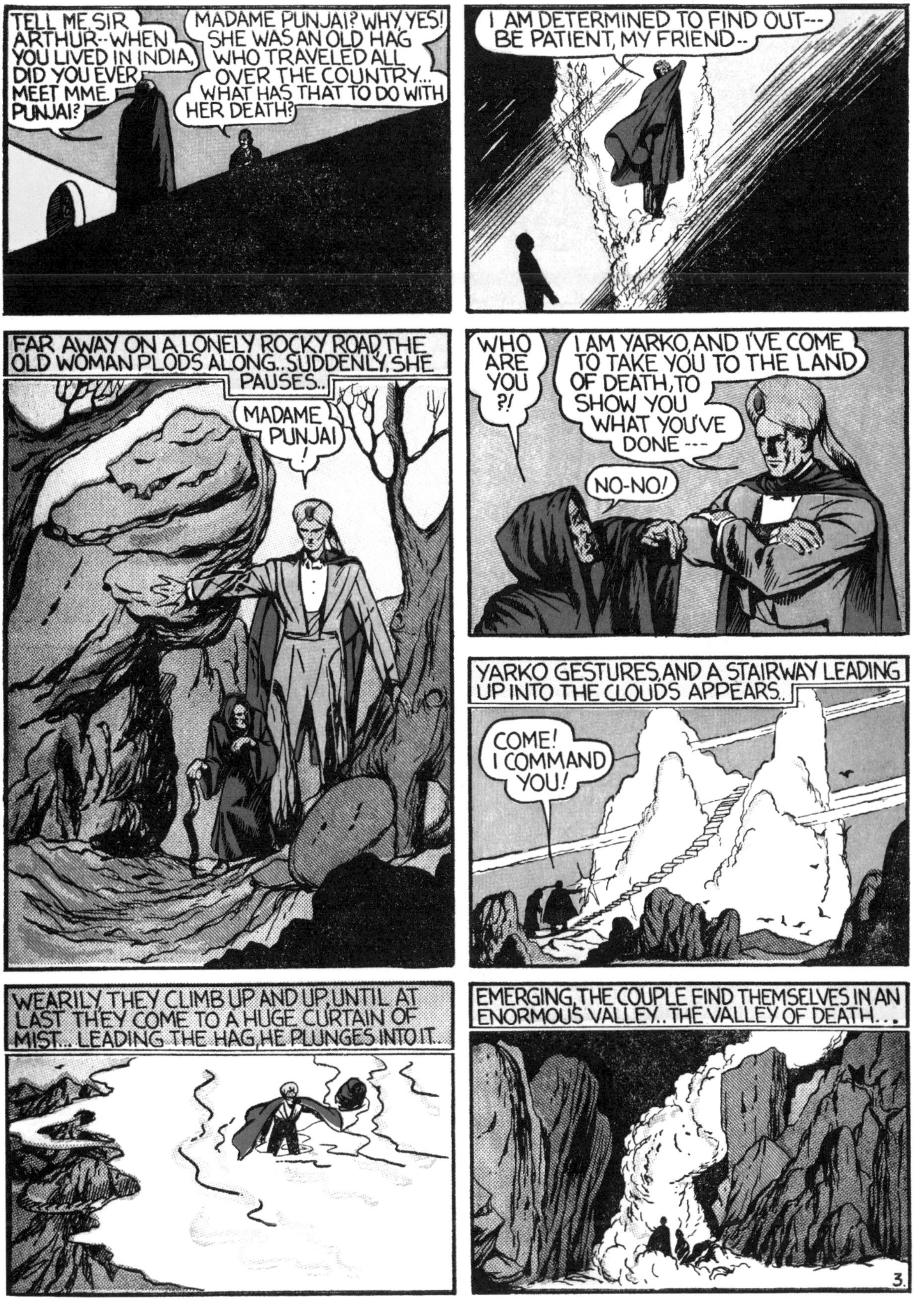
TELL ME, SIR ARTHUR-- WHEN YOU LIVED IN INDIA, DID YOU EVER MEET MME. PUNJAI?
MADAME PUNJAI? WHY, YES! SHE WAS AN OLD HAG WHO TRAVELED ALL OVER THE COUNTRY... WHAT HAS THAT TO DO WITH HER DEATH?
I AM DETERMINED TO FIND OUT--- BE PATIENT, MY FRIEND--
FAR AWAY ON A LONELY ROCKY ROAD THE OLD WOMAN PLODS ALONG.. SUDDENLY, SHE PAUSES..
MADAME PUNJAI!
WHO ARE YOU ?!
I AM YARKO, AND I'VE COME TO TAKE YOU TO THE LAND OF DEATH, TO SHOW YOU WHAT YOU'VE DONE ---
NO-NO!
YARKO GESTURES, AND A STAIRWAY LEADING UP INTO THE CLOUDS APPEARS..
COME! I COMMAND YOU!
WEARILY, THEY CLIMB UP AND UP, UNTIL AT LAST THEY COME TO A HUGE CURTAIN OF MIST... LEADING THE HAG, HE PLUNGES INTO IT..
EMERGING, THE COUPLE FIND THEMSELVES IN AN ENORMOUS VALLEY.. THE VALLEY OF DEATH...
3.

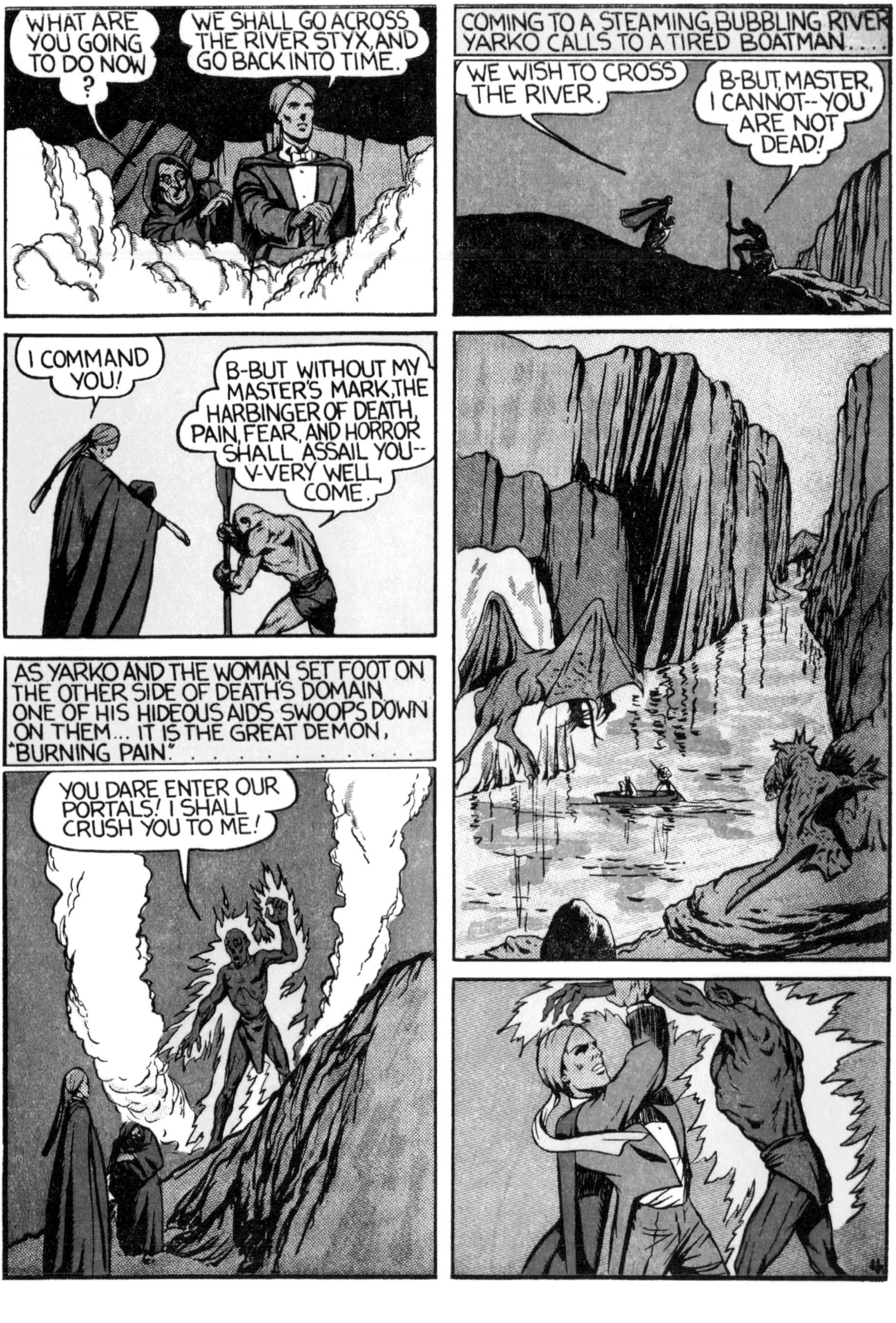
WHAT ARE YOU GOING TO DO NOW ?
WE SHALL GO ACROSS THE RIVER STYX, AND GO BACK INTO TIME.
COMING TO A STEAMING, BUBBLING RIVER YARKO CALLS TO A TIRED BOATMAN. . . .
WE WISH TO CROSS THE RIVER.
B-BUT, MASTER, I CANNOT--YOU ARE NOT DEAD!
I COMMAND YOU!
B-BUT WITHOUT MY MASTER'S MARK, THE HARBINGER OF DEATH, PAIN, FEAR, AND HORROR SHALL ASSAIL YOU-- V-VERY WELL, COME.
AS YARKO AND THE WOMAN SET FOOT ON THE OTHER SIDE OF DEATH'S DOMAIN ONE OF HIS HIDEOUS AIDS SWOOPS DOWN ON THEM... IT IS THE GREAT DEMON, "BURNING PAIN." . . . . . . . . . .
YOU DARE ENTER OUR PORTALS! I SHALL CRUSH YOU TO ME!

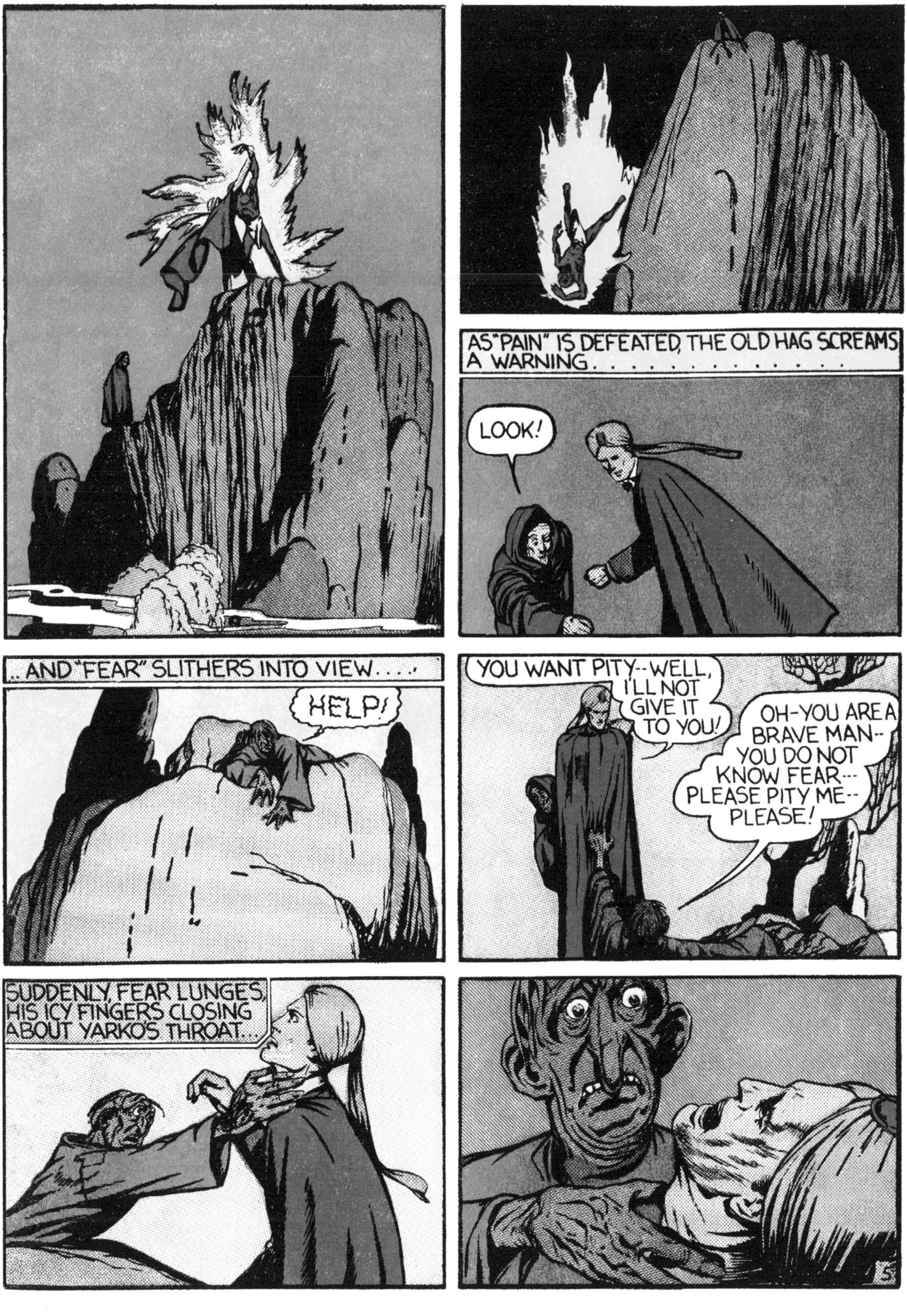
AS "PAIN" IS DEFEATED, THE OLD HAG SCREAMS A WARNING . . . . . . . . . . . .
LOOK!
.. AND "FEAR" SLITHERS INTO VIEW . . . .
HELP!
YOU WANT PITY--WELL, I'LL NOT GIVE IT TO YOU!
OH-YOU ARE A BRAVE MAN-- YOU DO NOT KNOW FEAR--- PLEASE PITY ME-- PLEASE!
SUDDENLY, FEAR LUNGES, HIS ICY FINGERS CLOSING ABOUT YARKO'S THROAT...
5

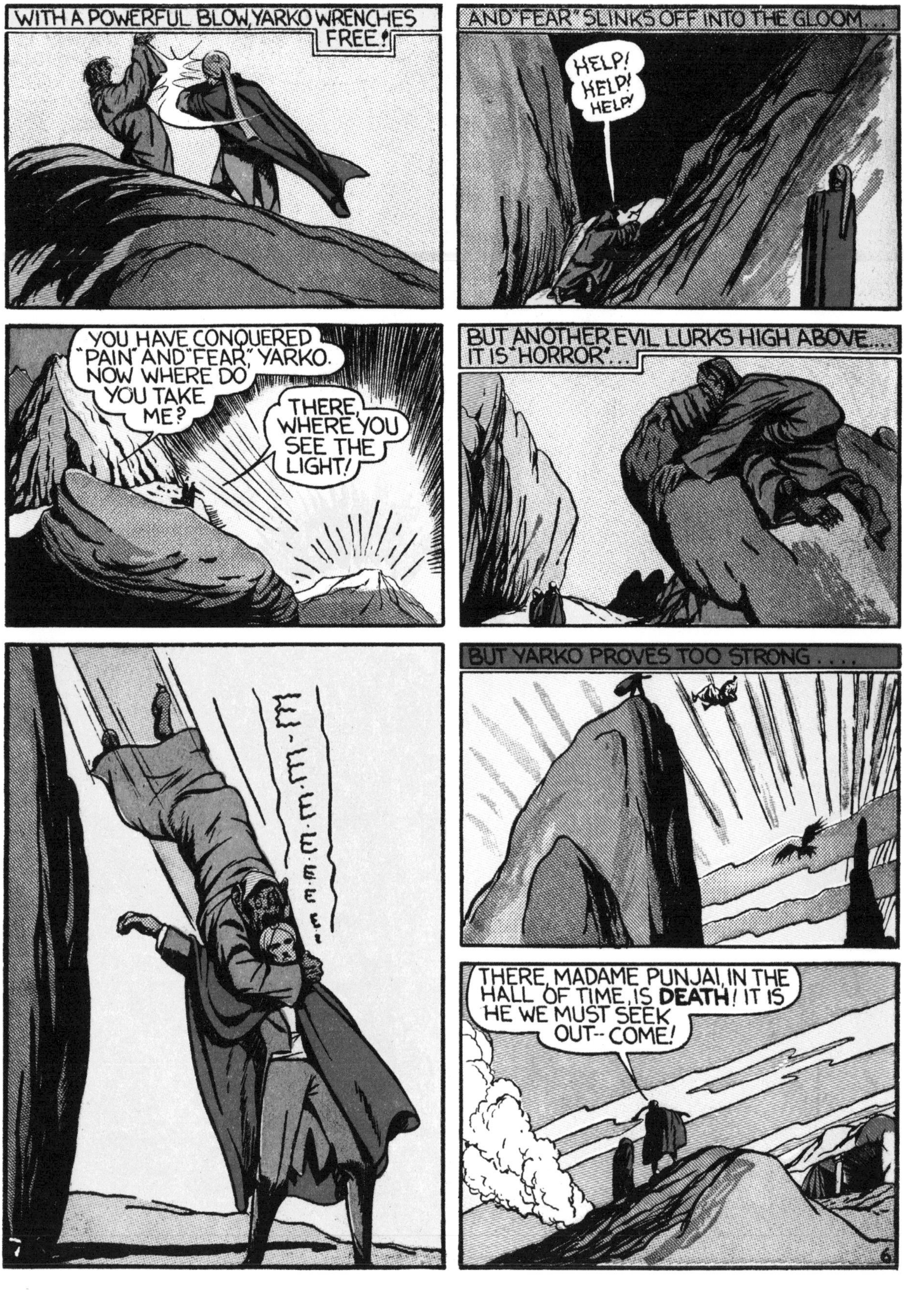
WITH A POWERFUL BLOW, YARKO WRENCHES FREE!
AND "FEAR" SLINKS OFF INTO THE GLOOM...
HELP! HELP! HELP!
YOU HAVE CONQUERED "PAIN" AND "FEAR," YARKO. NOW WHERE DO YOU TAKE ME?
THERE, WHERE YOU SEE THE LIGHT!
BUT ANOTHER EVIL LURKS HIGH ABOVE... IT IS "HORROR"...
E-E-E-E-E-E-E-E-E
BUT YARKO PROVES TOO STRONG....
THERE, MADAME PUNJAI, IN THE HALL OF TIME, IS **DEATH**! IT IS HE WE MUST SEEK OUT-- COME!

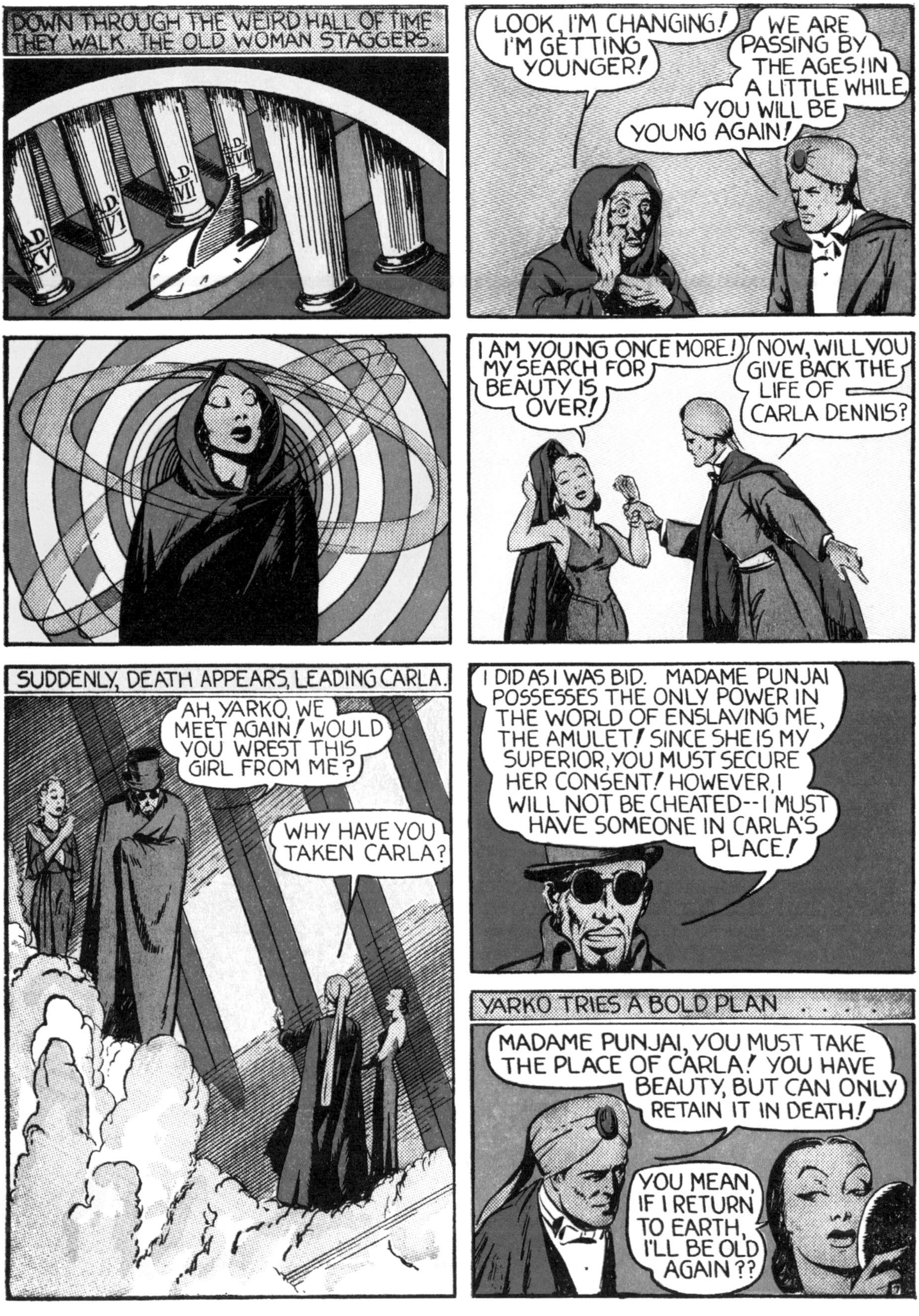
DOWN THROUGH THE WEIRD HALL OF TIME THEY WALK. THE OLD WOMAN STAGGERS.
A.D. XV
A.D. XVI
A.D. XVII
A.D. XVIII
LOOK, I'M CHANGING! I'M GETTING YOUNGER!
WE ARE PASSING BY THE AGES! IN A LITTLE WHILE YOU WILL BE YOUNG AGAIN!
I AM YOUNG ONCE MORE! MY SEARCH FOR BEAUTY IS OVER!
NOW, WILL YOU GIVE BACK THE LIFE OF CARLA DENNIS?
SUDDENLY, DEATH APPEARS, LEADING CARLA.
AH, YARKO, WE MEET AGAIN! WOULD YOU WREST THIS GIRL FROM ME?
WHY HAVE YOU TAKEN CARLA?
I DID AS I WAS BID. MADAME PUNJAI POSSESSES THE ONLY POWER IN THE WORLD OF ENSLAVING ME, THE AMULET! SINCE SHE IS MY SUPERIOR, YOU MUST SECURE HER CONSENT! HOWEVER, I WILL NOT BE CHEATED--I MUST HAVE SOMEONE IN CARLA'S PLACE!
YARKO TRIES A BOLD PLAN . . . .
MADAME PUNJAI, YOU MUST TAKE THE PLACE OF CARLA! YOU HAVE BEAUTY, BUT CAN ONLY RETAIN IT IN DEATH!
YOU MEAN, IF I RETURN TO EARTH, I'LL BE OLD AGAIN??

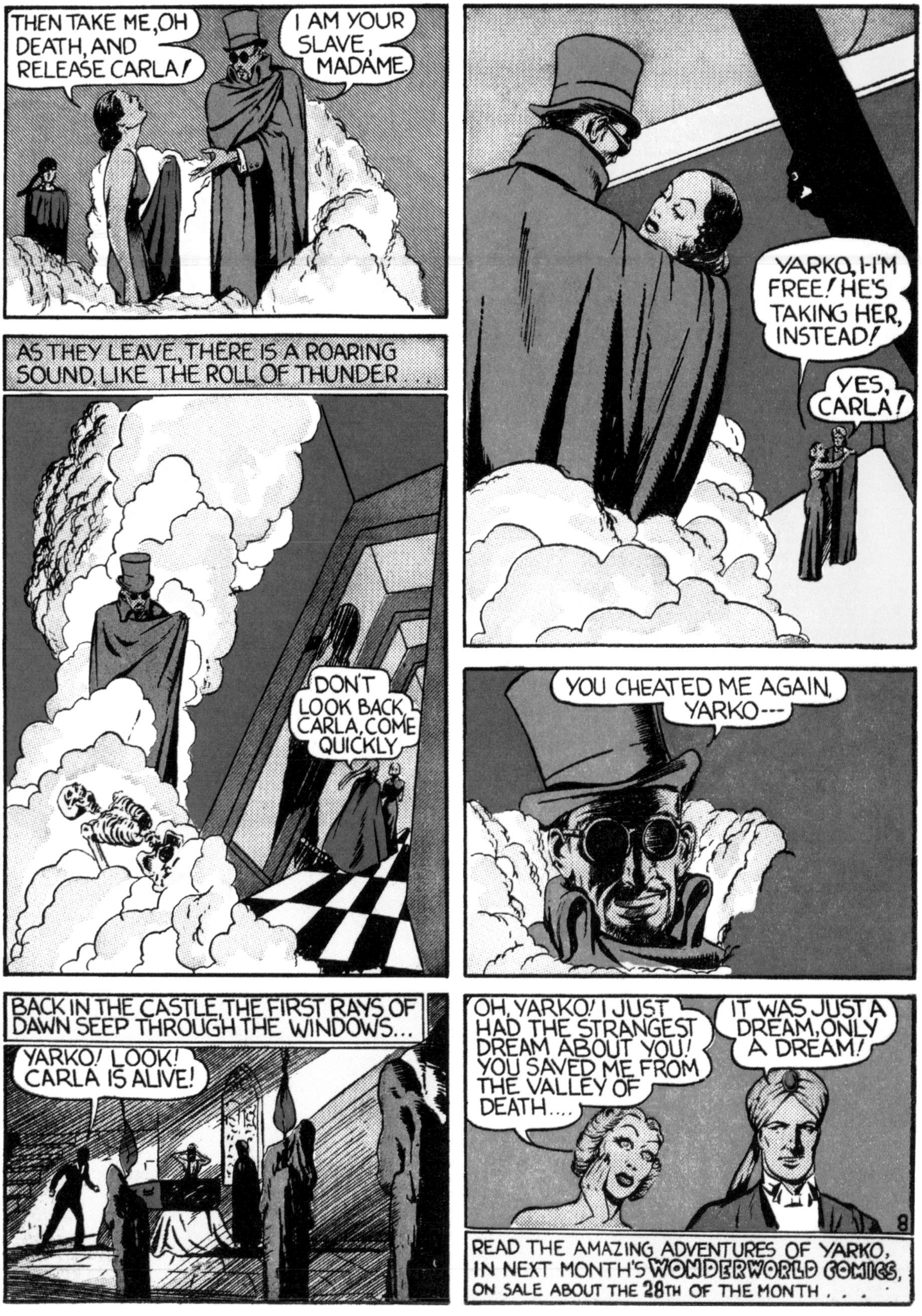
THEN TAKE ME, OH DEATH, AND RELEASE CARLA!
I AM YOUR SLAVE, MADAME.
YARKO, I-I'M FREE! HE'S TAKING HER, INSTEAD!
YES, CARLA!
AS THEY LEAVE, THERE IS A ROARING SOUND, LIKE THE ROLL OF THUNDER . . .
DON'T LOOK BACK, CARLA, COME QUICKLY
YOU CHEATED ME AGAIN, YARKO---
BACK IN THE CASTLE, THE FIRST RAYS OF DAWN SEEP THROUGH THE WINDOWS...
YARKO! LOOK! CARLA IS ALIVE!
OH, YARKO! I JUST HAD THE STRANGEST DREAM ABOUT YOU! YOU SAVED ME FROM THE VALLEY OF DEATH....
IT WAS JUST A DREAM, ONLY A DREAM!
8
READ THE AMAZING ADVENTURES OF YARKO, IN NEXT MONTH'S WONDERWORLD COMICS, ON SALE ABOUT THE 28TH OF THE MONTH . . .

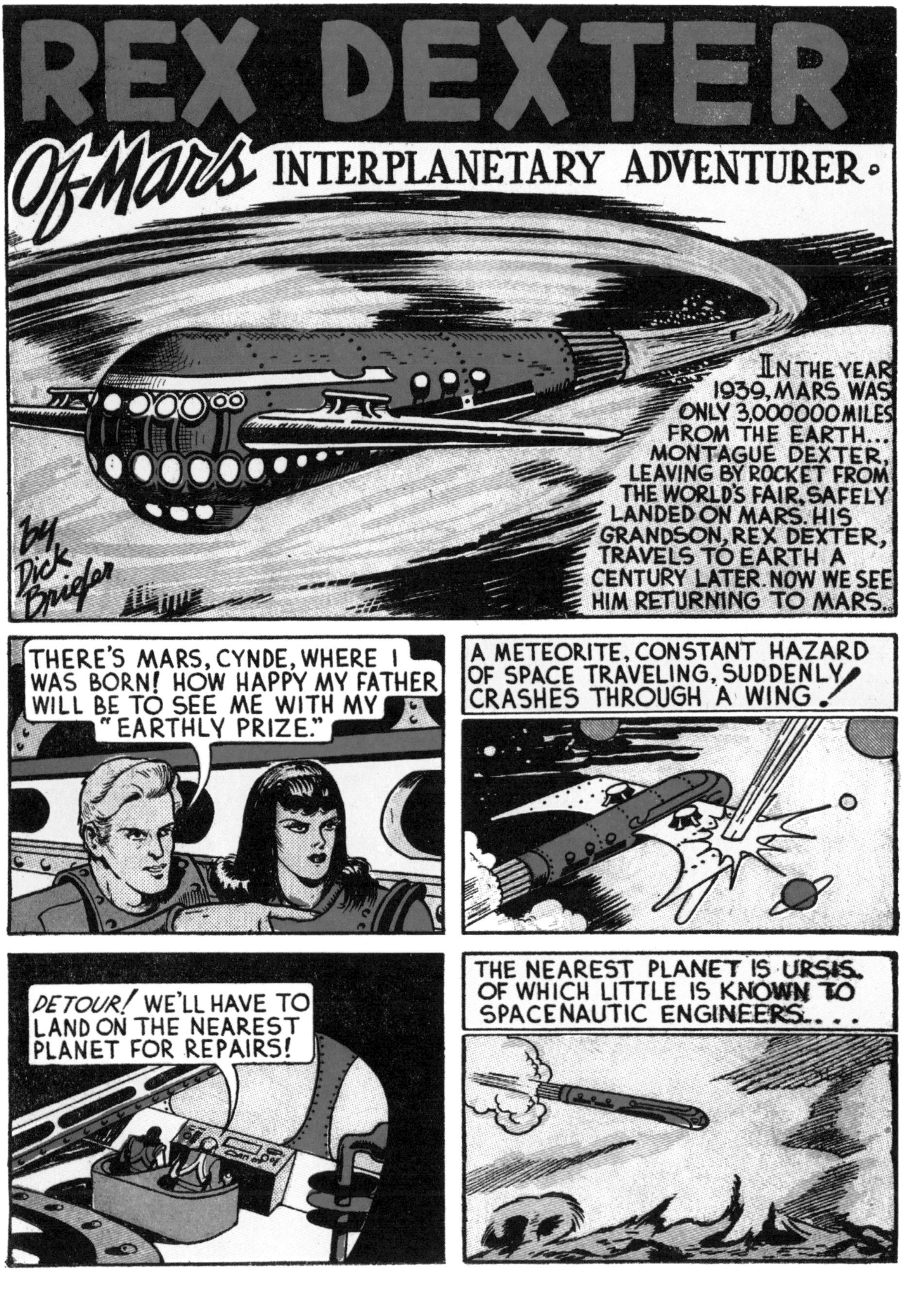
REX DEXTER
Of Mars INTERPLANETARY ADVENTURER
IN THE YEAR 1939, MARS WAS ONLY 3,000000 MILES FROM THE EARTH... MONTAGUE DEXTER, LEAVING BY ROCKET FROM THE WORLD'S FAIR, SAFELY LANDED ON MARS. HIS GRANDSON, REX DEXTER, TRAVELS TO EARTH A CENTURY LATER. NOW WE SEE HIM RETURNING TO MARS..
by Dick Briefer
THERE'S MARS, CYNDE, WHERE I WAS BORN! HOW HAPPY MY FATHER WILL BE TO SEE ME WITH MY "EARTHLY PRIZE."
A METEORITE, CONSTANT HAZARD OF SPACE TRAVELING, SUDDENLY CRASHES THROUGH A WING!
DETOUR! WE'LL HAVE TO LAND ON THE NEAREST PLANET FOR REPAIRS!
THE NEAREST PLANET IS URSIS. OF WHICH LITTLE IS KNOWN TO SPACENAUTIC ENGINEERS...

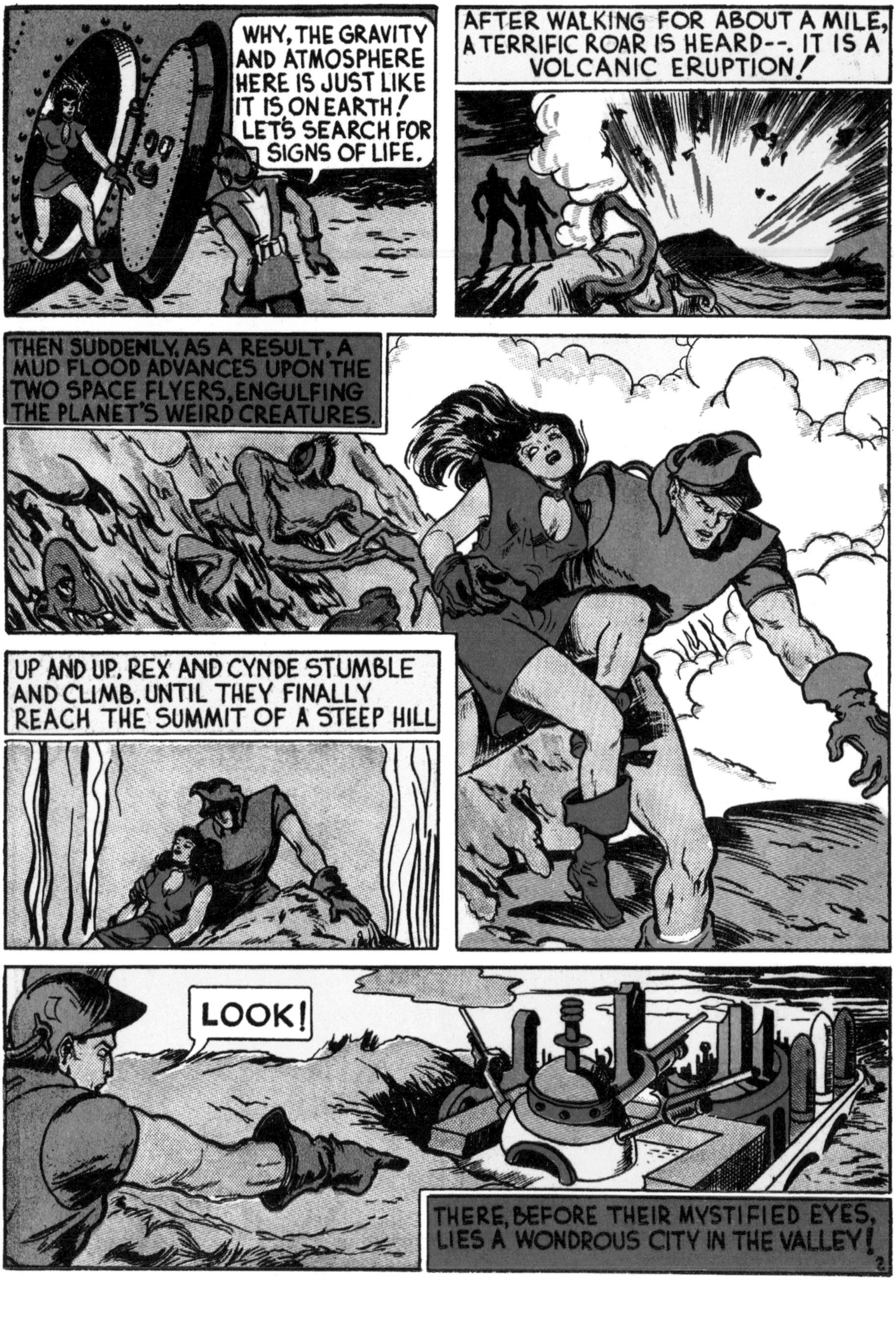
WHY, THE GRAVITY AND ATMOSPHERE HERE IS JUST LIKE IT IS ON EARTH! LET'S SEARCH FOR SIGNS OF LIFE.
AFTER WALKING FOR ABOUT A MILE, A TERRIFIC ROAR IS HEARD--. IT IS A VOLCANIC ERUPTION!
THEN SUDDENLY, AS A RESULT, A MUD FLOOD ADVANCES UPON THE TWO SPACE FLYERS, ENGULFING THE PLANET'S WEIRD CREATURES.
UP AND UP, REX AND CYNDE STUMBLE AND CLIMB, UNTIL THEY FINALLY REACH THE SUMMIT OF A STEEP HILL
LOOK!
THERE, BEFORE THEIR MYSTIFIED EYES, LIES A WONDROUS CITY IN THE VALLEY!
2

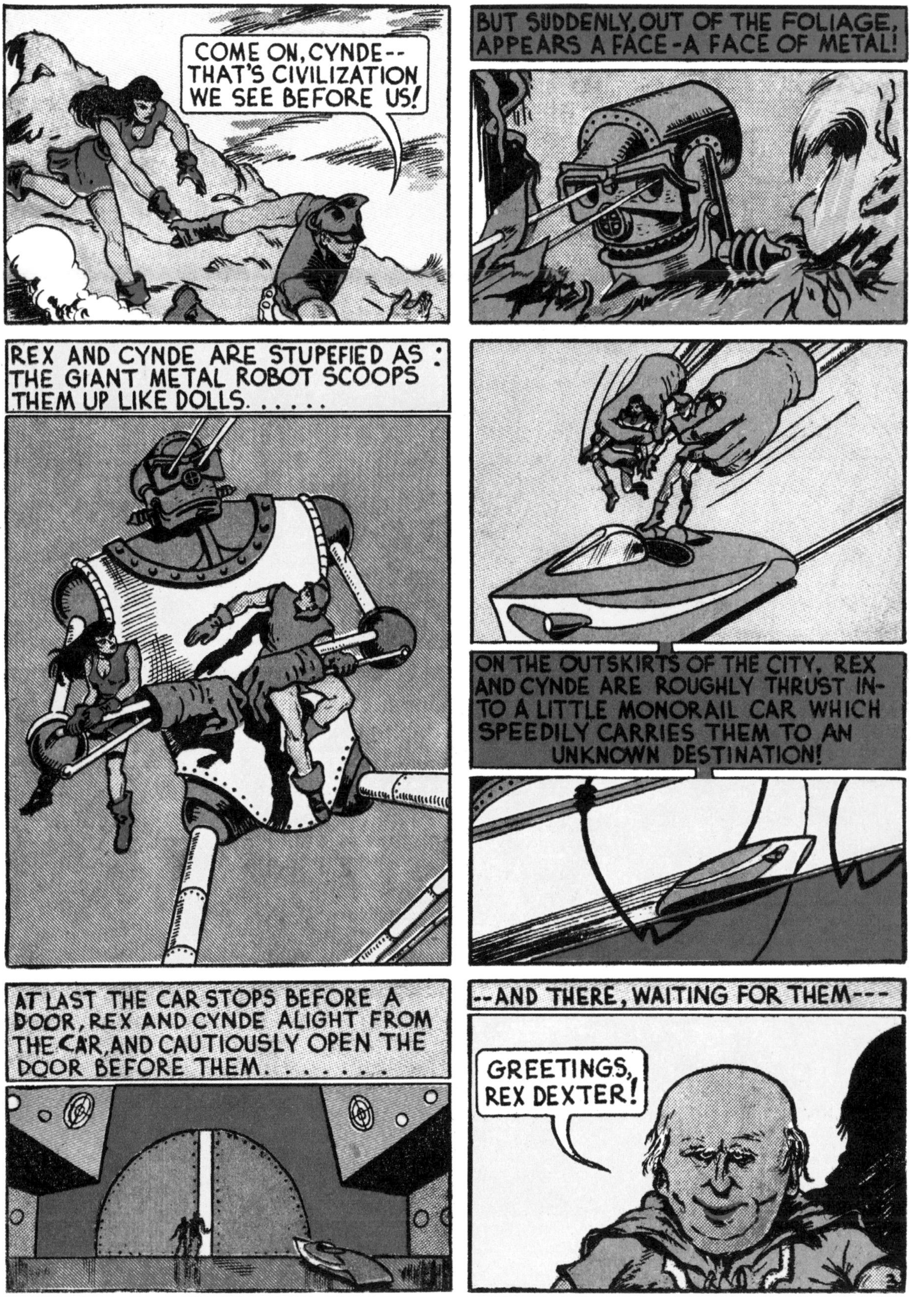
COME ON, CYNDE-- THAT'S CIVILIZATION WE SEE BEFORE US!
BUT SUDDENLY, OUT OF THE FOLIAGE, APPEARS A FACE-A FACE OF METAL!
REX AND CYNDE ARE STUPEFIED AS THE GIANT METAL ROBOT SCOOPS THEM UP LIKE DOLLS.....
ON THE OUTSKIRTS OF THE CITY, REX AND CYNDE ARE ROUGHLY THRUST INTO A LITTLE MONORAIL CAR WHICH SPEEDILY CARRIES THEM TO AN UNKNOWN DESTINATION!
AT LAST THE CAR STOPS BEFORE A DOOR, REX AND CYNDE ALIGHT FROM THE CAR, AND CAUTIOUSLY OPEN THE DOOR BEFORE THEM.......
--AND THERE, WAITING FOR THEM---
GREETINGS, REX DEXTER!

I AM LORD MARVEL- RULER OF URSIS, AND, SOON WILL RULE ALL PLANETS! BY THE AID OF MY INSTRUMENTS, I SAW YOU LEAVE EARTH. IT WAS NO MERE ACCIDENT THAT A METEORITE CROSSED YOUR PATH--IT WAS CONTROLLED BY ME TO BRING YOU TWO HERE!
LET ME EXPLAIN— YEARS AGO I TOO CAME FROM THE EARTH- THE DULL, MONOTONOUS, EARTH. THAT WORLD WAS NOT BIG ENOUGH FOR ME, SO I CAME TO URSIS DETERMINED TO RULE THE UNIVERSE. MY INSTRUMENTS AND ROBOTS CAN NOW CONTROL THE PLANETARY SYSTEM, WHICH I NOW INTEND TO REARRANGE TO SUIT MY OWN REQUIREMENTS!
NOW OBSERVE HOW I CAN CONTROL THE SYSTEM!
AS ONE PLANET MOVES NEAR. ANOTHER BLOWS UP! I WANT THE MOON UNDER MY COMMAND! UNFORTUNATELY, IT IS THE SATELITE OF THE EARTH--- CONSEQUENTLY, THE EARTH WILL PERISH!
YOU, LUNATIC! YOU CAN'T GET AWAY WITH IT!!- I'LL SEE THAT YOU DON'T CARRY OUT YOUR NEFARIOUS PLAN!
I AM ACCUSTOMED TO BEING OBEYED, DEXTER! I SEE YOU ONLY WILL BE A NUISANCE--- THEREFORE-OUT YOU GO!
SUDDENLY, AS IF BY A MAGNETIC CURRENT, REX SOARS FROM THE ROOM
4.

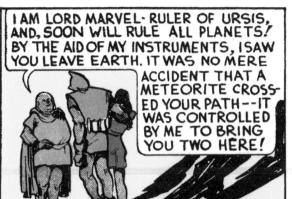

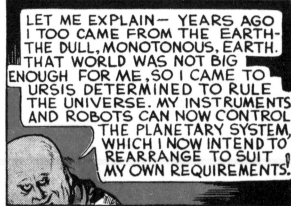

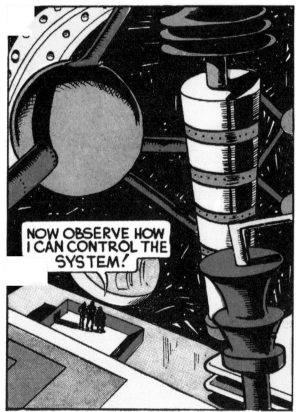

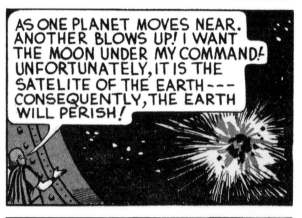

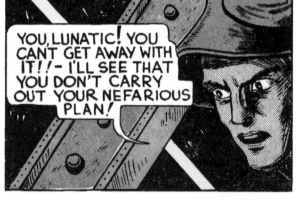

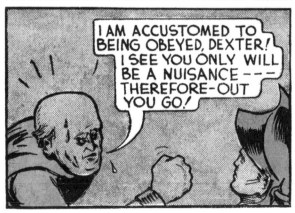

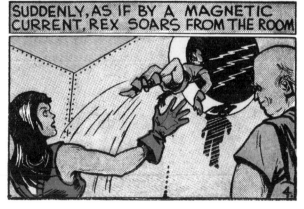

LOOK AT REX! LOOK AT THAT ROBOT HEADING FOR HIM! IN ONE MINUTE YOUR MARSMAN WILL BE DEAD! IRONICALLY, THAT VERY ROBOT WAS MANUFACTURED ON MARS!! COME, LET US TURN AWAY FROM THIS.

THERE IN THE ROOM BELOW, REX SEES THE ROBOT ADVANCING UPON HIM............

THAT METAL-MAN---- I'VE SEEN IT BEFORE! *I KNOW!!* --THE PLANS MY FATHER WAS WORKING ON!-- IS THIS HIS VERY INVENTION?

REX SPEAKS IN MARTIAN LANGUAGE TO THE ROBOT!

IF YOU UNDERSTAND-- TAKE ME TO THE LORD!

IN REPLY, THE ROBOT CRASHES DOWN THE STEEL WALLS, AS REX COMMANDS.

MEANWHILE, LORD MARVEL PREPARES TO REARRANGE THE SYSTEM!

NOW, MY DEAR, WATCH THE MOON COME TO ME-- WHILE THE EARTH CRUMBLES!

THE LEVER IS PULLED!! THE MOON STARTS MOVING AS THE EARTH TREMBLES!!

BUT SUDDENLY, FROM BEHIND THE LORD, A POWERFUL ARM SHOOTS OUT AND SLAMS BACK THE DESTRUCTIVE LEVER!

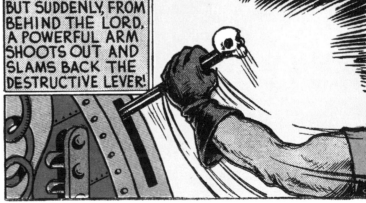

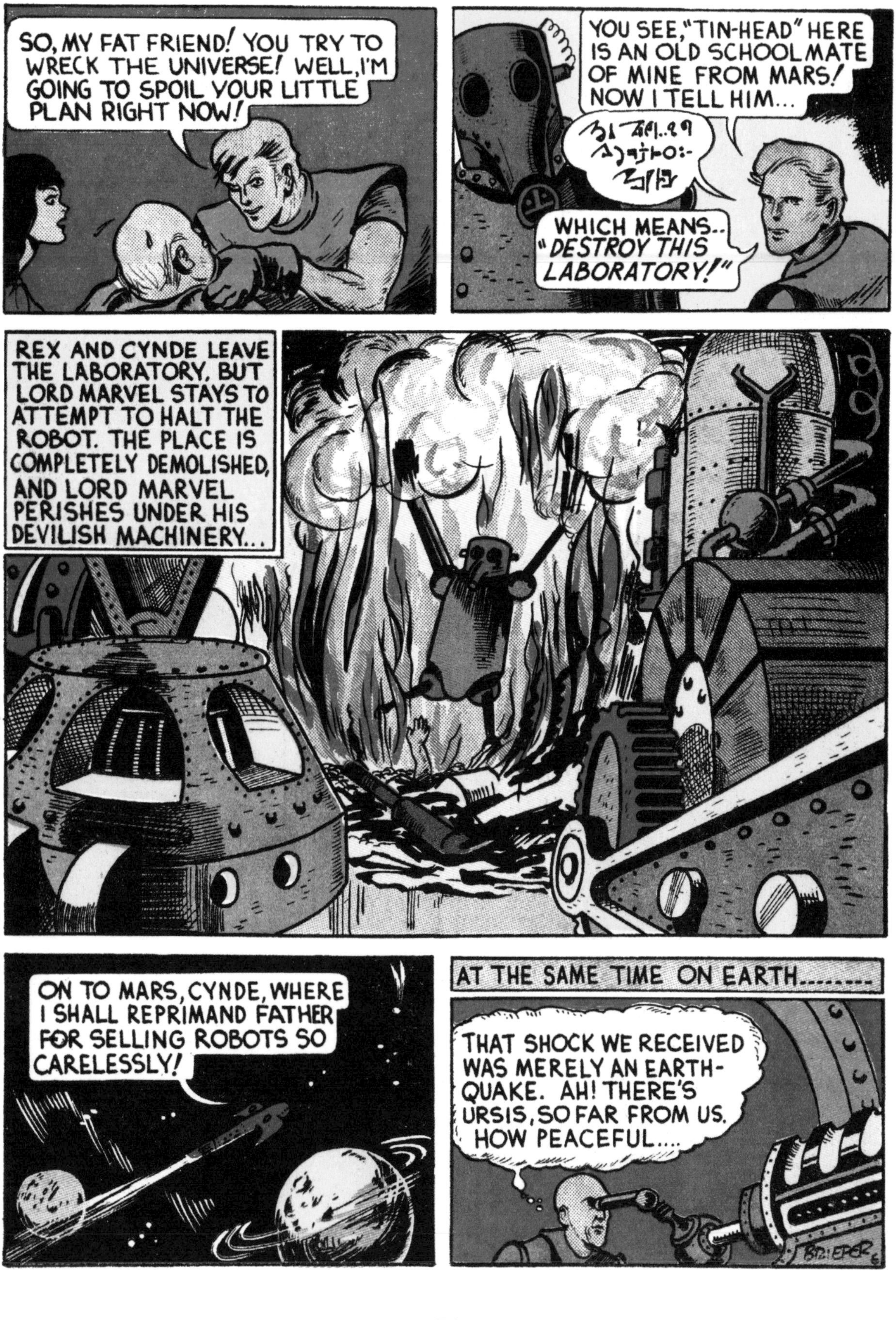
SO, MY FAT FRIEND! YOU TRY TO WRECK THE UNIVERSE! WELL, I'M GOING TO SPOIL YOUR LITTLE PLAN RIGHT NOW!
YOU SEE, "TIN-HEAD" HERE IS AN OLD SCHOOLMATE OF MINE FROM MARS! NOW I TELL HIM...
WHICH MEANS.. "DESTROY THIS LABORATORY!"
REX AND CYNDE LEAVE THE LABORATORY, BUT LORD MARVEL STAYS TO ATTEMPT TO HALT THE ROBOT. THE PLACE IS COMPLETELY DEMOLISHED, AND LORD MARVEL PERISHES UNDER HIS DEVILISH MACHINERY...
ON TO MARS, CYNDE, WHERE I SHALL REPRIMAND FATHER FOR SELLING ROBOTS SO CARELESSLY!
AT THE SAME TIME ON EARTH........
THAT SHOCK WE RECEIVED WAS MERELY AN EARTH-QUAKE. AH! THERE'S URSIS, SO FAR FROM US. HOW PEACEFUL....
BRIEFER

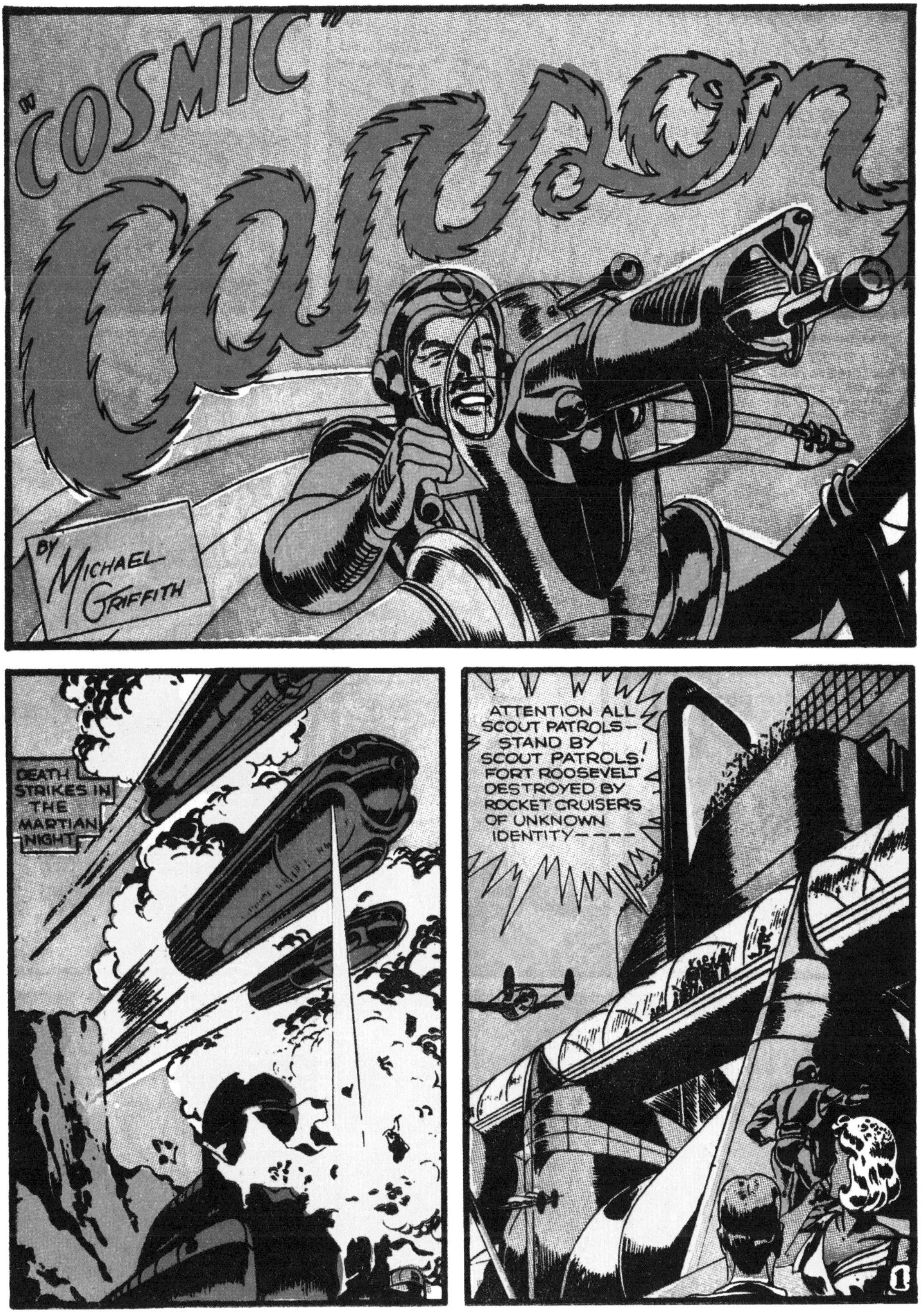
"COSMIC" CARSON
BY MICHAEL GRIFFITH
DEATH STRIKES IN THE MARTIAN NIGHT
ATTENTION ALL SCOUT PATROLS— STAND BY SCOUT PATROLS! FORT ROOSEVELT DESTROYED BY ROCKET CRUISERS OF UNKNOWN IDENTITY————
1

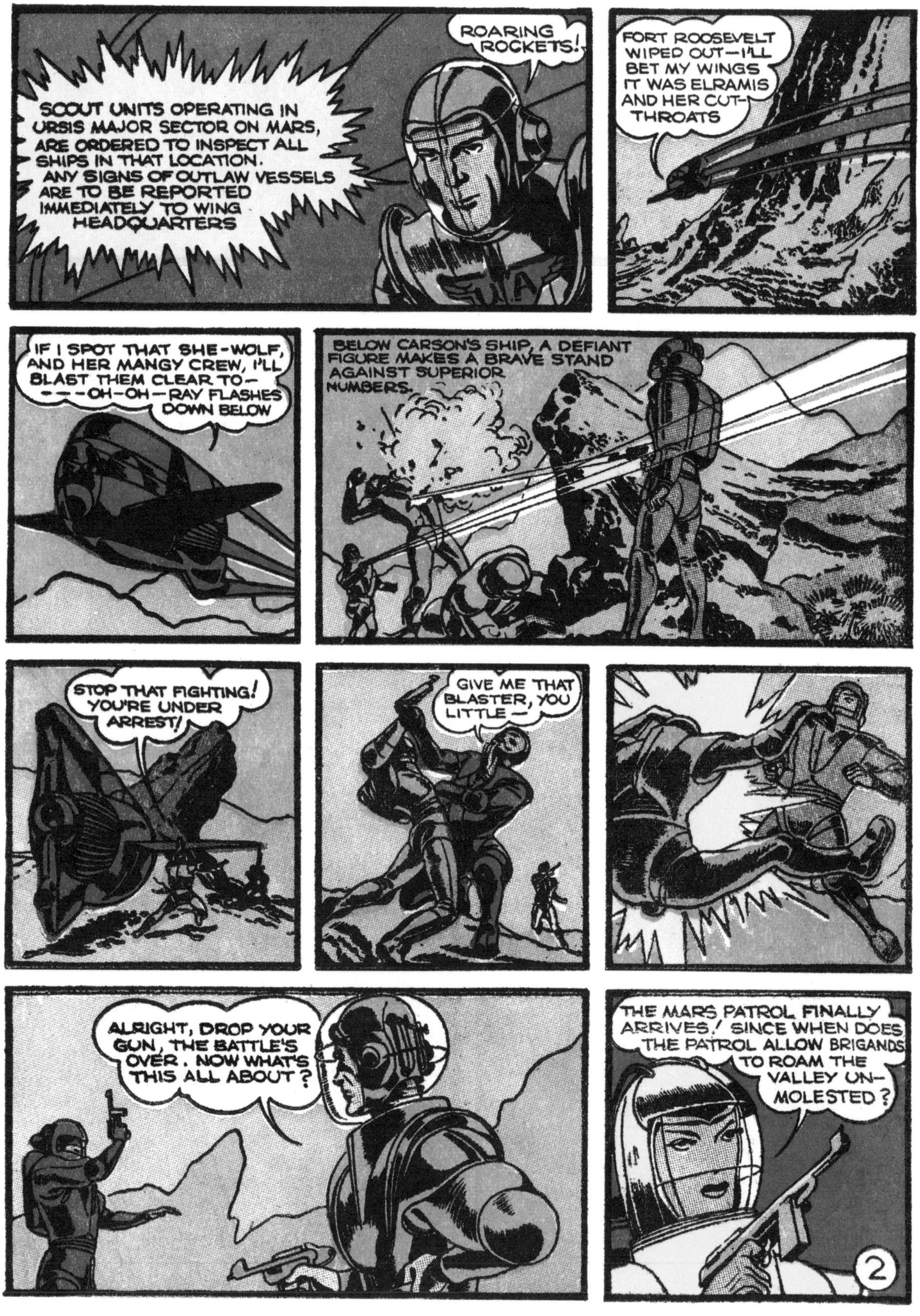
ROARING ROCKETS!
SCOUT UNITS OPERATING IN URSIS MAJOR SECTOR ON MARS, ARE ORDERED TO INSPECT ALL SHIPS IN THAT LOCATION. ANY SIGNS OF OUTLAW VESSELS ARE TO BE REPORTED IMMEDIATELY TO WING HEADQUARTERS
FORT ROOSEVELT WIPED OUT—I'LL BET MY WINGS IT WAS ELRAMIS AND HER CUT-THROATS
IF I SPOT THAT SHE-WOLF, AND HER MANGY CREW, I'LL BLAST THEM CLEAR TO— ---OH-OH—RAY FLASHES DOWN BELOW
BELOW CARSON'S SHIP, A DEFIANT FIGURE MAKES A BRAVE STAND AGAINST SUPERIOR NUMBERS.
STOP THAT FIGHTING! YOU'RE UNDER ARREST!
GIVE ME THAT BLASTER, YOU LITTLE —
ALRIGHT, DROP YOUR GUN, THE BATTLE'S OVER. NOW WHAT'S THIS ALL ABOUT?
THE MARS PATROL FINALLY ARRIVES! SINCE WHEN DOES THE PATROL ALLOW BRIGANDS TO ROAM THE VALLEY UN-MOLESTED?
2

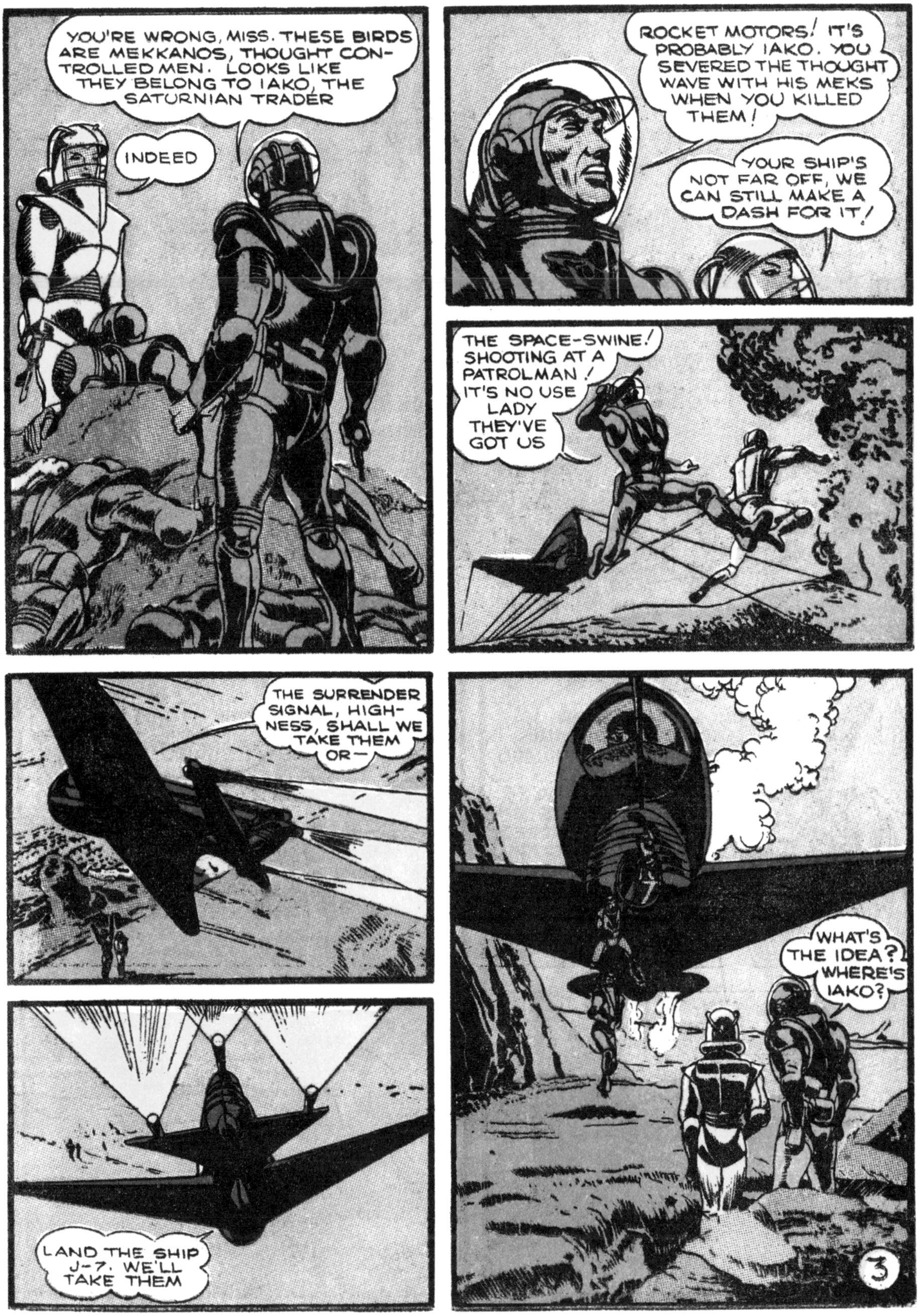
YOU'RE WRONG, MISS. THESE BIRDS ARE MEKKANOS, THOUGHT CONTROLLED MEN. LOOKS LIKE THEY BELONG TO IAKO, THE SATURNIAN TRADER
INDEED
ROCKET MOTORS! IT'S PROBABLY IAKO. YOU SEVERED THE THOUGHT WAVE WITH HIS MEKS WHEN YOU KILLED THEM!
YOUR SHIP'S NOT FAR OFF, WE CAN STILL MAKE A DASH FOR IT!
THE SPACE-SWINE! SHOOTING AT A PATROLMAN! IT'S NO USE LADY THEY'VE GOT US
THE SURRENDER SIGNAL, HIGHNESS, SHALL WE TAKE THEM OR—
LAND THE SHIP J-7. WE'LL TAKE THEM
WHAT'S THE IDEA? WHERE'S IAKO?
3

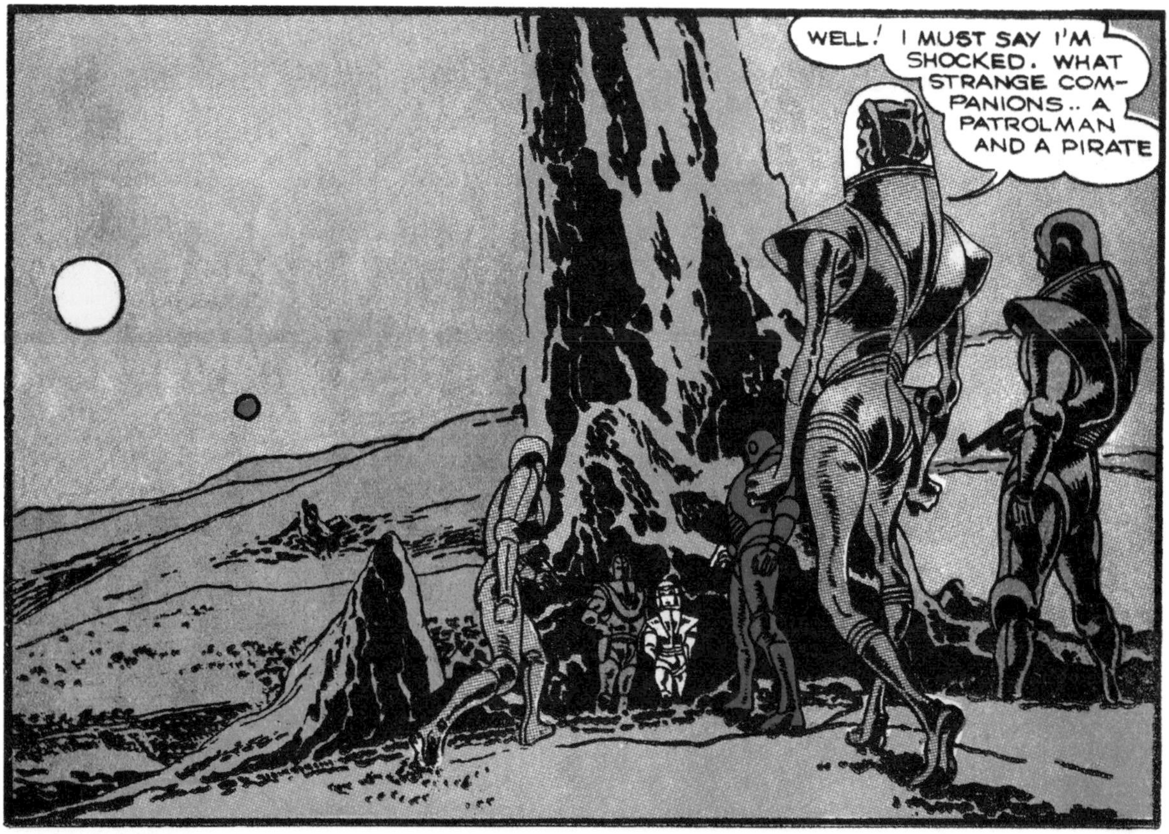
WELL! I MUST SAY I'M SHOCKED. WHAT STRANGE COMPANIONS.. A PATROLMAN AND A PIRATE

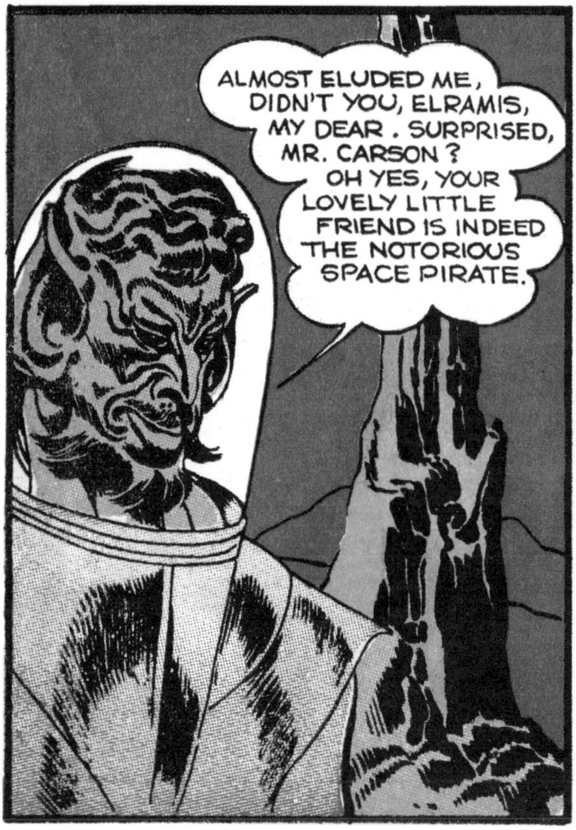
ALMOST ELUDED ME, DIDN'T YOU, ELRAMIS, MY DEAR. SURPRISED, MR. CARSON? OH YES, YOUR LOVELY LITTLE FRIEND IS INDEED THE NOTORIOUS SPACE PIRATE.

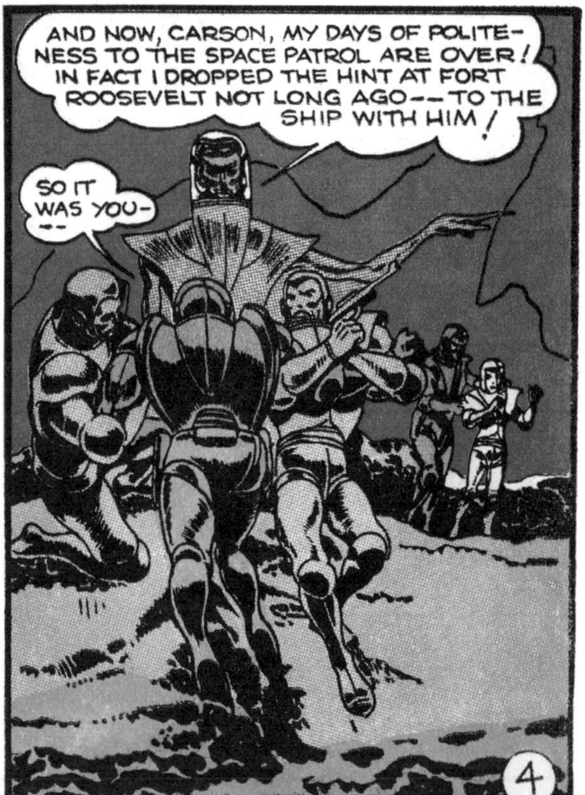
AND NOW, CARSON, MY DAYS OF POLITENESS TO THE SPACE PATROL ARE OVER! IN FACT I DROPPED THE HINT AT FORT ROOSEVELT NOT LONG AGO--TO THE SHIP WITH HIM!
SO IT WAS YOU---
4

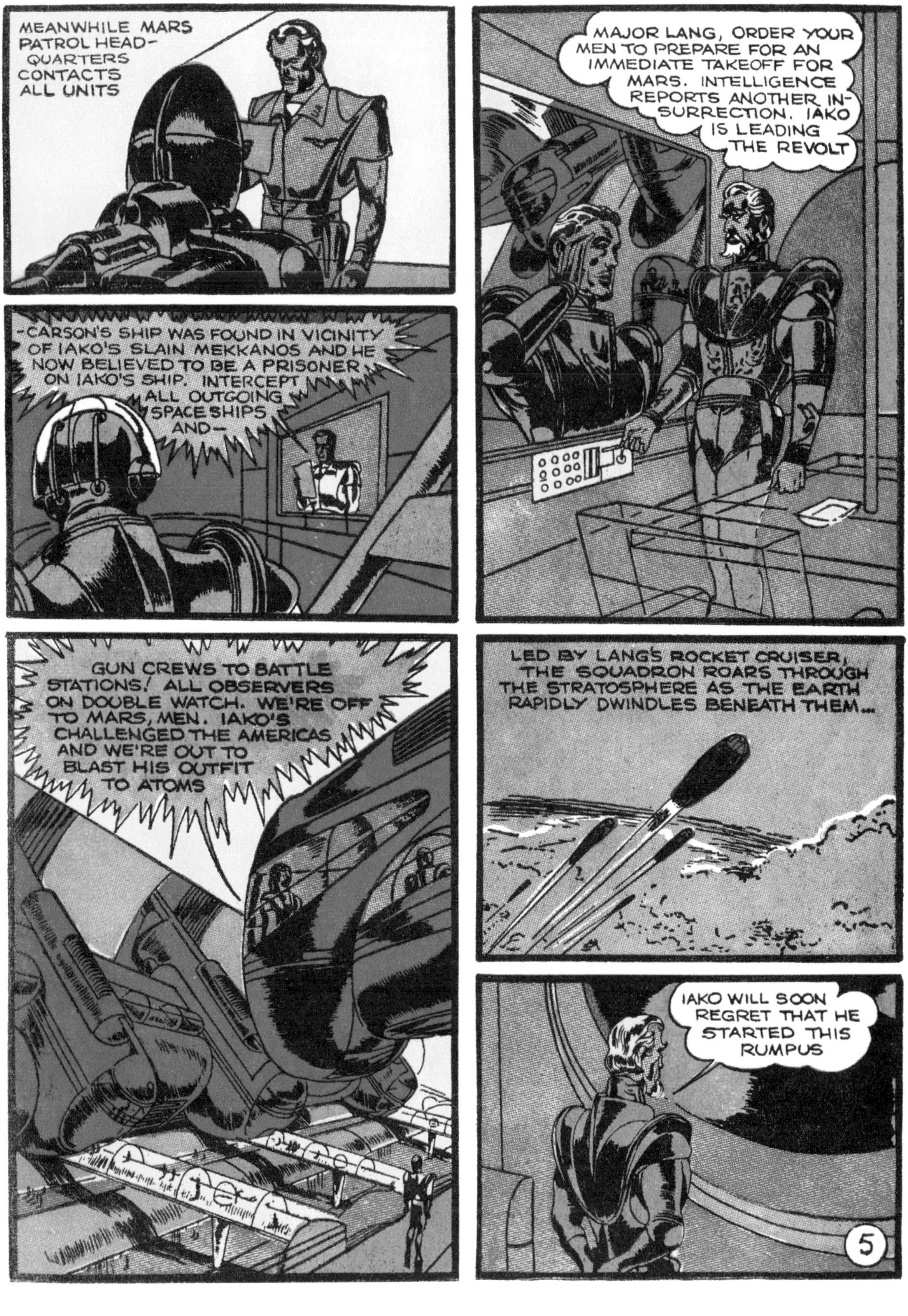
MEANWHILE MARS PATROL HEAD-QUARTERS CONTACTS ALL UNITS
MAJOR LANG, ORDER YOUR MEN TO PREPARE FOR AN IMMEDIATE TAKEOFF FOR MARS. INTELLIGENCE REPORTS ANOTHER IN-SURRECTION. IAKO IS LEADING THE REVOLT
-CARSON'S SHIP WAS FOUND IN VICINITY OF IAKO'S SLAIN MEKKANOS AND HE NOW BELIEVED TO BE A PRISONER ON IAKO'S SHIP. INTERCEPT ALL OUTGOING SPACE SHIPS AND-
GUN CREWS TO BATTLE STATIONS! ALL OBSERVERS ON DOUBLE WATCH. WE'RE OFF TO MARS, MEN. IAKO'S CHALLENGED THE AMERICAS AND WE'RE OUT TO BLAST HIS OUTFIT TO ATOMS
LED BY LANG'S ROCKET CRUISER, THE SQUADRON ROARS THROUGH THE STRATOSPHERE AS THE EARTH RAPIDLY DWINDLES BENEATH THEM...
IAKO WILL SOON REGRET THAT HE STARTED THIS RUMPUS
5

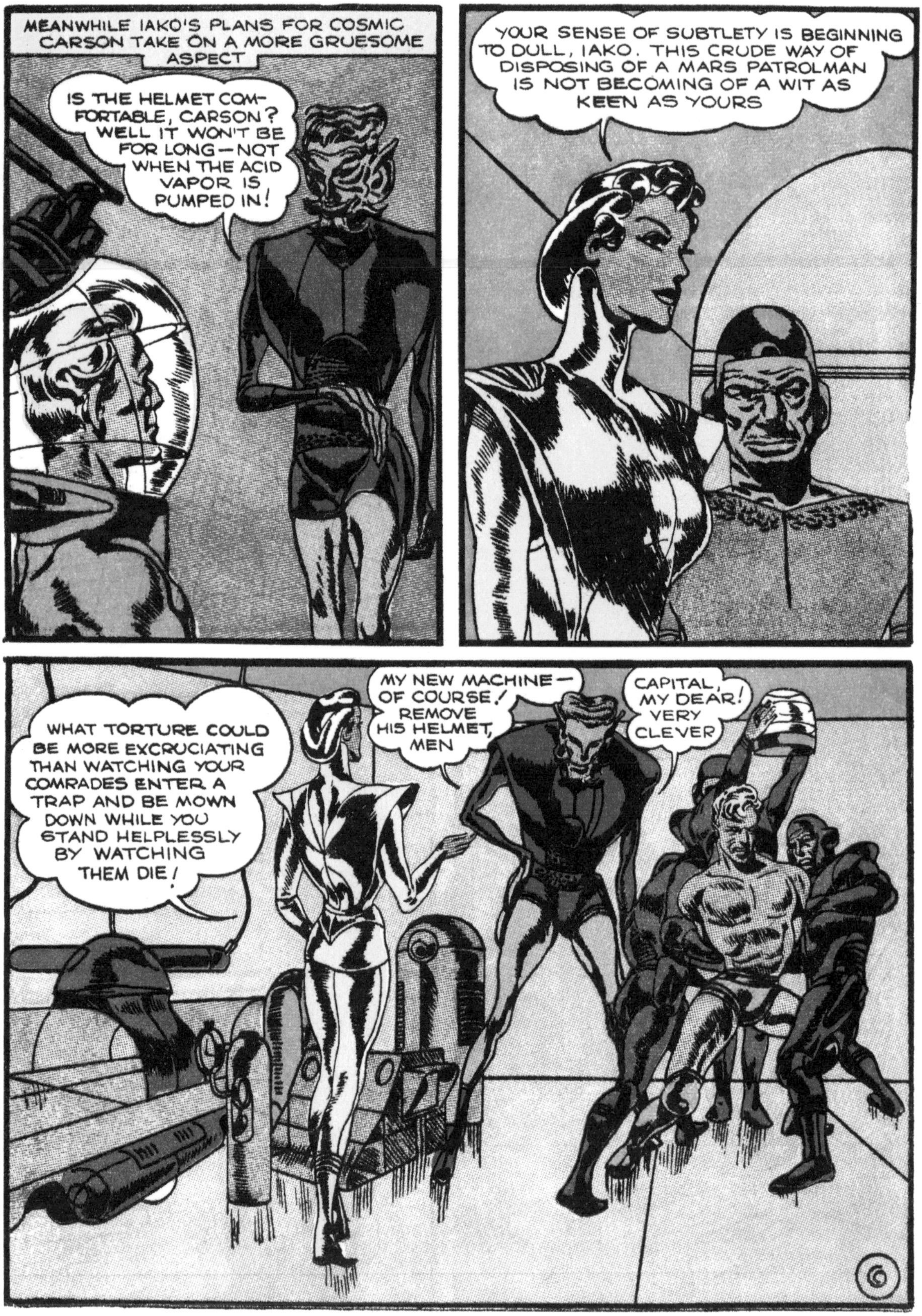
MEANWHILE IAKO'S PLANS FOR COSMIC CARSON TAKE ON A MORE GRUESOME ASPECT
IS THE HELMET COMFORTABLE, CARSON? WELL IT WON'T BE FOR LONG—NOT WHEN THE ACID VAPOR IS PUMPED IN!
YOUR SENSE OF SUBTLETY IS BEGINNING TO DULL, IAKO. THIS CRUDE WAY OF DISPOSING OF A MARS PATROLMAN IS NOT BECOMING OF A WIT AS KEEN AS YOURS
WHAT TORTURE COULD BE MORE EXCRUCIATING THAN WATCHING YOUR COMRADES ENTER A TRAP AND BE MOWN DOWN WHILE YOU STAND HELPLESSLY BY WATCHING THEM DIE!
MY NEW MACHINE—OF COURSE! REMOVE HIS HELMET, MEN
CAPITAL, MY DEAR! VERY CLEVER
6

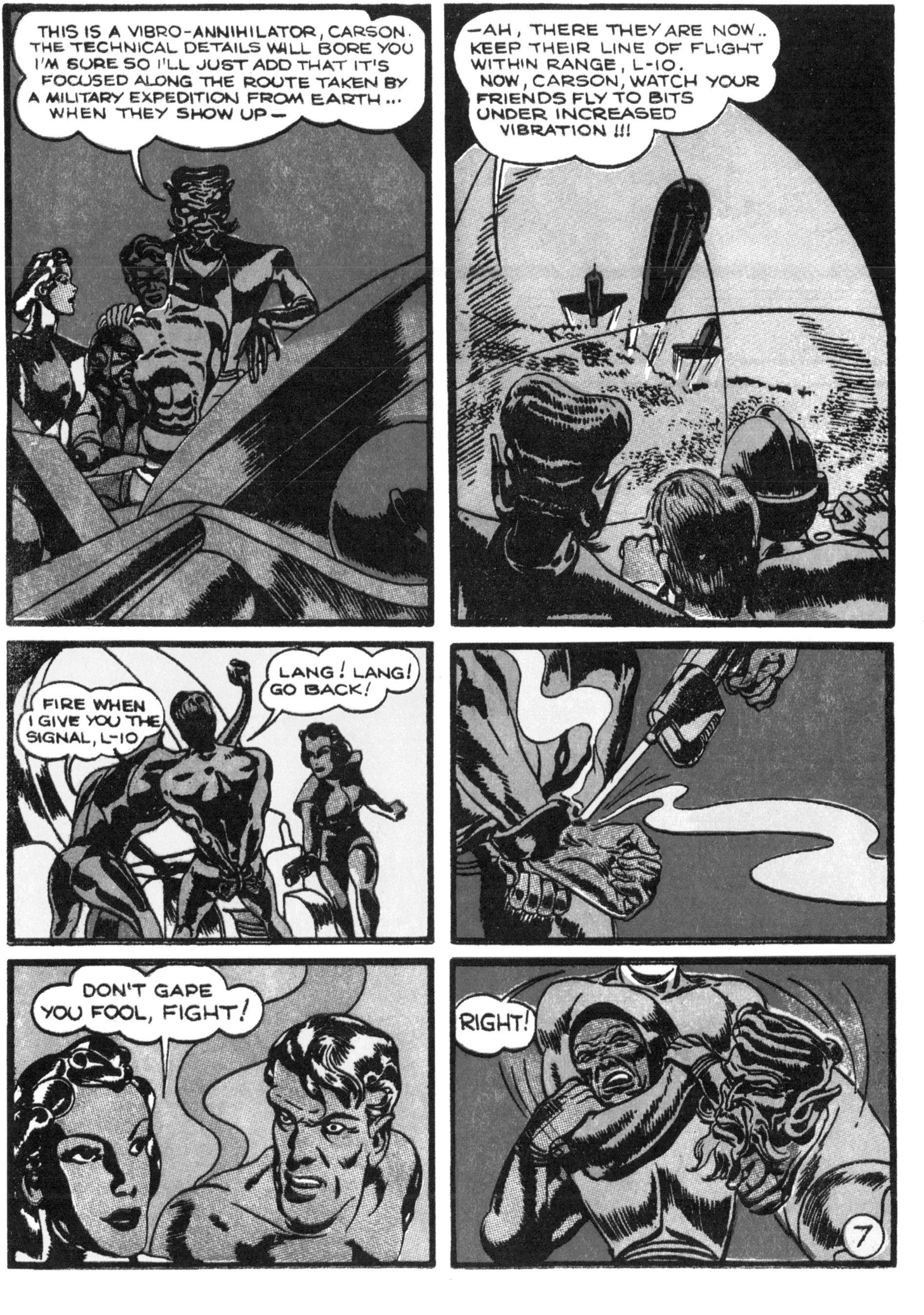
THIS IS A VIBRO-ANNIHILATOR, CARSON. THE TECHNICAL DETAILS WILL BORE YOU I'M SURE SO I'LL JUST ADD THAT IT'S FOCUSED ALONG THE ROUTE TAKEN BY A MILITARY EXPEDITION FROM EARTH ... WHEN THEY SHOW UP—
—AH, THERE THEY ARE NOW.. KEEP THEIR LINE OF FLIGHT WITHIN RANGE, L-10. NOW, CARSON, WATCH YOUR FRIENDS FLY TO BITS UNDER INCREASED VIBRATION !!!
FIRE WHEN I GIVE YOU THE SIGNAL, L-10
LANG! LANG! GO BACK!
DON'T GAPE YOU FOOL, FIGHT!
RIGHT!
7

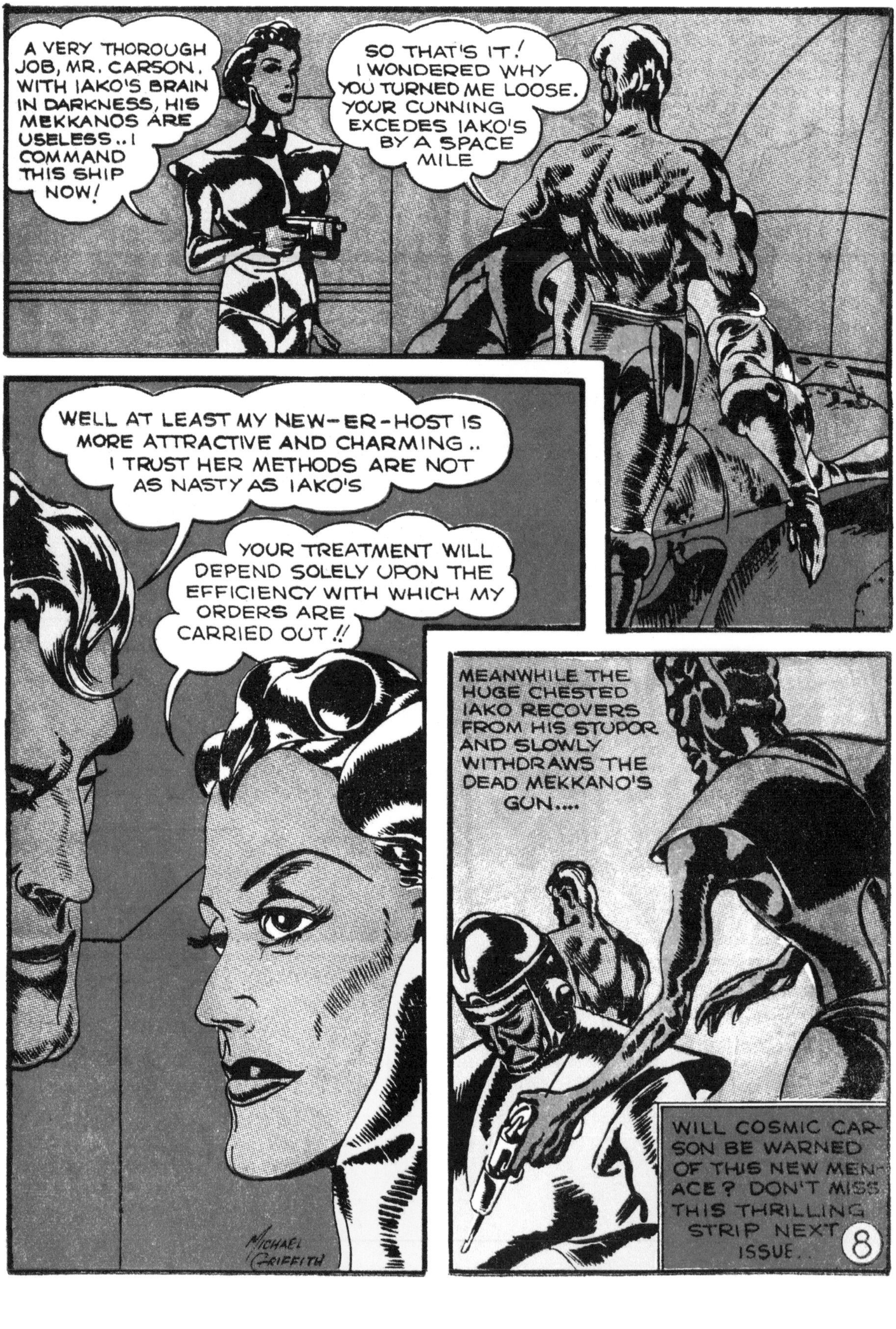
A VERY THOROUGH JOB, MR. CARSON. WITH IAKO'S BRAIN IN DARKNESS, HIS MEKKANOS ARE USELESS..I COMMAND THIS SHIP NOW!
SO THAT'S IT! I WONDERED WHY YOU TURNED ME LOOSE. YOUR CUNNING EXCEDES IAKO'S BY A SPACE MILE
WELL AT LEAST MY NEW-ER-HOST IS MORE ATTRACTIVE AND CHARMING.. I TRUST HER METHODS ARE NOT AS NASTY AS IAKO'S
YOUR TREATMENT WILL DEPEND SOLELY UPON THE EFFICIENCY WITH WHICH MY ORDERS ARE CARRIED OUT!!
MICHAEL GRIFFITH
MEANWHILE THE HUGE CHESTED IAKO RECOVERS FROM HIS STUPOR AND SLOWLY WITHDRAWS THE DEAD MEKKANO'S GUN....
WILL COSMIC CARSON BE WARNED OF THIS NEW MENACE? DON'T MISS THIS THRILLING STRIP NEXT ISSUE..
8

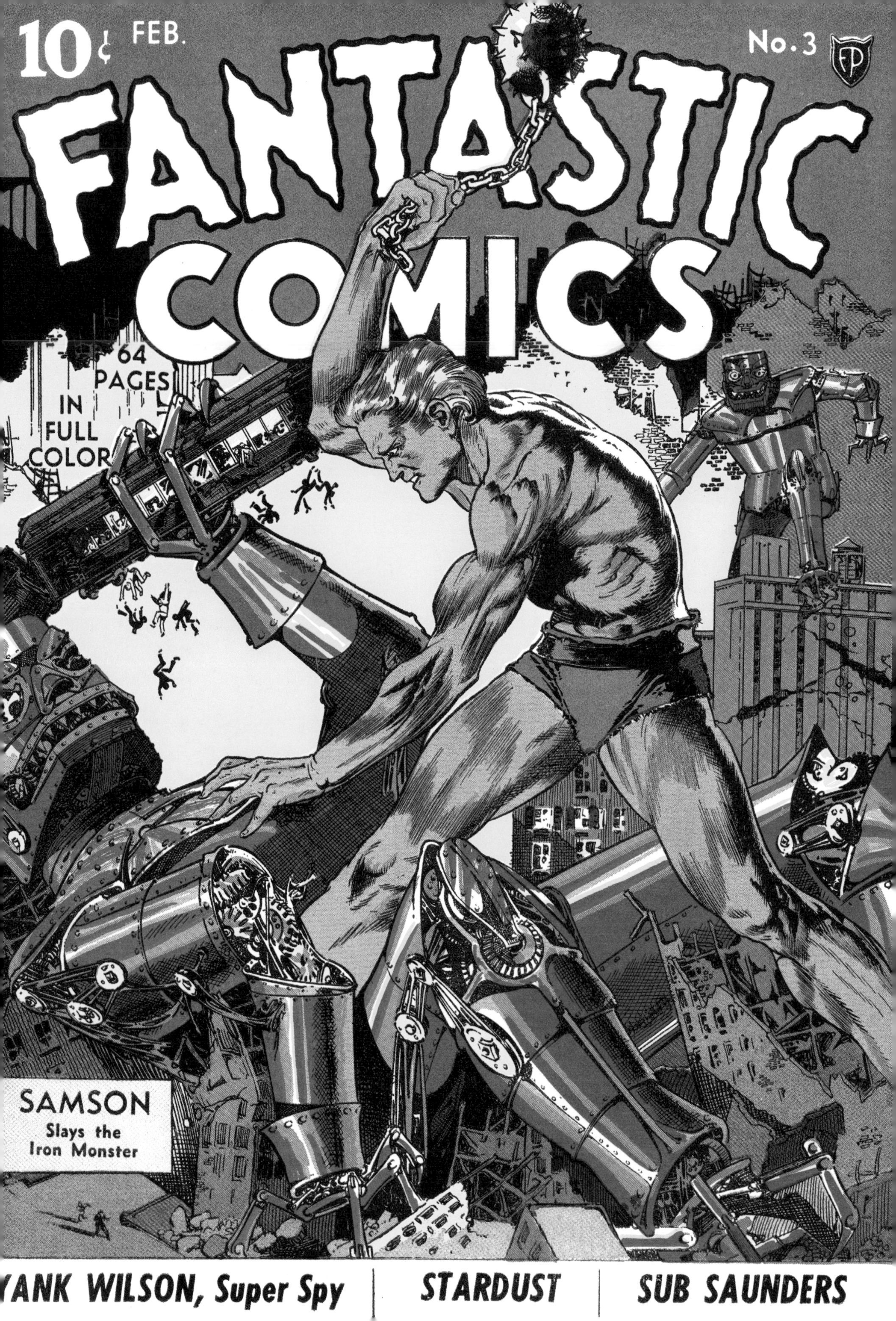
10¢ FEB.
No.3
FP
FANTASTIC COMICS
64 PAGES IN FULL COLOR
SAMSON
Slays the Iron Monster
YANK WILSON, Super Spy
STARDUST
SUB SAUNDERS

# PRESENTING

**BRAND NEW ADVENTURES OF THESE 2 HEADLINE FEATURES IN 2 OF AMERICA'S LEADING COMIC MAGAZINES!**

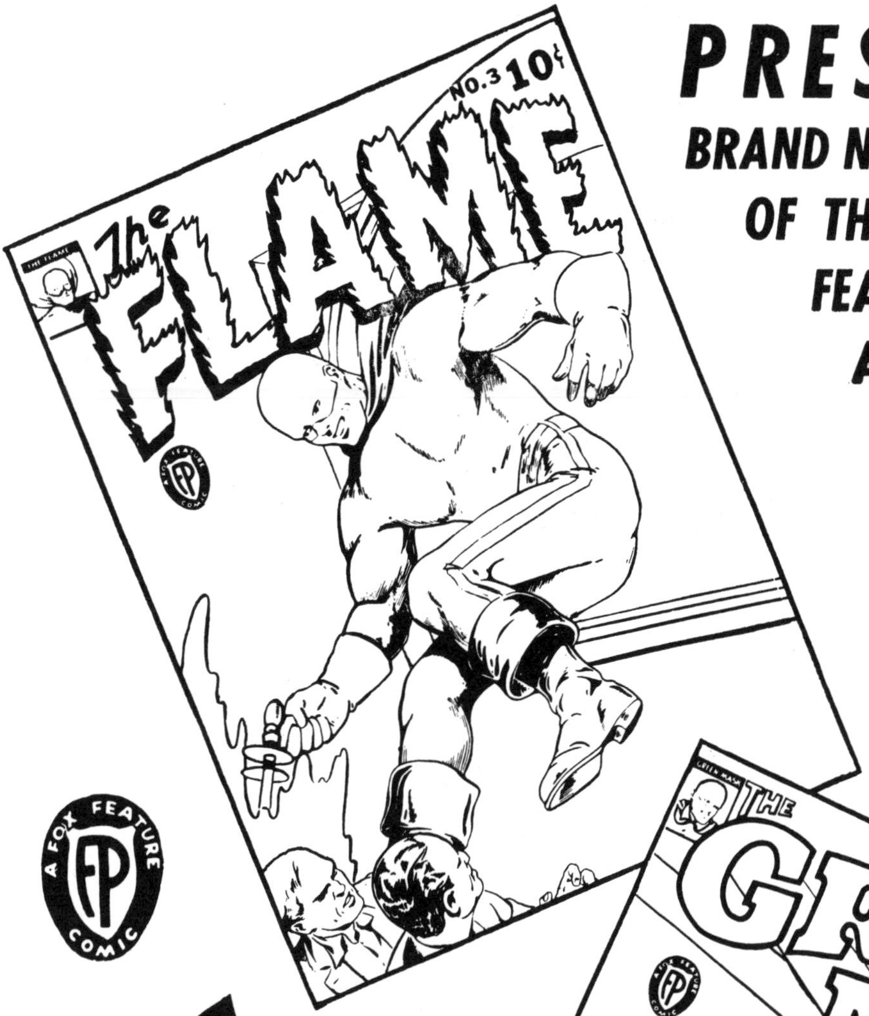

NO.3 10¢
The FLAME


DON'T MISS THESE TWO THRILLERS!

GET THESE MAGAZINES AT YOUR FAVORITE NEWSSTAND

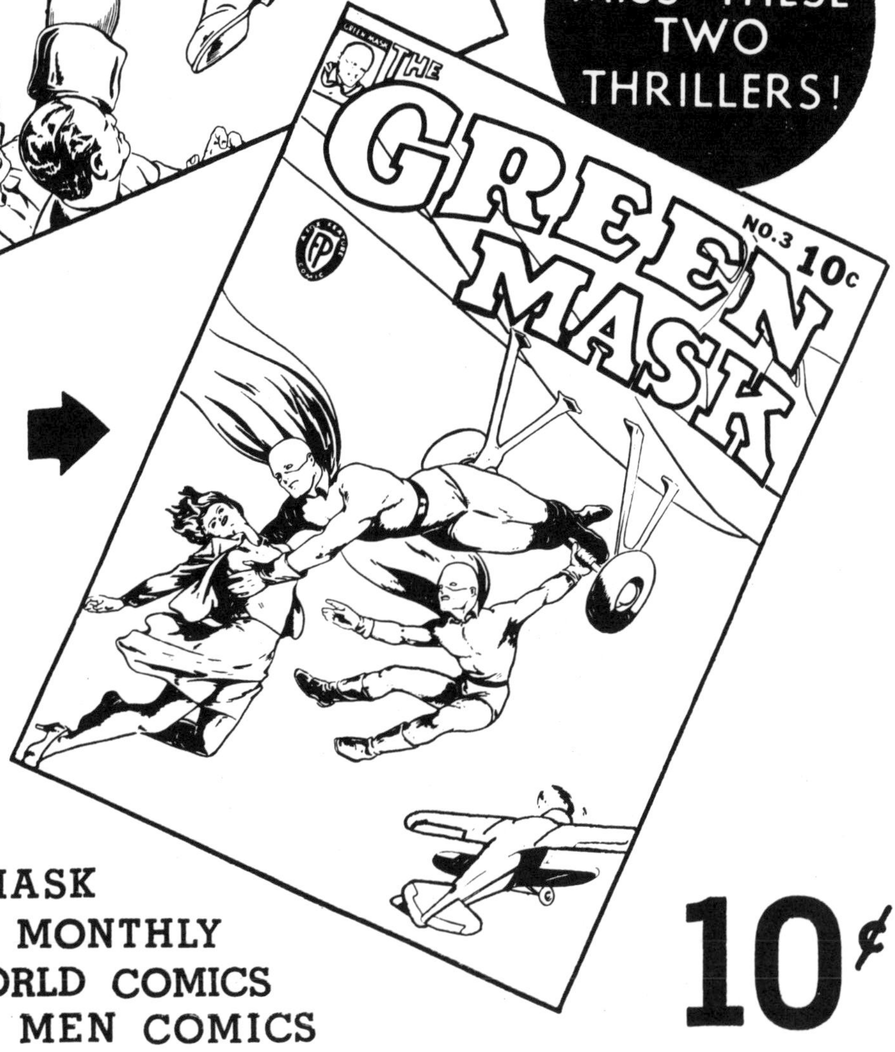

THE GREEN MASK
NO.3 10c


THE
FLAME AND
THE GREEN MASK
ALSO APPEAR MONTHLY
IN WONDERWORLD COMICS
AND MYSTERY MEN COMICS

**10¢**

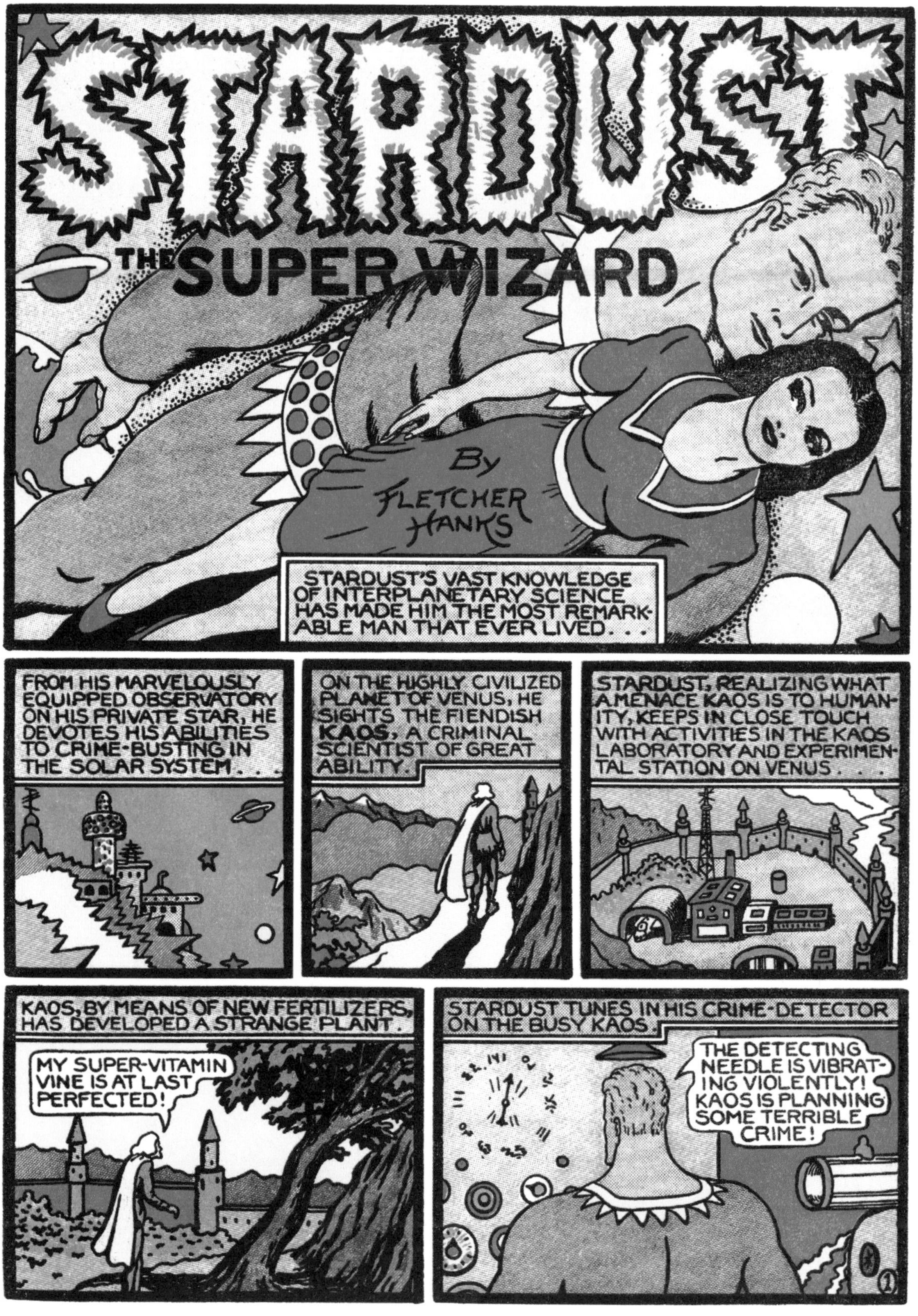
STARDUST
THE SUPER WIZARD
By FLETCHER HANKS
STARDUST'S VAST KNOWLEDGE OF INTERPLANETARY SCIENCE HAS MADE HIM THE MOST REMARKABLE MAN THAT EVER LIVED. . .
FROM HIS MARVELOUSLY EQUIPPED OBSERVATORY ON HIS PRIVATE STAR, HE DEVOTES HIS ABILITIES TO CRIME-BUSTING IN THE SOLAR SYSTEM. . .
ON THE HIGHLY CIVILIZED PLANET OF VENUS, HE SIGHTS THE FIENDISH KAOS, A CRIMINAL SCIENTIST OF GREAT ABILITY.
STARDUST, REALIZING WHAT A MENACE KAOS IS TO HUMANITY, KEEPS IN CLOSE TOUCH WITH ACTIVITIES IN THE KAOS LABORATORY AND EXPERIMENTAL STATION ON VENUS. . .
KAOS, BY MEANS OF NEW FERTILIZERS, HAS DEVELOPED A STRANGE PLANT.
MY SUPER-VITAMIN VINE IS AT LAST PERFECTED!
STARDUST TUNES IN HIS CRIME-DETECTOR ON THE BUSY KAOS.
THE DETECTING NEEDLE IS VIBRATING VIOLENTLY! KAOS IS PLANNING SOME TERRIBLE CRIME!
1

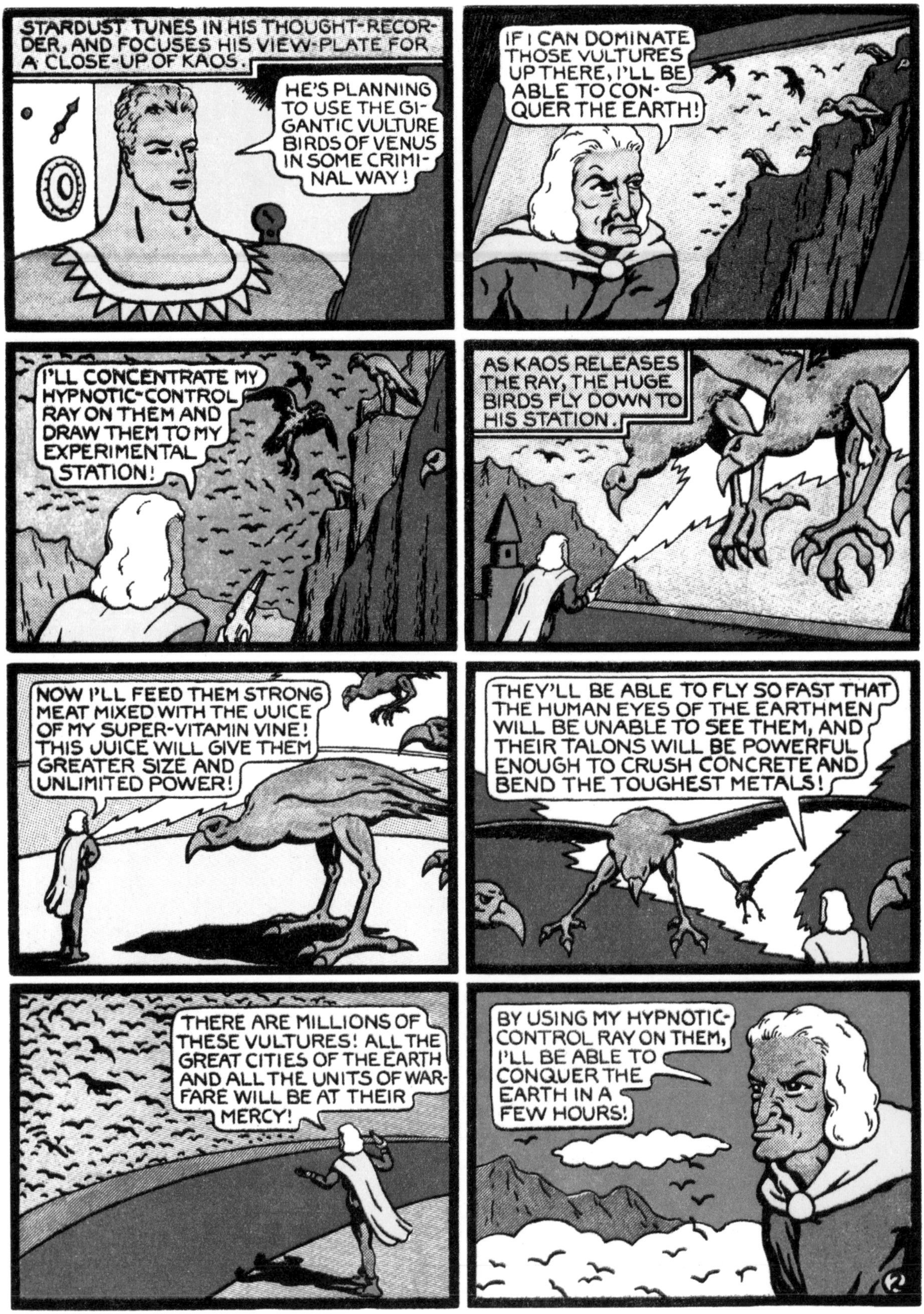
STARDUST TUNES IN HIS THOUGHT-RECORDER, AND FOCUSES HIS VIEW-PLATE FOR A CLOSE-UP OF KAOS.
HE'S PLANNING TO USE THE GIGANTIC VULTURE BIRDS OF VENUS IN SOME CRIMINAL WAY!
IF I CAN DOMINATE THOSE VULTURES UP THERE, I'LL BE ABLE TO CONQUER THE EARTH!
I'LL CONCENTRATE MY HYPNOTIC-CONTROL RAY ON THEM AND DRAW THEM TO MY EXPERIMENTAL STATION!
AS KAOS RELEASES THE RAY, THE HUGE BIRDS FLY DOWN TO HIS STATION.
NOW I'LL FEED THEM STRONG MEAT MIXED WITH THE JUICE OF MY SUPER-VITAMIN VINE! THIS JUICE WILL GIVE THEM GREATER SIZE AND UNLIMITED POWER!
THEY'LL BE ABLE TO FLY SO FAST THAT THE HUMAN EYES OF THE EARTHMEN WILL BE UNABLE TO SEE THEM, AND THEIR TALONS WILL BE POWERFUL ENOUGH TO CRUSH CONCRETE AND BEND THE TOUGHEST METALS!
THERE ARE MILLIONS OF THESE VULTURES! ALL THE GREAT CITIES OF THE EARTH AND ALL THE UNITS OF WARFARE WILL BE AT THEIR MERCY!
BY USING MY HYPNOTIC-CONTROL RAY ON THEM, I'LL BE ABLE TO CONQUER THE EARTH IN A FEW HOURS!
2

AS KAOS FEEDS THE VULTURES THE JUICE OF HIS SUPER-VITAMIN VINE, THE BIRDS DEVELOP RAPIDLY IN POWER AND SIZE.

I MUST KEEP THEM UNDER COMPLETE CONTROL!

STARDUST FOLLOWS THE PLOT CLOSELY...

KAOS IS GOING TO TRANSMIT THEM TO THE EARTH'S ATMOSPHERE ON CONCENTRATED THOUGHT-WAVES! I MUST INTERCEPT THEM!

STARDUST'S PRIVATE STAR IS MUCH FURTHER FROM THE EARTH THAN VENUS IS, SO THE MILLIONS OF DEMONIZED VULTURES HAVE THE ADVANTAGE....

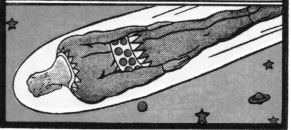

IN HIS TUBULAR SPACIAL, TRAVELING AT TERRIFIC SPEED ON ACCELERATED SUPERSOLAR LIGHT-WAVES, STARDUST STARTS HIS RACE TO SAVE THE EARTH FROM DESTRUCTIVE CONQUEST...

MEANWHILE, KAOS HAS ASSEMBLED THE VULTURES, READY FOR TRANSMISSION TO THE EARTH'S ATMOSPHERE.....

SOON, UNDER CONTROL OF THE HYPNOTIC RAY, THE POWERFUL BIRDS ZOOM OUT OF THE VENUS VAPOR INTO SPACE.

CONTROLLING THEM FROM THE REAR IN HIS SUPER-SPEED ROCKET-DART, KAOS GLOATS MADLY.

THE EARTH WILL SOON BE MINE!

STARDUST SEES THE VULTURES APPROACH THE EARTH'S ATMOSPHERE...

IF THEY REACH THE EARTH, IT WILL MEAN A HORRIBLE DESTRUCTION OF LIFE AND PROPERTY!

③

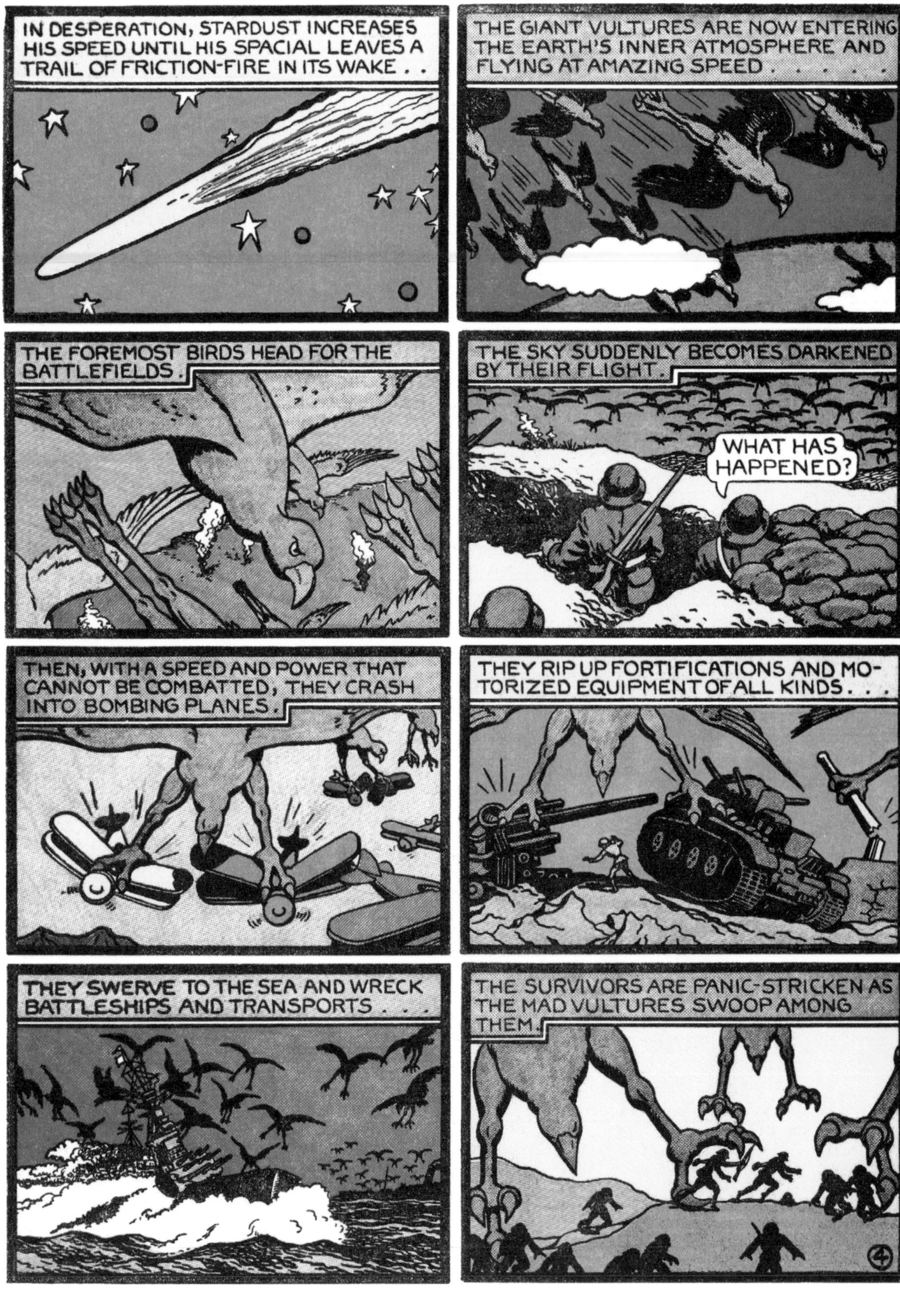
IN DESPERATION, STARDUST INCREASES HIS SPEED UNTIL HIS SPACIAL LEAVES A TRAIL OF FRICTION-FIRE IN ITS WAKE . .
THE GIANT VULTURES ARE NOW ENTERING THE EARTH'S INNER ATMOSPHERE AND FLYING AT AMAZING SPEED . . . . .
THE FOREMOST BIRDS HEAD FOR THE BATTLEFIELDS.
THE SKY SUDDENLY BECOMES DARKENED BY THEIR FLIGHT.
WHAT HAS HAPPENED?
THEN, WITH A SPEED AND POWER THAT CANNOT BE COMBATTED, THEY CRASH INTO BOMBING PLANES.
THEY RIP UP FORTIFICATIONS AND MOTORIZED EQUIPMENT OF ALL KINDS . . .
THEY SWERVE TO THE SEA AND WRECK BATTLESHIPS AND TRANSPORTS . . .
THE SURVIVORS ARE PANIC-STRICKEN AS THE MAD VULTURES SWOOP AMONG THEM.
4

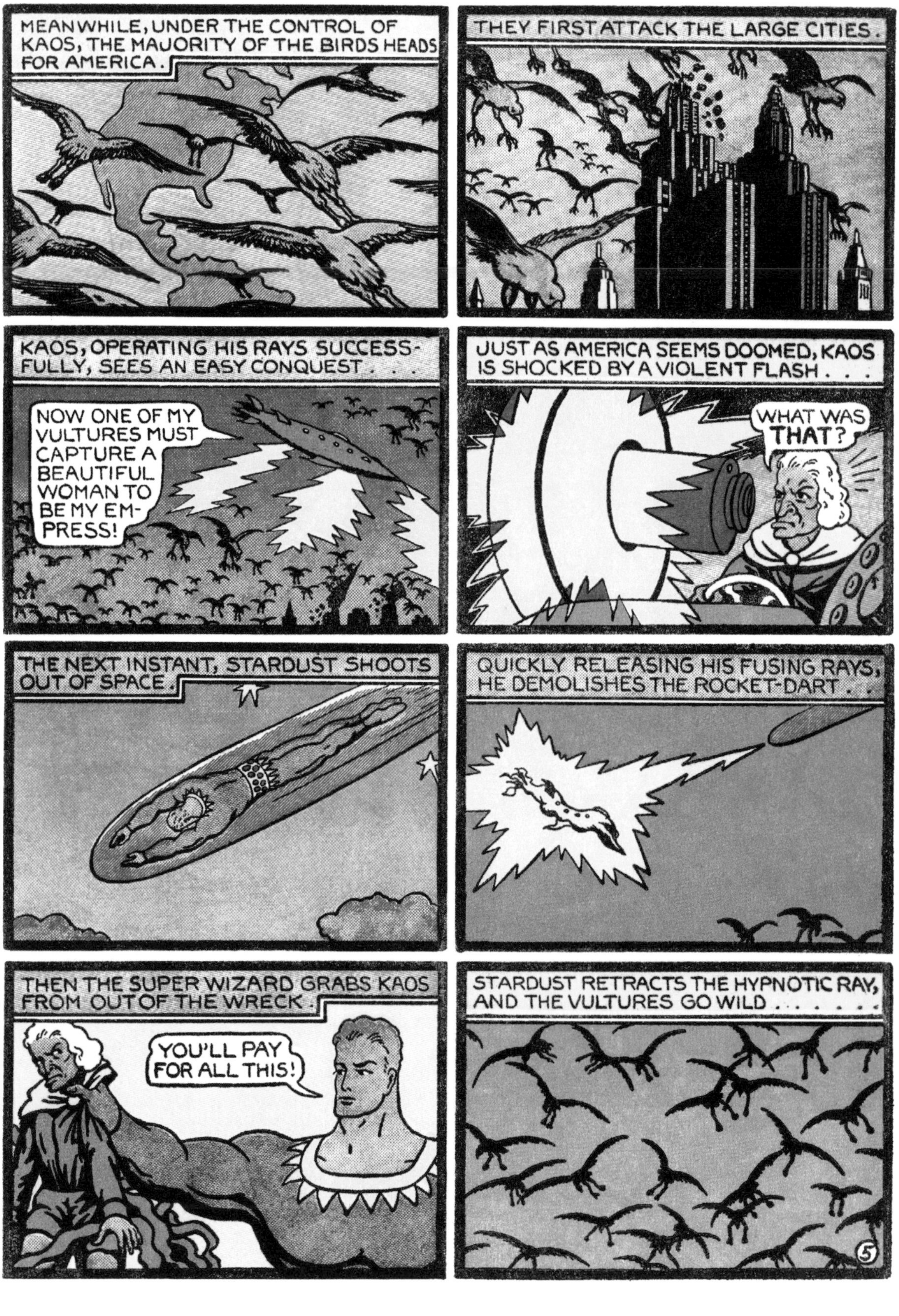
MEANWHILE, UNDER THE CONTROL OF KAOS, THE MAJORITY OF THE BIRDS HEADS FOR AMERICA.
THEY FIRST ATTACK THE LARGE CITIES.
KAOS, OPERATING HIS RAYS SUCCESSFULLY, SEES AN EASY CONQUEST . . .
NOW ONE OF MY VULTURES MUST CAPTURE A BEAUTIFUL WOMAN TO BE MY EMPRESS!
JUST AS AMERICA SEEMS DOOMED, KAOS IS SHOCKED BY A VIOLENT FLASH . . .
WHAT WAS THAT?
THE NEXT INSTANT, STARDUST SHOOTS OUT OF SPACE.
QUICKLY RELEASING HIS FUSING RAYS, HE DEMOLISHES THE ROCKET-DART . . .
THEN THE SUPER WIZARD GRABS KAOS FROM OUT OF THE WRECK.
YOU'LL PAY FOR ALL THIS!
STARDUST RETRACTS THE HYPNOTIC RAY, AND THE VULTURES GO WILD . . . . . . .
5

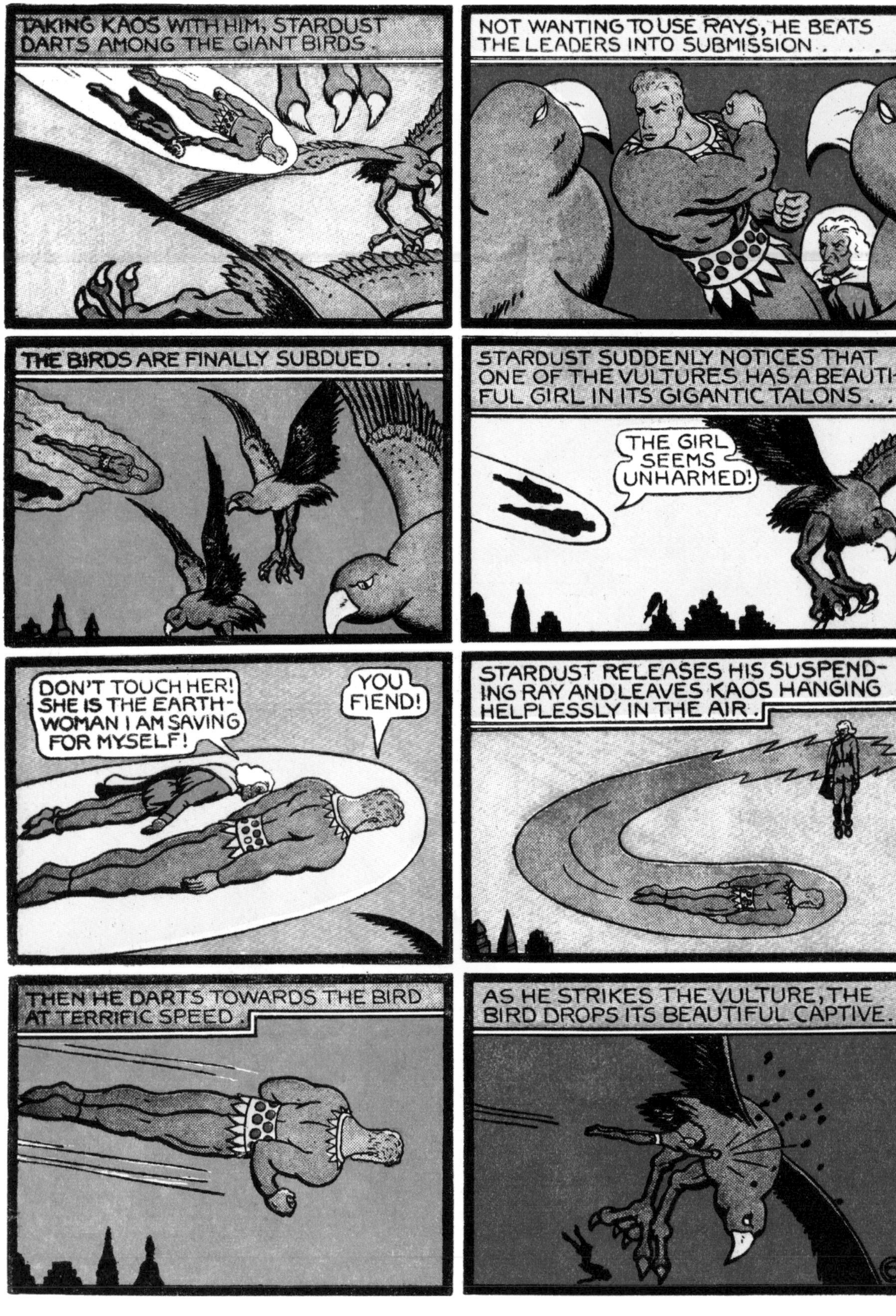
TAKING KAOS WITH HIM, STARDUST DARTS AMONG THE GIANT BIRDS.
NOT WANTING TO USE RAYS, HE BEATS THE LEADERS INTO SUBMISSION . . . .
THE BIRDS ARE FINALLY SUBDUED . . .
STARDUST SUDDENLY NOTICES THAT ONE OF THE VULTURES HAS A BEAUTIFUL GIRL IN ITS GIGANTIC TALONS . .
THE GIRL SEEMS UNHARMED!
DON'T TOUCH HER! SHE IS THE EARTH-WOMAN I AM SAVING FOR MYSELF!
YOU FIEND!
STARDUST RELEASES HIS SUSPENDING RAY AND LEAVES KAOS HANGING HELPLESSLY IN THE AIR.
THEN HE DARTS TOWARDS THE BIRD AT TERRIFIC SPEED.
AS HE STRIKES THE VULTURE, THE BIRD DROPS ITS BEAUTIFUL CAPTIVE.
6

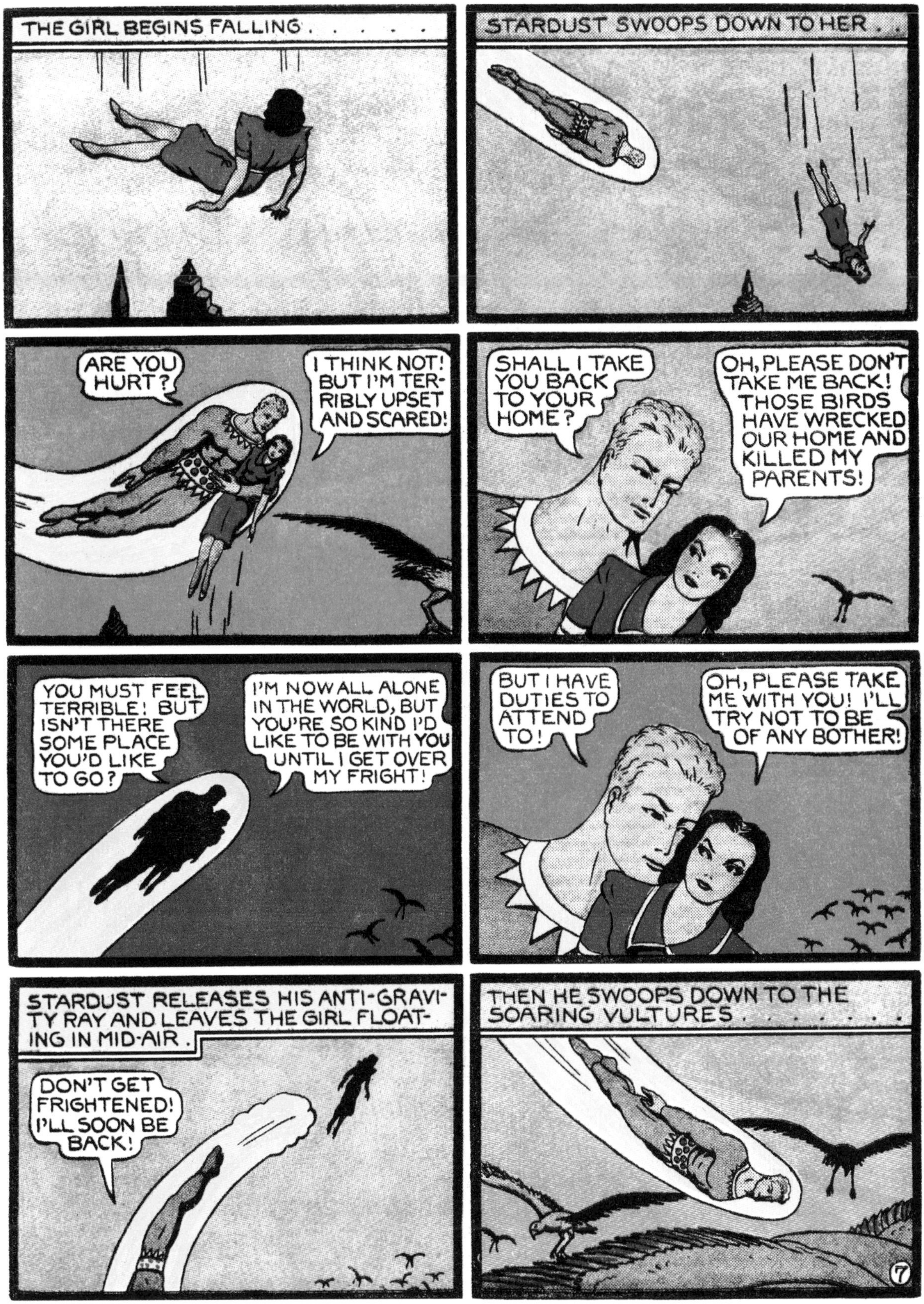

THE GIRL BEGINS FALLING . . . . .
STARDUST SWOOPS DOWN TO HER . .
ARE YOU HURT?
I THINK NOT! BUT I'M TERRIBLY UPSET AND SCARED!
SHALL I TAKE YOU BACK TO YOUR HOME?
OH, PLEASE DON'T TAKE ME BACK! THOSE BIRDS HAVE WRECKED OUR HOME AND KILLED MY PARENTS!
YOU MUST FEEL TERRIBLE! BUT ISN'T THERE SOME PLACE YOU'D LIKE TO GO?
I'M NOW ALL ALONE IN THE WORLD, BUT YOU'RE SO KIND I'D LIKE TO BE WITH YOU UNTIL I GET OVER MY FRIGHT!
BUT I HAVE DUTIES TO ATTEND TO!
OH, PLEASE TAKE ME WITH YOU! I'LL TRY NOT TO BE OF ANY BOTHER!
STARDUST RELEASES HIS ANTI-GRAVITY RAY AND LEAVES THE GIRL FLOATING IN MID-AIR.
DON'T GET FRIGHTENED! I'LL SOON BE BACK!
THEN HE SWOOPS DOWN TO THE SOARING VULTURES . . . . . .
7

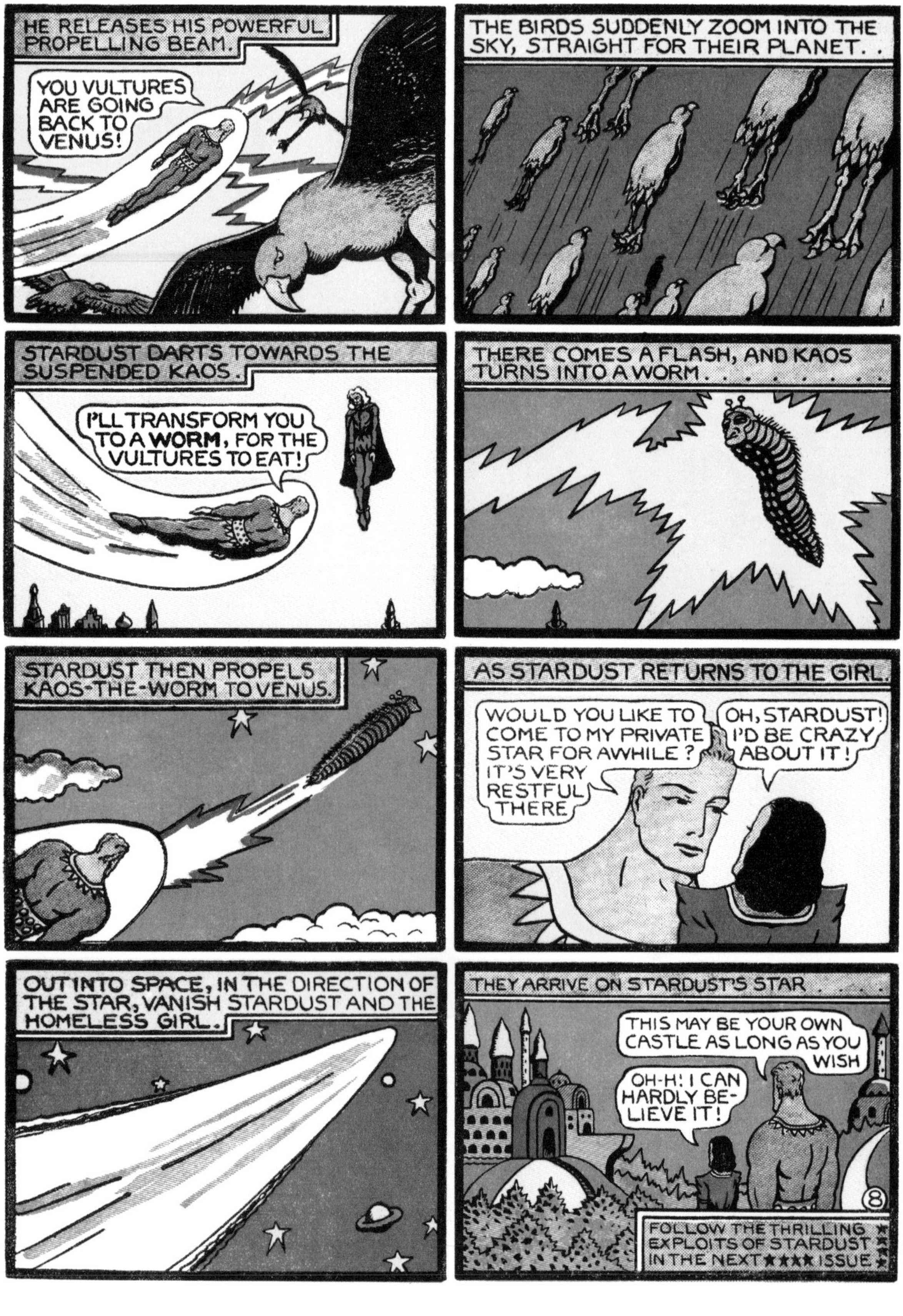
HE RELEASES HIS POWERFUL PROPELLING BEAM.
YOU VULTURES ARE GOING BACK TO VENUS!
THE BIRDS SUDDENLY ZOOM INTO THE SKY, STRAIGHT FOR THEIR PLANET . .
STARDUST DARTS TOWARDS THE SUSPENDED KAOS.
I'LL TRANSFORM YOU TO A WORM, FOR THE VULTURES TO EAT!
THERE COMES A FLASH, AND KAOS TURNS INTO A WORM . . . . . . .
STARDUST THEN PROPELS KAOS-THE-WORM TO VENUS.
AS STARDUST RETURNS TO THE GIRL.
WOULD YOU LIKE TO COME TO MY PRIVATE STAR FOR AWHILE? IT'S VERY RESTFUL THERE
OH, STARDUST! I'D BE CRAZY ABOUT IT!
OUT INTO SPACE, IN THE DIRECTION OF THE STAR, VANISH STARDUST AND THE HOMELESS GIRL.
THEY ARRIVE ON STARDUST'S STAR . . . .
THIS MAY BE YOUR OWN CASTLE AS LONG AS YOU WISH
OH-H! I CAN HARDLY BE-LIEVE IT!
8
FOLLOW THE THRILLING EXPLOITS OF STARDUST IN THE NEXT ★★★ ISSUE.

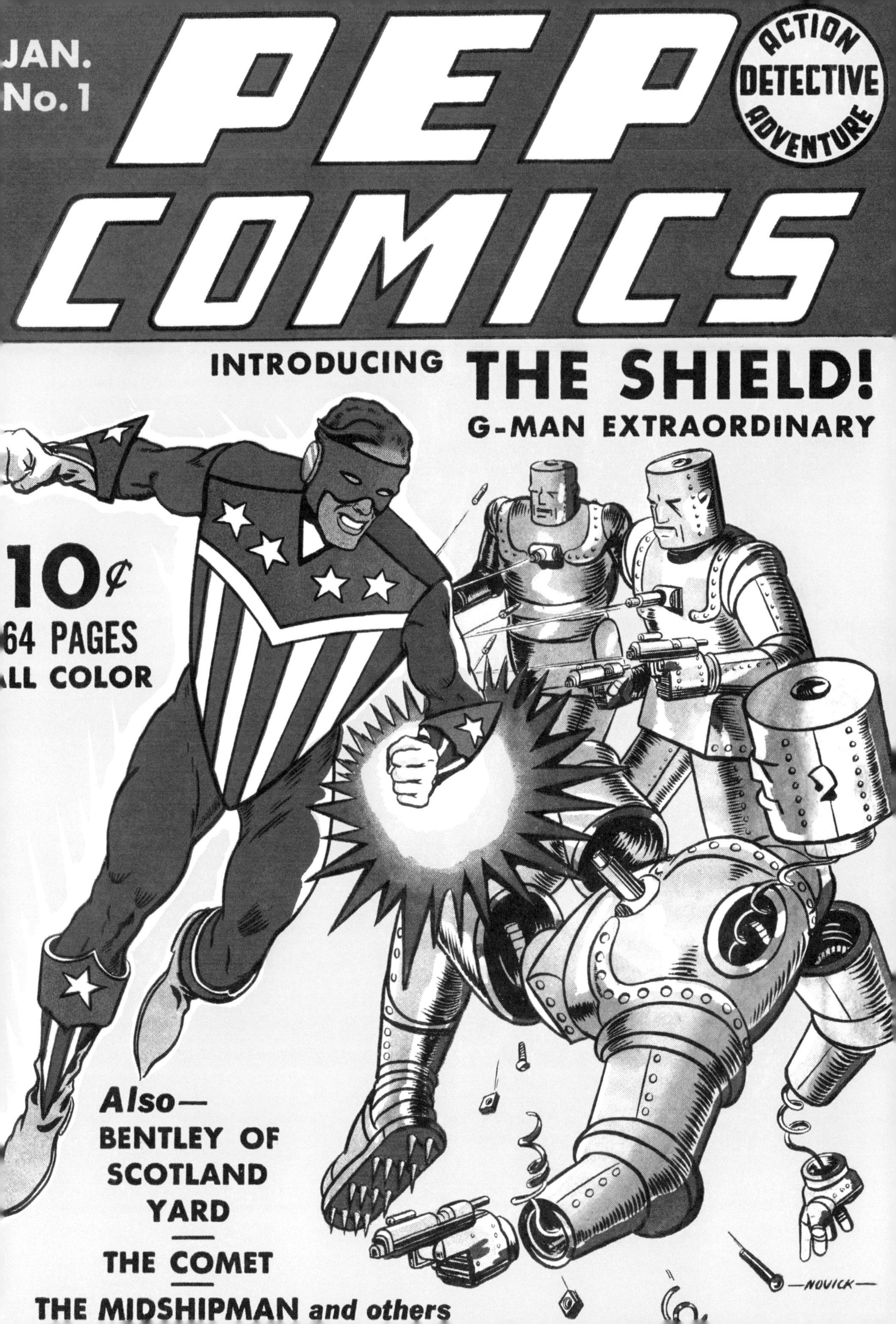
JAN.
No. 1
PEP COMICS
ACTION
DETECTIVE
ADVENTURE
INTRODUCING THE SHIELD!
G-MAN EXTRAORDINARY
10¢
64 PAGES
LL COLOR
Also—
BENTLEY OF
SCOTLAND
YARD
THE COMET
THE MIDSHIPMAN and others
—NOVICK—

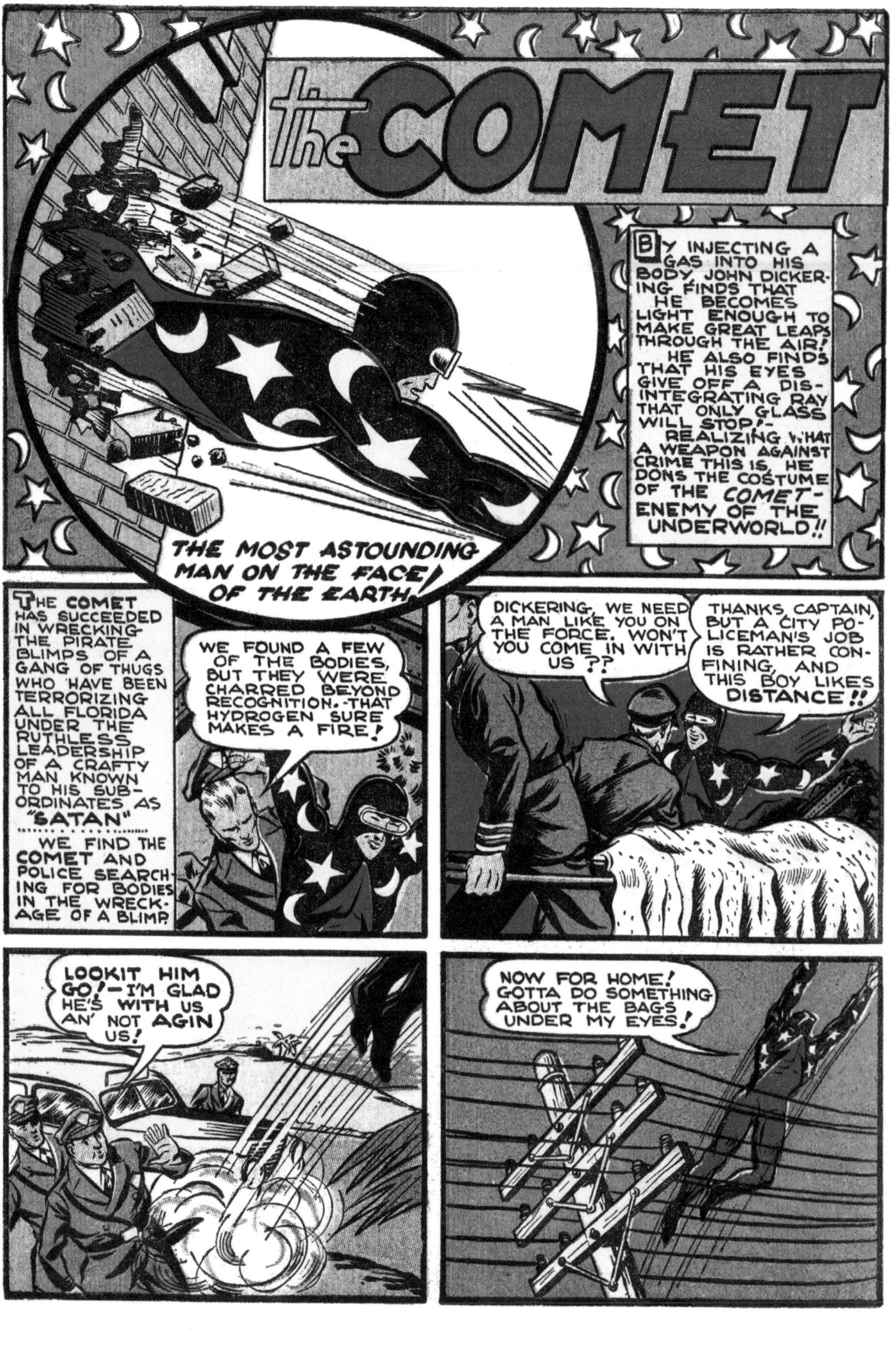

THE COMET
BY INJECTING A GAS INTO HIS BODY, JOHN DICKERING FINDS THAT HE BECOMES LIGHT ENOUGH TO MAKE GREAT LEAPS THROUGH THE AIR! HE ALSO FINDS THAT HIS EYES GIVE OFF A DISINTEGRATING RAY THAT ONLY GLASS WILL STOP! REALIZING WHAT A WEAPON AGAINST CRIME THIS IS, HE DONS THE COSTUME OF THE COMET - ENEMY OF THE UNDERWORLD!!
THE MOST ASTOUNDING MAN ON THE FACE OF THE EARTH!
THE COMET HAS SUCCEEDED IN WRECKING THE PIRATE BLIMPS OF A GANG OF THUGS WHO HAVE BEEN TERRORIZING ALL FLORIDA UNDER THE RUTHLESS LEADERSHIP OF A CRAFTY MAN KNOWN TO HIS SUBORDINATES AS "SATAN" ......... WE FIND THE COMET AND POLICE SEARCHING FOR BODIES IN THE WRECKAGE OF A BLIMP.
WE FOUND A FEW OF THE BODIES, BUT THEY WERE CHARRED BEYOND RECOGNITION.-THAT HYDROGEN SURE MAKES A FIRE!
DICKERING, WE NEED A MAN LIKE YOU ON THE FORCE. WON'T YOU COME IN WITH US ??
THANKS CAPTAIN, BUT A CITY POLICEMAN'S JOB IS RATHER CONFINING, AND THIS BOY LIKES DISTANCE!!
LOOKIT HIM GO!-I'M GLAD HE'S WITH US AN' NOT AGIN US!
NOW FOR HOME! GOTTA DO SOMETHING ABOUT THE BAGS UNDER MY EYES!

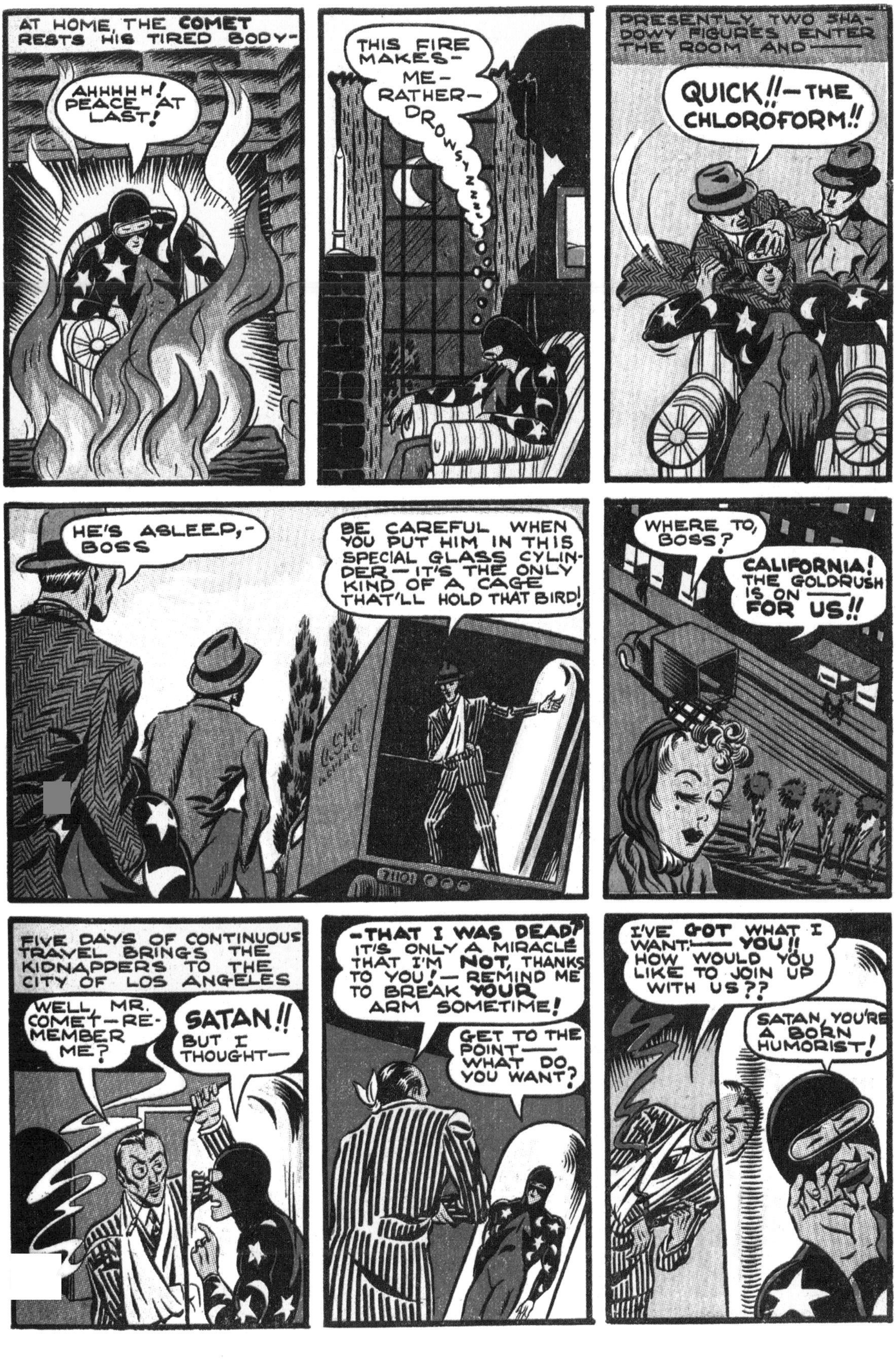
AT HOME, THE COMET RESTS HIS TIRED BODY-
AHHHHH! PEACE AT LAST!
THIS FIRE MAKES- ME- RATHER- DROWSY ZZZZ
PRESENTLY, TWO SHADOWY FIGURES ENTER THE ROOM AND——
QUICK!!—THE CHLOROFORM!!
HE'S ASLEEP,- BOSS
BE CAREFUL WHEN YOU PUT HIM IN THIS SPECIAL GLASS CYLINDER—IT'S THE ONLY KIND OF A CAGE THAT'LL HOLD THAT BIRD!
WHERE TO, BOSS?
CALIFORNIA! THE GOLDRUSH IS ON —— FOR US!!
FIVE DAYS OF CONTINUOUS TRAVEL BRINGS THE KIDNAPPERS TO THE CITY OF LOS ANGELES
WELL, MR. COMET—REMEMBER ME?
SATAN!! BUT I THOUGHT—
—THAT I WAS DEAD? IT'S ONLY A MIRACLE THAT I'M NOT, THANKS TO YOU!—REMIND ME TO BREAK YOUR ARM SOMETIME!
GET TO THE POINT—— WHAT DO YOU WANT?
I'VE GOT WHAT I WANT.—— YOU!! HOW WOULD YOU LIKE TO JOIN UP WITH US??
SATAN, YOU'RE A BORN HUMORIST!

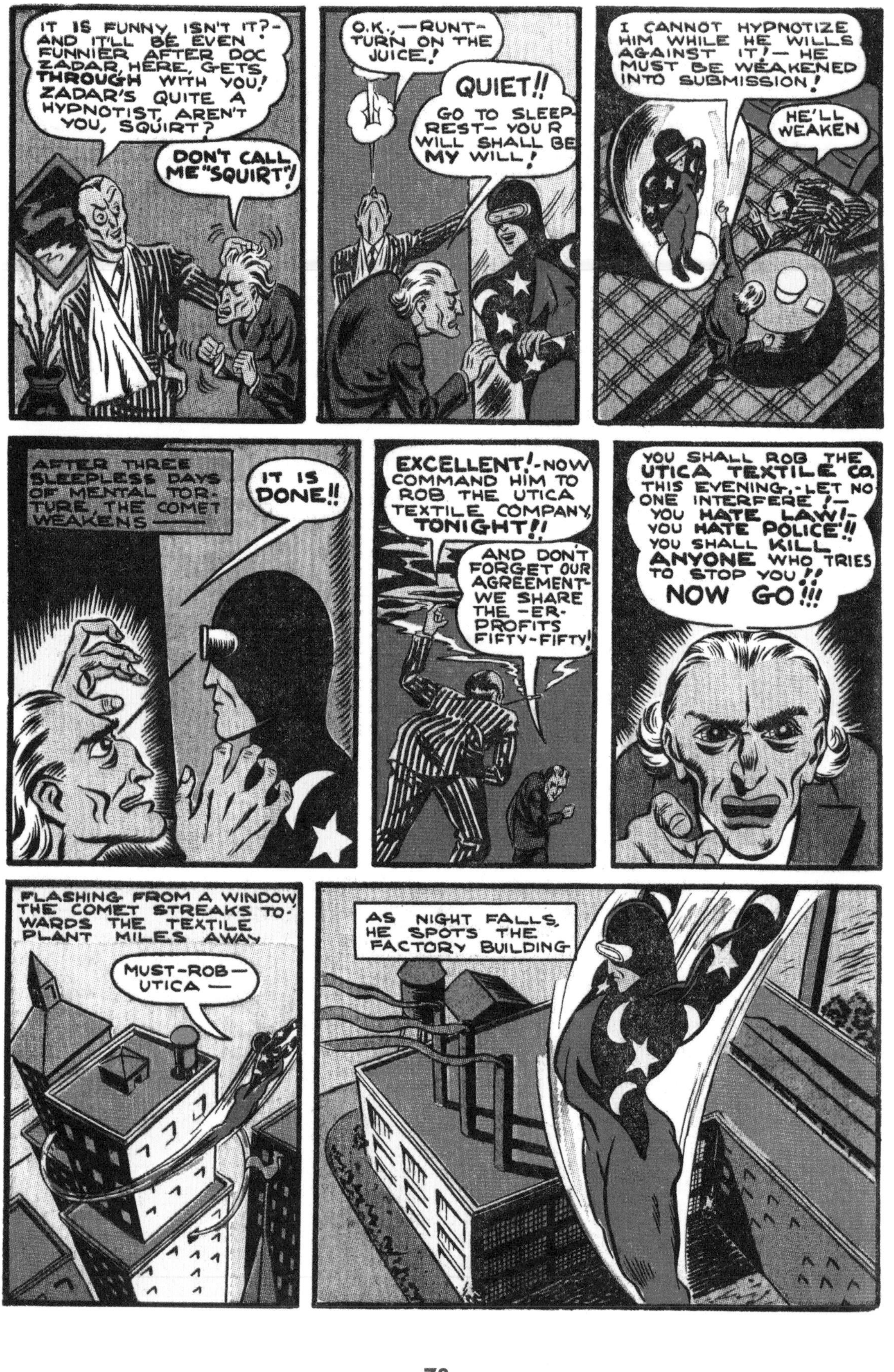
IT IS FUNNY, ISN'T IT?- AND IT'LL BE EVEN FUNNIER AFTER DOC ZADAR, HERE, GETS THROUGH WITH YOU! ZADAR'S QUITE A HYPNOTIST, AREN'T YOU, SQUIRT?
DON'T CALL ME "SQUIRT"!
O.K., —RUNT- TURN ON THE JUICE!
QUIET!! GO TO SLEEP- REST- YOUR WILL SHALL BE MY WILL!
I CANNOT HYPNOTIZE HIM WHILE HE WILLS AGAINST IT!— HE MUST BE WEAKENED INTO SUBMISSION!
HE'LL WEAKEN
AFTER THREE SLEEPLESS DAYS OF MENTAL TORTURE, THE COMET WEAKENS —
IT IS DONE!!
EXCELLENT!-NOW COMMAND HIM TO ROB THE UTICA TEXTILE COMPANY, TONIGHT!!
AND DON'T FORGET OUR AGREEMENT- WE SHARE THE -ER- PROFITS FIFTY-FIFTY!
YOU SHALL ROB THE UTICA TEXTILE CO. THIS EVENING,-LET NO ONE INTERFERE!— YOU HATE LAW!- YOU HATE POLICE!! YOU SHALL KILL ANYONE WHO TRIES TO STOP YOU!! NOW GO!!!
FLASHING FROM A WINDOW THE COMET STREAKS TOWARDS THE TEXTILE PLANT MILES AWAY
MUST-ROB— UTICA —
AS NIGHT FALLS, HE SPOTS THE FACTORY BUILDING

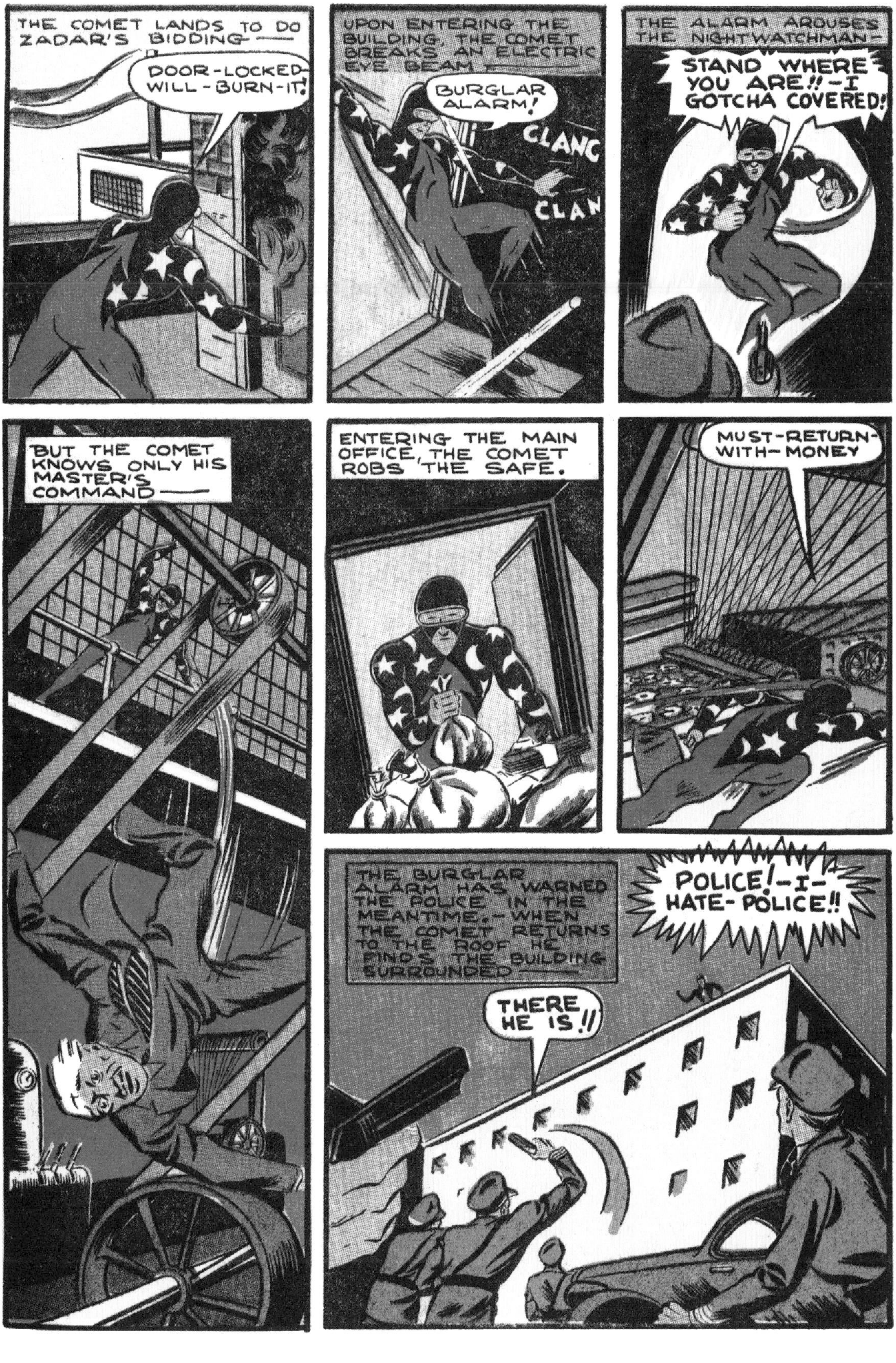
THE COMET LANDS TO DO ZADAR'S BIDDING——
DOOR-LOCKED-WILL-BURN-IT!
UPON ENTERING THE BUILDING, THE COMET BREAKS AN ELECTRIC EYE BEAM——
BURGLAR ALARM!
CLANG
CLAN
THE ALARM AROUSES THE NIGHTWATCHMAN-
STAND WHERE YOU ARE!!-I GOTCHA COVERED!
BUT THE COMET KNOWS ONLY HIS MASTER'S COMMAND——
ENTERING THE MAIN OFFICE, THE COMET ROBS THE SAFE.
MUST-RETURN-WITH-MONEY
THE BURGLAR ALARM HAS WARNED THE POLICE IN THE MEANTIME.-WHEN THE COMET RETURNS TO THE ROOF HE FINDS THE BUILDING SURROUNDED——
POLICE!-I-HATE-POLICE!!
THERE HE IS!!

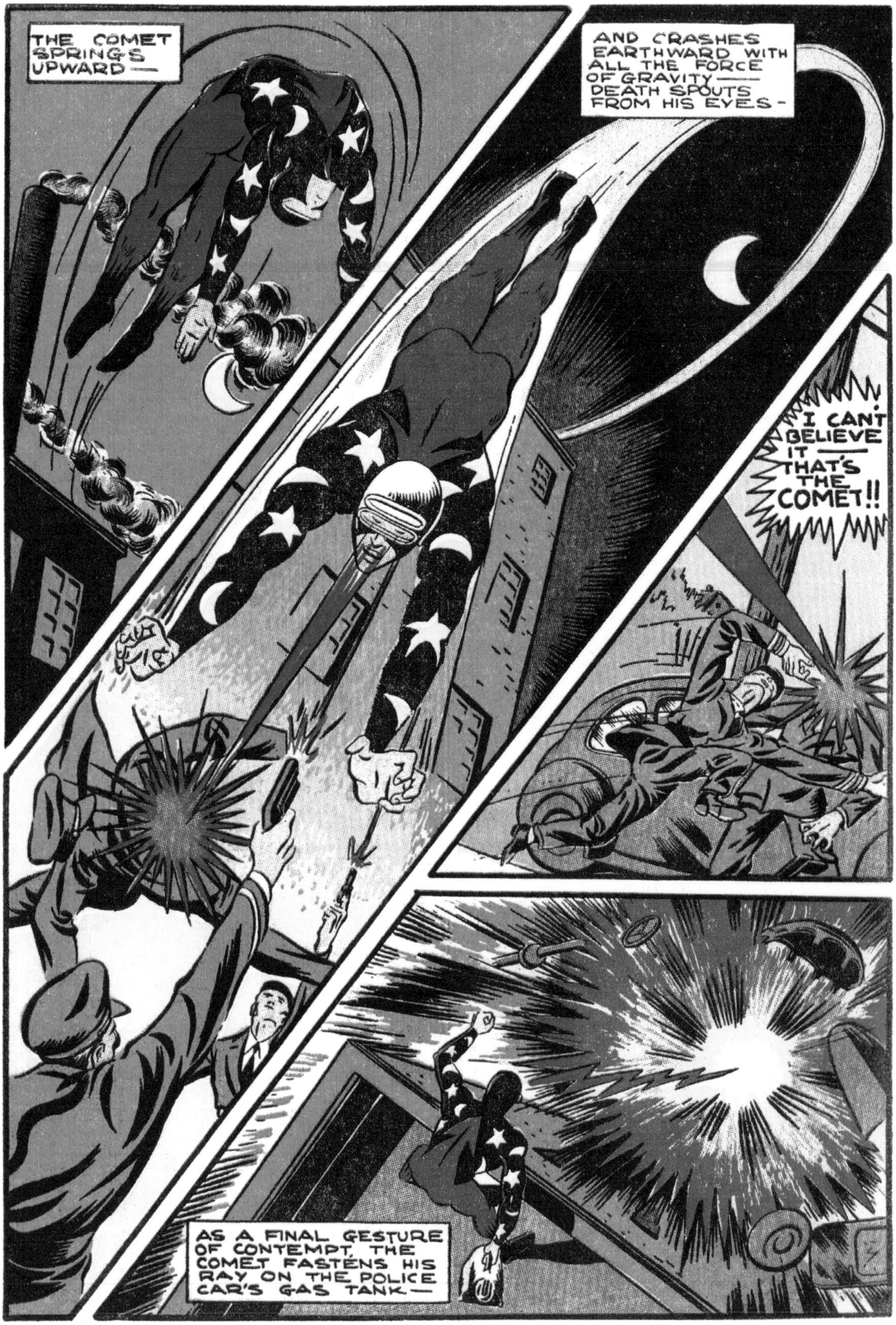
THE COMET SPRINGS UPWARD —
AND CRASHES EARTHWARD WITH ALL THE FORCE OF GRAVITY —— DEATH SPOUTS FROM HIS EYES -
I CAN'T BELIEVE IT — THAT'S THE COMET!!
AS A FINAL GESTURE OF CONTEMPT, THE COMET FASTENS HIS RAY ON THE POLICE CAR'S GAS TANK —

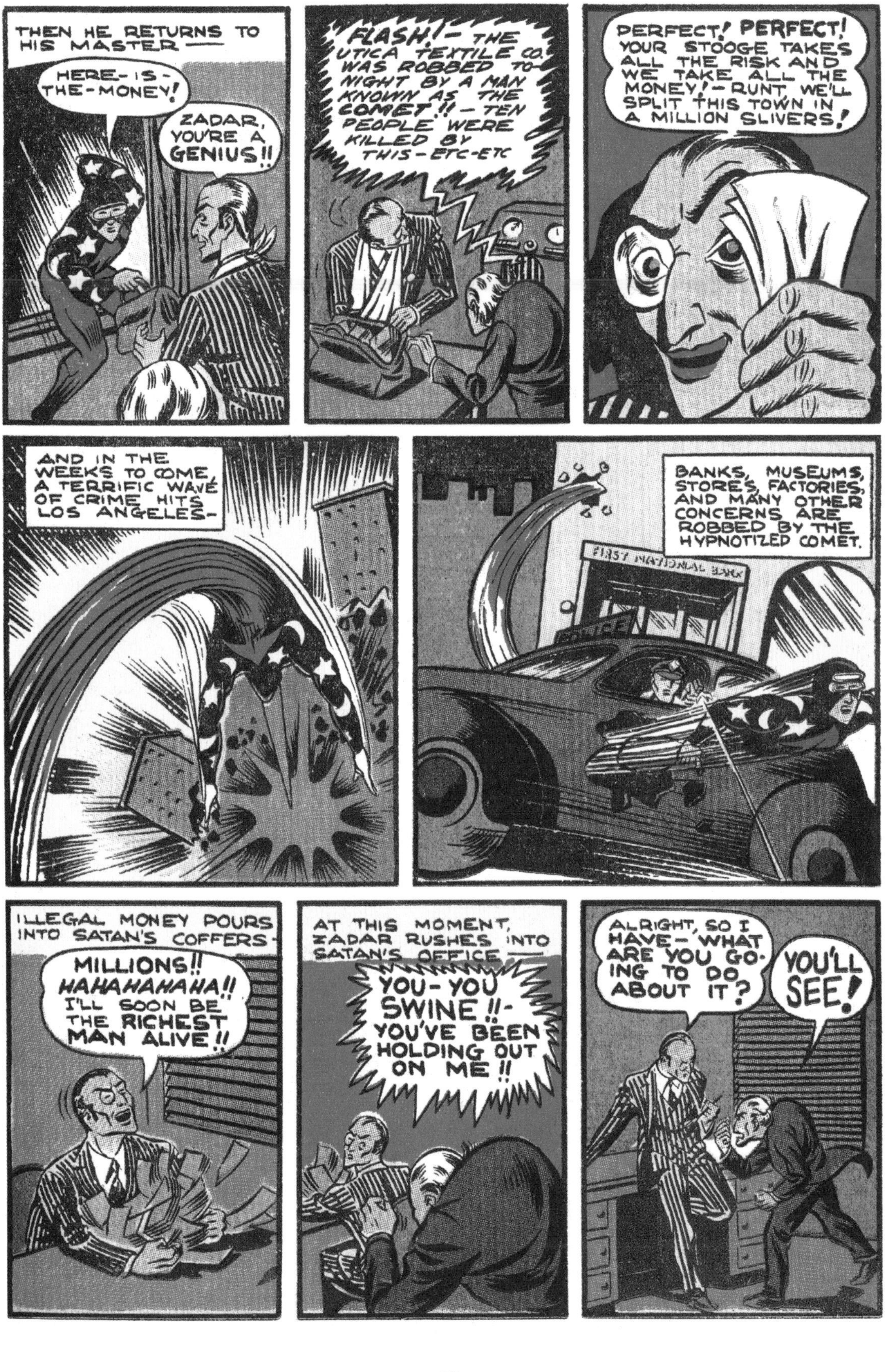
THEN HE RETURNS TO HIS MASTER—
HERE-IS-THE-MONEY!
ZADAR, YOU'RE A GENIUS!!
FLASH!— THE UTICA TEXTILE CO. WAS ROBBED TO-NIGHT BY A MAN KNOWN AS THE COMET!!— TEN PEOPLE WERE KILLED BY THIS-ETC-ETC
PERFECT! PERFECT! YOUR STOOGE TAKES ALL THE RISK AND WE TAKE ALL THE MONEY!— RUNT WE'LL SPLIT THIS TOWN IN A MILLION SLIVERS!
AND IN THE WEEKS TO COME, A TERRIFIC WAVE OF CRIME HITS LOS ANGELES-
BANKS, MUSEUMS, STORES, FACTORIES, AND MANY OTHER CONCERNS ARE ROBBED BY THE HYPNOTIZED COMET.
FIRST NATIONAL BANK
ILLEGAL MONEY POURS INTO SATAN'S COFFERS-
MILLIONS!! HAHAHAHAHA!! I'LL SOON BE THE RICHEST MAN ALIVE!!
AT THIS MOMENT, ZADAR RUSHES INTO SATAN'S OFFICE—
YOU- YOU SWINE!!- YOU'VE BEEN HOLDING OUT ON ME!!
ALRIGHT, SO I HAVE- WHAT ARE YOU GO-ING TO DO ABOUT IT?
YOU'LL SEE!

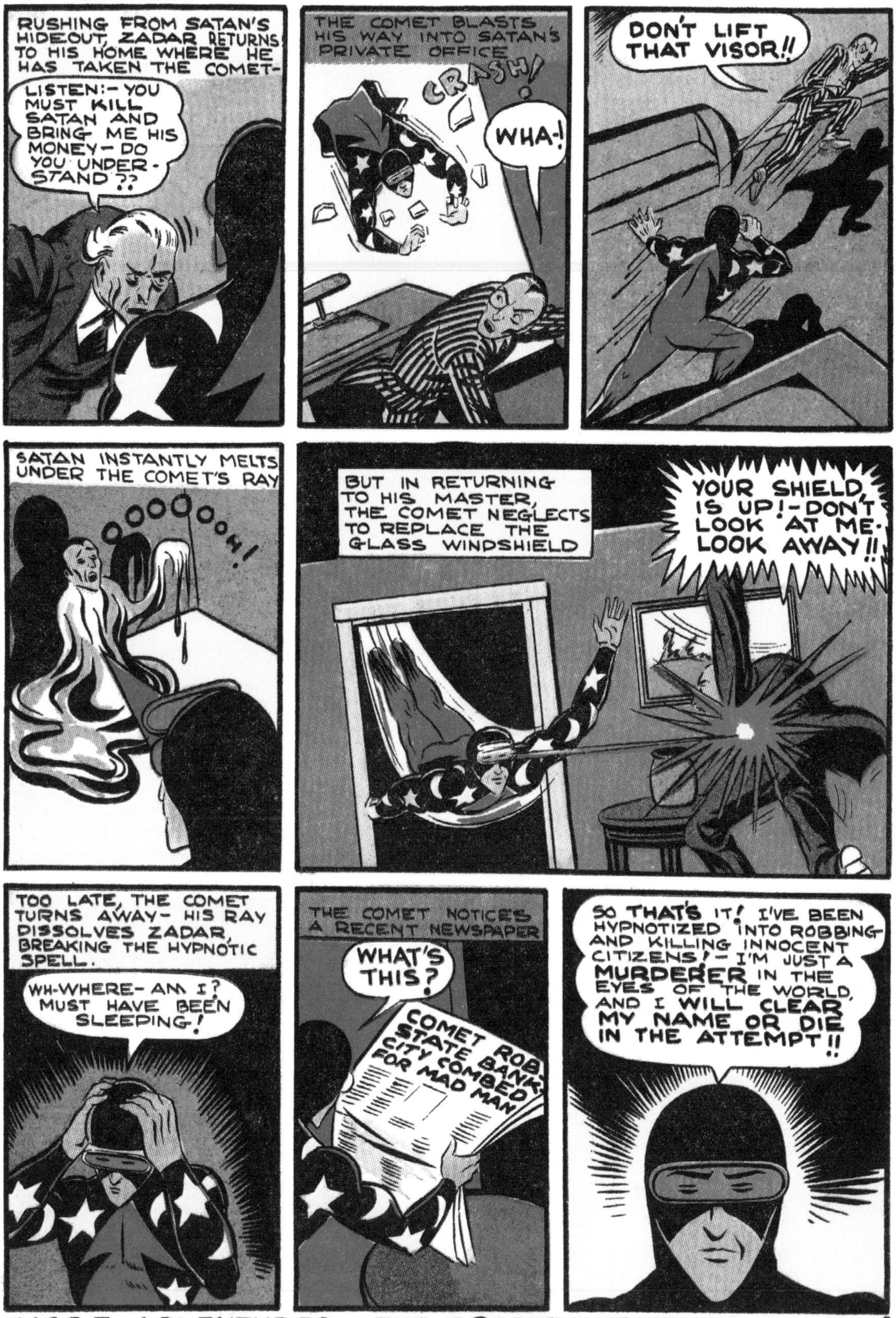
RUSHING FROM SATAN'S HIDEOUT, ZADAR RETURNS TO HIS HOME WHERE HE HAS TAKEN THE COMET-
LISTEN:- YOU MUST KILL SATAN AND BRING ME HIS MONEY- DO YOU UNDER-STAND ??
THE COMET BLASTS HIS WAY INTO SATAN'S PRIVATE OFFICE
CRASH!
WHA-!
DON'T LIFT THAT VISOR!!
SATAN INSTANTLY MELTS UNDER THE COMET'S RAY
OOOOOOOH!
BUT IN RETURNING TO HIS MASTER, THE COMET NEGLECTS TO REPLACE THE GLASS WINDSHIELD
YOUR SHIELD IS UP!- DON'T LOOK AT ME- LOOK AWAY!!
TOO LATE, THE COMET TURNS AWAY- HIS RAY DISSOLVES ZADAR, BREAKING THE HYPNOTIC SPELL.
WH-WHERE- AM I? MUST HAVE BEEN SLEEPING!
THE COMET NOTICES A RECENT NEWSPAPER
WHAT'S THIS?
COMET ROBS STATE BANK. CITY COMBED FOR MAD MAN
SO THAT'S IT! I'VE BEEN HYPNOTIZED INTO ROBBING AND KILLING INNOCENT CITIZENS!- I'M JUST A MURDERER IN THE EYES OF THE WORLD, AND I WILL CLEAR MY NAME OR DIE IN THE ATTEMPT!!
MORE ADVENTURES OF THE COMET IN THE NEXT ISSUE OF PEP COMICS!

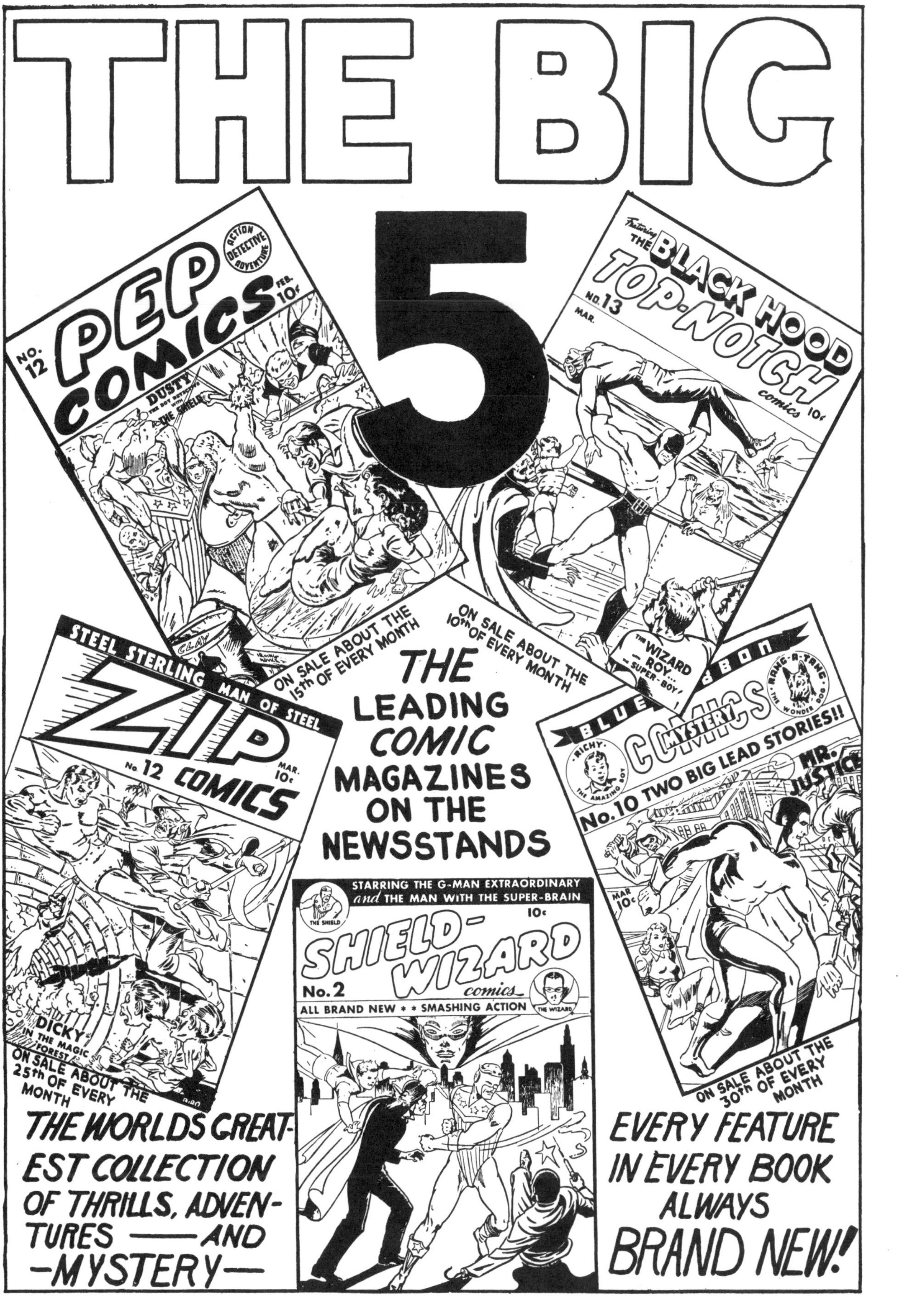

THE BIG
5
PEP COMICS
NO. 12
FEB. 10¢
ACTION DETECTIVE ADVENTURE
DUSTY THE BOY DETECTIVE WITH THE SHIELD
Featuring THE BLACK HOOD
TOP-NOTCH comics
NO. 13
MAR.
10¢
THE WIZARD ROY... THE SUPER-BOY!
ON SALE ABOUT THE 15th OF EVERY MONTH
ON SALE ABOUT THE 10th OF EVERY MONTH
STEEL STERLING MAN OF STEEL
ZIP
No. 12 COMICS
MAR. 10¢
DICKY IN THE MAGIC FOREST
ON SALE ABOUT THE 25th OF EVERY MONTH
THE LEADING COMIC MAGAZINES ON THE NEWSSTANDS
BLUE RIBBON
MYSTERY
COMICS
BANG-A-TANG THE WONDER DOG
RICHY THE AMAZING BOY
No. 10 TWO BIG LEAD STORIES!!
MR. JUSTICE
MAR 10¢
ON SALE ABOUT THE 30th OF EVERY MONTH
STARRING THE G-MAN EXTRAORDINARY and THE MAN WITH THE SUPER-BRAIN
THE SHIELD
10¢
SHIELD-WIZARD comics
No. 2
THE WIZARD
ALL BRAND NEW * * SMASHING ACTION
THE WORLDS GREATEST COLLECTION OF THRILLS, ADVENTURES —— AND —MYSTERY—
EVERY FEATURE IN EVERY BOOK ALWAYS BRAND NEW!

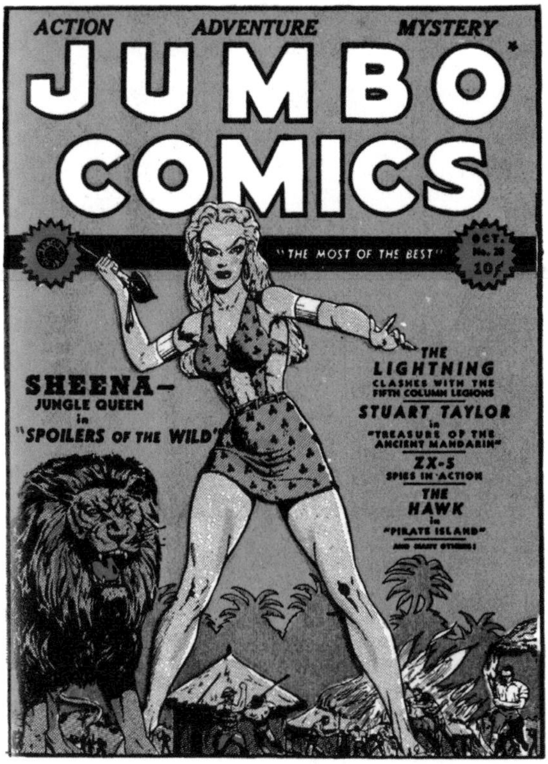
ACTION ADVENTURE MYSTERY
JUMBO COMICS
"THE MOST OF THE BEST"
OCT.
10¢
SHEENA—JUNGLE QUEEN in "SPOILERS OF THE WILD"
THE LIGHTNING CLASHES WITH THE FIFTH COLUMN LEGIONS
STUART TAYLOR in "TREASURE OF THE ANCIENT MANDARIN"
ZX-5 SPIES IN ACTION
THE HAWK in "PIRATE ISLAND"
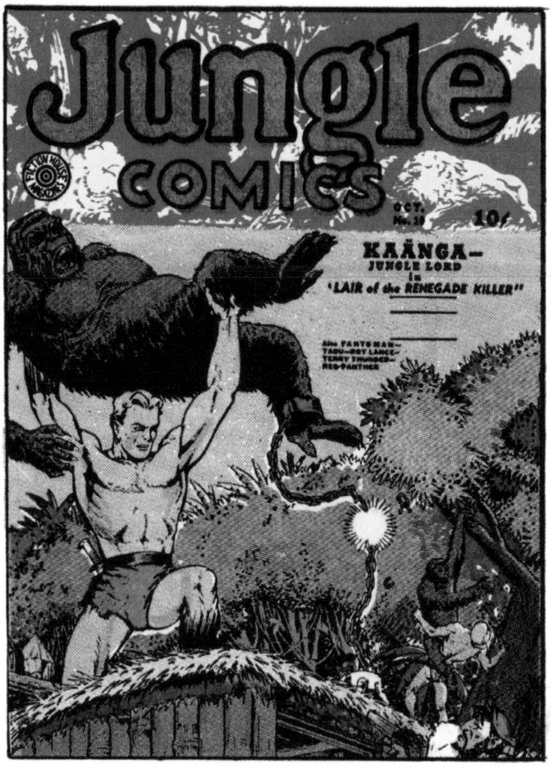
Jungle COMICS
OCT.
10¢
KAÄNGA—JUNGLE LORD in "LAIR of the RENEGADE KILLER"
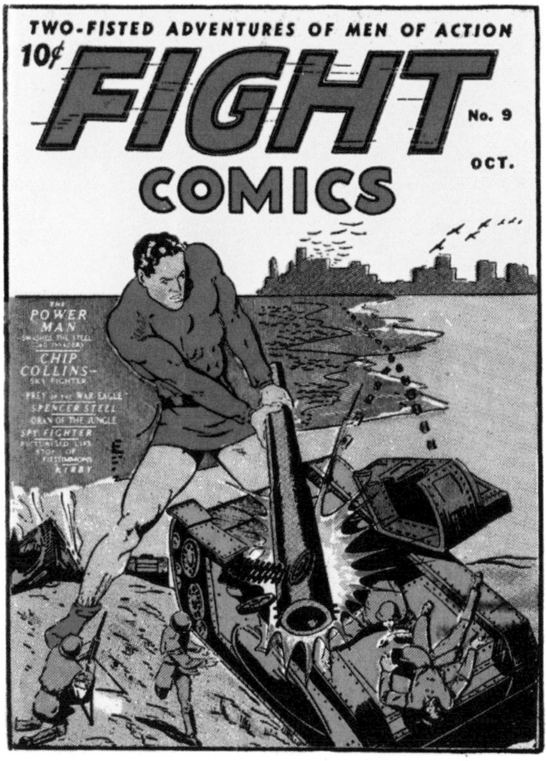
TWO-FISTED ADVENTURES OF MEN OF ACTION
10¢
FIGHT
No. 9
OCT.
COMICS
THE POWER MAN
CHIP COLLINS—SKY FIGHTER
SPENCER STEEL
SPY FIGHTER
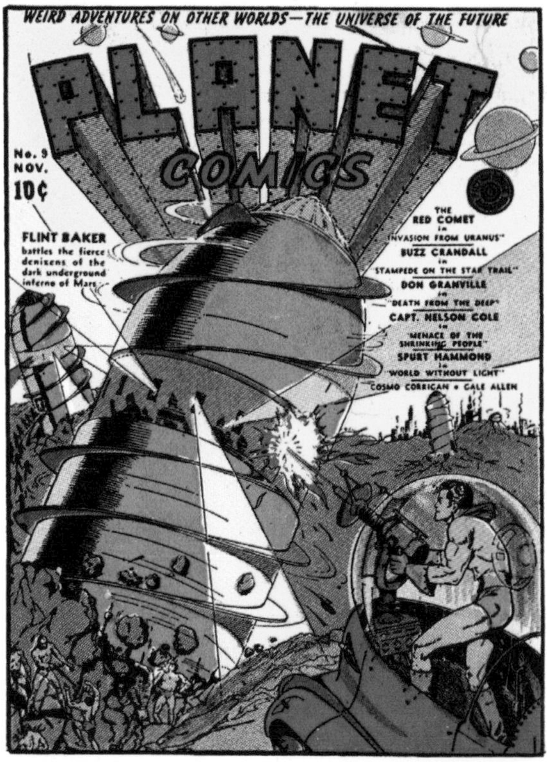
WEIRD ADVENTURES ON OTHER WORLDS—THE UNIVERSE OF THE FUTURE
PLANET COMICS
No. 9
NOV.
10¢
FLINT BAKER battles the fierce denizens of the dark underground inferno of Mars
THE RED COMET in "INVASION FROM URANUS"
BUZZ CRANDALL in "STAMPEDE ON THE STAR TRAIL"
DON GRANVILLE in "DEATH FROM THE DEEP"
CAPT. NELSON COLE in "MENACE OF THE SHRINKING PEOPLE"
SPURT HAMMOND in "WORLD WITHOUT LIGHT"
COSMO CORRIGAN • GALE ALLEN

The Bull's-Eye on the Cover means

TOP-FLIGHT QUALITY—SMASHING ACTION-ADVENTURE!

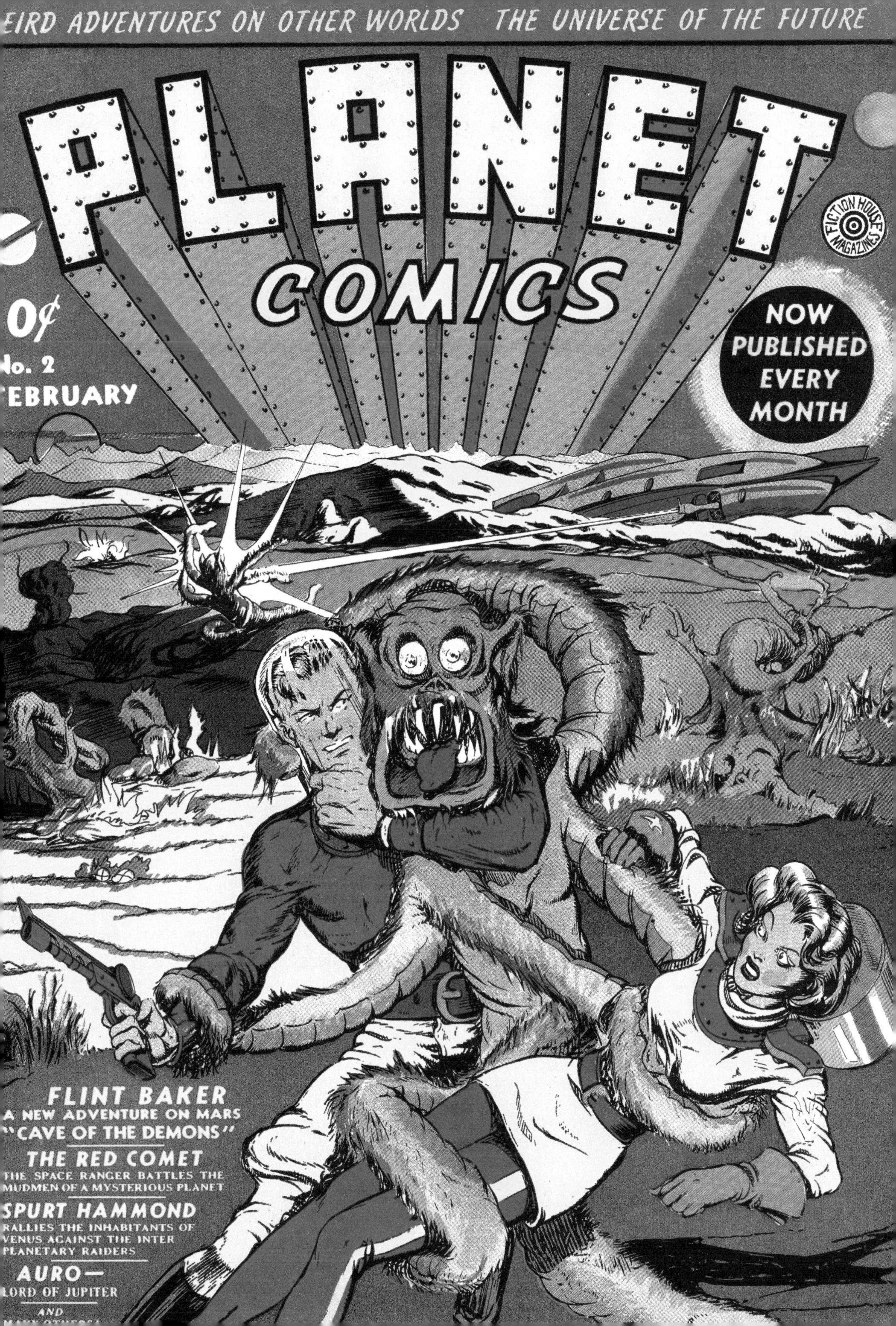
EIRD ADVENTURES ON OTHER WORLDS
THE UNIVERSE OF THE FUTURE
PLANET
COMICS
FICTION HOUSE MAGAZINES
10¢
No. 2
FEBRUARY
NOW PUBLISHED EVERY MONTH
FLINT BAKER
A NEW ADVENTURE ON MARS
"CAVE OF THE DEMONS"
THE RED COMET
THE SPACE RANGER BATTLES THE MUDMEN OF A MYSTERIOUS PLANET
SPURT HAMMOND
RALLIES THE INHABITANTS OF VENUS AGAINST THE INTER PLANETARY RAIDERS
AURO—
LORD OF JUPITER
AND

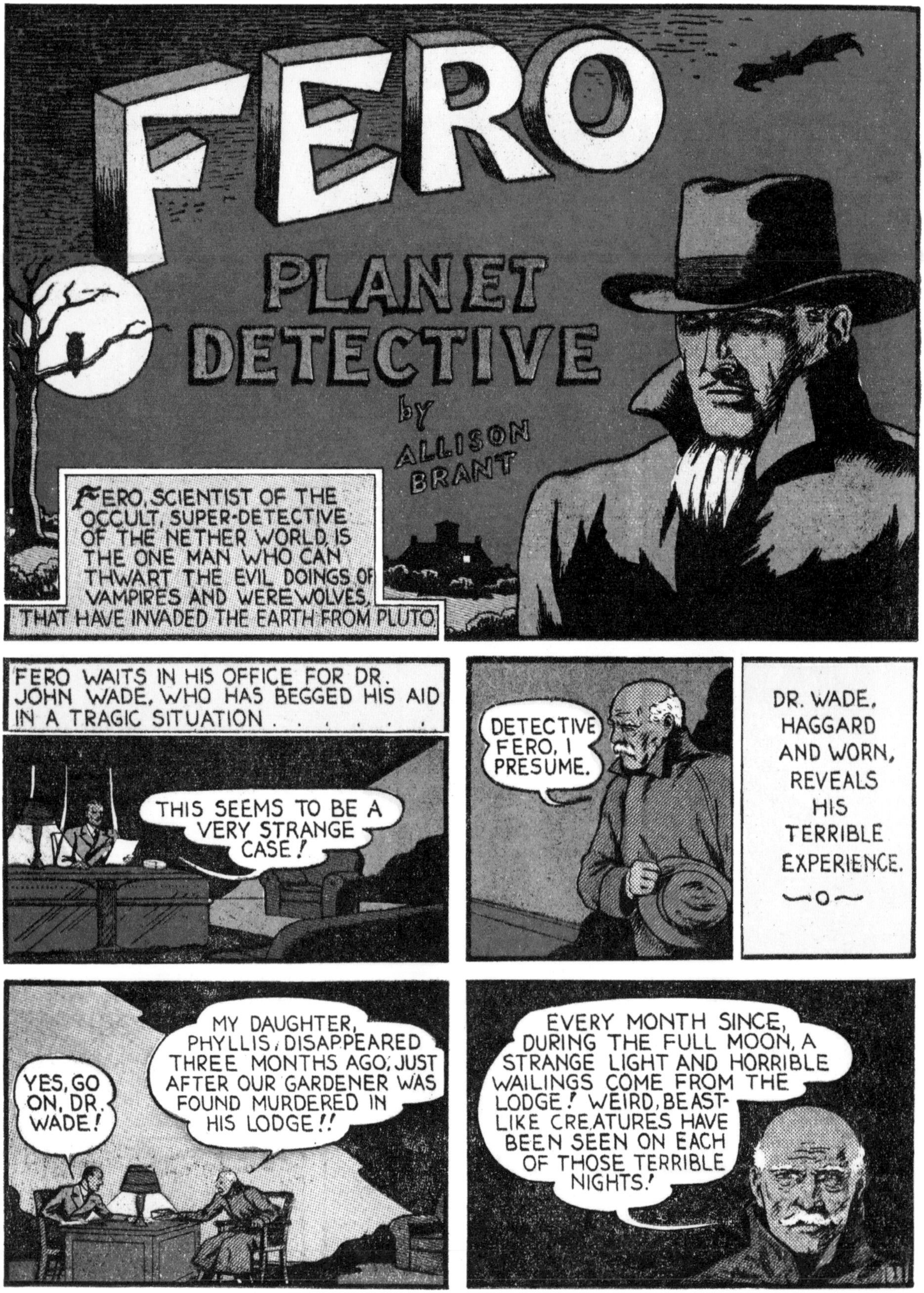
FERO
PLANET DETECTIVE
by ALLISON BRANT
FERO, SCIENTIST OF THE OCCULT, SUPER-DETECTIVE OF THE NETHER WORLD, IS THE ONE MAN WHO CAN THWART THE EVIL DOINGS OF VAMPIRES AND WEREWOLVES, THAT HAVE INVADED THE EARTH FROM PLUTO.
FERO WAITS IN HIS OFFICE FOR DR. JOHN WADE, WHO HAS BEGGED HIS AID IN A TRAGIC SITUATION . . . . . .
THIS SEEMS TO BE A VERY STRANGE CASE!
DETECTIVE FERO, I PRESUME.
DR. WADE, HAGGARD AND WORN, REVEALS HIS TERRIBLE EXPERIENCE.
YES, GO ON, DR. WADE!
MY DAUGHTER, PHYLLIS, DISAPPEARED THREE MONTHS AGO, JUST AFTER OUR GARDENER WAS FOUND MURDERED IN HIS LODGE!!
EVERY MONTH SINCE, DURING THE FULL MOON, A STRANGE LIGHT AND HORRIBLE WAILINGS COME FROM THE LODGE! WEIRD, BEAST-LIKE CREATURES HAVE BEEN SEEN ON EACH OF THOSE TERRIBLE NIGHTS!

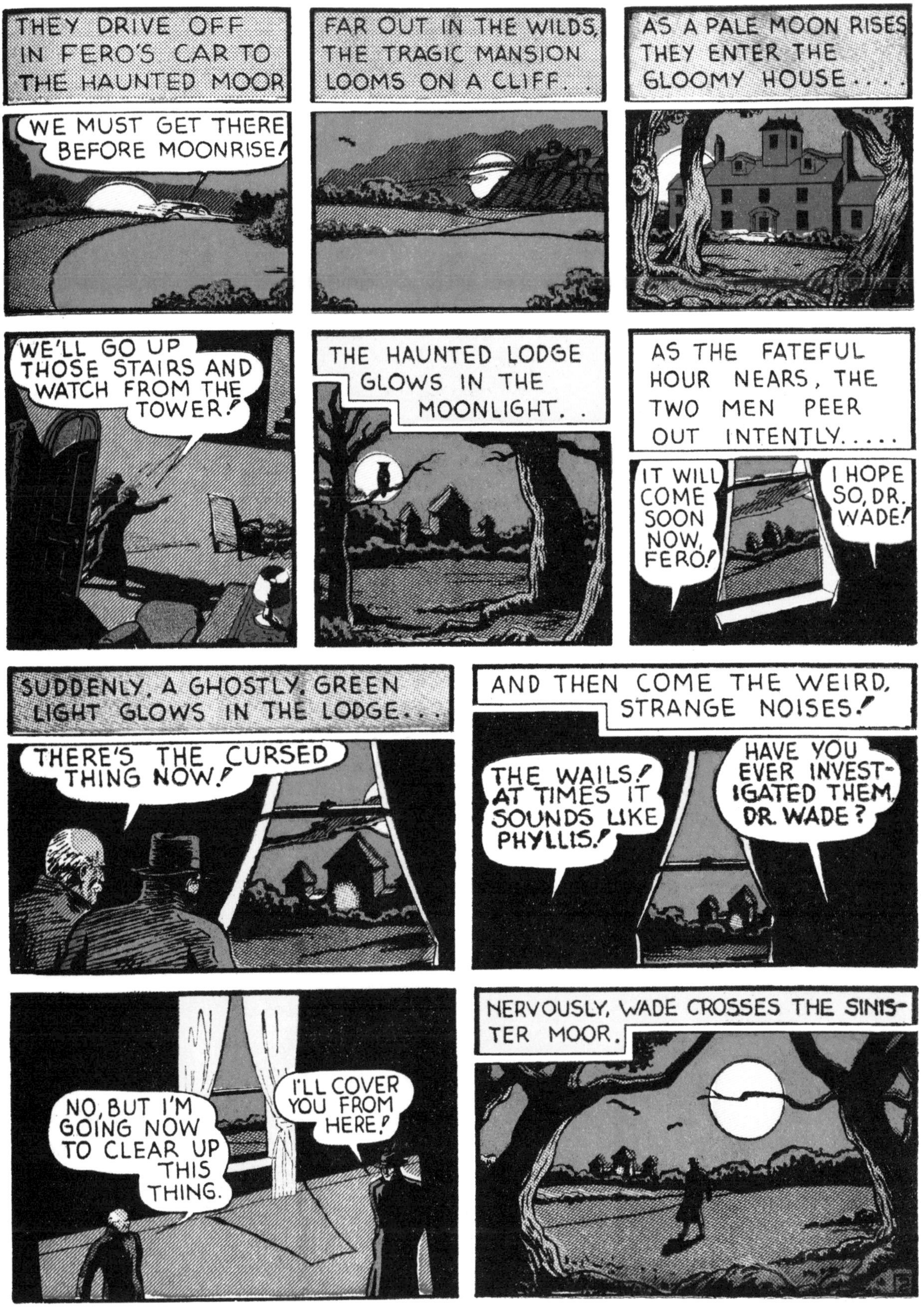
THEY DRIVE OFF IN FERO'S CAR TO THE HAUNTED MOOR
WE MUST GET THERE BEFORE MOONRISE!
FAR OUT IN THE WILDS, THE TRAGIC MANSION LOOMS ON A CLIFF. .
AS A PALE MOON RISES THEY ENTER THE GLOOMY HOUSE. . . .
WE'LL GO UP THOSE STAIRS AND WATCH FROM THE TOWER!
THE HAUNTED LODGE GLOWS IN THE MOONLIGHT. .
AS THE FATEFUL HOUR NEARS, THE TWO MEN PEER OUT INTENTLY. . . . .
IT WILL COME SOON NOW, FERO!
I HOPE SO, DR. WADE!
SUDDENLY, A GHOSTLY, GREEN LIGHT GLOWS IN THE LODGE. . .
THERE'S THE CURSED THING NOW!
AND THEN COME THE WEIRD, STRANGE NOISES!
THE WAILS! AT TIMES IT SOUNDS LIKE PHYLLIS!
HAVE YOU EVER INVESTIGATED THEM, DR. WADE?
NO, BUT I'M GOING NOW TO CLEAR UP THIS THING.
I'LL COVER YOU FROM HERE!
NERVOUSLY, WADE CROSSES THE SINISTER MOOR.

FERO HEARS A VICIOUS SNARL AND SEES A GHOSTLY LIGHT MOVE TOWARDS DR. WADE.

THE LIGHT SUDDENLY CHANGES INTO A HORRIBLE WEREWOLF, HALF-MAN AND HALF VICIOUS WOLF.

A TERRIBLE STRUGGLE ENSUES, AS THE BEAST ATTACKS THE DEFENSELESS WADE.

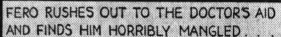
FERO RUSHES OUT TO THE DOCTOR'S AID AND FINDS HIM HORRIBLY MANGLED...

HE'S DONE FOR, POOR FELLOW!

I'LL CLEAN UP THAT LODGE MYSELF!

AS HE APPROACHES, THE LIGHT MOVES TOWARD FERO, AND A SINISTER VOICE SPEAKS.

KEEP AWAY, OR I'LL—

SUDDENLY, THE WEREWOLF LEAPS AT FERO....

TAKE THAT, YOU DEMON!

FERO ENTERS THE LODGE AS THE LIGHT GROWS DIM......

HE STUMBLES ACROSS A BEAUTIFUL GIRL....

HELLO! WHAT'S THIS?

HE FINDS SHE IS STILL ALIVE, THOUGH UNCONSCIOUS.

THIS MUST BE PHYLLIS!

NOW TO GET HER OUT OF THIS DEN OF FIENDS!

A HIDEOUS DWARF APPEARS DOWN THE DARK CORRIDOR . . . . .

DROP THAT BODY, OR YOU DIE YOURSELF!

FERO DRAWS HIS GUN AS THE FOUL CREATURE ADVANCES MENACINGLY...

THE GIRL BELONGS TO ME! I AM GOING TO TAKE HER BACK TO PLUTO!

THE GUN IS MYSTERIOUSLY KNOCKED FROM HIS HAND AS THE DWARF LAUGHS IN GLEE!

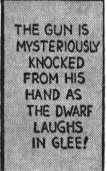

THEY GRAPPLE IN DEADLY COMBAT . . .

BUT FERO PROVES TOO STRONG FOR HIM.

THAT TAKES CARE OF YOU!

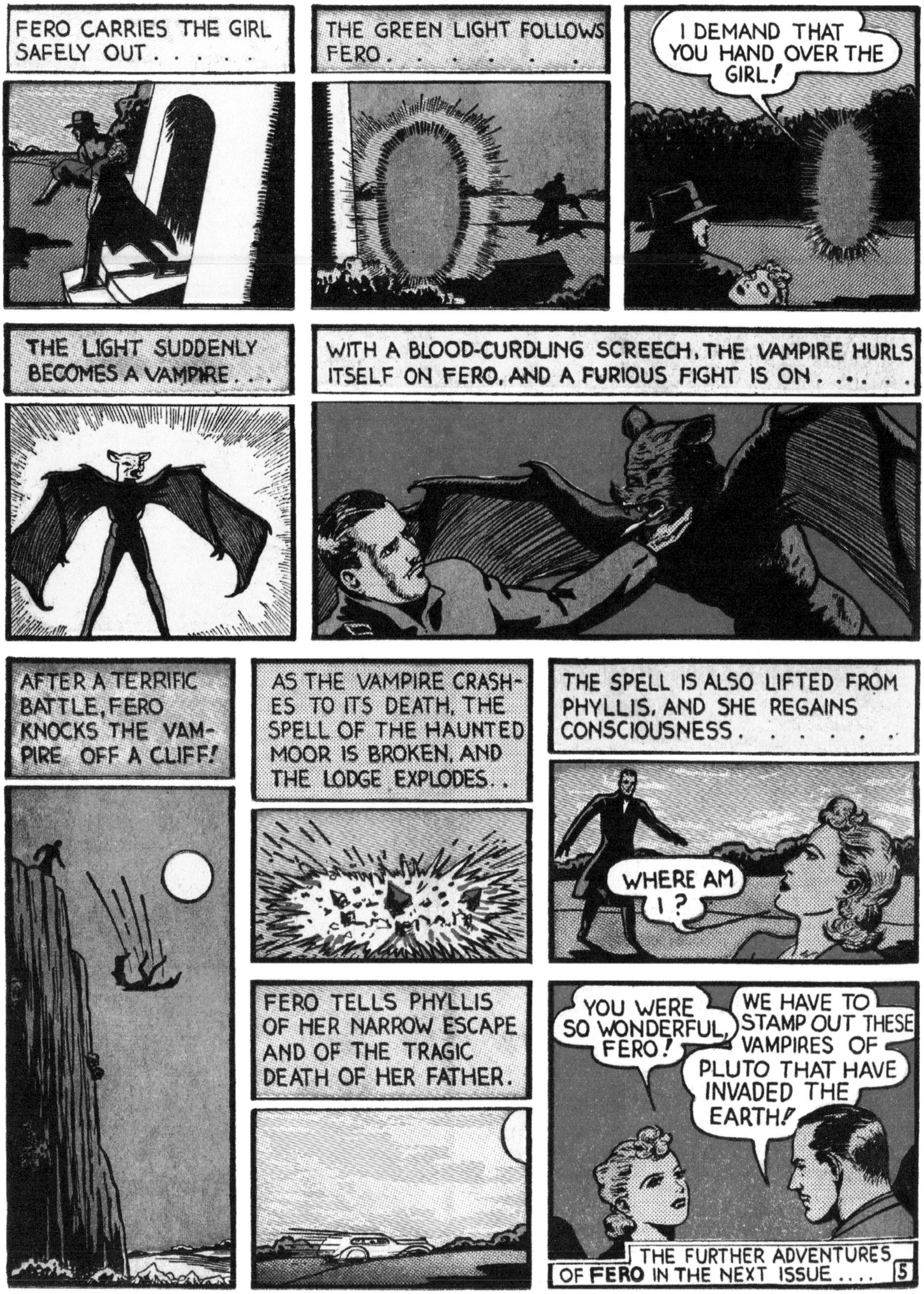
FERO CARRIES THE GIRL SAFELY OUT . . . . .
THE GREEN LIGHT FOLLOWS FERO . . . . . .
I DEMAND THAT YOU HAND OVER THE GIRL!
THE LIGHT SUDDENLY BECOMES A VAMPIRE . . .
WITH A BLOOD-CURDLING SCREECH, THE VAMPIRE HURLS ITSELF ON FERO, AND A FURIOUS FIGHT IS ON . . . . .
AFTER A TERRIFIC BATTLE, FERO KNOCKS THE VAMPIRE OFF A CLIFF!
AS THE VAMPIRE CRASHES TO ITS DEATH, THE SPELL OF THE HAUNTED MOOR IS BROKEN, AND THE LODGE EXPLODES . .
THE SPELL IS ALSO LIFTED FROM PHYLLIS, AND SHE REGAINS CONSCIOUSNESS . . . . . .
WHERE AM I?
FERO TELLS PHYLLIS OF HER NARROW ESCAPE AND OF THE TRAGIC DEATH OF HER FATHER.
YOU WERE SO WONDERFUL, FERO!
WE HAVE TO STAMP OUT THESE VAMPIRES OF PLUTO THAT HAVE INVADED THE EARTH!
THE FURTHER ADVENTURES OF FERO IN THE NEXT ISSUE . . . .
5

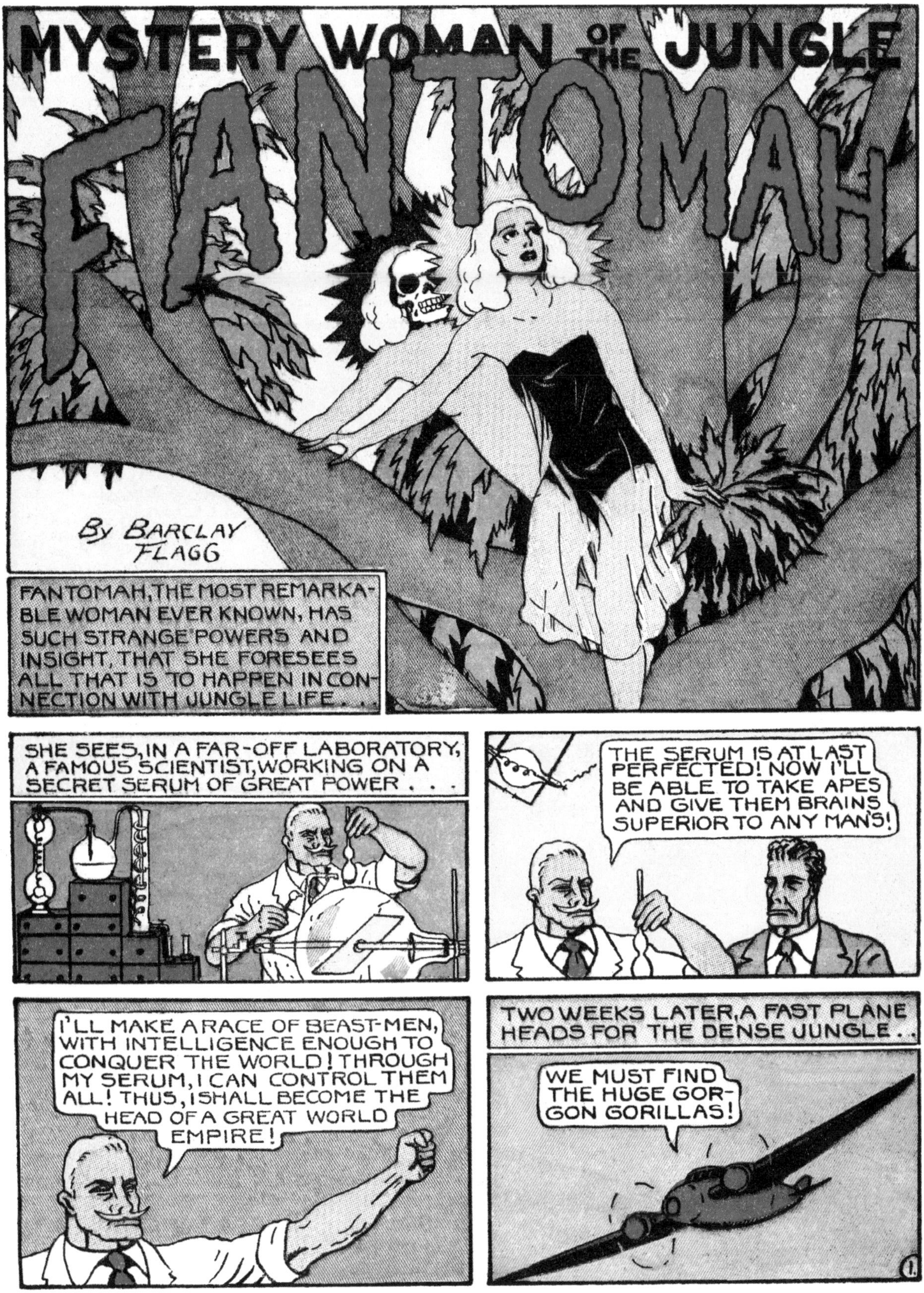
MYSTERY WOMAN OF THE JUNGLE
FANTOMAH
BY BARCLAY FLAGG
FANTOMAH, THE MOST REMARKABLE WOMAN EVER KNOWN, HAS SUCH STRANGE POWERS AND INSIGHT, THAT SHE FORESEES ALL THAT IS TO HAPPEN IN CONNECTION WITH JUNGLE LIFE . . .
SHE SEES, IN A FAR-OFF LABORATORY, A FAMOUS SCIENTIST, WORKING ON A SECRET SERUM OF GREAT POWER . . .
THE SERUM IS AT LAST PERFECTED! NOW I'LL BE ABLE TO TAKE APES AND GIVE THEM BRAINS SUPERIOR TO ANY MAN'S!
I'LL MAKE A RACE OF BEAST-MEN, WITH INTELLIGENCE ENOUGH TO CONQUER THE WORLD! THROUGH MY SERUM, I CAN CONTROL THEM ALL! THUS, I SHALL BECOME THE HEAD OF A GREAT WORLD EMPIRE!
TWO WEEKS LATER, A FAST PLANE HEADS FOR THE DENSE JUNGLE . .
WE MUST FIND THE HUGE GORGON GORILLAS!
1.

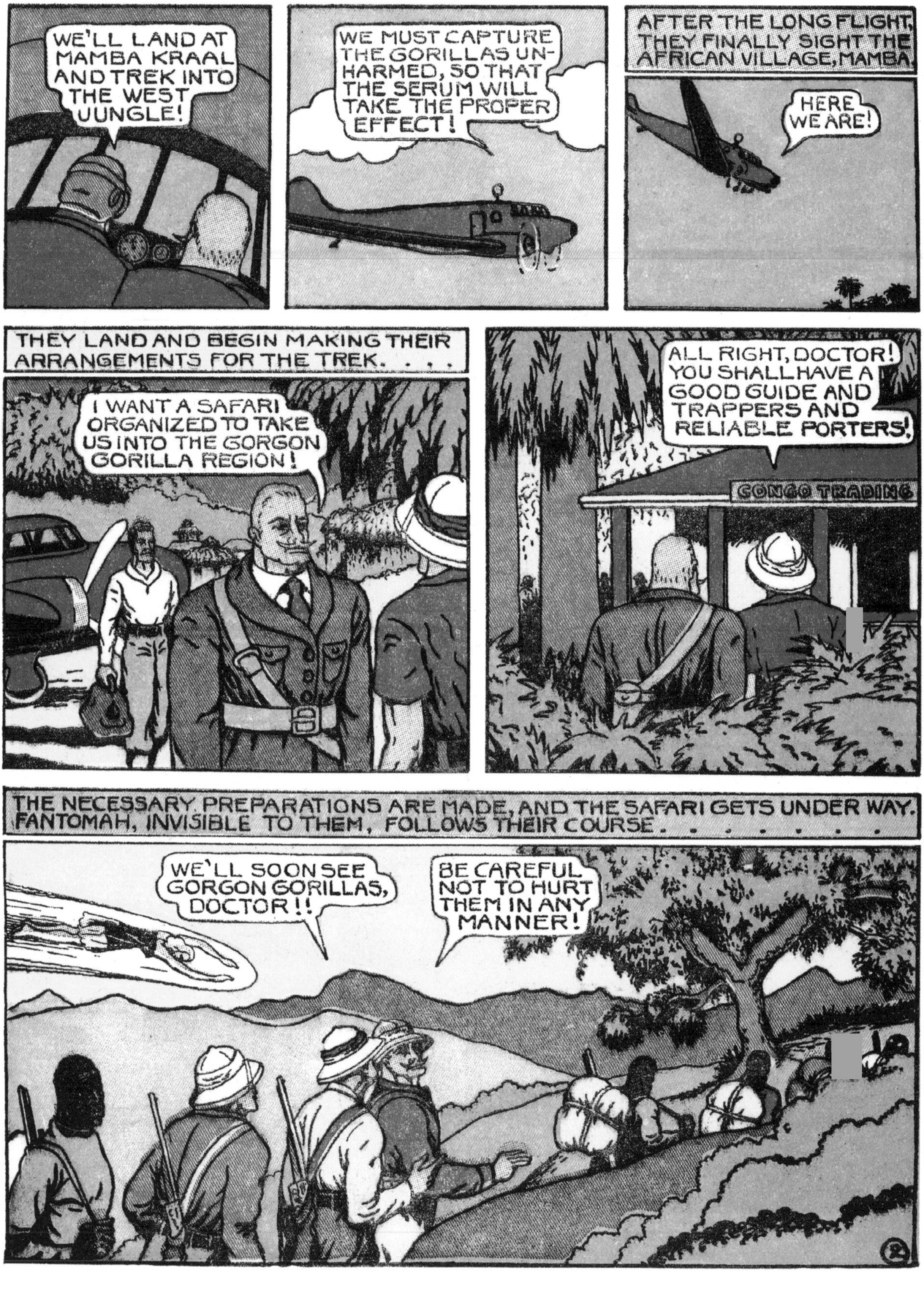
WE'LL LAND AT MAMBA KRAAL AND TREK INTO THE WEST UUNGLE!
WE MUST CAPTURE THE GORILLAS UN-HARMED, SO THAT THE SERUM WILL TAKE THE PROPER EFFECT!
AFTER THE LONG FLIGHT, THEY FINALLY SIGHT THE AFRICAN VILLAGE, MAMBA.
HERE WE ARE!
THEY LAND AND BEGIN MAKING THEIR ARRANGEMENTS FOR THE TREK. . . .
I WANT A SAFARI ORGANIZED TO TAKE US INTO THE GORGON GORILLA REGION!
ALL RIGHT, DOCTOR! YOU SHALL HAVE A GOOD GUIDE AND TRAPPERS AND RELIABLE PORTERS!
CONGO TRADING
THE NECESSARY PREPARATIONS ARE MADE, AND THE SAFARI GETS UNDER WAY. FANTOMAH, INVISIBLE TO THEM, FOLLOWS THEIR COURSE . . . . . . .
WE'LL SOON SEE GORGON GORILLAS, DOCTOR!!
BE CAREFUL NOT TO HURT THEM IN ANY MANNER!
2

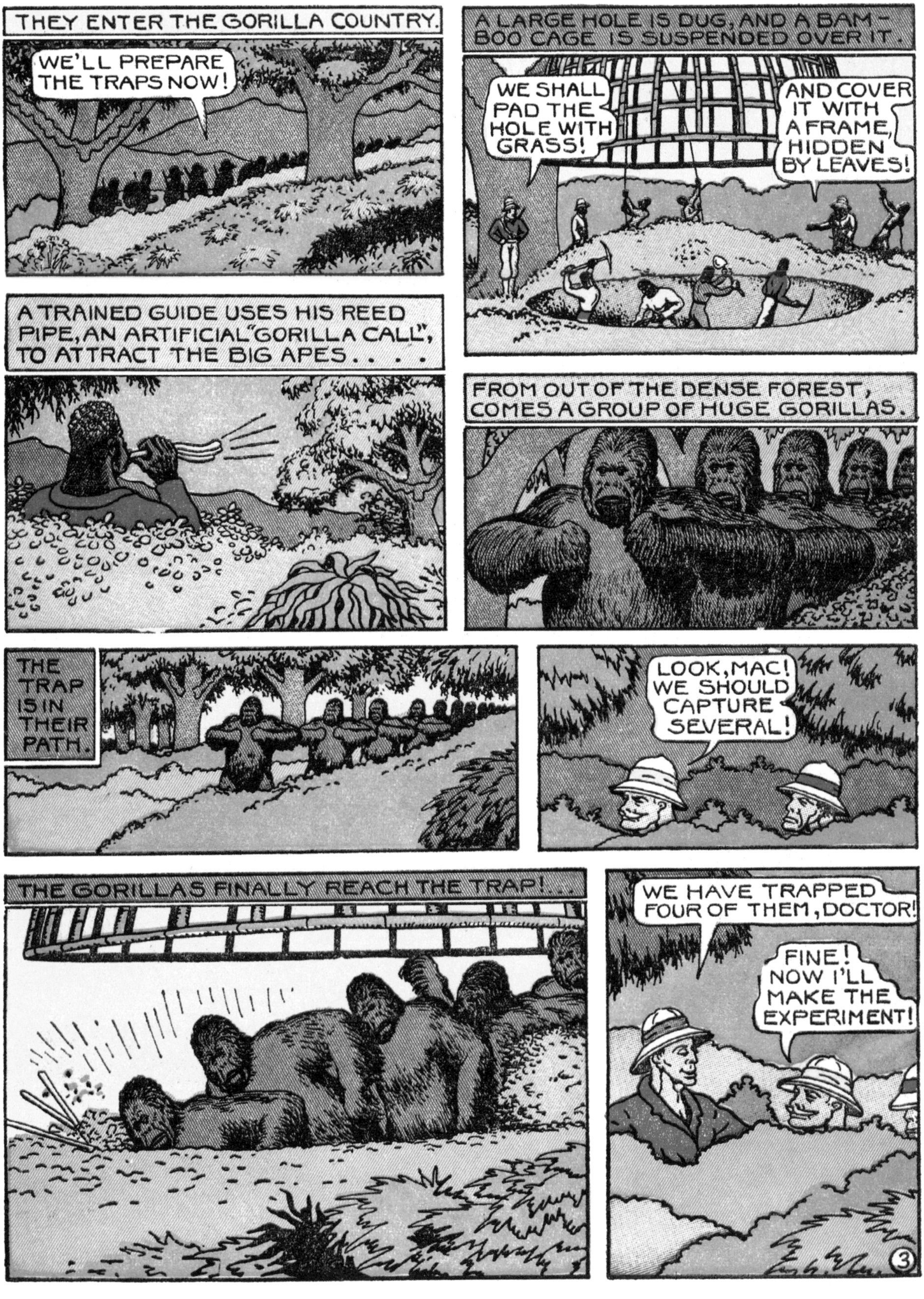
THEY ENTER THE GORILLA COUNTRY.
WE'LL PREPARE THE TRAPS NOW!
A LARGE HOLE IS DUG, AND A BAMBOO CAGE IS SUSPENDED OVER IT.
WE SHALL PAD THE HOLE WITH GRASS!
AND COVER IT WITH A FRAME, HIDDEN BY LEAVES!
A TRAINED GUIDE USES HIS REED PIPE, AN ARTIFICIAL "GORILLA CALL", TO ATTRACT THE BIG APES . . . .
FROM OUT OF THE DENSE FOREST, COMES A GROUP OF HUGE GORILLAS.
THE TRAP IS IN THEIR PATH.
LOOK, MAC! WE SHOULD CAPTURE SEVERAL!
THE GORILLAS FINALLY REACH THE TRAP!
WE HAVE TRAPPED FOUR OF THEM, DOCTOR!
FINE! NOW I'LL MAKE THE EXPERIMENT!
3

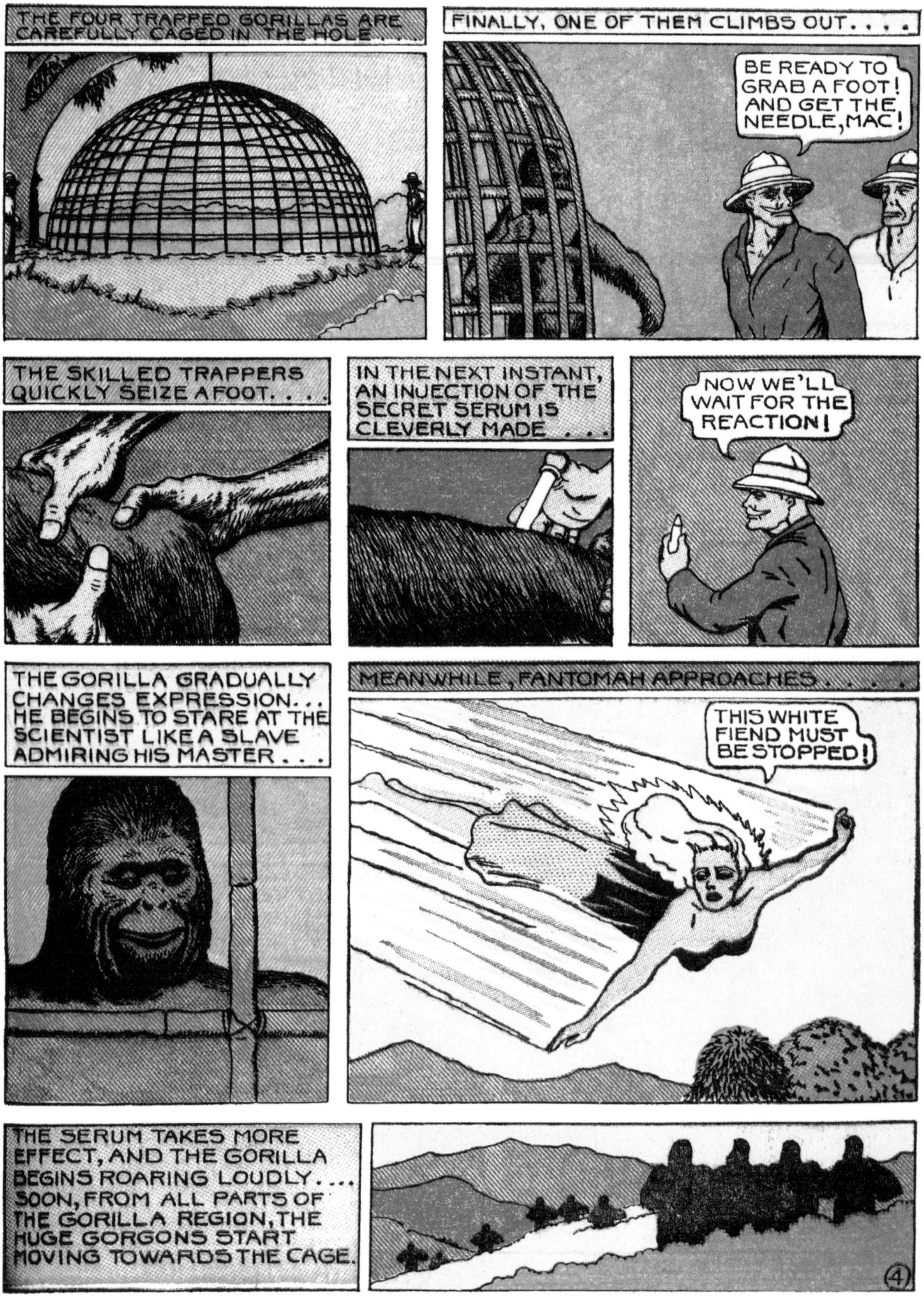
THE FOUR TRAPPED GORILLAS ARE CAREFULLY CAGED IN THE HOLE . . .
FINALLY, ONE OF THEM CLIMBS OUT . . . .
BE READY TO GRAB A FOOT! AND GET THE NEEDLE, MAC!
THE SKILLED TRAPPERS QUICKLY SEIZE A FOOT . . .
IN THE NEXT INSTANT, AN INJECTION OF THE SECRET SERUM IS CLEVERLY MADE . . .
NOW WE'LL WAIT FOR THE REACTION!
THE GORILLA GRADUALLY CHANGES EXPRESSION... HE BEGINS TO STARE AT THE SCIENTIST LIKE A SLAVE ADMIRING HIS MASTER . . .
MEANWHILE, FANTOMAH APPROACHES . . . .
THIS WHITE FIEND MUST BE STOPPED!
THE SERUM TAKES MORE EFFECT, AND THE GORILLA BEGINS ROARING LOUDLY.... SOON, FROM ALL PARTS OF THE GORILLA REGION, THE HUGE GORGONS START MOVING TOWARDS THE CAGE.
4

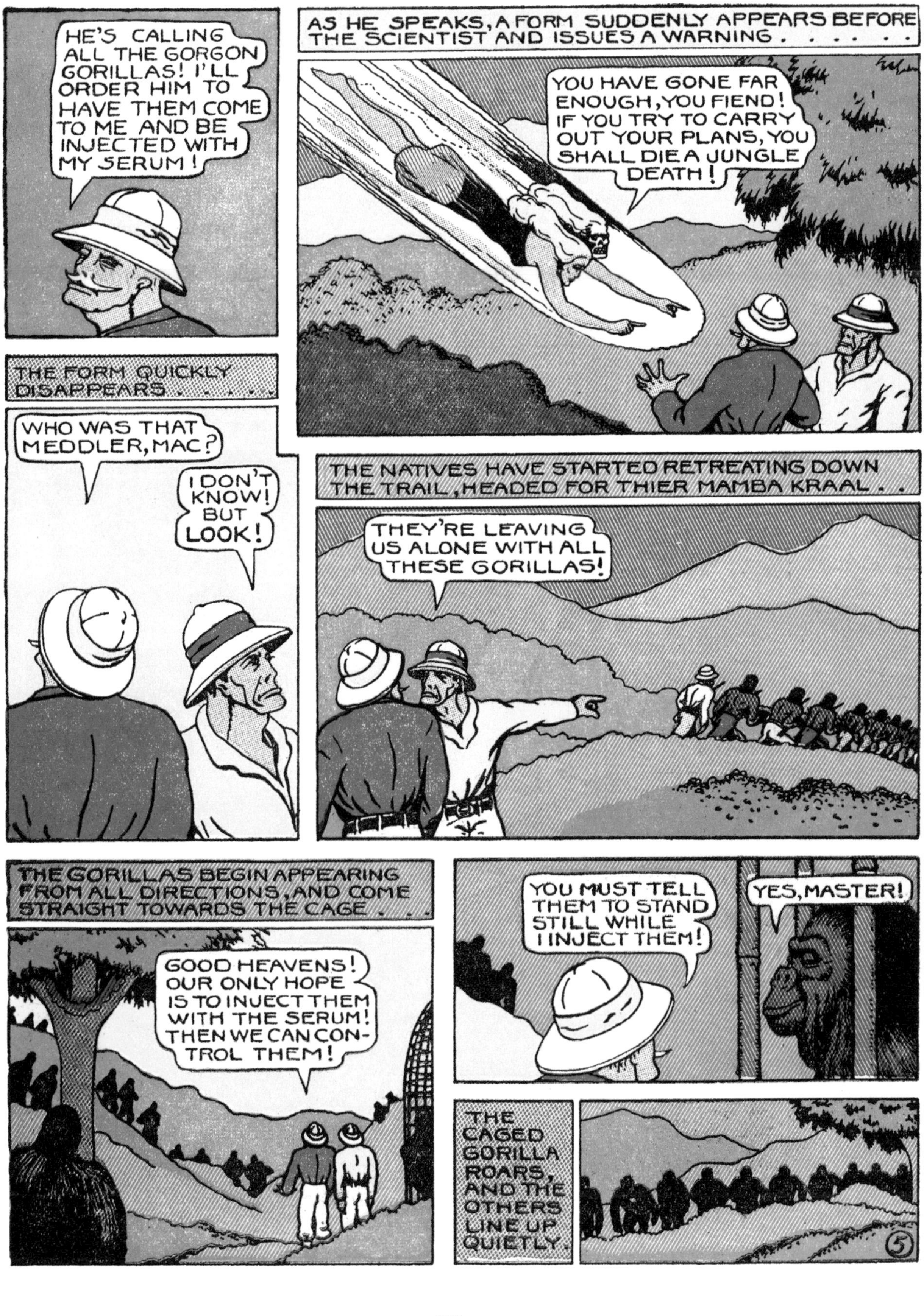
HE'S CALLING ALL THE GORGON GORILLAS! I'LL ORDER HIM TO HAVE THEM COME TO ME AND BE INJECTED WITH MY SERUM!
AS HE SPEAKS, A FORM SUDDENLY APPEARS BEFORE THE SCIENTIST AND ISSUES A WARNING . . . . .
YOU HAVE GONE FAR ENOUGH, YOU FIEND! IF YOU TRY TO CARRY OUT YOUR PLANS, YOU SHALL DIE A JUNGLE DEATH!
THE FORM QUICKLY DISAPPEARS . . . .
WHO WAS THAT MEDDLER, MAC?
I DON'T KNOW! BUT LOOK!
THE NATIVES HAVE STARTED RETREATING DOWN THE TRAIL, HEADED FOR THIER MAMBA KRAAL . .
THEY'RE LEAVING US ALONE WITH ALL THESE GORILLAS!
THE GORILLAS BEGIN APPEARING FROM ALL DIRECTIONS, AND COME STRAIGHT TOWARDS THE CAGE . . .
GOOD HEAVENS! OUR ONLY HOPE IS TO INJECT THEM WITH THE SERUM! THEN WE CAN CONTROL THEM!
YOU MUST TELL THEM TO STAND STILL WHILE I INJECT THEM!
YES, MASTER!
THE CAGED GORILLA ROARS, AND THE OTHERS LINE UP QUIETLY.
5

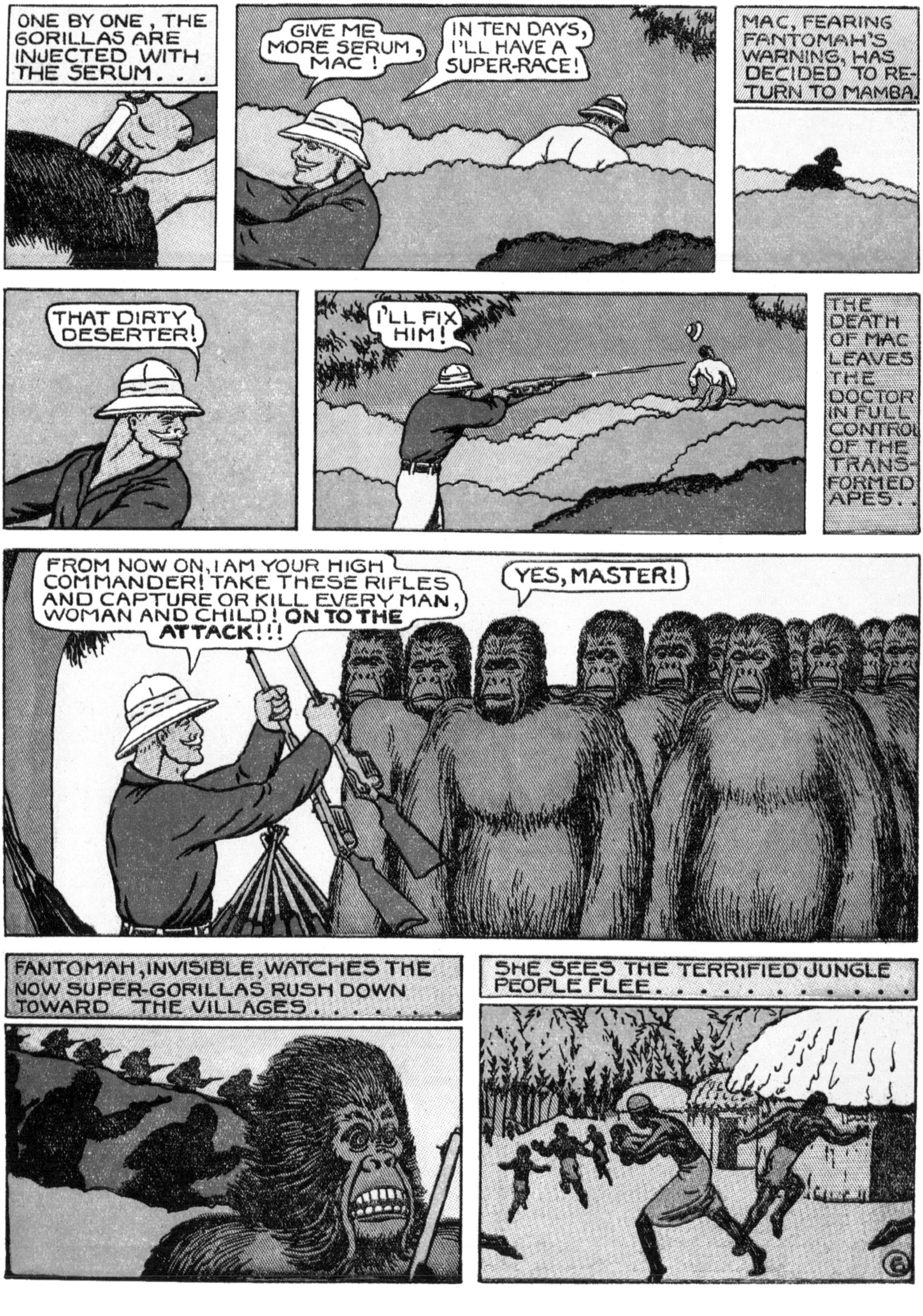

ONE BY ONE, THE GORILLAS ARE INJECTED WITH THE SERUM...
GIVE ME MORE SERUM, MAC!
IN TEN DAYS, I'LL HAVE A SUPER-RACE!
MAC, FEARING FANTOMAH'S WARNING, HAS DECIDED TO RETURN TO MAMBA.
THAT DIRTY DESERTER!
I'LL FIX HIM!
THE DEATH OF MAC LEAVES THE DOCTOR IN FULL CONTROL OF THE TRANSFORMED APES...
FROM NOW ON, I AM YOUR HIGH COMMANDER! TAKE THESE RIFLES AND CAPTURE OR KILL EVERY MAN, WOMAN AND CHILD! ON TO THE ATTACK!!!
YES, MASTER!
FANTOMAH, INVISIBLE, WATCHES THE NOW SUPER-GORILLAS RUSH DOWN TOWARD THE VILLAGES.......
SHE SEES THE TERRIFIED JUNGLE PEOPLE FLEE...........
6

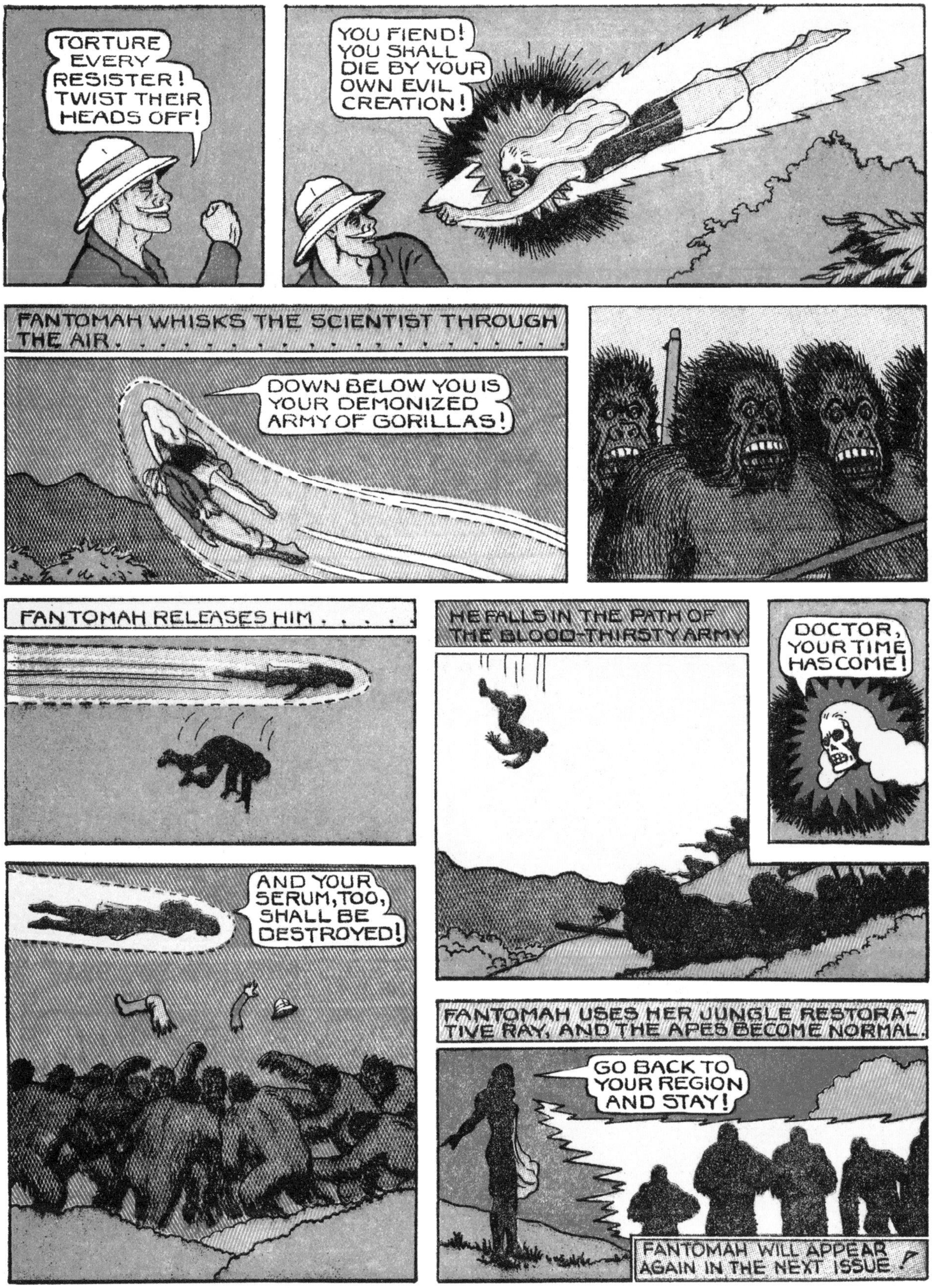
TORTURE EVERY RESISTER! TWIST THEIR HEADS OFF!
YOU FIEND! YOU SHALL DIE BY YOUR OWN EVIL CREATION!
FANTOMAH WHISKS THE SCIENTIST THROUGH THE AIR . . . . . . . . . . . . . . . . .
DOWN BELOW YOU IS YOUR DEMONIZED ARMY OF GORILLAS!
FANTOMAH RELEASES HIM . . . . .
AND YOUR SERUM, TOO, SHALL BE DESTROYED!
HE FALLS IN THE PATH OF THE BLOOD-THIRSTY ARMY
DOCTOR, YOUR TIME HAS COME!
FANTOMAH USES HER JUNGLE RESTORATIVE RAY, AND THE APES BECOME NORMAL.
GO BACK TO YOUR REGION AND STAY!
FANTOMAH WILL APPEAR AGAIN IN THE NEXT ISSUE!

**A BIG FULL COLOR PICTURE OF SKYMAN SUITABLE FOR FRAMING!**

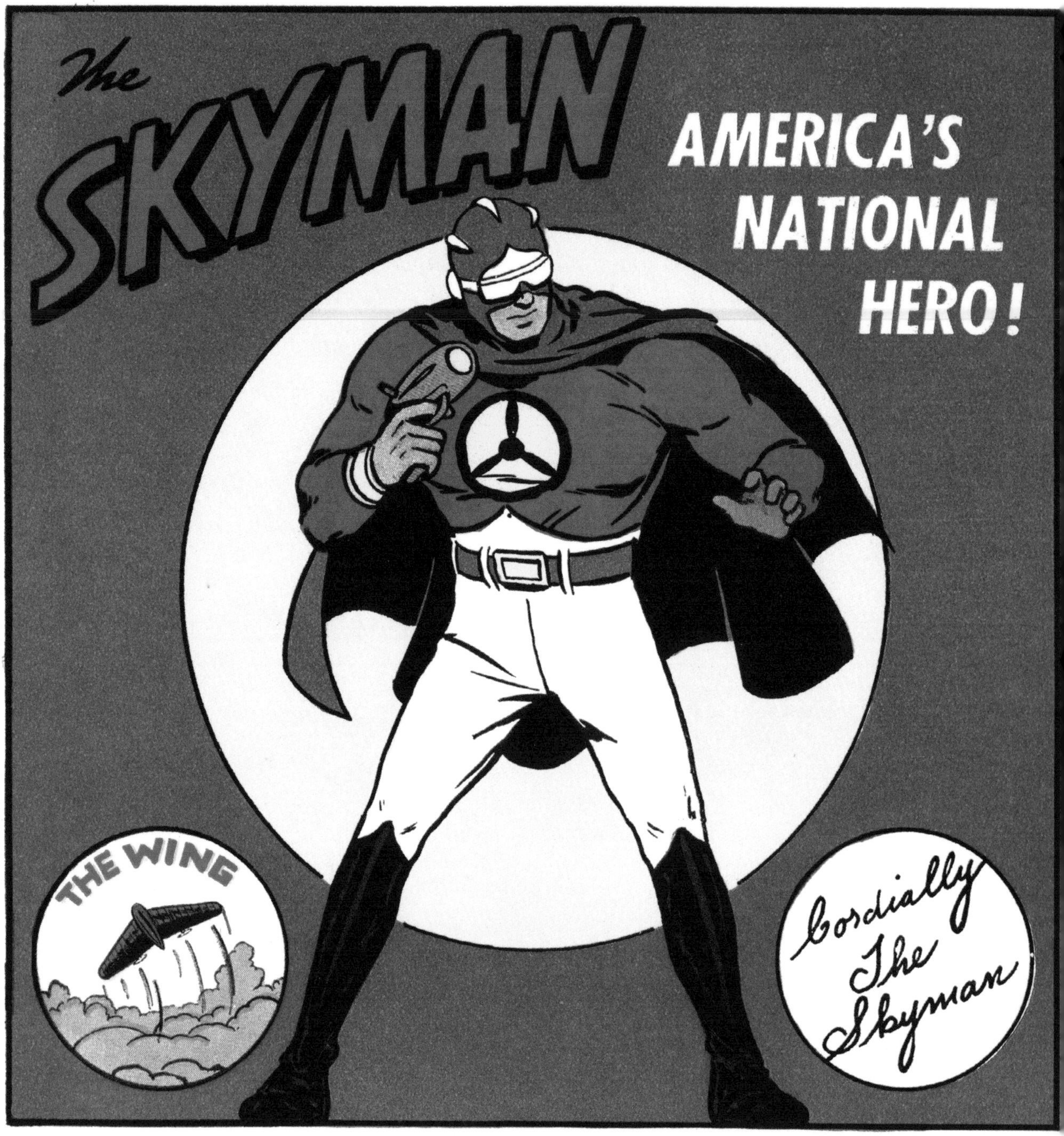

The SKYMAN
AMERICA'S NATIONAL HERO!
THE WING
Cordially The Skyman


SUBSCRIPTION

BIG SHOT COMICS,
369 Lexington Avenue,
New York City.

CANADA AND FOREIGN $1.50

Enclosed is my dollar. Mail me BIG SHOT COMICS every month for one year.

Name ........................................................................

Address ....................................................................

City.......................................... State ..................

**THE SKYMAN SAYS:**

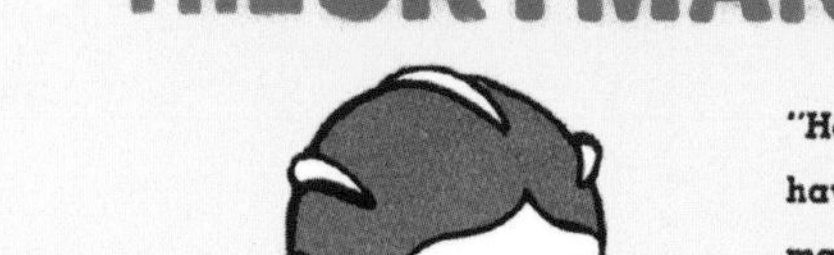

"Here's an opportunity to have BIG SHOT COMICS mailed to you every month for a year for only $1.00. Take advantage of it—fill in the coupon, enclose your $1.00 and mail it in right away!"

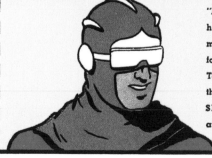

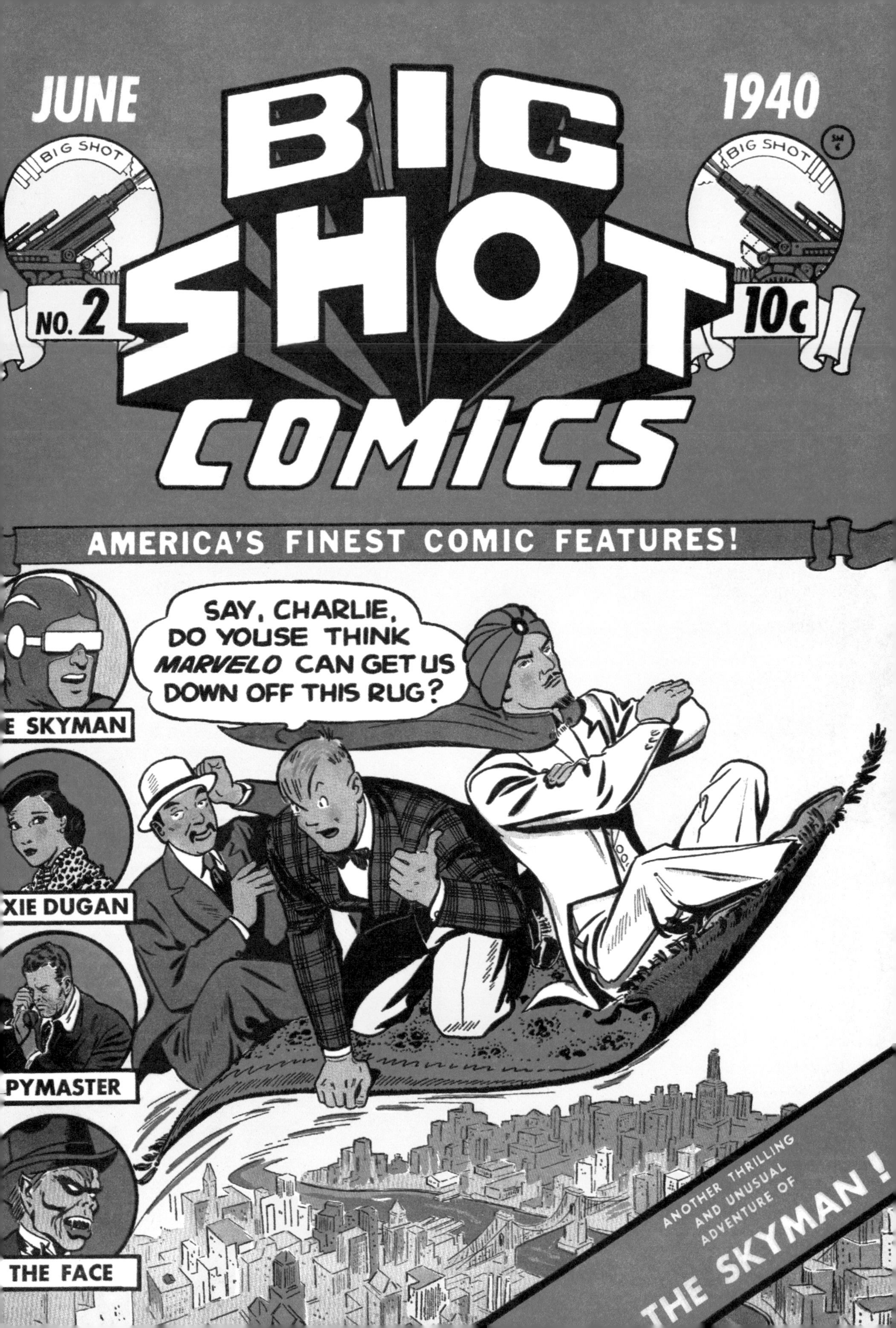
JUNE
BIG SHOT
BIG SHOT COMICS
1940
BIG SHOT
NO. 2
10c
AMERICA'S FINEST COMIC FEATURES!
SAY, CHARLIE, DO YOUSE THINK *MARVELO* CAN GET US DOWN OFF THIS RUG?
E SKYMAN
XIE DUGAN
PYMASTER
THE FACE
ANOTHER THRILLING AND UNUSUAL ADVENTURE OF
THE SKYMAN!

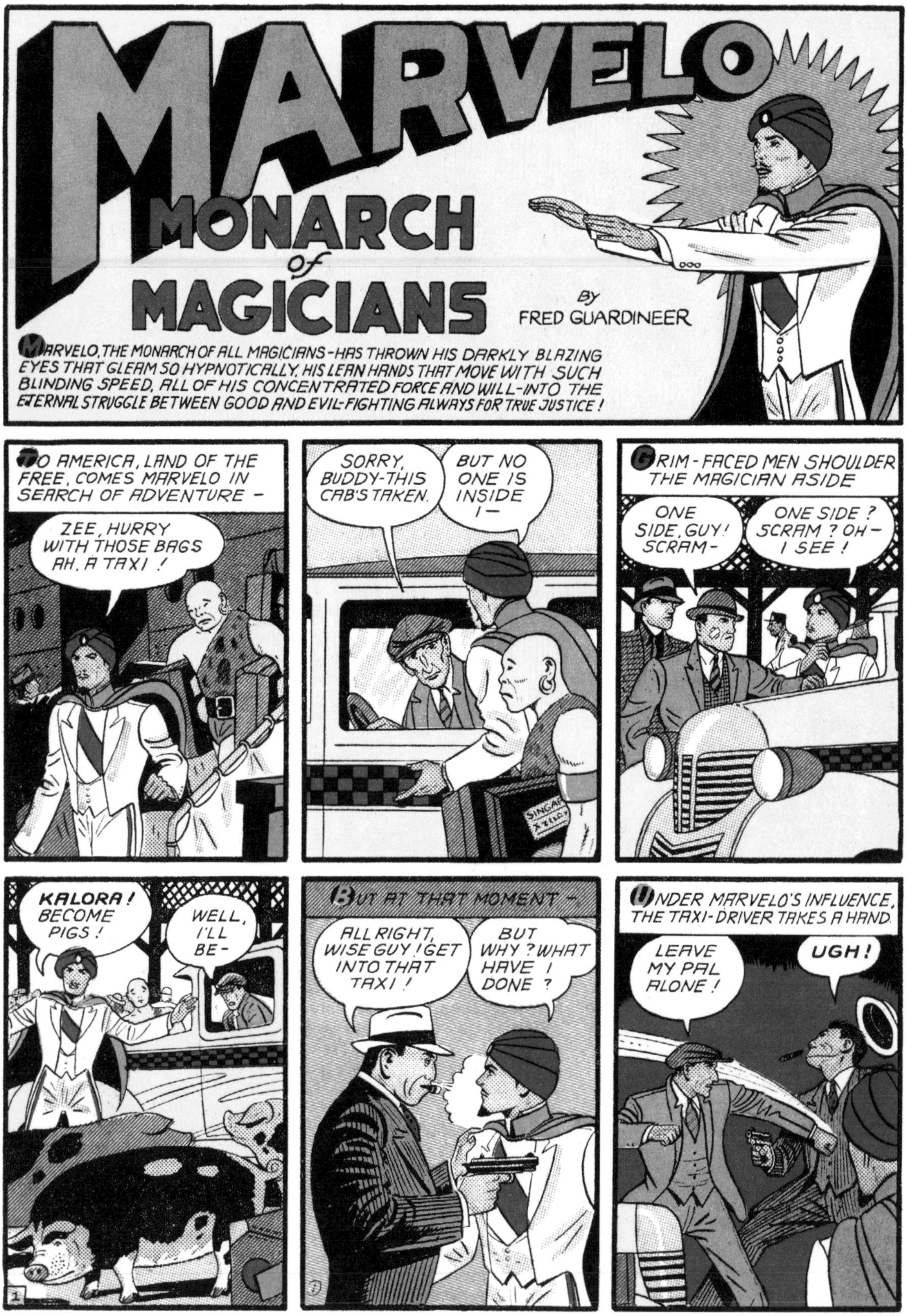
MARVELO
MONARCH of MAGICIANS
BY FRED GUARDINEER
MARVELO, THE MONARCH OF ALL MAGICIANS - HAS THROWN HIS DARKLY BLAZING EYES THAT GLEAM SO HYPNOTICALLY, HIS LEAN HANDS THAT MOVE WITH SUCH BLINDING SPEED, ALL OF HIS CONCENTRATED FORCE AND WILL - INTO THE ETERNAL STRUGGLE BETWEEN GOOD AND EVIL - FIGHTING ALWAYS FOR TRUE JUSTICE!
TO AMERICA, LAND OF THE FREE, COMES MARVELO IN SEARCH OF ADVENTURE -
ZEE, HURRY WITH THOSE BAGS AH, A TAXI!
SORRY, BUDDY-THIS CAB'S TAKEN.
BUT NO ONE IS INSIDE I—
GRIM - FACED MEN SHOULDER THE MAGICIAN ASIDE
ONE SIDE, GUY! SCRAM-
ONE SIDE? SCRAM? OH - I SEE!
KALORA! BECOME PIGS!
WELL, I'LL BE-
BUT AT THAT MOMENT -
ALL RIGHT, WISE GUY! GET INTO THAT TAXI!
BUT WHY? WHAT HAVE I DONE?
UNDER MARVELO'S INFLUENCE, THE TAXI-DRIVER TAKES A HAND.
LEAVE MY PAL ALONE!
UGH!

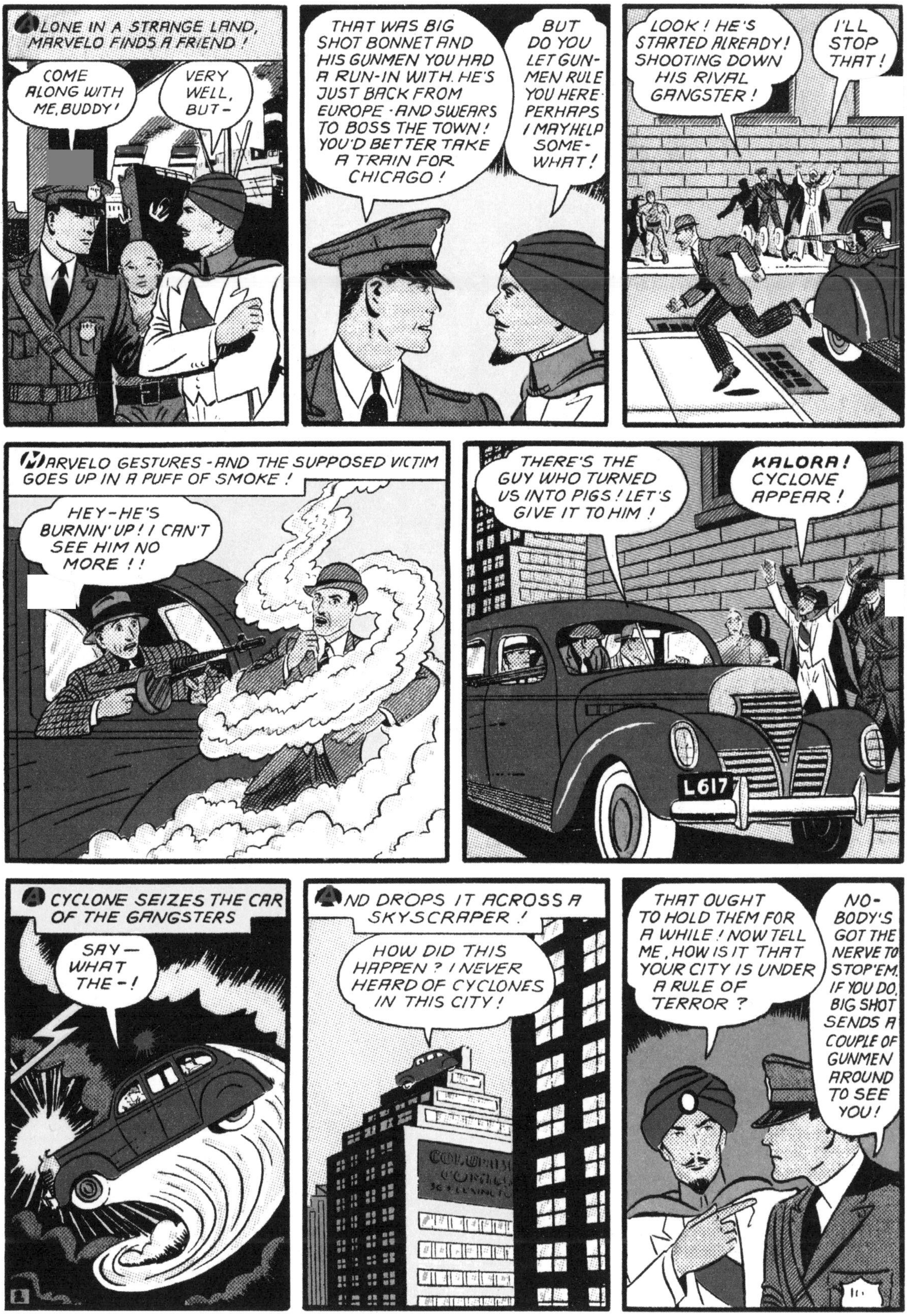
ALONE IN A STRANGE LAND, MARVELO FINDS A FRIEND!
COME ALONG WITH ME, BUDDY!
VERY WELL, BUT -
THAT WAS BIG SHOT BONNET AND HIS GUNMEN YOU HAD A RUN-IN WITH. HE'S JUST BACK FROM EUROPE - AND SWEARS TO BOSS THE TOWN! YOU'D BETTER TAKE A TRAIN FOR CHICAGO!
BUT DO YOU LET GUNMEN RULE YOU HERE. PERHAPS I MAY HELP SOMEWHAT!
LOOK! HE'S STARTED ALREADY! SHOOTING DOWN HIS RIVAL GANGSTER!
I'LL STOP THAT!
MARVELO GESTURES - AND THE SUPPOSED VICTIM GOES UP IN A PUFF OF SMOKE!
HEY-HE'S BURNIN' UP!! I CAN'T SEE HIM NO MORE!!
THERE'S THE GUY WHO TURNED US INTO PIGS! LET'S GIVE IT TO HIM!
KALORA! CYCLONE APPEAR!
L617
A CYCLONE SEIZES THE CAR OF THE GANGSTERS
SAY— WHAT THE -!
AND DROPS IT ACROSS A SKYSCRAPER!
HOW DID THIS HAPPEN? I NEVER HEARD OF CYCLONES IN THIS CITY!
THAT OUGHT TO HOLD THEM FOR A WHILE! NOW TELL ME, HOW IS IT THAT YOUR CITY IS UNDER A RULE OF TERROR?
NOBODY'S GOT THE NERVE TO STOP'EM. IF YOU DO, BIG SHOT SENDS A COUPLE OF GUNMEN AROUND TO SEE YOU!

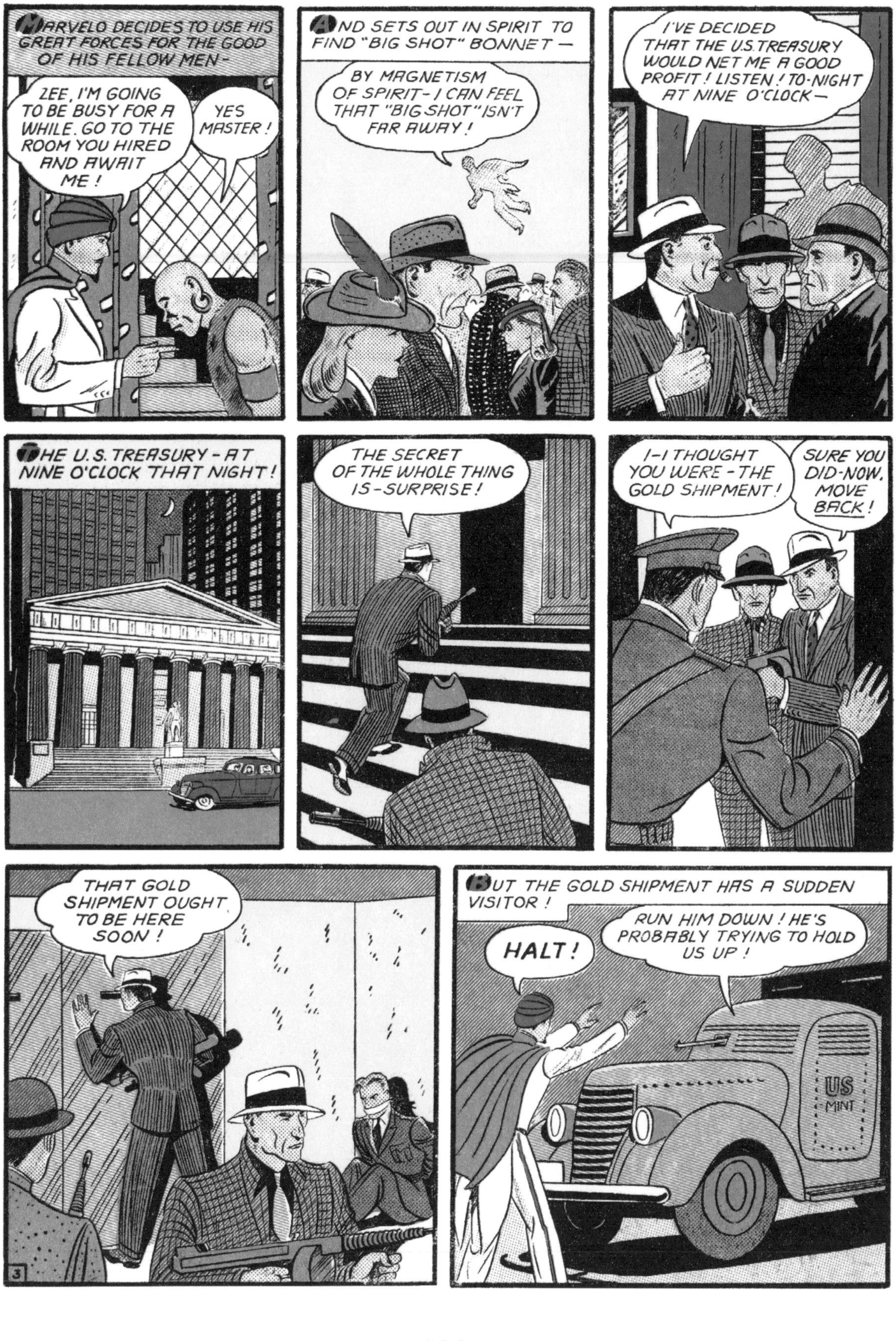
MARVELO DECIDES TO USE HIS GREAT FORCES FOR THE GOOD OF HIS FELLOW MEN-
ZEE, I'M GOING TO BE BUSY FOR A WHILE. GO TO THE ROOM YOU HIRED AND AWAIT ME!
YES MASTER!
AND SETS OUT IN SPIRIT TO FIND "BIG SHOT" BONNET —
BY MAGNETISM OF SPIRIT- I CAN FEEL THAT "BIG SHOT" ISN'T FAR AWAY!
I'VE DECIDED THAT THE U.S. TREASURY WOULD NET ME A GOOD PROFIT! LISTEN! TO-NIGHT AT NINE O'CLOCK—
THE U.S. TREASURY - AT NINE O'CLOCK THAT NIGHT!
THE SECRET OF THE WHOLE THING IS-SURPRISE!
I-I THOUGHT YOU WERE - THE GOLD SHIPMENT!
SURE YOU DID-NOW, MOVE BACK!
THAT GOLD SHIPMENT OUGHT TO BE HERE SOON!
3
BUT THE GOLD SHIPMENT HAS A SUDDEN VISITOR!
HALT!
RUN HIM DOWN! HE'S PROBABLY TRYING TO HOLD US UP!
US MINT

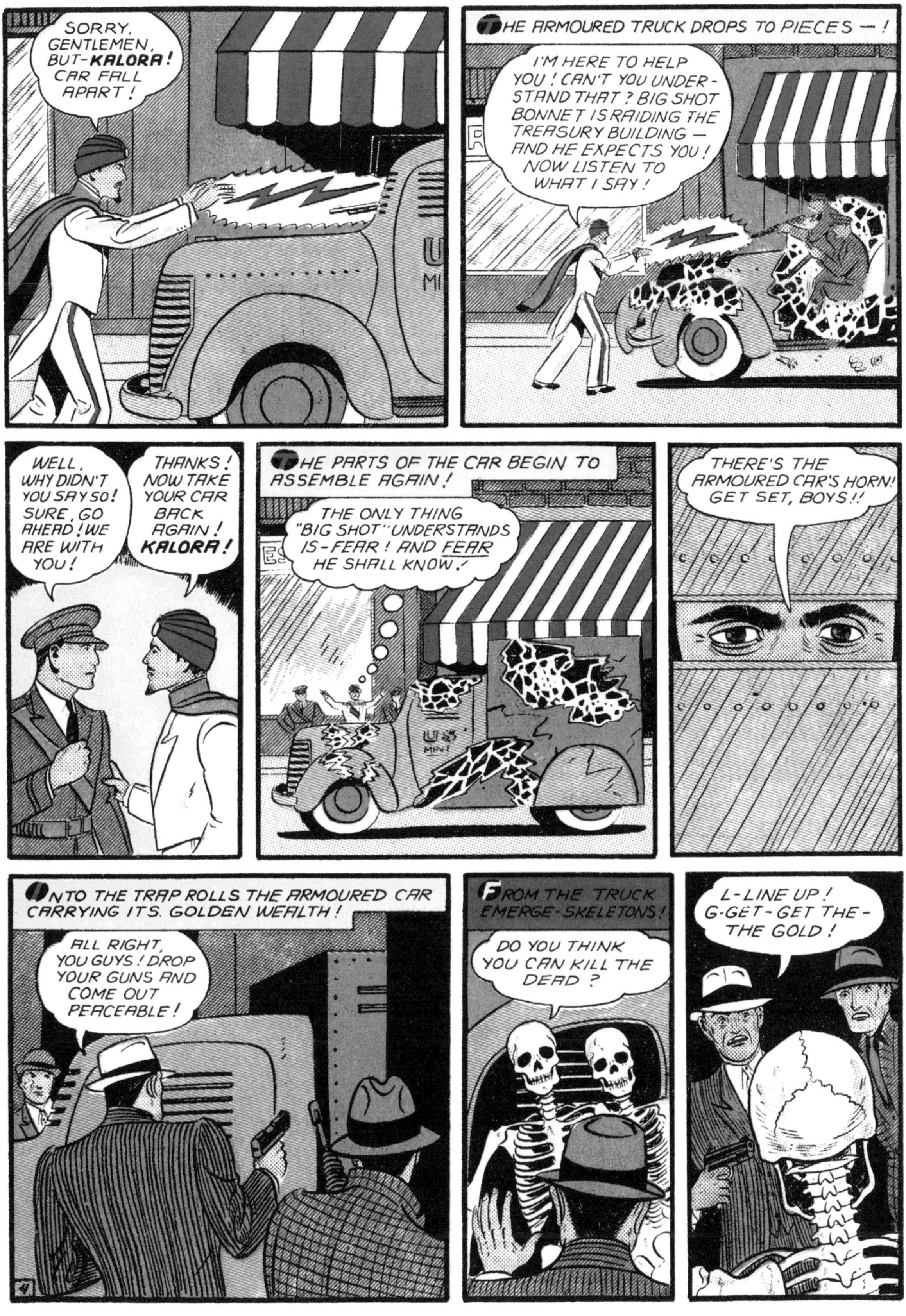
SORRY, GENTLEMEN, BUT-KALORA! CAR FALL APART!
THE ARMOURED TRUCK DROPS TO PIECES—!
I'M HERE TO HELP YOU! CAN'T YOU UNDERSTAND THAT? BIG SHOT BONNET IS RAIDING THE TREASURY BUILDING—AND HE EXPECTS YOU! NOW LISTEN TO WHAT I SAY!
WELL, WHY DIDN'T YOU SAY SO! SURE, GO AHEAD! WE ARE WITH YOU!
THANKS! NOW TAKE YOUR CAR BACK AGAIN! KALORA!
THE PARTS OF THE CAR BEGIN TO ASSEMBLE AGAIN!
THE ONLY THING "BIG SHOT" UNDERSTANDS IS-FEAR! AND FEAR HE SHALL KNOW.!
U.S. MINT
THERE'S THE ARMOURED CAR'S HORN! GET SET, BOYS!!
INTO THE TRAP ROLLS THE ARMOURED CAR CARRYING ITS GOLDEN WEALTH!
ALL RIGHT, YOU GUYS! DROP YOUR GUNS AND COME OUT PEACEABLE!
FROM THE TRUCK EMERGE-SKELETONS!
DO YOU THINK YOU CAN KILL THE DEAD?
L-LINE UP! G-GET-GET THE-THE GOLD!

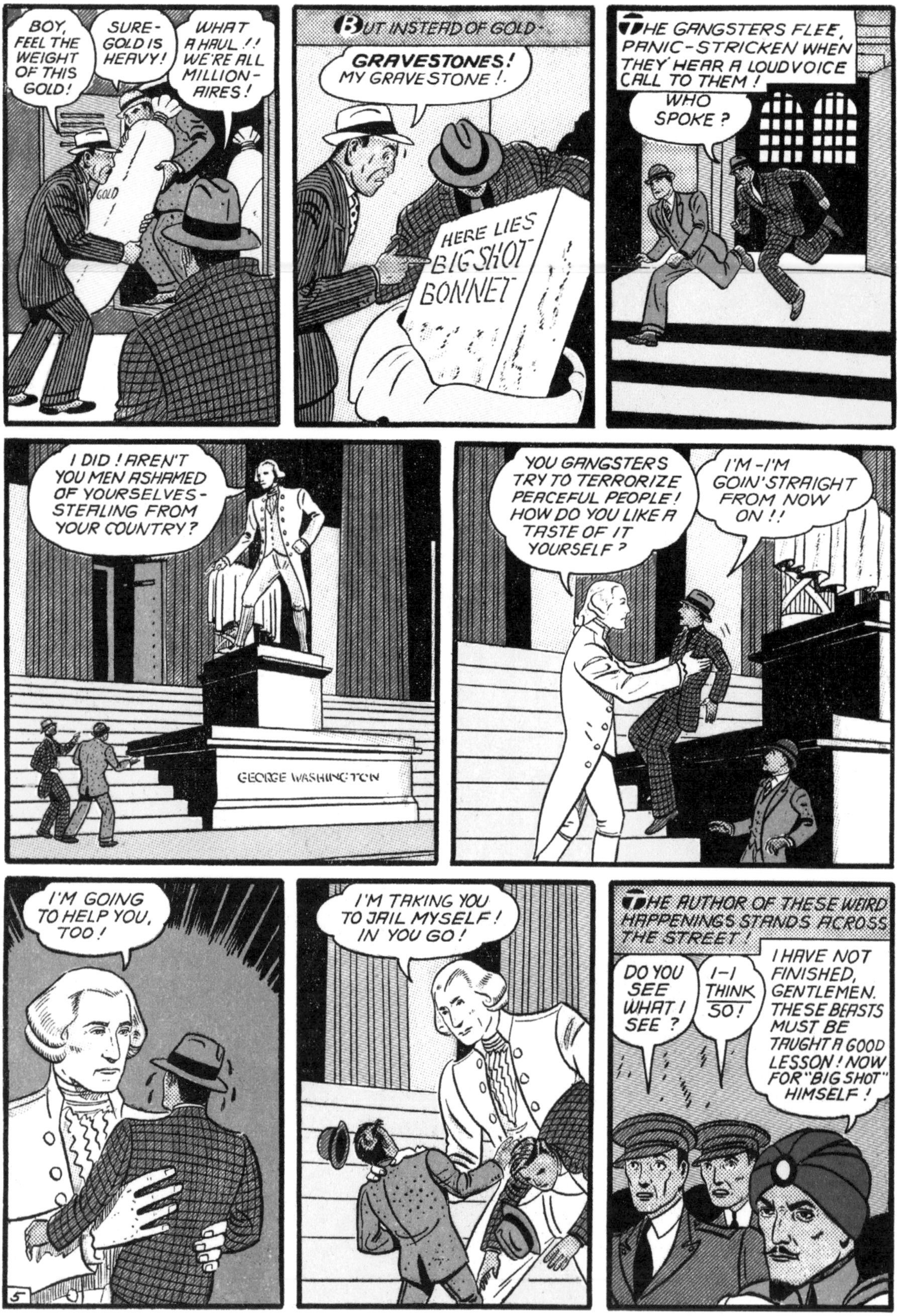
BOY, FEEL THE WEIGHT OF THIS GOLD!
SURE-GOLD IS HEAVY!
WHAT A HAUL!! WE'RE ALL MILLION-AIRES!
GOLD
BUT INSTEAD OF GOLD-
GRAVESTONES! MY GRAVESTONE!
HERE LIES BIG SHOT BONNET
THE GANGSTERS FLEE, PANIC-STRICKEN WHEN THEY HEAR A LOUD VOICE CALL TO THEM!
WHO SPOKE?
I DID! AREN'T YOU MEN ASHAMED OF YOURSELVES-STEALING FROM YOUR COUNTRY?
GEORGE WASHINGTON
YOU GANGSTERS TRY TO TERRORIZE PEACEFUL PEOPLE! HOW DO YOU LIKE A TASTE OF IT YOURSELF?
I'M-I'M GOIN' STRAIGHT FROM NOW ON!!
I'M GOING TO HELP YOU, TOO!
5
I'M TAKING YOU TO JAIL MYSELF! IN YOU GO!
THE AUTHOR OF THESE WEIRD HAPPENINGS STANDS ACROSS THE STREET!
DO YOU SEE WHAT I SEE?
I-I THINK SO!
I HAVE NOT FINISHED, GENTLEMEN. THESE BEASTS MUST BE TAUGHT A GOOD LESSON! NOW FOR "BIG SHOT" HIMSELF!

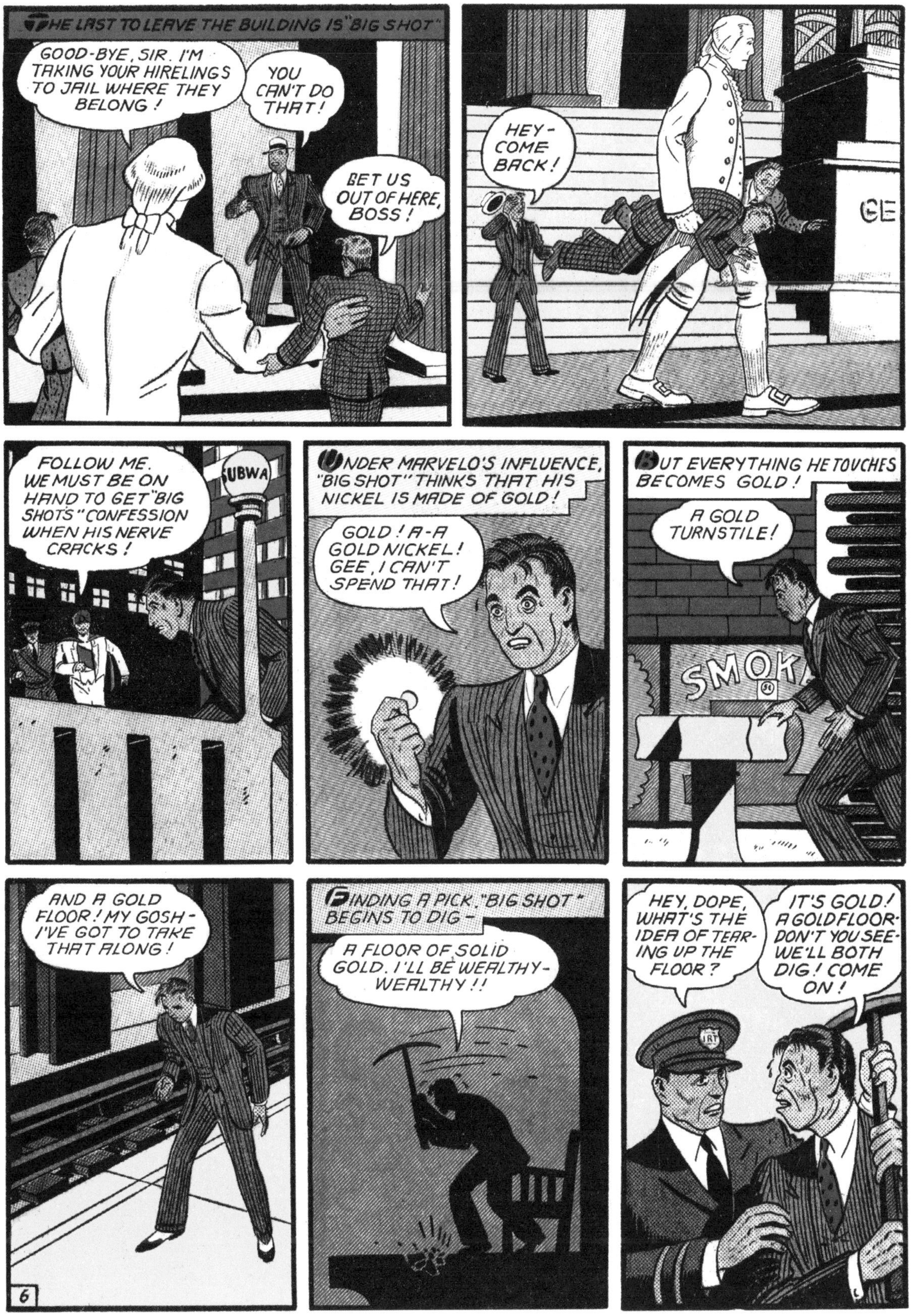
THE LAST TO LEAVE THE BUILDING IS "BIG SHOT"
GOOD-BYE, SIR. I'M TAKING YOUR HIRELINGS TO JAIL WHERE THEY BELONG!
YOU CAN'T DO THAT!
GET US OUT OF HERE, BOSS!
HEY- COME BACK!
GE
FOLLOW ME. WE MUST BE ON HAND TO GET "BIG SHOT'S" CONFESSION WHEN HIS NERVE CRACKS!
SUBWA
UNDER MARVELO'S INFLUENCE, "BIG SHOT" THINKS THAT HIS NICKEL IS MADE OF GOLD!
GOLD! A-A GOLD NICKEL! GEE, I CAN'T SPEND THAT!
BUT EVERYTHING HE TOUCHES BECOMES GOLD!
A GOLD TURNSTILE!
SMOK
AND A GOLD FLOOR! MY GOSH- I'VE GOT TO TAKE THAT ALONG!
6
FINDING A PICK, "BIG SHOT" BEGINS TO DIG-
A FLOOR OF SOLID GOLD. I'LL BE WEALTHY- WEALTHY!!
HEY, DOPE, WHAT'S THE IDEA OF TEARING UP THE FLOOR?
IT'S GOLD! A GOLD FLOOR- DON'T YOU SEE- WE'LL BOTH DIG! COME ON!
IRT

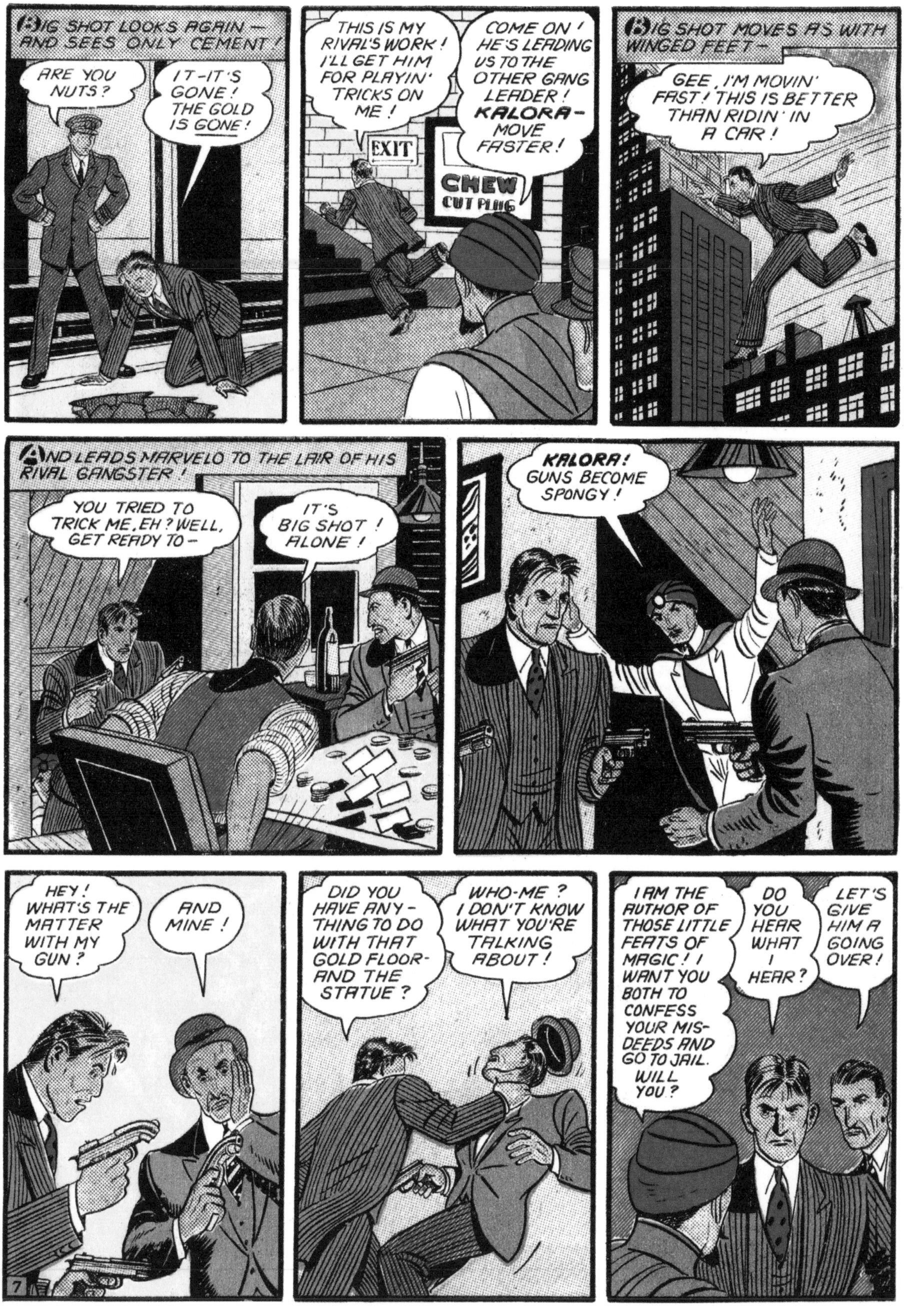
BIG SHOT LOOKS AGAIN — AND SEES ONLY CEMENT!
ARE YOU NUTS?
IT-IT'S GONE! THE GOLD IS GONE!
THIS IS MY RIVAL'S WORK! I'LL GET HIM FOR PLAYIN' TRICKS ON ME!
COME ON! HE'S LEADING US TO THE OTHER GANG LEADER! KALORA — MOVE FASTER!
EXIT
CHEW CUT PLUG
BIG SHOT MOVES AS WITH WINGED FEET —
GEE, I'M MOVIN' FAST! THIS IS BETTER THAN RIDIN' IN A CAR!
AND LEADS MARVELO TO THE LAIR OF HIS RIVAL GANGSTER!
YOU TRIED TO TRICK ME, EH? WELL, GET READY TO —
IT'S BIG SHOT! ALONE!
KALORA! GUNS BECOME SPONGY!
HEY! WHAT'S THE MATTER WITH MY GUN?
AND MINE!
7
DID YOU HAVE ANY-THING TO DO WITH THAT GOLD FLOOR-AND THE STATUE?
WHO-ME? I DON'T KNOW WHAT YOU'RE TALKING ABOUT!
I AM THE AUTHOR OF THOSE LITTLE FEATS OF MAGIC! I WANT YOU BOTH TO CONFESS YOUR MIS-DEEDS AND GO TO JAIL. WILL YOU?
DO YOU HEAR WHAT I HEAR?
LET'S GIVE HIM A GOING OVER!

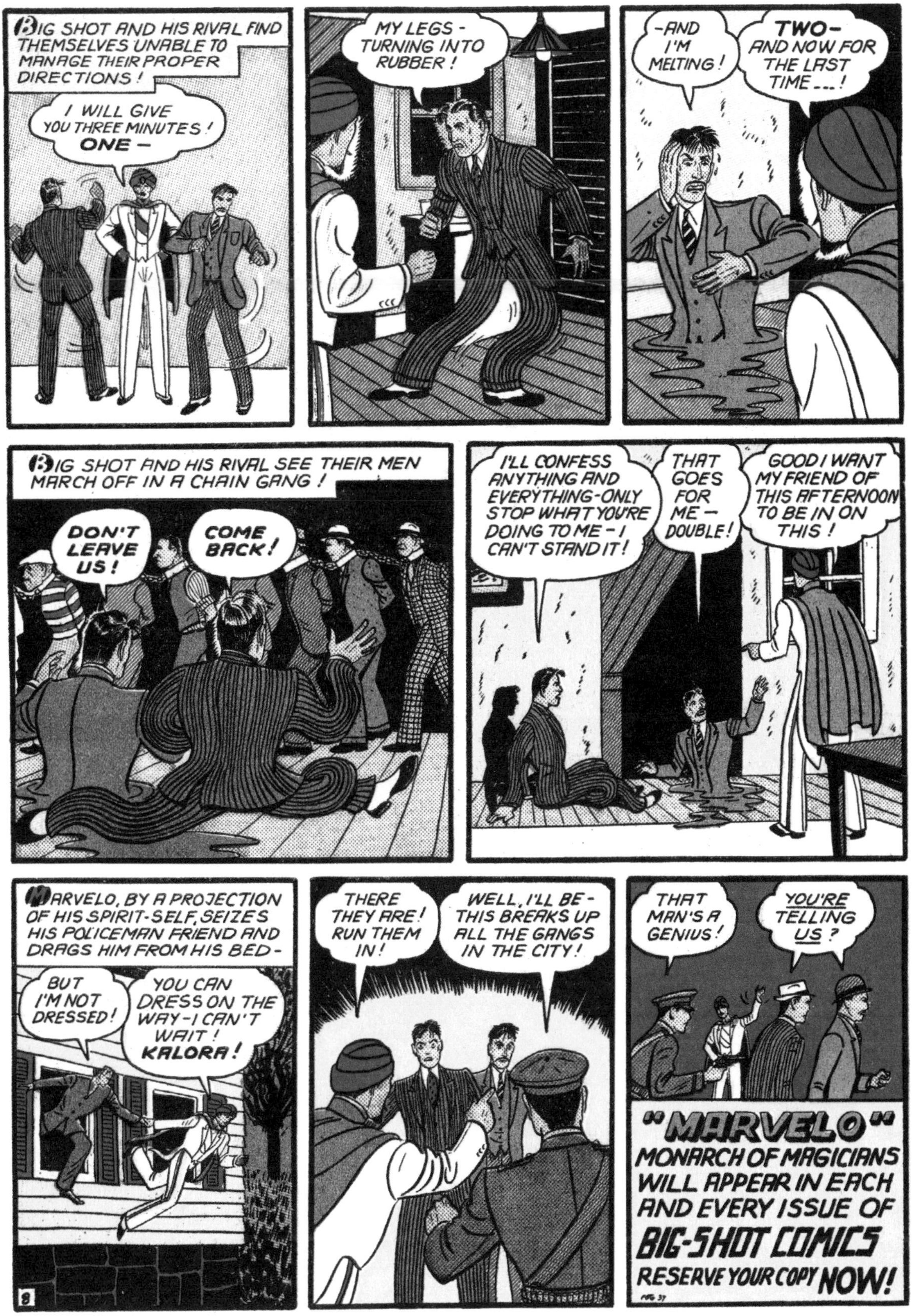
BIG SHOT AND HIS RIVAL FIND THEMSELVES UNABLE TO MANAGE THEIR PROPER DIRECTIONS!
I WILL GIVE YOU THREE MINUTES! ONE –
MY LEGS - TURNING INTO RUBBER!
–AND I'M MELTING!
TWO– AND NOW FOR THE LAST TIME ---!
BIG SHOT AND HIS RIVAL SEE THEIR MEN MARCH OFF IN A CHAIN GANG!
DON'T LEAVE US!
COME BACK!
I'LL CONFESS ANYTHING AND EVERYTHING-ONLY STOP WHAT YOU'RE DOING TO ME - I CAN'T STAND IT!
THAT GOES FOR ME – DOUBLE!
GOOD I WANT MY FRIEND OF THIS AFTERNOON TO BE IN ON THIS!
MARVELO, BY A PROJECTION OF HIS SPIRIT-SELF, SEIZES HIS POLICEMAN FRIEND AND DRAGS HIM FROM HIS BED-
BUT I'M NOT DRESSED!
YOU CAN DRESS ON THE WAY-I CAN'T WAIT! KALORA!
8
THERE THEY ARE! RUN THEM IN!
WELL, I'LL BE- THIS BREAKS UP ALL THE GANGS IN THE CITY!
THAT MAN'S A GENIUS!
YOU'RE TELLING US?
"MARVELO"
MONARCH OF MAGICIANS WILL APPEAR IN EACH AND EVERY ISSUE OF
BIG-SHOT COMICS
RESERVE YOUR COPY NOW!

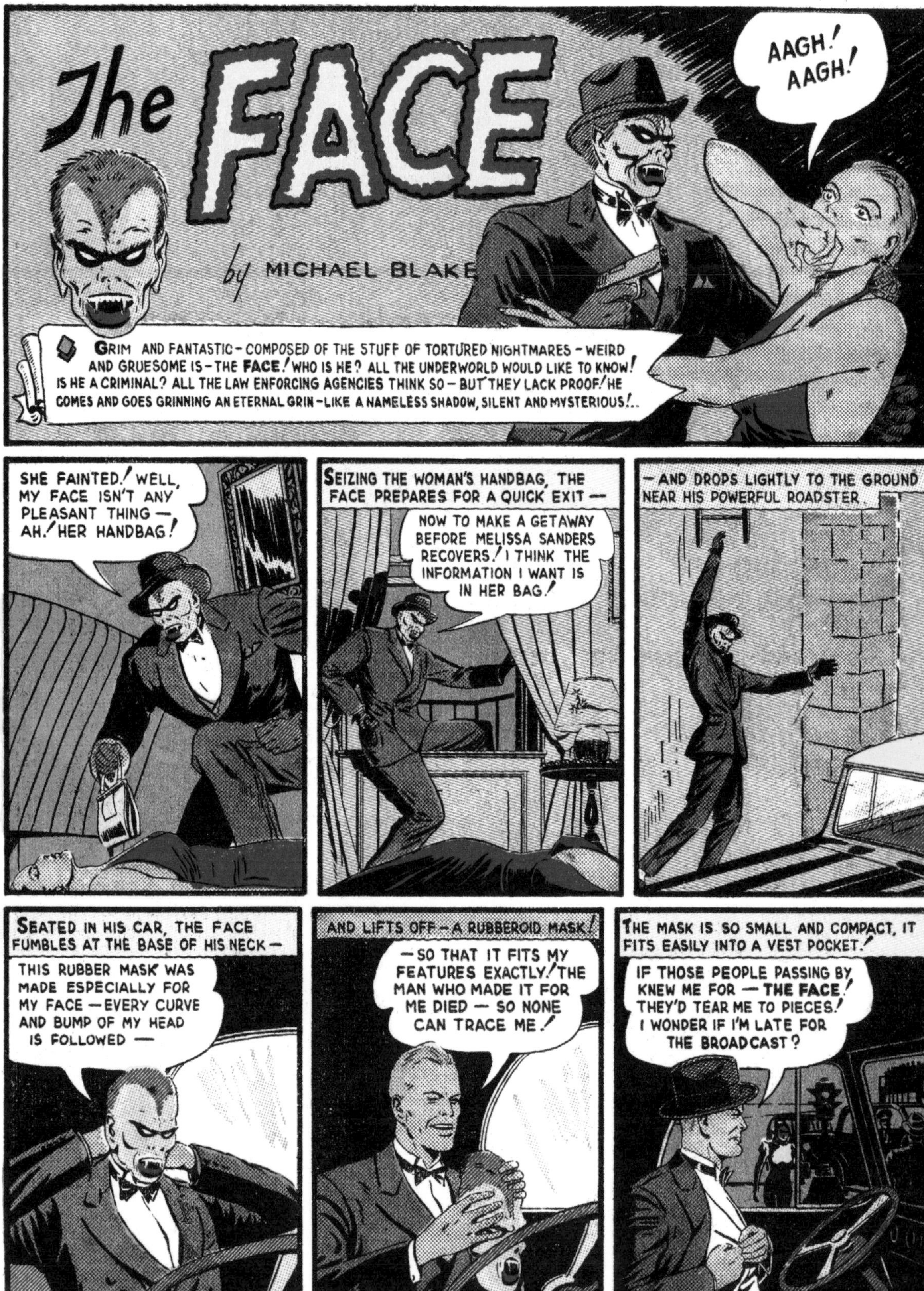

The FACE
by MICHAEL BLAKE
AAGH! AAGH!
GRIM AND FANTASTIC - COMPOSED OF THE STUFF OF TORTURED NIGHTMARES - WEIRD AND GRUESOME IS - THE FACE! WHO IS HE? ALL THE UNDERWORLD WOULD LIKE TO KNOW! IS HE A CRIMINAL? ALL THE LAW ENFORCING AGENCIES THINK SO - BUT THEY LACK PROOF! HE COMES AND GOES GRINNING AN ETERNAL GRIN - LIKE A NAMELESS SHADOW, SILENT AND MYSTERIOUS!..
SHE FAINTED! WELL, MY FACE ISN'T ANY PLEASANT THING — AH! HER HANDBAG!
SEIZING THE WOMAN'S HANDBAG, THE FACE PREPARES FOR A QUICK EXIT —
NOW TO MAKE A GETAWAY BEFORE MELISSA SANDERS RECOVERS! I THINK THE INFORMATION I WANT IS IN HER BAG!
— AND DROPS LIGHTLY TO THE GROUND NEAR HIS POWERFUL ROADSTER.
SEATED IN HIS CAR, THE FACE FUMBLES AT THE BASE OF HIS NECK —
THIS RUBBER MASK WAS MADE ESPECIALLY FOR MY FACE — EVERY CURVE AND BUMP OF MY HEAD IS FOLLOWED —
AND LIFTS OFF — A RUBBEROID MASK!
— SO THAT IT FITS MY FEATURES EXACTLY! THE MAN WHO MADE IT FOR ME DIED — SO NONE CAN TRACE ME!
THE MASK IS SO SMALL AND COMPACT, IT FITS EASILY INTO A VEST POCKET!
IF THOSE PEOPLE PASSING BY KNEW ME FOR — THE FACE! THEY'D TEAR ME TO PIECES! I WONDER IF I'M LATE FOR THE BROADCAST?
1

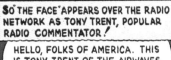

AT RADIO STATION WBSC, OWNED BY TONY TRENT (THE FACE) —

**TONY TRENT!** YOU'RE LATE AGAIN! **HURRY** — YOU SHOULD BE ON THE AIR! OH, YOU'RE IMPOSSIBLE!

HELLO, BABS! MY, WHAT AN EFFICIENT SECRETARY! OKAY — I'M READY!

SO THE FACE APPEARS OVER THE RADIO NETWORK AS TONY TRENT, POPULAR RADIO COMMENTATOR!

HELLO, FOLKS OF AMERICA. THIS IS TONY TRENT OF THE AIRWAVES COMING TO YOU — THAT **FOOD SHORTAGE** IN THE CITY I WAS TELLING YOU ABOUT YESTERDAY IS **NO JOKE**. LISTEN —

I GOT HOLD OF SOMETHING — THE BILL OF SALE FROM A WESTERN FARMER TO — THE CITY'S CRIME CHIEF — GRUDGE GROGAN — **FOR THOSE TURKEYS THAT MADE THE POOR ORPHAN ASYLUM CHILDREN SICK THIS WEEK-END!**

HOW DID YOU LIKE THAT, BABS? I TOLD YOU I'D GET THE PROOF AND THE TRUTH — ABOUT THOSE TURKEYS!

TONY — GROGAN WILL GET YOU FOR THIS! HE'LL **KILL YOU!**

I'M GOING TO PAY A FLYING VISIT TO THE ORPHAN ASYLUM TO CHECK UP ON THIS POISONED TURKEY FOOD!

TONY — BE **CAREFUL!**

THE FACE ARRIVES AT THE ASYLUM!

THIS IS THE ORPHAN ASYLUM — I'LL CHECK ON THE POISONED TURKEY MEAT FIRST!

HE INVESTIGATES THE BAD MEAT —

THIS MEAT IS RANK! GROGAN OUGHT TO BE SENT TO JAIL FOR THIS!

AND LOOKS IN ON THE SICK WARD OF THE ASYLUM —

POOR LITTLE TYKES — ALL SICK! I'LL SEE THAT GROGAN **PAYS FOR THIS!**

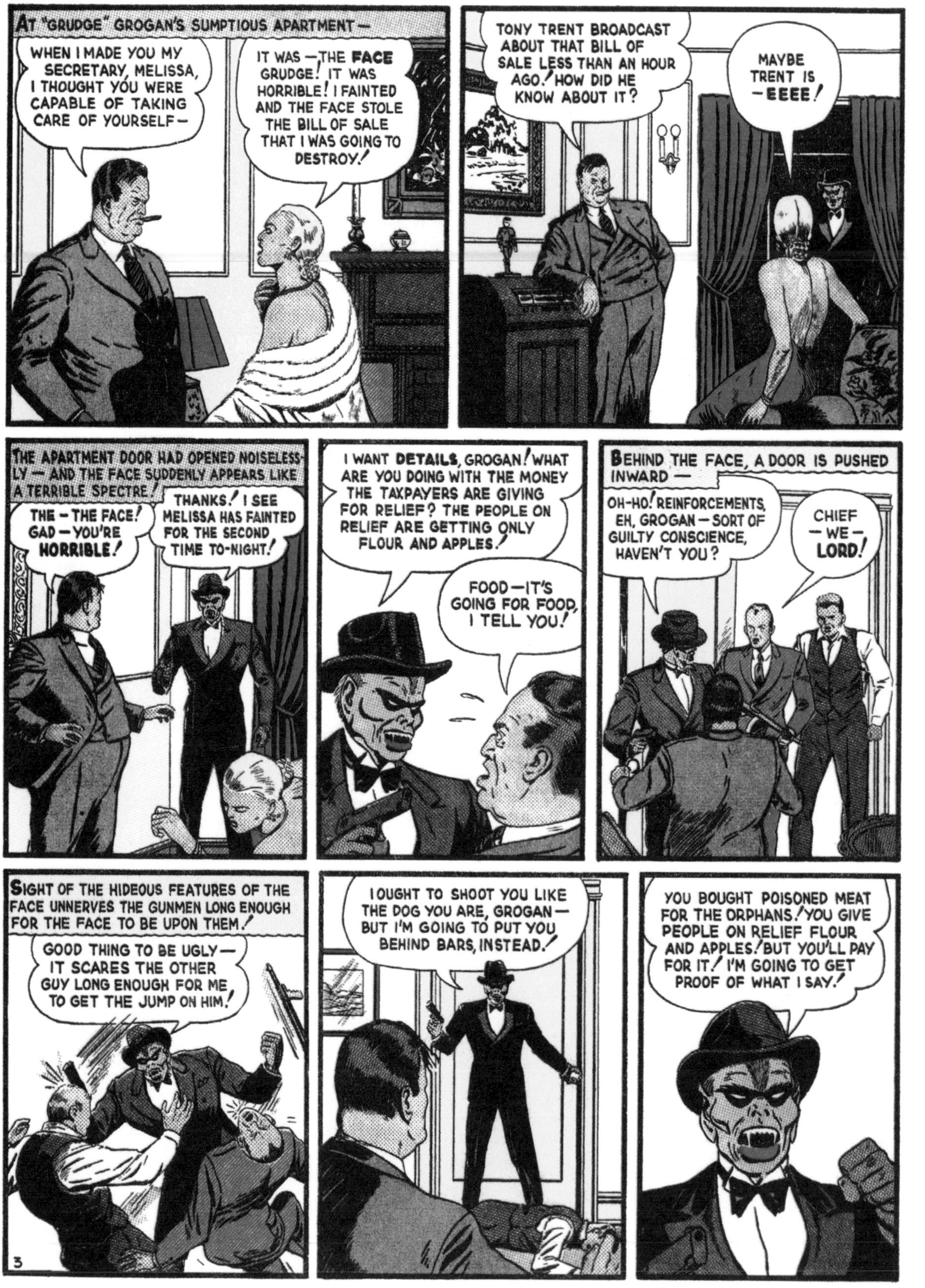
AT "GRUDGE" GROGAN'S SUMPTIOUS APARTMENT—
WHEN I MADE YOU MY SECRETARY, MELISSA, I THOUGHT YOU WERE CAPABLE OF TAKING CARE OF YOURSELF—
IT WAS—THE FACE GRUDGE! IT WAS HORRIBLE! I FAINTED AND THE FACE STOLE THE BILL OF SALE THAT I WAS GOING TO DESTROY!
TONY TRENT BROADCAST ABOUT THAT BILL OF SALE LESS THAN AN HOUR AGO! HOW DID HE KNOW ABOUT IT?
MAYBE TRENT IS —EEEE!
THE APARTMENT DOOR HAD OPENED NOISELESSLY — AND THE FACE SUDDENLY APPEARS LIKE A TERRIBLE SPECTRE!
THE — THE FACE! GAD — YOU'RE HORRIBLE!
THANKS! I SEE MELISSA HAS FAINTED FOR THE SECOND TIME TO-NIGHT!
I WANT DETAILS, GROGAN! WHAT ARE YOU DOING WITH THE MONEY THE TAXPAYERS ARE GIVING FOR RELIEF? THE PEOPLE ON RELIEF ARE GETTING ONLY FLOUR AND APPLES!
FOOD—IT'S GOING FOR FOOD, I TELL YOU!
BEHIND THE FACE, A DOOR IS PUSHED INWARD —
OH-HO! REINFORCEMENTS, EH, GROGAN — SORT OF GUILTY CONSCIENCE, HAVEN'T YOU?
CHIEF —WE— LORD!
SIGHT OF THE HIDEOUS FEATURES OF THE FACE UNNERVES THE GUNMEN LONG ENOUGH FOR THE FACE TO BE UPON THEM!
GOOD THING TO BE UGLY— IT SCARES THE OTHER GUY LONG ENOUGH FOR ME TO GET THE JUMP ON HIM!
3
I OUGHT TO SHOOT YOU LIKE THE DOG YOU ARE, GROGAN— BUT I'M GOING TO PUT YOU BEHIND BARS, INSTEAD!
YOU BOUGHT POISONED MEAT FOR THE ORPHANS! YOU GIVE PEOPLE ON RELIEF FLOUR AND APPLES! BUT YOU'LL PAY FOR IT! I'M GOING TO GET PROOF OF WHAT I SAY!

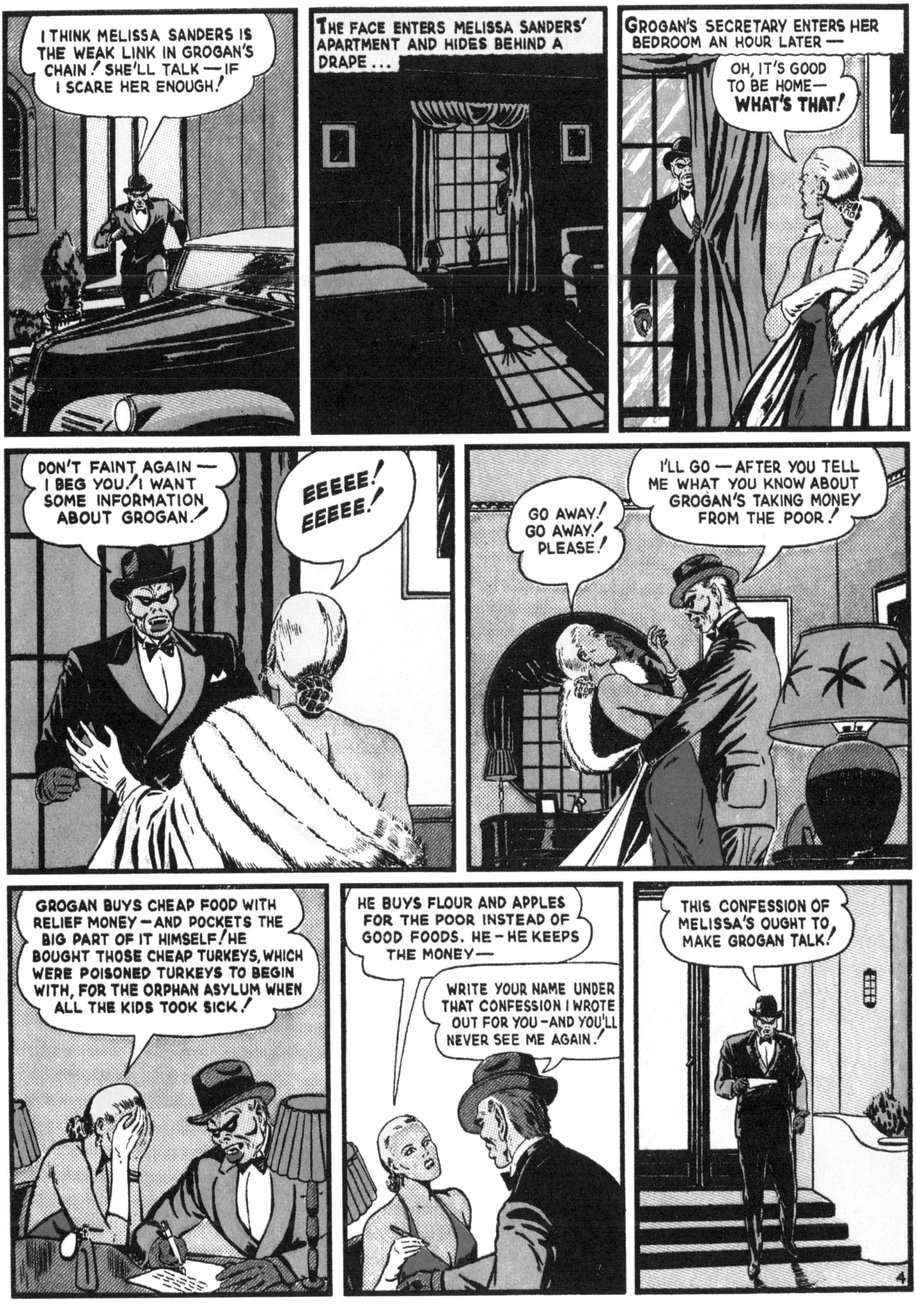
I THINK MELISSA SANDERS IS THE WEAK LINK IN GROGAN'S CHAIN! SHE'LL TALK — IF I SCARE HER ENOUGH!
THE FACE ENTERS MELISSA SANDERS' APARTMENT AND HIDES BEHIND A DRAPE ...
GROGAN'S SECRETARY ENTERS HER BEDROOM AN HOUR LATER —
OH, IT'S GOOD TO BE HOME— WHAT'S THAT!
DON'T FAINT AGAIN — I BEG YOU! I WANT SOME INFORMATION ABOUT GROGAN!
EEEEE! EEEEE!
GO AWAY! GO AWAY! PLEASE!
I'LL GO — AFTER YOU TELL ME WHAT YOU KNOW ABOUT GROGAN'S TAKING MONEY FROM THE POOR!
GROGAN BUYS CHEAP FOOD WITH RELIEF MONEY — AND POCKETS THE BIG PART OF IT HIMSELF! HE BOUGHT THOSE CHEAP TURKEYS, WHICH WERE POISONED TURKEYS TO BEGIN WITH, FOR THE ORPHAN ASYLUM WHEN ALL THE KIDS TOOK SICK!
HE BUYS FLOUR AND APPLES FOR THE POOR INSTEAD OF GOOD FOODS. HE - HE KEEPS THE MONEY—
WRITE YOUR NAME UNDER THAT CONFESSION I WROTE OUT FOR YOU - AND YOU'LL NEVER SEE ME AGAIN!
THIS CONFESSION OF MELISSA'S OUGHT TO MAKE GROGAN TALK!
4

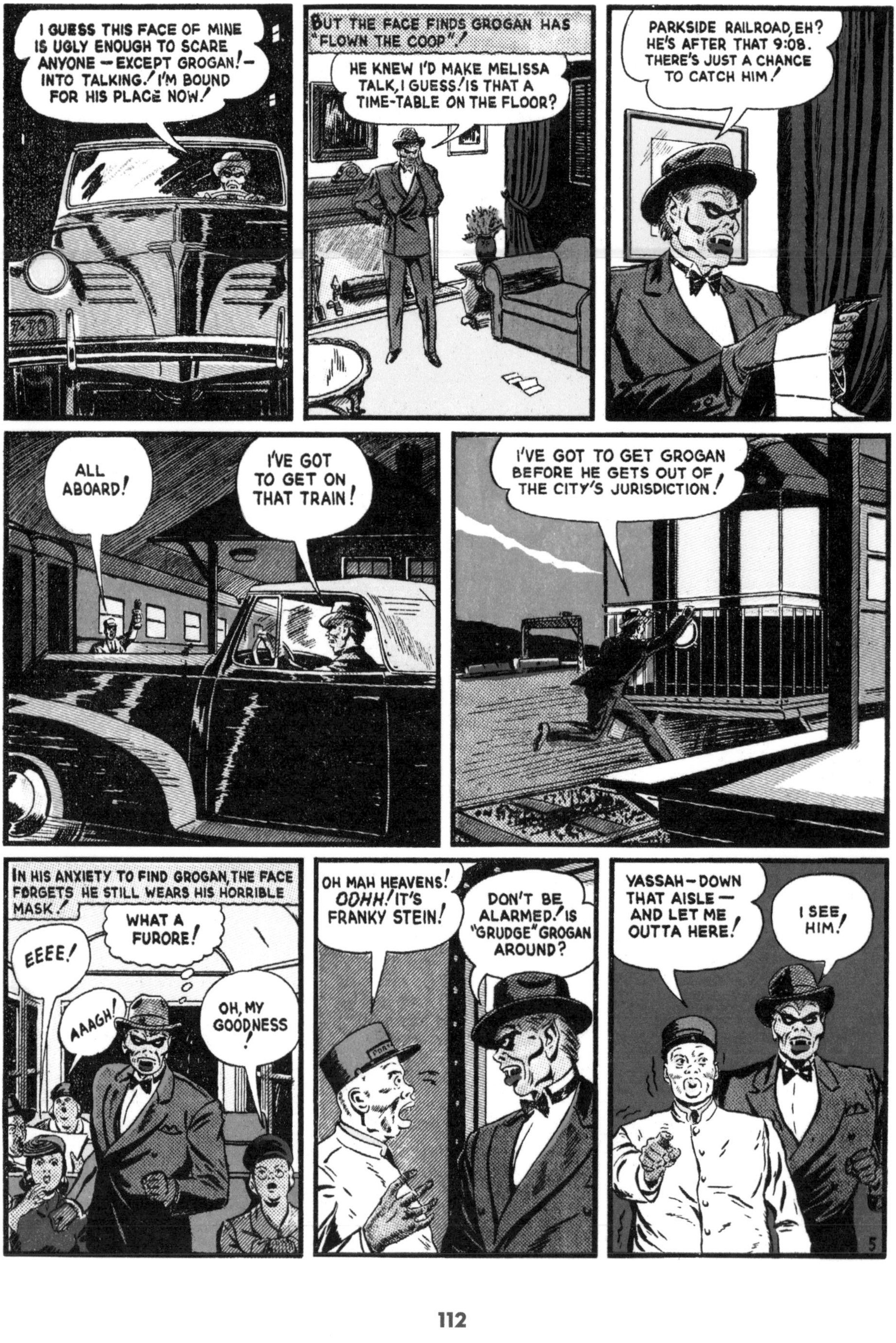
I GUESS THIS FACE OF MINE IS UGLY ENOUGH TO SCARE ANYONE — EXCEPT GROGAN! — INTO TALKING! I'M BOUND FOR HIS PLACE NOW!
BUT THE FACE FINDS GROGAN HAS "FLOWN THE COOP"!
HE KNEW I'D MAKE MELISSA TALK, I GUESS! IS THAT A TIME-TABLE ON THE FLOOR?
PARKSIDE RAILROAD, EH? HE'S AFTER THAT 9:08. THERE'S JUST A CHANCE TO CATCH HIM!
ALL ABOARD!
I'VE GOT TO GET ON THAT TRAIN!
I'VE GOT TO GET GROGAN BEFORE HE GETS OUT OF THE CITY'S JURISDICTION!
IN HIS ANXIETY TO FIND GROGAN, THE FACE FORGETS HE STILL WEARS HIS HORRIBLE MASK!
WHAT A FURORE!
EEEE!
AAAGH!
OH, MY GOODNESS!
OH MAH HEAVENS! OOHH! IT'S FRANKY STEIN!
DON'T BE ALARMED! IS "GRUDGE" GROGAN AROUND?
YASSAH — DOWN THAT AISLE — AND LET ME OUTTA HERE!
I SEE HIM!

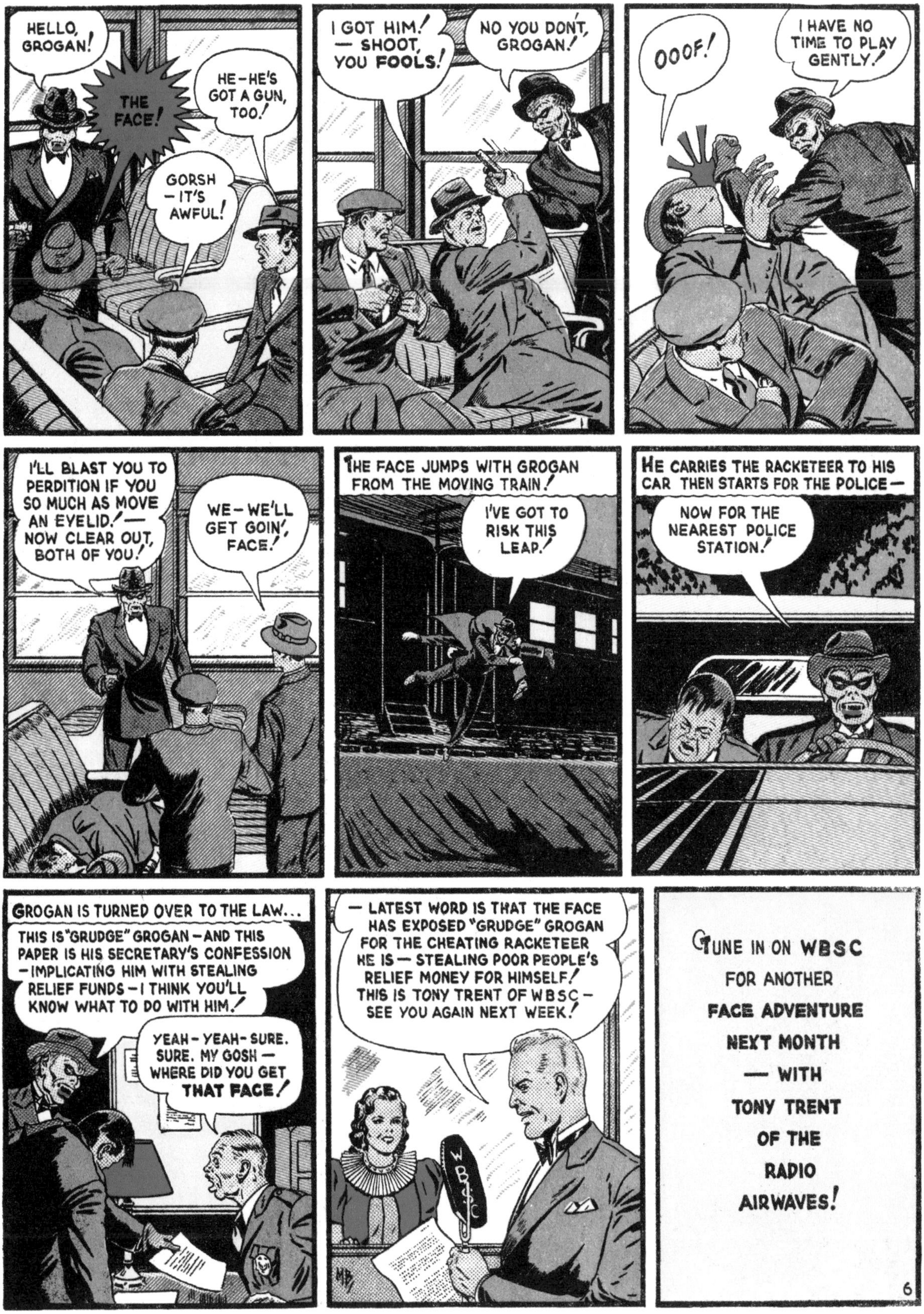
HELLO, GROGAN!
THE FACE!
HE-HE'S GOT A GUN, TOO!
GORSH - IT'S AWFUL!
I GOT HIM! — SHOOT, YOU FOOLS!
NO YOU DON'T, GROGAN!
OOOF!
I HAVE NO TIME TO PLAY GENTLY!
I'LL BLAST YOU TO PERDITION IF YOU SO MUCH AS MOVE AN EYELID! — NOW CLEAR OUT, BOTH OF YOU!
WE-WE'LL GET GOIN', FACE!
THE FACE JUMPS WITH GROGAN FROM THE MOVING TRAIN!
I'VE GOT TO RISK THIS LEAP!
HE CARRIES THE RACKETEER TO HIS CAR THEN STARTS FOR THE POLICE—
NOW FOR THE NEAREST POLICE STATION!
GROGAN IS TURNED OVER TO THE LAW...
THIS IS "GRUDGE" GROGAN—AND THIS PAPER IS HIS SECRETARY'S CONFESSION—IMPLICATING HIM WITH STEALING RELIEF FUNDS—I THINK YOU'LL KNOW WHAT TO DO WITH HIM!
YEAH-YEAH-SURE. SURE. MY GOSH— WHERE DID YOU GET THAT FACE!
— LATEST WORD IS THAT THE FACE HAS EXPOSED "GRUDGE" GROGAN FOR THE CHEATING RACKETEER HE IS — STEALING POOR PEOPLE'S RELIEF MONEY FOR HIMSELF! THIS IS TONY TRENT OF WBSC — SEE YOU AGAIN NEXT WEEK!
WBSC
TUNE IN ON WBSC
FOR ANOTHER
FACE ADVENTURE
NEXT MONTH
— WITH
TONY TRENT
OF THE
RADIO
AIRWAVES!
6

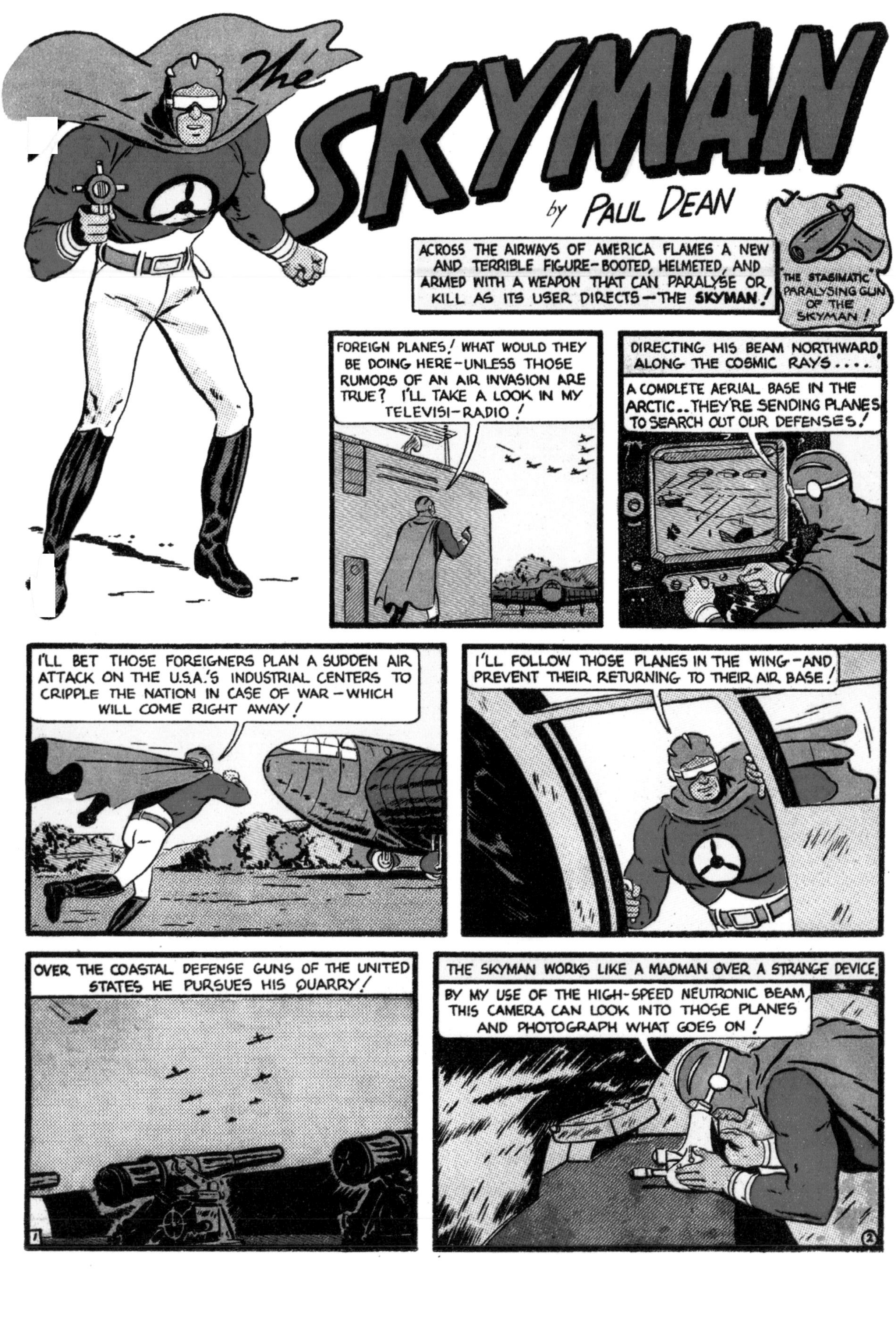
The SKYMAN
by PAUL DEAN
ACROSS THE AIRWAYS OF AMERICA FLAMES A NEW AND TERRIBLE FIGURE—BOOTED, HELMETED, AND ARMED WITH A WEAPON THAT CAN PARALYSE OR KILL AS ITS USER DIRECTS—THE SKYMAN!
"THE STASIMATIC" PARALYSING GUN OF THE SKYMAN!
FOREIGN PLANES! WHAT WOULD THEY BE DOING HERE—UNLESS THOSE RUMORS OF AN AIR INVASION ARE TRUE? I'LL TAKE A LOOK IN MY TELEVISI-RADIO!
DIRECTING HIS BEAM NORTHWARD, ALONG THE COSMIC RAYS....
A COMPLETE AERIAL BASE IN THE ARCTIC..THEY'RE SENDING PLANES TO SEARCH OUT OUR DEFENSES!
I'LL BET THOSE FOREIGNERS PLAN A SUDDEN AIR ATTACK ON THE U.S.A.'S INDUSTRIAL CENTERS TO CRIPPLE THE NATION IN CASE OF WAR—WHICH WILL COME RIGHT AWAY!
I'LL FOLLOW THOSE PLANES IN THE WING—AND PREVENT THEIR RETURNING TO THEIR AIR BASE!
OVER THE COASTAL DEFENSE GUNS OF THE UNITED STATES HE PURSUES HIS QUARRY!
1
THE SKYMAN WORKS LIKE A MADMAN OVER A STRANGE DEVICE.
BY MY USE OF THE HIGH-SPEED NEUTRONIC BEAM, THIS CAMERA CAN LOOK INTO THOSE PLANES AND PHOTOGRAPH WHAT GOES ON!
2

USING A RADIUM RAY THE SKYMAN DEVELOPS HIS PICTURES IN AN INSTANT AND SEES THE PLANES' INTERIORS!

THEY'RE TAKING SHOTS OF OUR COASTAL DEFENSES! I'VE GOT TO STOP THEM BEFORE THEY GET BACK TO THEIR AIR BASE WITH THE INFORMATION!

HE DECLARES HIS OWN WAR IN THE MODERN MANNER, TREATING SPIES AS THEY DESERVE!

THE ENEMY FLEET IS SHOT OUT OF THE SKY, ALL EXCEPT ONE!

I'LL FOLLOW HIM TO THE AIR BASE — I WANT TO KNOW ITS EXACT LOCATION!

WE'RE OVER JONES SOUND — OUR DESTINATION MUST BE GRANT LAND! THAT PLANE MUST NEVER REACH THERE —

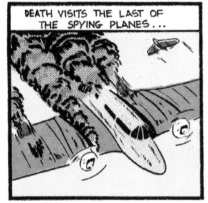

DEATH VISITS THE LAST OF THE SPYING PLANES...

SCREENED BEHIND TALL FUR TREES THE WING LANDS NEAR THE AERIAL BASE.

I BROUGHT SKIIS ALONG TO GET ME OVER THE ICE AND SNOW FASTER. I MAY NEED TO GET AWAY IN A HURRY!

WHEN NIGHTFALL DARKENS THE SKY, A WEIRD FIGURE CREEPS CLOSE TO THE LOG CABINS —

THIS IS THE COMMANDER'S CABIN —

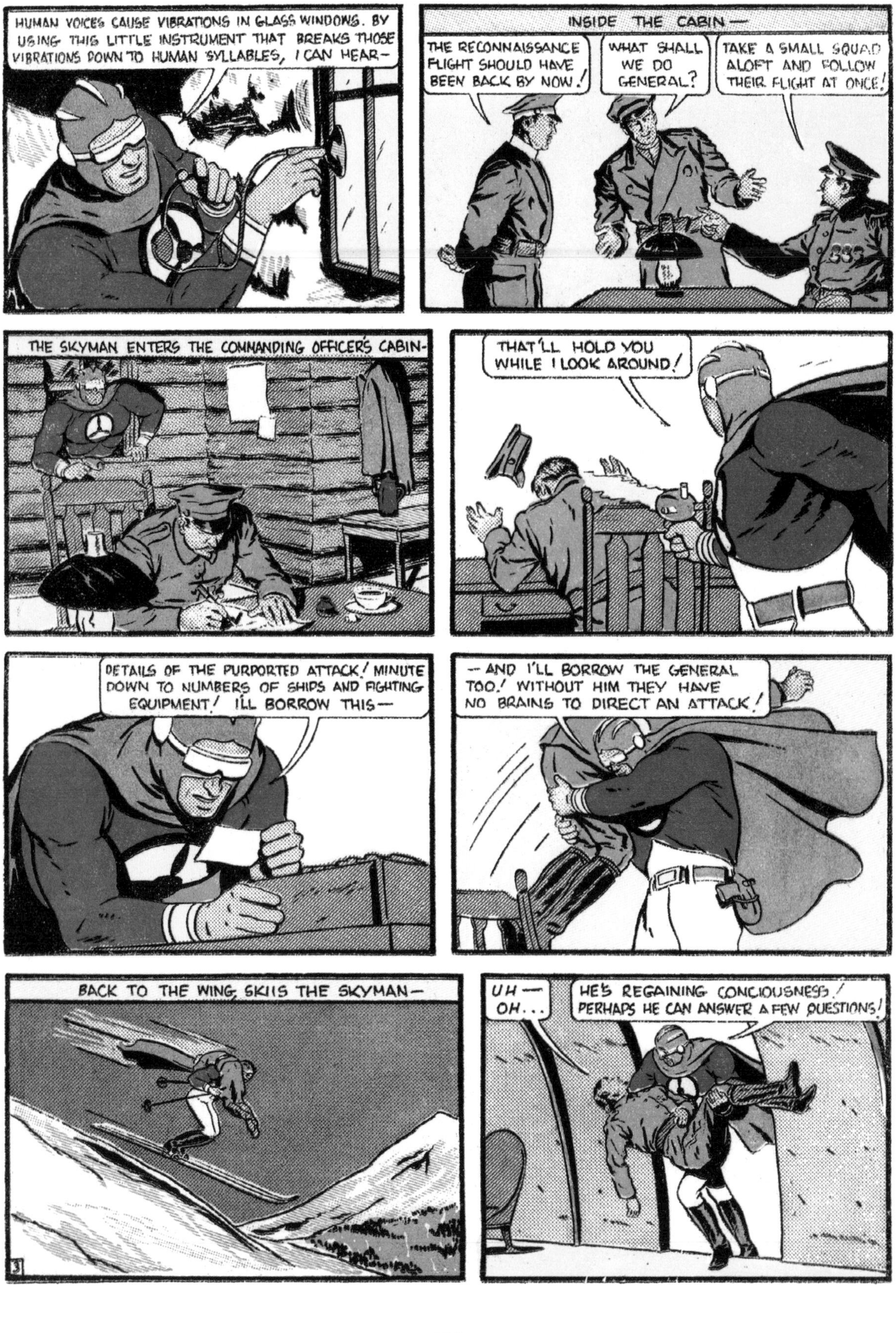
HUMAN VOICES CAUSE VIBRATIONS IN GLASS WINDOWS. BY USING THIS LITTLE INSTRUMENT THAT BREAKS THOSE VIBRATIONS DOWN TO HUMAN SYLLABLES, I CAN HEAR—
INSIDE THE CABIN—
THE RECONNAISSANCE FLIGHT SHOULD HAVE BEEN BACK BY NOW!
WHAT SHALL WE DO GENERAL?
TAKE A SMALL SQUAD ALOFT AND FOLLOW THEIR FLIGHT AT ONCE!
THE SKYMAN ENTERS THE COMMANDING OFFICER'S CABIN—
THAT'LL HOLD YOU WHILE I LOOK AROUND!
DETAILS OF THE PURPORTED ATTACK! MINUTE DOWN TO NUMBERS OF SHIPS AND FIGHTING EQUIPMENT! I'LL BORROW THIS—
—AND I'LL BORROW THE GENERAL TOO! WITHOUT HIM THEY HAVE NO BRAINS TO DIRECT AN ATTACK!
BACK TO THE WING, SKIIS THE SKYMAN—
3
UH—OH...
HE'S REGAINING CONCIOUSNESS! PERHAPS HE CAN ANSWER A FEW QUESTIONS!

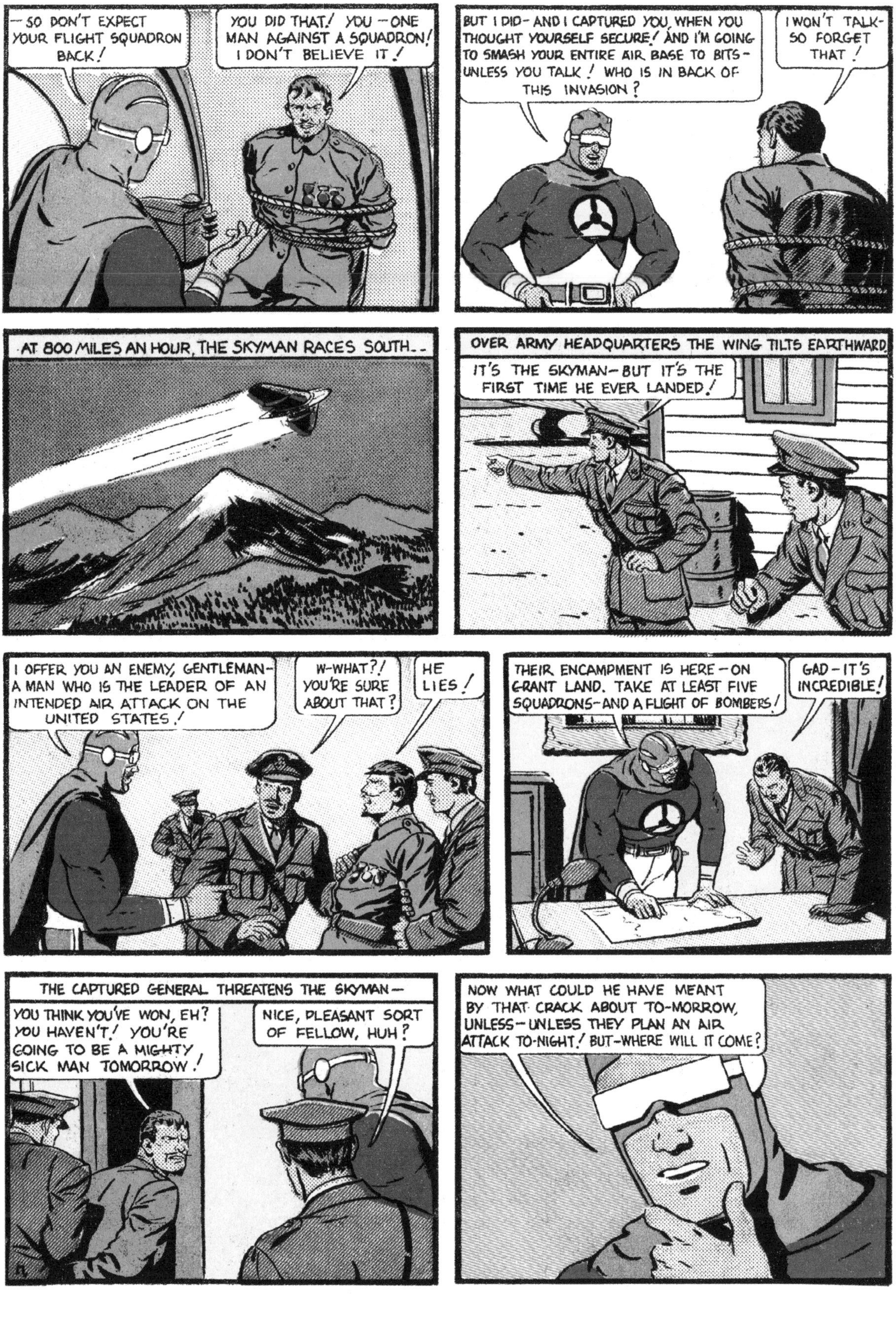
—SO DON'T EXPECT YOUR FLIGHT SQUADRON BACK!
YOU DID THAT! YOU—ONE MAN AGAINST A SQUADRON! I DON'T BELIEVE IT!
BUT I DID—AND I CAPTURED YOU, WHEN YOU THOUGHT YOURSELF SECURE! AND I'M GOING TO SMASH YOUR ENTIRE AIR BASE TO BITS—UNLESS YOU TALK! WHO IS IN BACK OF THIS INVASION?
I WON'T TALK—SO FORGET THAT!
AT 800 MILES AN HOUR, THE SKYMAN RACES SOUTH—
OVER ARMY HEADQUARTERS THE WING TILTS EARTHWARD.
IT'S THE SKYMAN—BUT IT'S THE FIRST TIME HE EVER LANDED!
I OFFER YOU AN ENEMY, GENTLEMAN—A MAN WHO IS THE LEADER OF AN INTENDED AIR ATTACK ON THE UNITED STATES!
W-WHAT?! YOU'RE SURE ABOUT THAT?
HE LIES!
THEIR ENCAMPMENT IS HERE—ON GRANT LAND. TAKE AT LEAST FIVE SQUADRONS—AND A FLIGHT OF BOMBERS!
GAD—IT'S INCREDIBLE!
THE CAPTURED GENERAL THREATENS THE SKYMAN—
YOU THINK YOU'VE WON, EH? YOU HAVEN'T! YOU'RE GOING TO BE A MIGHTY SICK MAN TOMORROW!
NICE, PLEASANT SORT OF FELLOW, HUH?
NOW WHAT COULD HE HAVE MEANT BY THAT CRACK ABOUT TO-MORROW, UNLESS—UNLESS THEY PLAN AN AIR ATTACK TO-NIGHT! BUT—WHERE WILL IT COME?

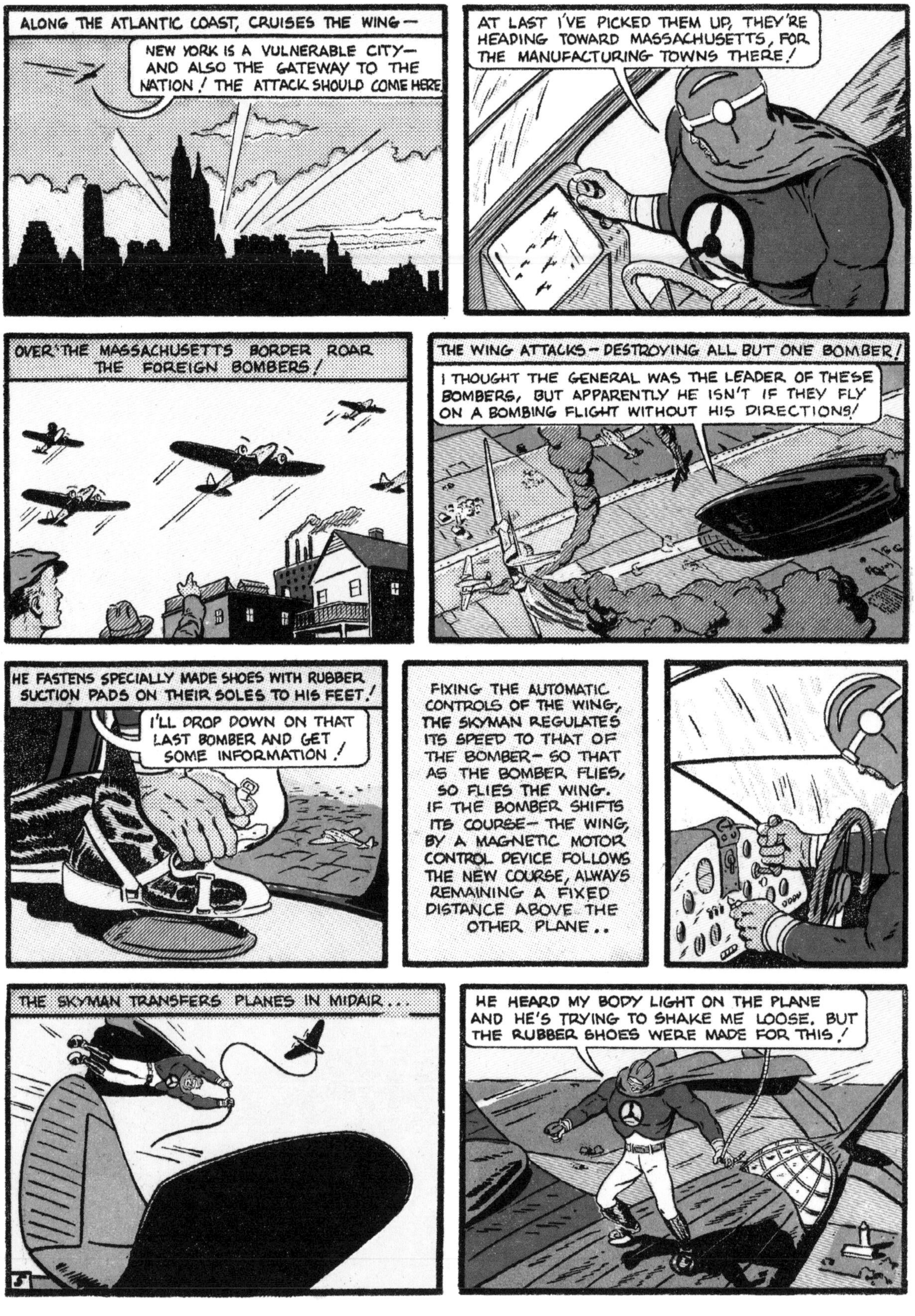
ALONG THE ATLANTIC COAST, CRUISES THE WING—
NEW YORK IS A VULNERABLE CITY— AND ALSO THE GATEWAY TO THE NATION! THE ATTACK SHOULD COME HERE!
AT LAST I'VE PICKED THEM UP, THEY'RE HEADING TOWARD MASSACHUSETTS, FOR THE MANUFACTURING TOWNS THERE!
OVER THE MASSACHUSETTS BORDER ROAR THE FOREIGN BOMBERS!
THE WING ATTACKS— DESTROYING ALL BUT ONE BOMBER!
I THOUGHT THE GENERAL WAS THE LEADER OF THESE BOMBERS, BUT APPARENTLY HE ISN'T IF THEY FLY ON A BOMBING FLIGHT WITHOUT HIS DIRECTIONS!
HE FASTENS SPECIALLY MADE SHOES WITH RUBBER SUCTION PADS ON THEIR SOLES TO HIS FEET!
I'LL DROP DOWN ON THAT LAST BOMBER AND GET SOME INFORMATION!
FIXING THE AUTOMATIC CONTROLS OF THE WING, THE SKYMAN REGULATES ITS SPEED TO THAT OF THE BOMBER— SO THAT AS THE BOMBER FLIES, SO FLIES THE WING. IF THE BOMBER SHIFTS ITS COURSE— THE WING, BY A MAGNETIC MOTOR CONTROL DEVICE FOLLOWS THE NEW COURSE, ALWAYS REMAINING A FIXED DISTANCE ABOVE THE OTHER PLANE..
THE SKYMAN TRANSFERS PLANES IN MIDAIR...
HE HEARD MY BODY LIGHT ON THE PLANE AND HE'S TRYING TO SHAKE ME LOOSE. BUT THE RUBBER SHOES WERE MADE FOR THIS!

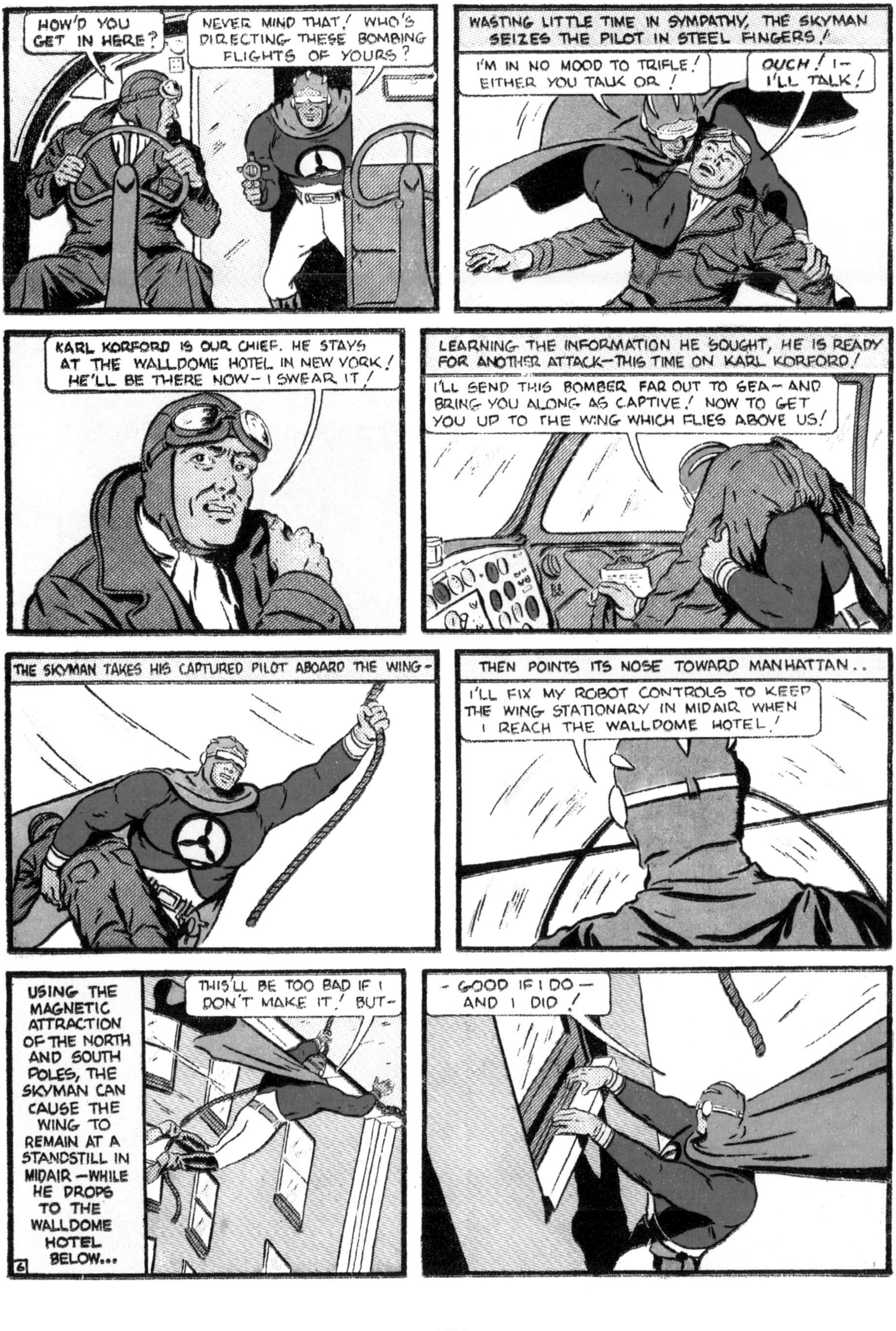
HOW'D YOU GET IN HERE?
NEVER MIND THAT! WHO'S DIRECTING THESE BOMBING FLIGHTS OF YOURS?
WASTING LITTLE TIME IN SYMPATHY, THE SKYMAN SEIZES THE PILOT IN STEEL FINGERS!
I'M IN NO MOOD TO TRIFLE! EITHER YOU TALK OR !
OUCH! I— I'LL TALK!
KARL KORFORD IS OUR CHIEF. HE STAYS AT THE WALLDOME HOTEL IN NEW YORK! HE'LL BE THERE NOW—I SWEAR IT!
LEARNING THE INFORMATION HE SOUGHT, HE IS READY FOR ANOTHER ATTACK—THIS TIME ON KARL KORFORD!
I'LL SEND THIS BOMBER FAR OUT TO SEA—AND BRING YOU ALONG AS CAPTIVE! NOW TO GET YOU UP TO THE WING WHICH FLIES ABOVE US!
THE SKYMAN TAKES HIS CAPTURED PILOT ABOARD THE WING—
THEN POINTS ITS NOSE TOWARD MANHATTAN..
I'LL FIX MY ROBOT CONTROLS TO KEEP THE WING STATIONARY IN MIDAIR WHEN I REACH THE WALLDOME HOTEL!
USING THE MAGNETIC ATTRACTION OF THE NORTH AND SOUTH POLES, THE SKYMAN CAN CAUSE THE WING TO REMAIN AT A STANDSTILL IN MIDAIR—WHILE HE DROPS TO THE WALLDOME HOTEL BELOW...
6
THIS'LL BE TOO BAD IF I DON'T MAKE IT! BUT—
—GOOD IF I DO— AND I DID!

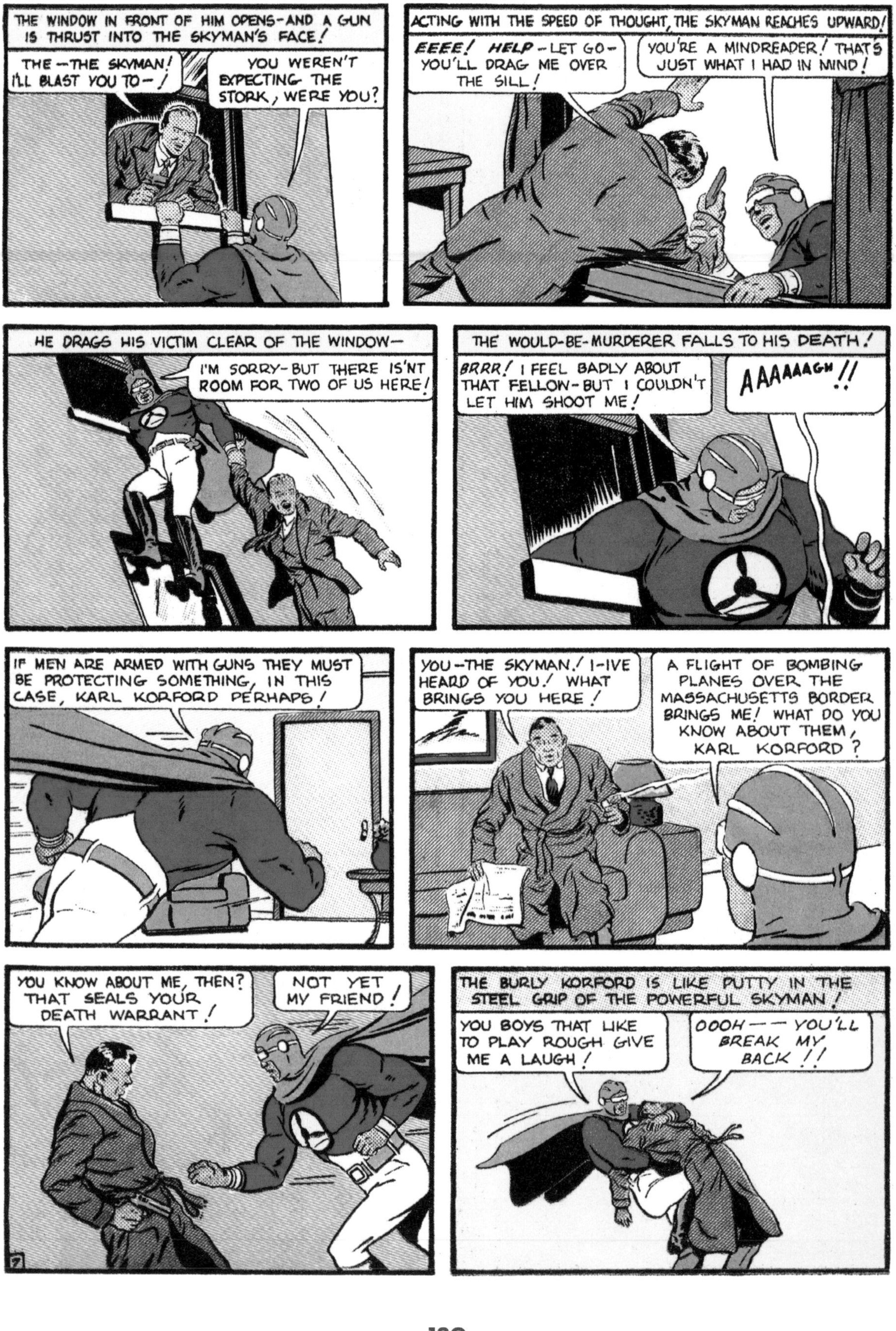
THE WINDOW IN FRONT OF HIM OPENS-AND A GUN IS THRUST INTO THE SKYMAN'S FACE!
THE --THE SKYMAN! I'LL BLAST YOU TO-!
YOU WEREN'T EXPECTING THE STORK, WERE YOU?
ACTING WITH THE SPEED OF THOUGHT, THE SKYMAN REACHES UPWARD!
EEEE! HELP-LET GO-YOU'LL DRAG ME OVER THE SILL!
YOU'RE A MINDREADER! THAT'S JUST WHAT I HAD IN MIND!
HE DRAGS HIS VICTIM CLEAR OF THE WINDOW-
I'M SORRY-BUT THERE IS'NT ROOM FOR TWO OF US HERE!
THE WOULD-BE-MURDERER FALLS TO HIS DEATH!
BRRR! I FEEL BADLY ABOUT THAT FELLOW-BUT I COULDN'T LET HIM SHOOT ME!
AAAAAAGH!!
IF MEN ARE ARMED WITH GUNS THEY MUST BE PROTECTING SOMETHING, IN THIS CASE, KARL KORFORD PERHAPS!
YOU-THE SKYMAN! I-IVE HEARD OF YOU! WHAT BRINGS YOU HERE!
A FLIGHT OF BOMBING PLANES OVER THE MASSACHUSETTS BORDER BRINGS ME! WHAT DO YOU KNOW ABOUT THEM, KARL KORFORD?
YOU KNOW ABOUT ME, THEN? THAT SEALS YOUR DEATH WARRANT!
NOT YET MY FRIEND!
THE BURLY KORFORD IS LIKE PUTTY IN THE STEEL GRIP OF THE POWERFUL SKYMAN!
YOU BOYS THAT LIKE TO PLAY ROUGH GIVE ME A LAUGH!
OOOH -- YOU'LL BREAK MY BACK!!

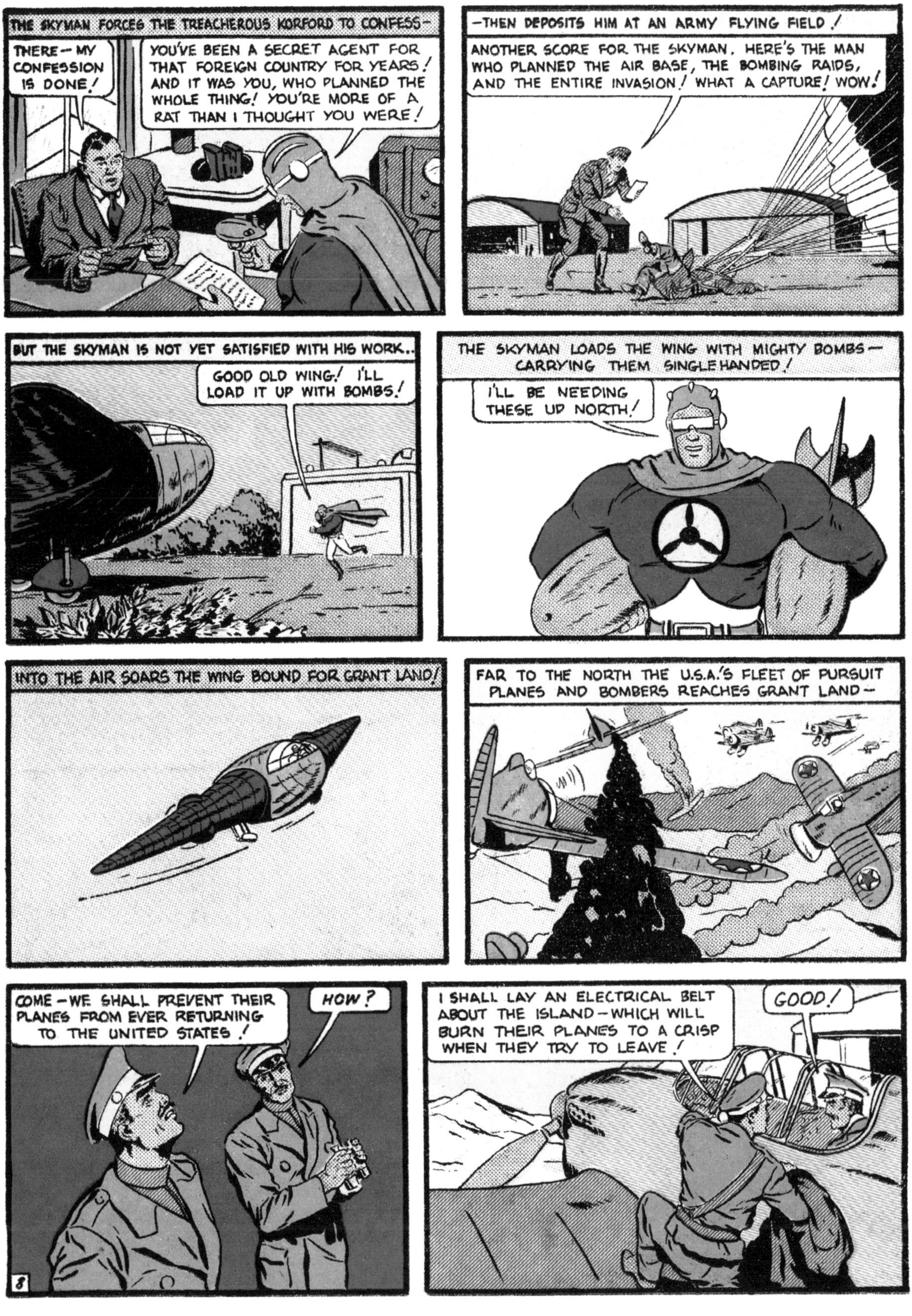
THE SKYMAN FORCES THE TREACHEROUS KORFORD TO CONFESS-
THERE-MY CONFESSION IS DONE!
YOU'VE BEEN A SECRET AGENT FOR THAT FOREIGN COUNTRY FOR YEARS! AND IT WAS YOU, WHO PLANNED THE WHOLE THING! YOU'RE MORE OF A RAT THAN I THOUGHT YOU WERE!
-THEN DEPOSITS HIM AT AN ARMY FLYING FIELD!
ANOTHER SCORE FOR THE SKYMAN. HERE'S THE MAN WHO PLANNED THE AIR BASE, THE BOMBING RAIDS, AND THE ENTIRE INVASION! WHAT A CAPTURE! WOW!
BUT THE SKYMAN IS NOT YET SATISFIED WITH HIS WORK..
GOOD OLD WING! I'LL LOAD IT UP WITH BOMBS!
THE SKYMAN LOADS THE WING WITH MIGHTY BOMBS—CARRYING THEM SINGLE HANDED!
I'LL BE NEEDING THESE UP NORTH!
INTO THE AIR SOARS THE WING BOUND FOR GRANT LAND!
FAR TO THE NORTH THE U.S.A.'S FLEET OF PURSUIT PLANES AND BOMBERS REACHES GRANT LAND—
COME-WE SHALL PREVENT THEIR PLANES FROM EVER RETURNING TO THE UNITED STATES!
HOW?
8
I SHALL LAY AN ELECTRICAL BELT ABOUT THE ISLAND-WHICH WILL BURN THEIR PLANES TO A CRISP WHEN THEY TRY TO LEAVE!
GOOD!

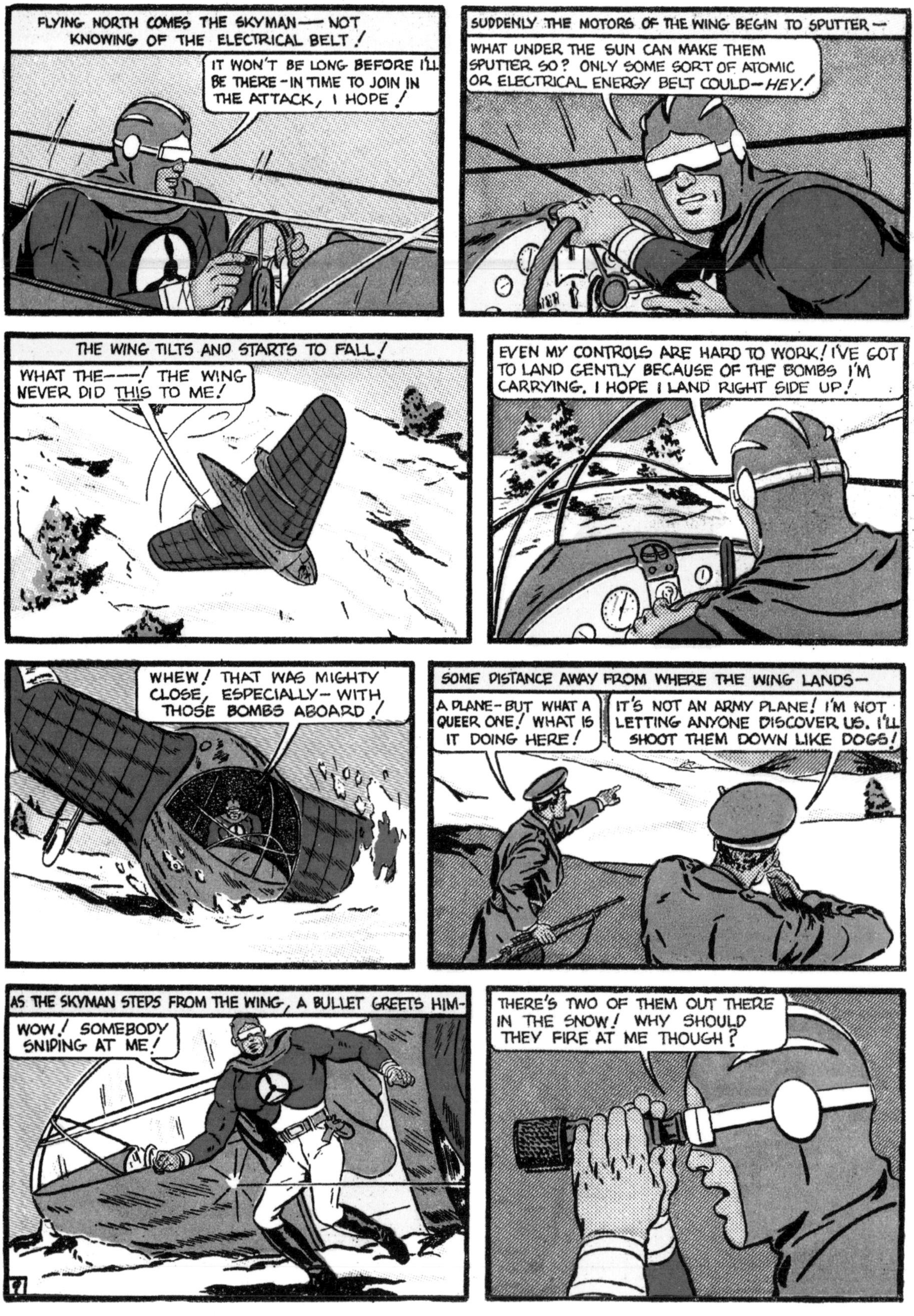
FLYING NORTH COMES THE SKYMAN— NOT KNOWING OF THE ELECTRICAL BELT!
IT WON'T BE LONG BEFORE I'LL BE THERE-IN TIME TO JOIN IN THE ATTACK, I HOPE!
SUDDENLY THE MOTORS OF THE WING BEGIN TO SPUTTER—
WHAT UNDER THE SUN CAN MAKE THEM SPUTTER SO? ONLY SOME SORT OF ATOMIC OR ELECTRICAL ENERGY BELT COULD—HEY!
THE WING TILTS AND STARTS TO FALL!
WHAT THE---! THE WING NEVER DID THIS TO ME!
EVEN MY CONTROLS ARE HARD TO WORK! I'VE GOT TO LAND GENTLY BECAUSE OF THE BOMBS I'M CARRYING. I HOPE I LAND RIGHT SIDE UP!
WHEW! THAT WAS MIGHTY CLOSE, ESPECIALLY- WITH THOSE BOMBS ABOARD!
SOME DISTANCE AWAY FROM WHERE THE WING LANDS—
A PLANE-BUT WHAT A QUEER ONE! WHAT IS IT DOING HERE!
IT'S NOT AN ARMY PLANE! I'M NOT LETTING ANYONE DISCOVER US. I'LL SHOOT THEM DOWN LIKE DOGS!
AS THE SKYMAN STEPS FROM THE WING, A BULLET GREETS HIM-
WOW! SOMEBODY SNIPING AT ME!
9
THERE'S TWO OF THEM OUT THERE IN THE SNOW! WHY SHOULD THEY FIRE AT ME THOUGH?

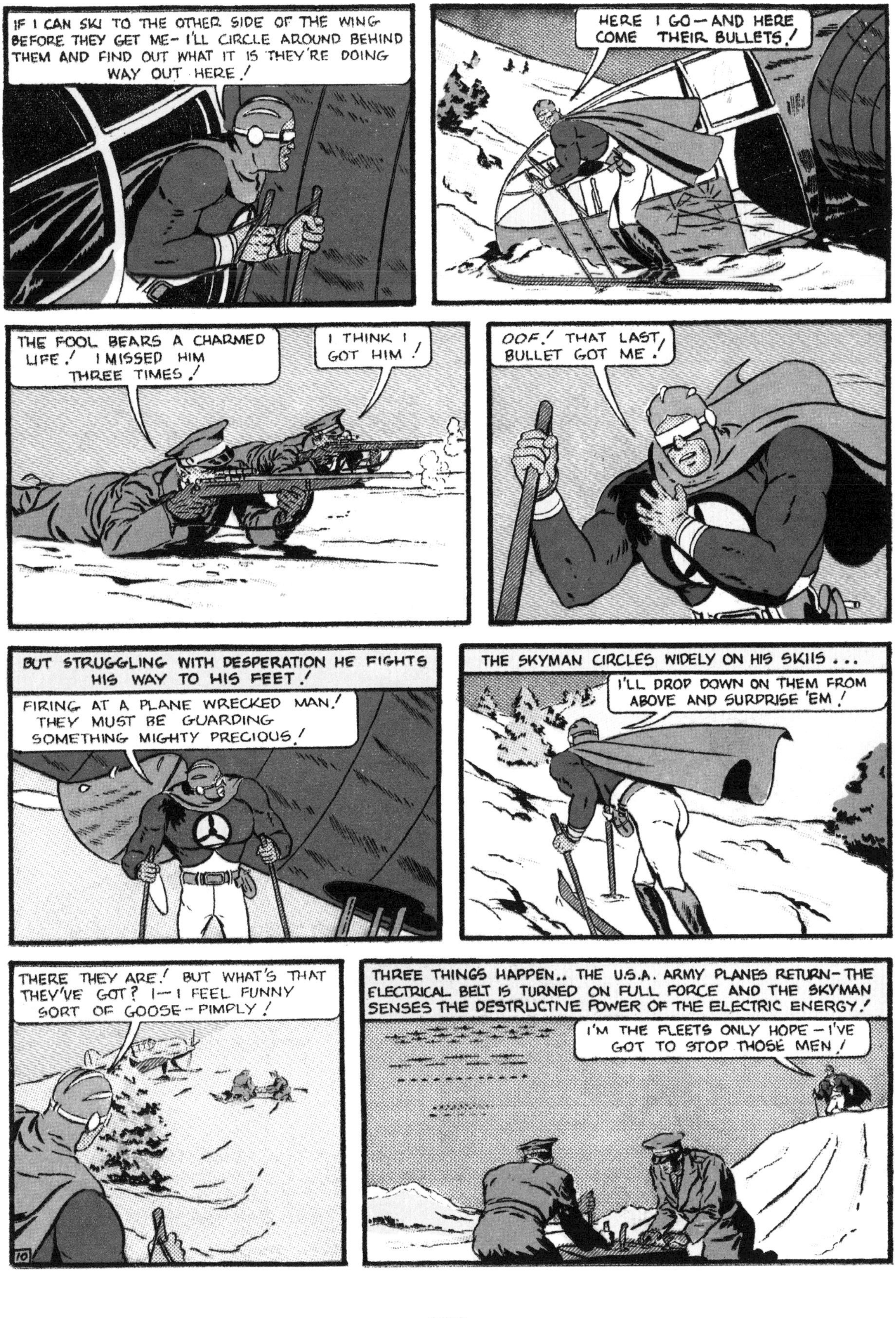
IF I CAN SKI TO THE OTHER SIDE OF THE WING BEFORE THEY GET ME– I'LL CIRCLE AROUND BEHIND THEM AND FIND OUT WHAT IT IS THEY'RE DOING WAY OUT HERE!
HERE I GO—AND HERE COME THEIR BULLETS!
THE FOOL BEARS A CHARMED LIFE! I MISSED HIM THREE TIMES!
I THINK I GOT HIM!
OOF! THAT LAST BULLET GOT ME!
BUT STRUGGLING WITH DESPERATION HE FIGHTS HIS WAY TO HIS FEET!
FIRING AT A PLANE WRECKED MAN! THEY MUST BE GUARDING SOMETHING MIGHTY PRECIOUS!
THE SKYMAN CIRCLES WIDELY ON HIS SKIIS . . .
I'LL DROP DOWN ON THEM FROM ABOVE AND SURPRISE 'EM!
THERE THEY ARE! BUT WHAT'S THAT THEY'VE GOT? I—I FEEL FUNNY SORT OF GOOSE-PIMPLY!
THREE THINGS HAPPEN.. THE U.S.A. ARMY PLANES RETURN—THE ELECTRICAL BELT IS TURNED ON FULL FORCE AND THE SKYMAN SENSES THE DESTRUCTIVE POWER OF THE ELECTRIC ENERGY!
I'M THE FLEETS ONLY HOPE—I'VE GOT TO STOP THOSE MEN!

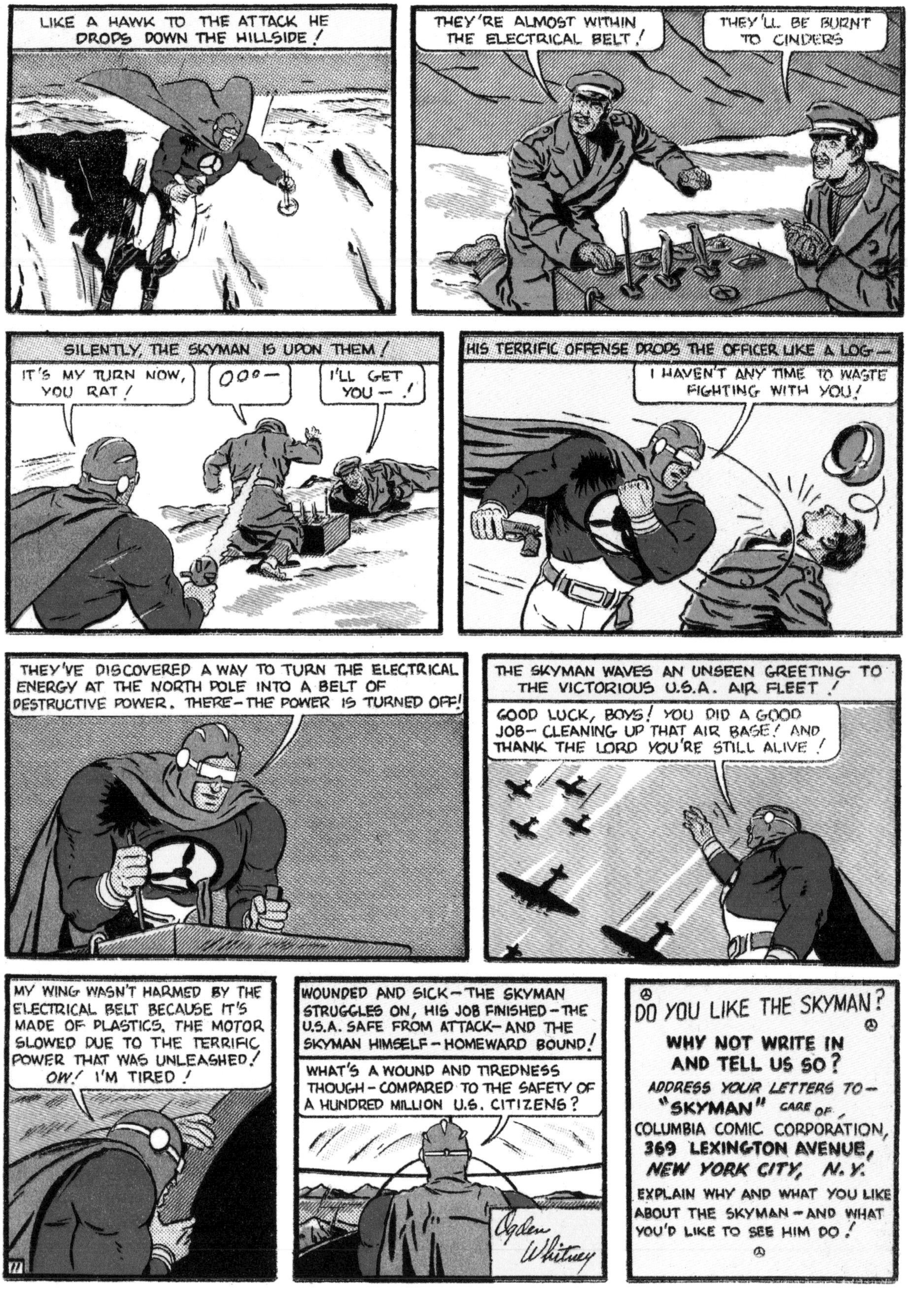
LIKE A HAWK TO THE ATTACK HE DROPS DOWN THE HILLSIDE!
THEY'RE ALMOST WITHIN THE ELECTRICAL BELT!
THEY'LL BE BURNT TO CINDERS
SILENTLY, THE SKYMAN IS UPON THEM!
IT'S MY TURN NOW, YOU RAT!
OOO—
I'LL GET YOU—!
HIS TERRIFIC OFFENSE DROPS THE OFFICER LIKE A LOG—
I HAVEN'T ANY TIME TO WASTE FIGHTING WITH YOU!
THEY'VE DISCOVERED A WAY TO TURN THE ELECTRICAL ENERGY AT THE NORTH POLE INTO A BELT OF DESTRUCTIVE POWER. THERE—THE POWER IS TURNED OFF!
THE SKYMAN WAVES AN UNSEEN GREETING TO THE VICTORIOUS U.S.A. AIR FLEET!
GOOD LUCK, BOYS! YOU DID A GOOD JOB—CLEANING UP THAT AIR BASE! AND THANK THE LORD YOU'RE STILL ALIVE!
MY WING WASN'T HARMED BY THE ELECTRICAL BELT BECAUSE IT'S MADE OF PLASTICS, THE MOTOR SLOWED DUE TO THE TERRIFIC POWER THAT WAS UNLEASHED! OW! I'M TIRED!
WOUNDED AND SICK—THE SKYMAN STRUGGLES ON, HIS JOB FINISHED—THE U.S.A. SAFE FROM ATTACK—AND THE SKYMAN HIMSELF—HOMEWARD BOUND!
WHAT'S A WOUND AND TIREDNESS THOUGH—COMPARED TO THE SAFETY OF A HUNDRED MILLION U.S. CITIZENS?
Ogden Whitney
DO YOU LIKE THE SKYMAN?
WHY NOT WRITE IN AND TELL US SO?
ADDRESS YOUR LETTERS TO—
"SKYMAN" CARE OF
COLUMBIA COMIC CORPORATION,
369 LEXINGTON AVENUE,
NEW YORK CITY, N.Y.
EXPLAIN WHY AND WHAT YOU LIKE ABOUT THE SKYMAN—AND WHAT YOU'D LIKE TO SEE HIM DO!

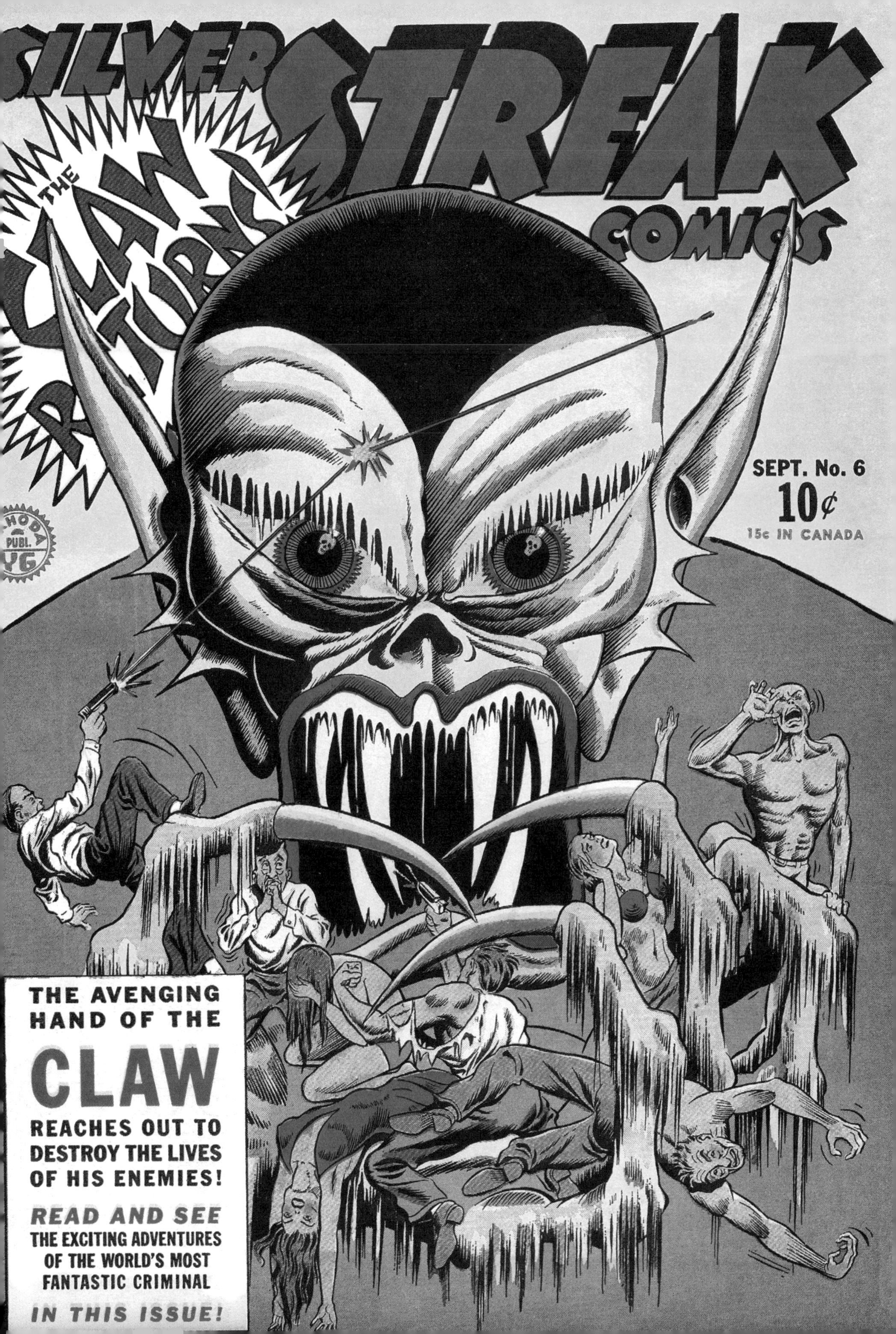
SILVER STREAK COMICS
THE CLAW RETURNS!
SEPT. No. 6
10¢
15c IN CANADA
THE AVENGING HAND OF THE
CLAW
REACHES OUT TO DESTROY THE LIVES OF HIS ENEMIES!
READ AND SEE
THE EXCITING ADVENTURES OF THE WORLD'S MOST FANTASTIC CRIMINAL
IN THIS ISSUE!

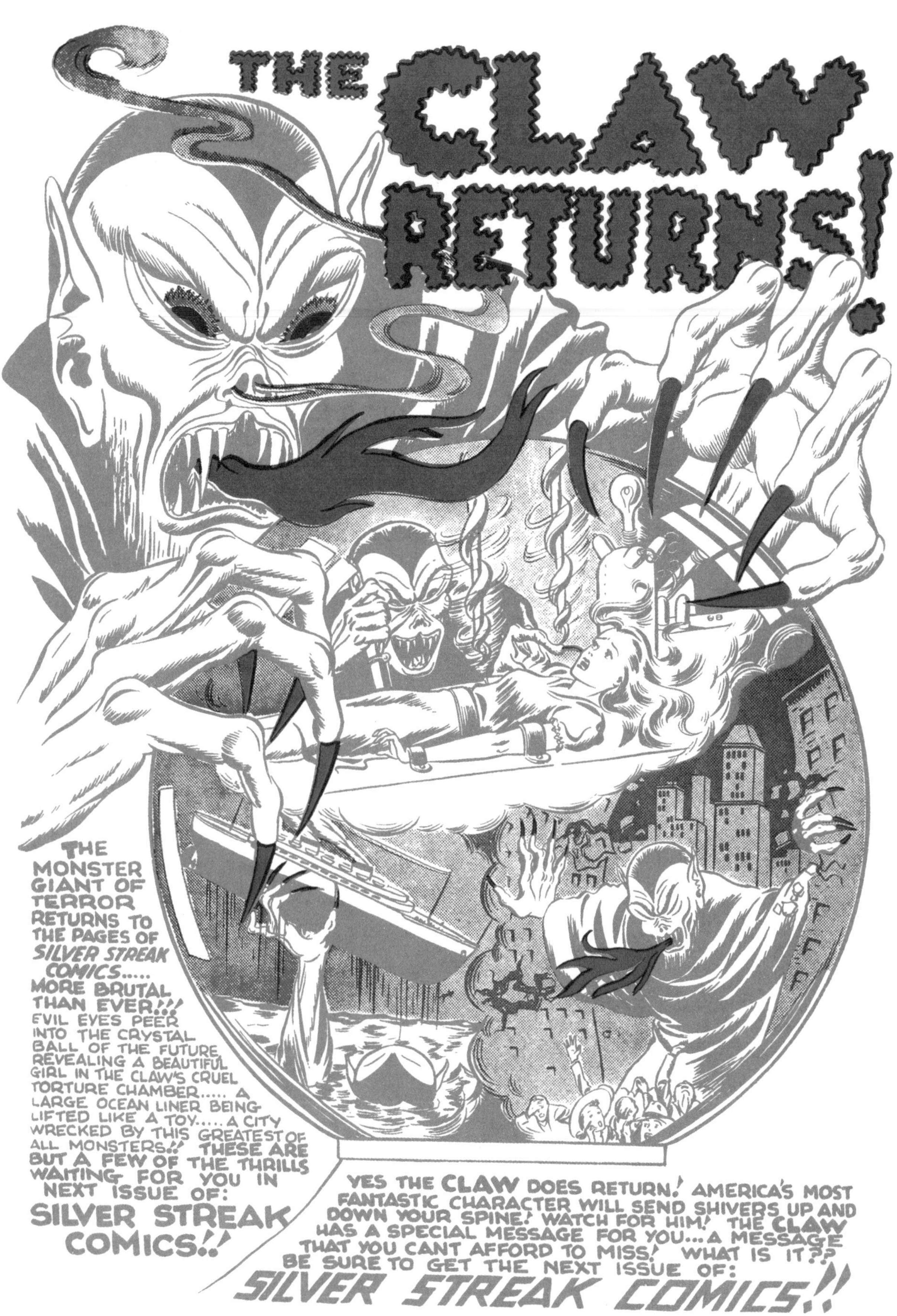

THE CLAW RETURNS!
THE MONSTER GIANT OF TERROR RETURNS TO THE PAGES OF SILVER STREAK COMICS..... MORE BRUTAL THAN EVER!!! EVIL EYES PEER INTO THE CRYSTAL BALL OF THE FUTURE REVEALING A BEAUTIFUL GIRL IN THE CLAW'S CRUEL TORTURE CHAMBER..... A LARGE OCEAN LINER BEING LIFTED LIKE A TOY..... A CITY WRECKED BY THIS GREATEST OF ALL MONSTERS!! THESE ARE BUT A FEW OF THE THRILLS WAITING FOR YOU IN NEXT ISSUE OF: SILVER STREAK COMICS!!
YES THE CLAW DOES RETURN! AMERICA'S MOST FANTASTIC CHARACTER WILL SEND SHIVERS UP AND DOWN YOUR SPINE! WATCH FOR HIM! THE CLAW HAS A SPECIAL MESSAGE FOR YOU... A MESSAGE THAT YOU CANT AFFORD TO MISS! WHAT IS IT?? BE SURE TO GET THE NEXT ISSUE OF:
SILVER STREAK COMICS!!


PRINIED IN U.S.A.

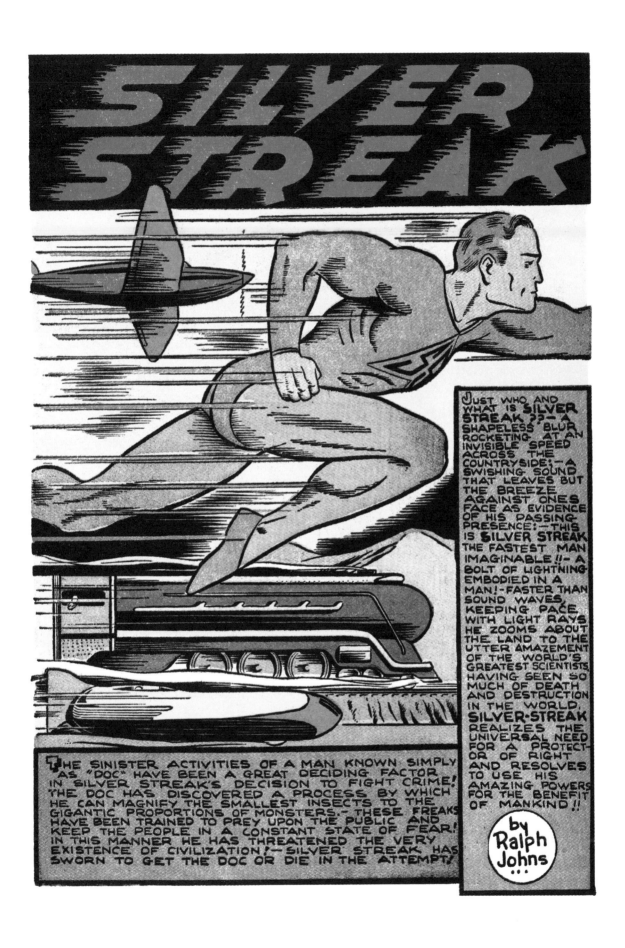

# SILVER STREAK

JUST WHO AND WHAT IS SILVER STREAK ??—A SHAPELESS BLUR ROCKETING AT AN INVISIBLE SPEED ACROSS THE COUNTRYSIDE;—A SWISHING SOUND THAT LEAVES BUT THE BREEZE AGAINST ONES FACE AS EVIDENCE OF HIS PASSING PRESENCE;—THIS IS SILVER STREAK, THE FASTEST MAN IMAGINABLE !!—A BOLT OF LIGHTNING EMBODIED IN A MAN!—FASTER THAN SOUND WAVES, KEEPING PACE WITH LIGHT RAYS HE ZOOMS ABOUT THE LAND TO THE UTTER AMAZEMENT OF THE WORLD'S GREATEST SCIENTISTS, HAVING SEEN SO MUCH OF DEATH AND DESTRUCTION IN THE WORLD SILVER-STREAK REALIZES THE UNIVERSAL NEED FOR A PROTECTOR OF RIGHT AND RESOLVES TO USE HIS AMAZING POWERS FOR THE BENEFIT OF MANKIND !!

THE SINISTER ACTIVITIES OF A MAN KNOWN SIMPLY AS "DOC" HAVE BEEN A GREAT DECIDING FACTOR IN SILVER STREAK'S DECISION TO FIGHT CRIME! THE DOC HAS DISCOVERED A PROCESS BY WHICH HE CAN MAGNIFY THE SMALLEST INSECTS TO THE GIGANTIC PROPORTIONS OF MONSTERS.—THESE FREAKS HAVE BEEN TRAINED TO PREY UPON THE PUBLIC AND KEEP THE PEOPLE IN A CONSTANT STATE OF FEAR! IN THIS MANNER HE HAS THREATENED THE VERY EXISTENCE OF CIVILIZATION!—SILVER STREAK HAS SWORN TO GET THE DOC OR DIE IN THE ATTEMPT!

by Ralph Johns ...

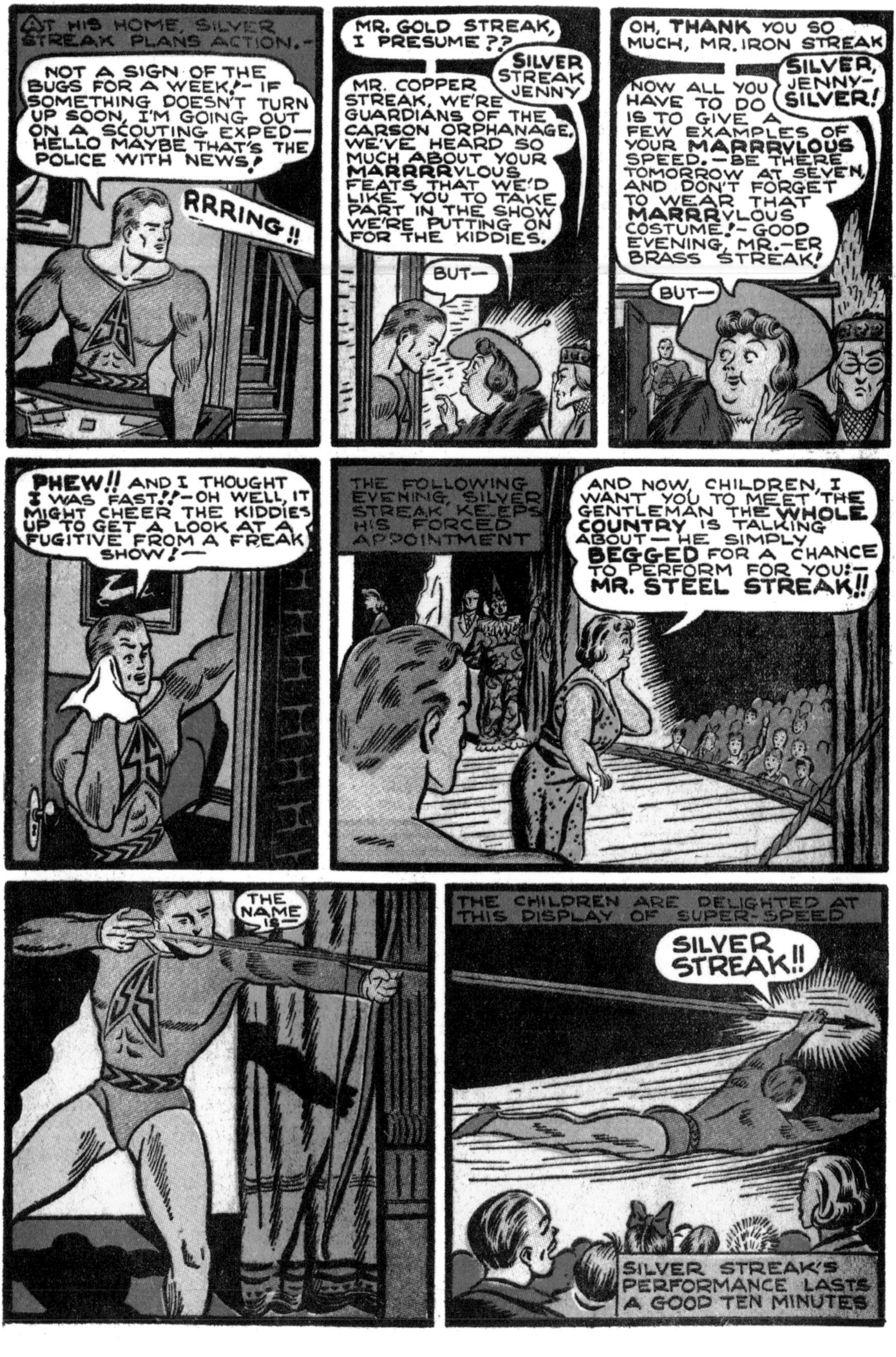
AT HIS HOME, SILVER STREAK PLANS ACTION.—
NOT A SIGN OF THE BUGS FOR A WEEK!—IF SOMETHING DOESN'T TURN UP SOON, I'M GOING OUT ON A SCOUTING EXPED— HELLO MAYBE THAT'S THE POLICE WITH NEWS!
RRRING!!
MR. GOLD STREAK, I PRESUME??
SILVER STREAK JENNY
MR. COPPER STREAK, WE'RE GUARDIANS OF THE CARSON ORPHANAGE. WE'VE HEARD SO MUCH ABOUT YOUR MARRRRVLOUS FEATS THAT WE'D LIKE YOU TO TAKE PART IN THE SHOW WE'RE PUTTING ON FOR THE KIDDIES.
BUT—
OH, THANK YOU SO MUCH, MR. IRON STREAK
SILVER, JENNY— SILVER!
NOW ALL YOU HAVE TO DO IS TO GIVE A FEW EXAMPLES OF YOUR MARRRVLOUS SPEED.—BE THERE TOMORROW AT SEVEN, AND DON'T FORGET TO WEAR THAT MARRRVLOUS COSTUME!—GOOD EVENING, MR.—ER BRASS STREAK!
BUT—
PHEW!! AND I THOUGHT I WAS FAST!!—OH WELL, IT MIGHT CHEER THE KIDDIES UP TO GET A LOOK AT A FUGITIVE FROM A FREAK SHOW!—
THE FOLLOWING EVENING, SILVER STREAK KEEPS HIS FORCED APPOINTMENT
AND NOW, CHILDREN, I WANT YOU TO MEET THE GENTLEMAN THE WHOLE COUNTRY IS TALKING ABOUT—HE SIMPLY BEGGED FOR A CHANCE TO PERFORM FOR YOU!— MR. STEEL STREAK!!
THE NAME IS—
THE CHILDREN ARE DELIGHTED AT THIS DISPLAY OF SUPER-SPEED
SILVER STREAK!!
SILVER STREAK'S PERFORMANCE LASTS A GOOD TEN MINUTES

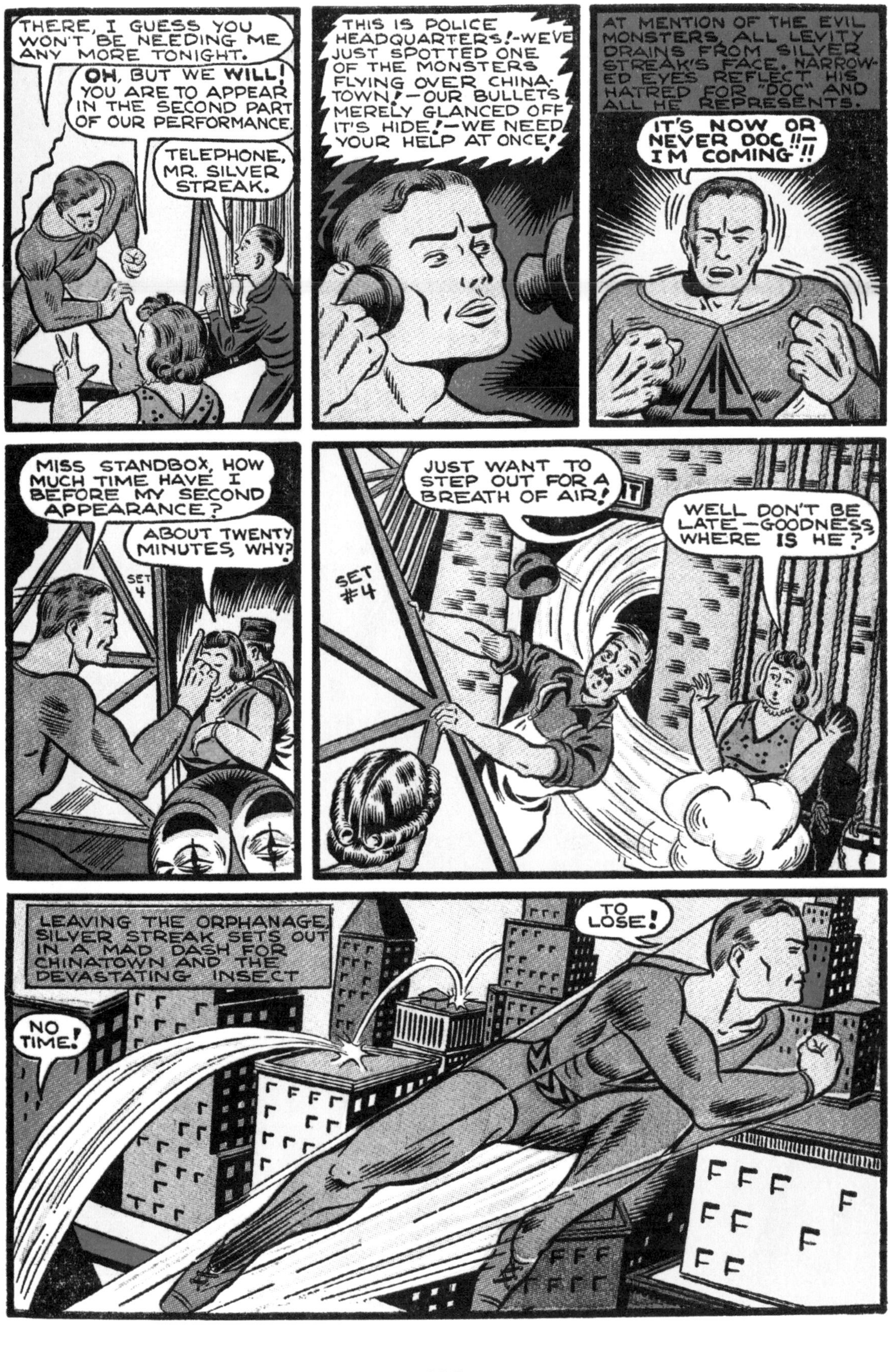
THERE, I GUESS YOU WON'T BE NEEDING ME ANY MORE TONIGHT.
OH, BUT WE WILL! YOU ARE TO APPEAR IN THE SECOND PART OF OUR PERFORMANCE.
TELEPHONE, MR. SILVER STREAK.
THIS IS POLICE HEADQUARTERS!-WE'VE JUST SPOTTED ONE OF THE MONSTERS FLYING OVER CHINA-TOWN!-OUR BULLETS MERELY GLANCED OFF IT'S HIDE!-WE NEED YOUR HELP AT ONCE!
AT MENTION OF THE EVIL MONSTERS, ALL LEVITY DRAINS FROM SILVER STREAK'S FACE. NARROW-ED EYES REFLECT HIS HATRED FOR "DOC" AND ALL HE REPRESENTS.
IT'S NOW OR NEVER DOC!!-I'M COMING!!
MISS STANDBOX, HOW MUCH TIME HAVE I BEFORE MY SECOND APPEARANCE?
ABOUT TWENTY MINUTES, WHY?
SET 4
JUST WANT TO STEP OUT FOR A BREATH OF AIR!
WELL DON'T BE LATE-GOODNESS WHERE IS HE?
SET #4
LEAVING THE ORPHANAGE, SILVER STREAK SETS OUT IN A MAD DASH FOR CHINATOWN AND THE DEVASTATING INSECT
NO TIME!
TO LOSE!

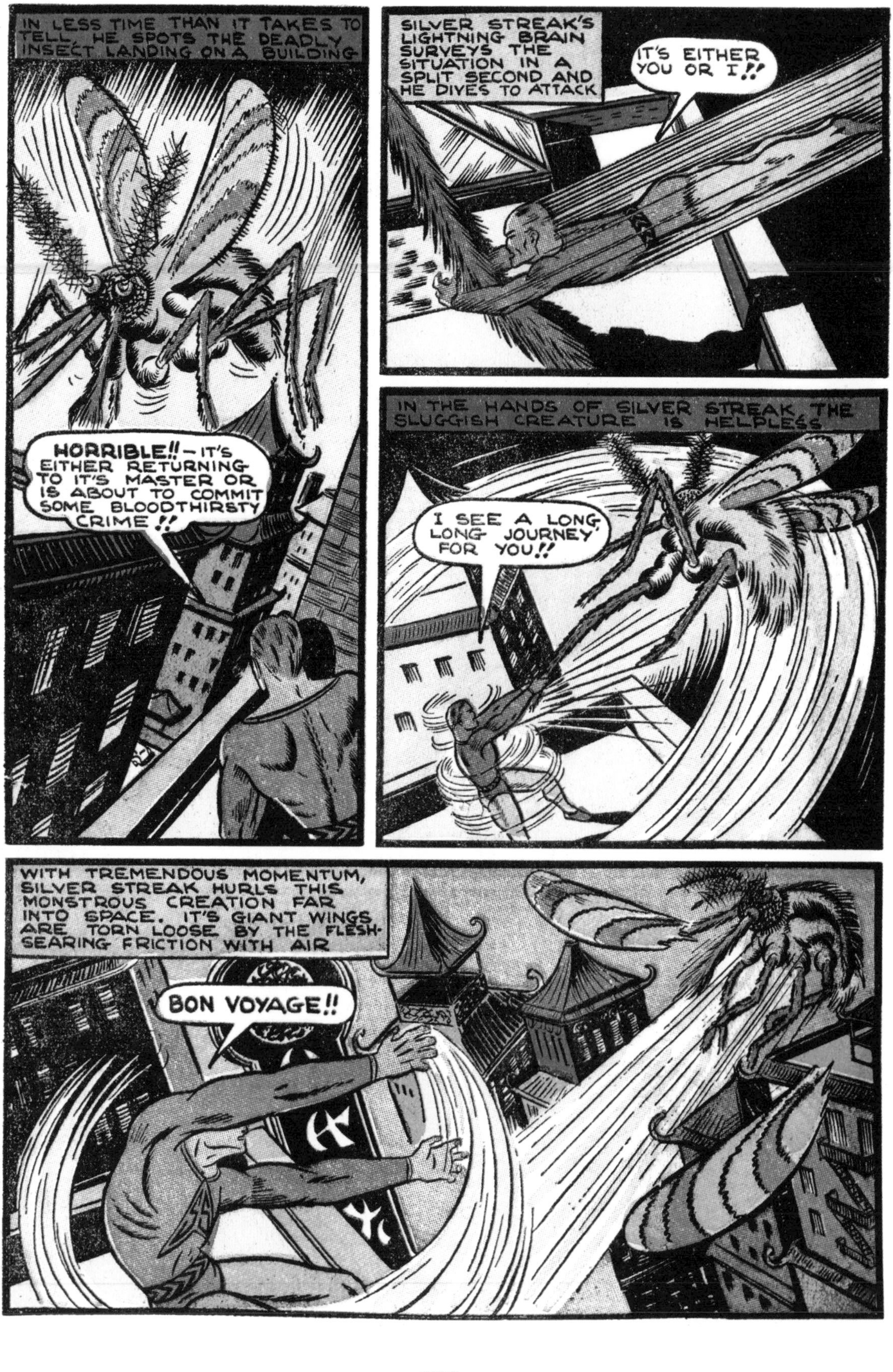
IN LESS TIME THAN IT TAKES TO TELL, HE SPOTS THE DEADLY INSECT LANDING ON A BUILDING
HORRIBLE!! – IT'S EITHER RETURNING TO IT'S MASTER OR IS ABOUT TO COMMIT SOME BLOODTHIRSTY CRIME!!
SILVER STREAK'S LIGHTNING BRAIN SURVEYS THE SITUATION IN A SPLIT SECOND AND HE DIVES TO ATTACK
IT'S EITHER YOU OR I!!
IN THE HANDS OF SILVER STREAK THE SLUGGISH CREATURE IS HELPLESS
I SEE A LONG, LONG JOURNEY FOR YOU!!
WITH TREMENDOUS MOMENTUM, SILVER STREAK HURLS THIS MONSTROUS CREATION FAR INTO SPACE. IT'S GIANT WINGS ARE TORN LOOSE BY THE FLESH-SEARING FRICTION WITH AIR
BON VOYAGE!!

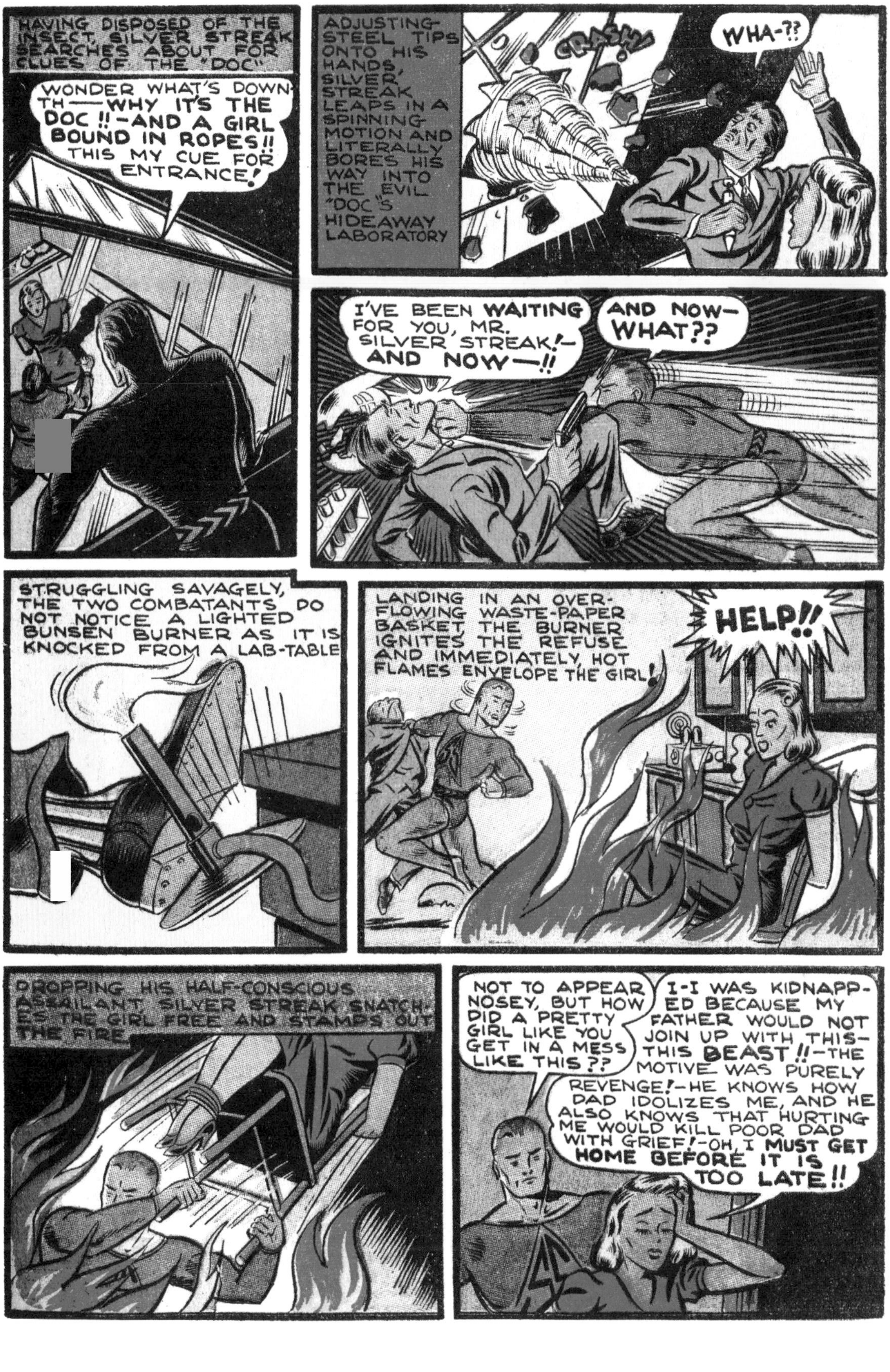
HAVING DISPOSED OF THE INSECT, SILVER STREAK SEARCHES ABOUT FOR CLUES OF THE "DOC"
WONDER WHAT'S DOWN-TH — WHY IT'S THE DOC !! -AND A GIRL BOUND IN ROPES!! THIS MY CUE FOR ENTRANCE!
ADJUSTING STEEL TIPS ONTO HIS HANDS, SILVER STREAK LEAPS IN A SPINNING MOTION AND LITERALLY BORES HIS WAY INTO THE EVIL "DOC'S" HIDEAWAY LABORATORY
CRASH!
WHA-??
I'VE BEEN WAITING FOR YOU, MR. SILVER STREAK!- AND NOW—!!
AND NOW— WHAT??
STRUGGLING SAVAGELY, THE TWO COMBATANTS DO NOT NOTICE A LIGHTED BUNSEN BURNER AS IT IS KNOCKED FROM A LAB-TABLE
LANDING IN AN OVER-FLOWING WASTE-PAPER BASKET, THE BURNER IGNITES THE REFUSE AND IMMEDIATELY, HOT FLAMES ENVELOPE THE GIRL!
HELP!!
DROPPING HIS HALF-CONSCIOUS ASSAILANT, SILVER STREAK SNATCHES THE GIRL FREE AND STAMPS OUT THE FIRE
NOT TO APPEAR NOSEY, BUT HOW DID A PRETTY GIRL LIKE YOU GET IN A MESS LIKE THIS ??
I-I WAS KIDNAPP-ED BECAUSE MY FATHER WOULD NOT JOIN UP WITH THIS- THIS BEAST!!-THE MOTIVE WAS PURELY REVENGE!-HE KNOWS HOW DAD IDOLIZES ME, AND HE ALSO KNOWS THAT HURTING ME WOULD KILL POOR DAD WITH GRIEF!-OH, I MUST GET HOME BEFORE IT IS TOO LATE!!

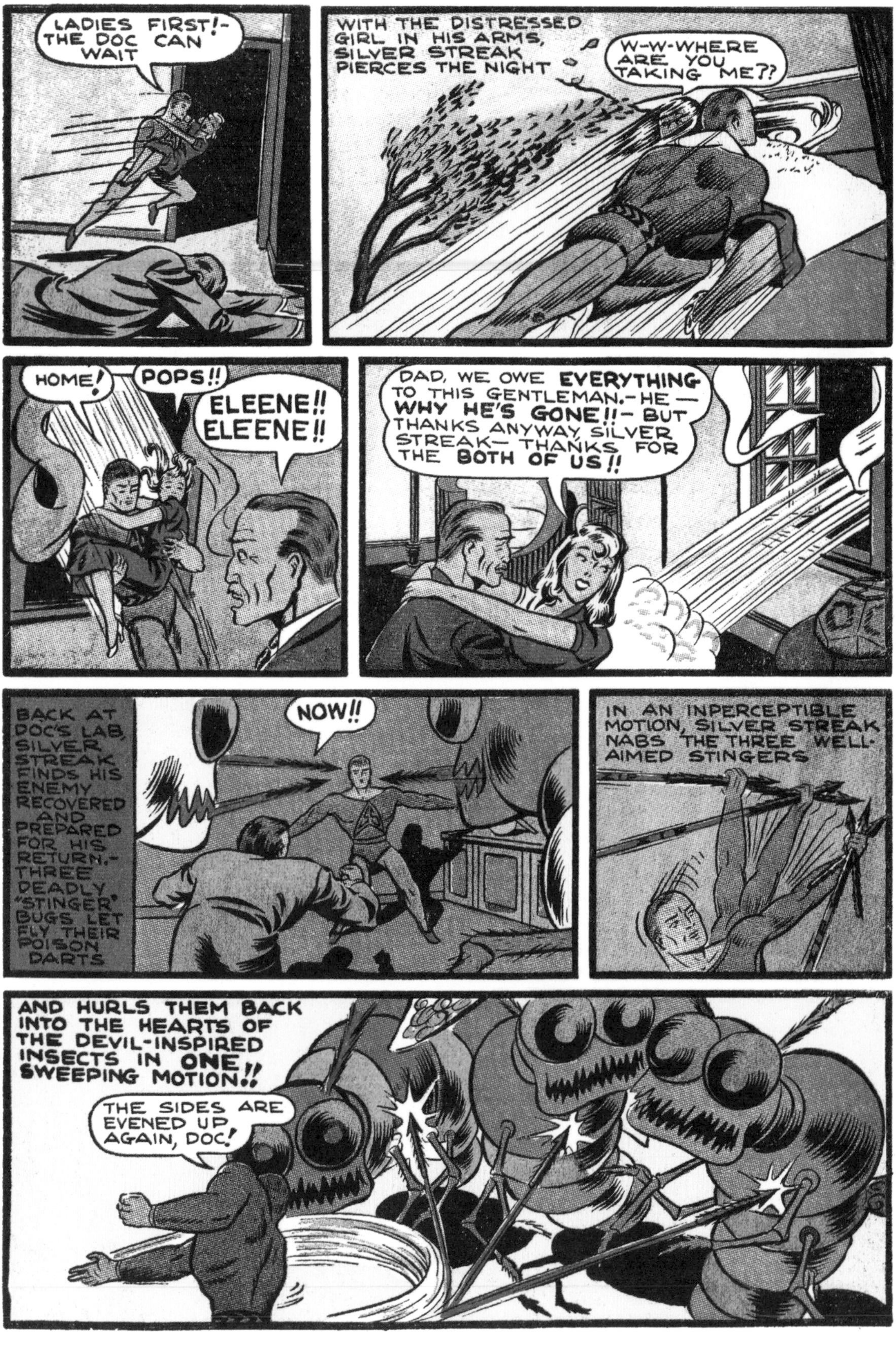
LADIES FIRST!- THE DOC CAN WAIT
WITH THE DISTRESSED GIRL IN HIS ARMS, SILVER STREAK PIERCES THE NIGHT
W-W-WHERE ARE YOU TAKING ME??
HOME!
POPS!!
ELEENE!! ELEENE!!
DAD, WE OWE EVERYTHING TO THIS GENTLEMAN.-HE — WHY HE'S GONE!!- BUT THANKS ANYWAY SILVER STREAK- THANKS FOR THE BOTH OF US!!
BACK AT DOC'S LAB, SILVER STREAK FINDS HIS ENEMY RECOVERED AND PREPARED FOR HIS RETURN.- THREE DEADLY "STINGER" BUGS LET FLY THEIR POISON DARTS
NOW!!
IN AN INPERCEPTIBLE MOTION, SILVER STREAK NABS THE THREE WELL-AIMED STINGERS
ZIP
AND HURLS THEM BACK INTO THE HEARTS OF THE DEVIL-INSPIRED INSECTS IN ONE SWEEPING MOTION!!
THE SIDES ARE EVENED UP AGAIN, DOC!

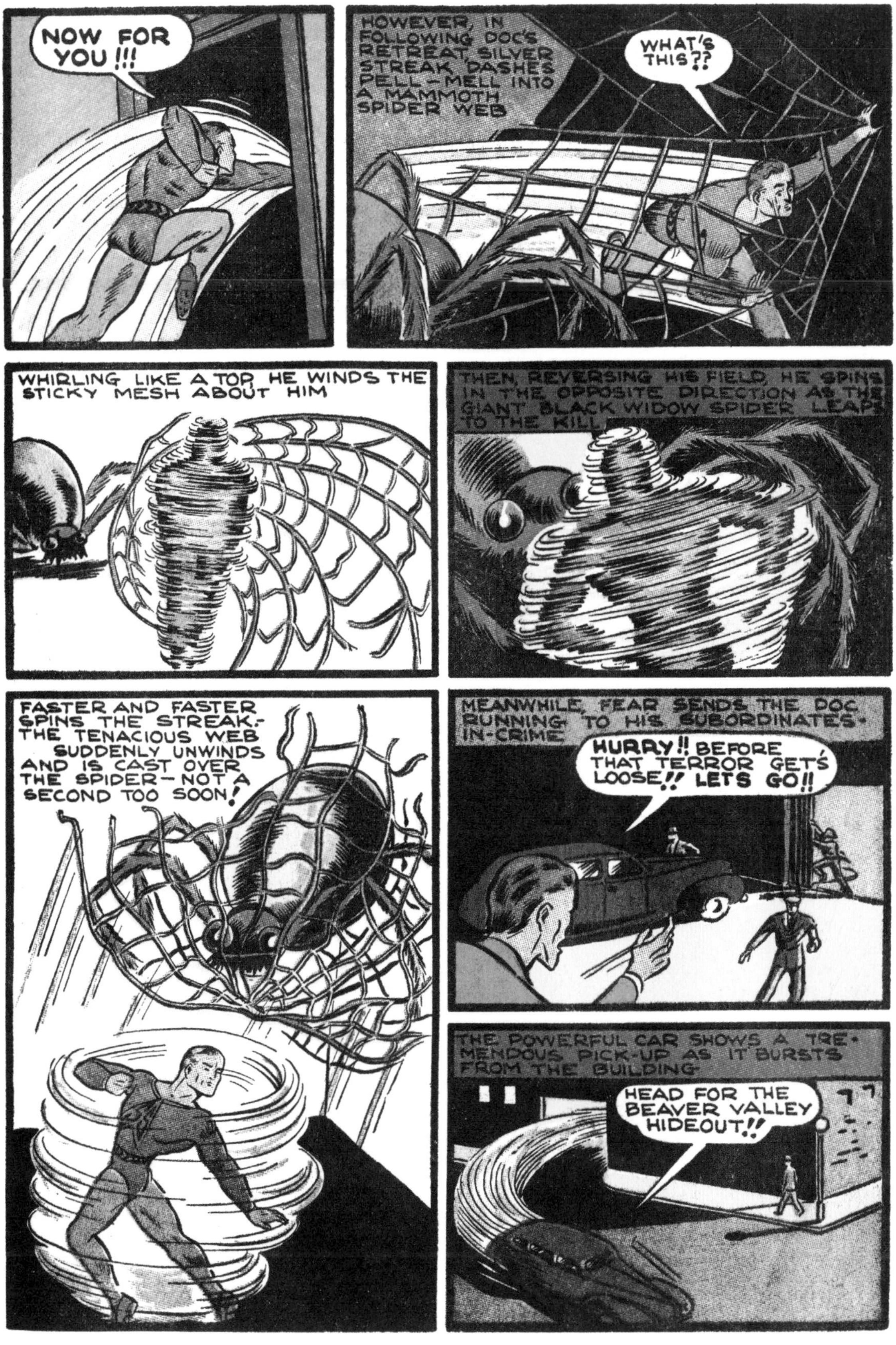
NOW FOR YOU!!!
HOWEVER, IN FOLLOWING DOC'S RETREAT SILVER STREAK DASHES PELL-MELL INTO A MAMMOTH SPIDER WEB
WHAT'S THIS??
WHIRLING LIKE A TOP HE WINDS THE STICKY MESH ABOUT HIM
THEN, REVERSING HIS FIELD, HE SPINS IN THE OPPOSITE DIRECTION AS THE GIANT BLACK WIDOW SPIDER LEAPS TO THE KILL
FASTER AND FASTER SPINS THE STREAK.- THE TENACIOUS WEB SUDDENLY UNWINDS AND IS CAST OVER THE SPIDER-NOT A SECOND TOO SOON!
MEANWHILE, FEAR SENDS THE DOC RUNNING TO HIS SUBORDINATES-IN-CRIME
HURRY!! BEFORE THAT TERROR GETS LOOSE!! LETS GO!!
THE POWERFUL CAR SHOWS A TRE-MENDOUS PICK-UP AS IT BURSTS FROM THE BUILDING
HEAD FOR THE BEAVER VALLEY HIDEOUT!!

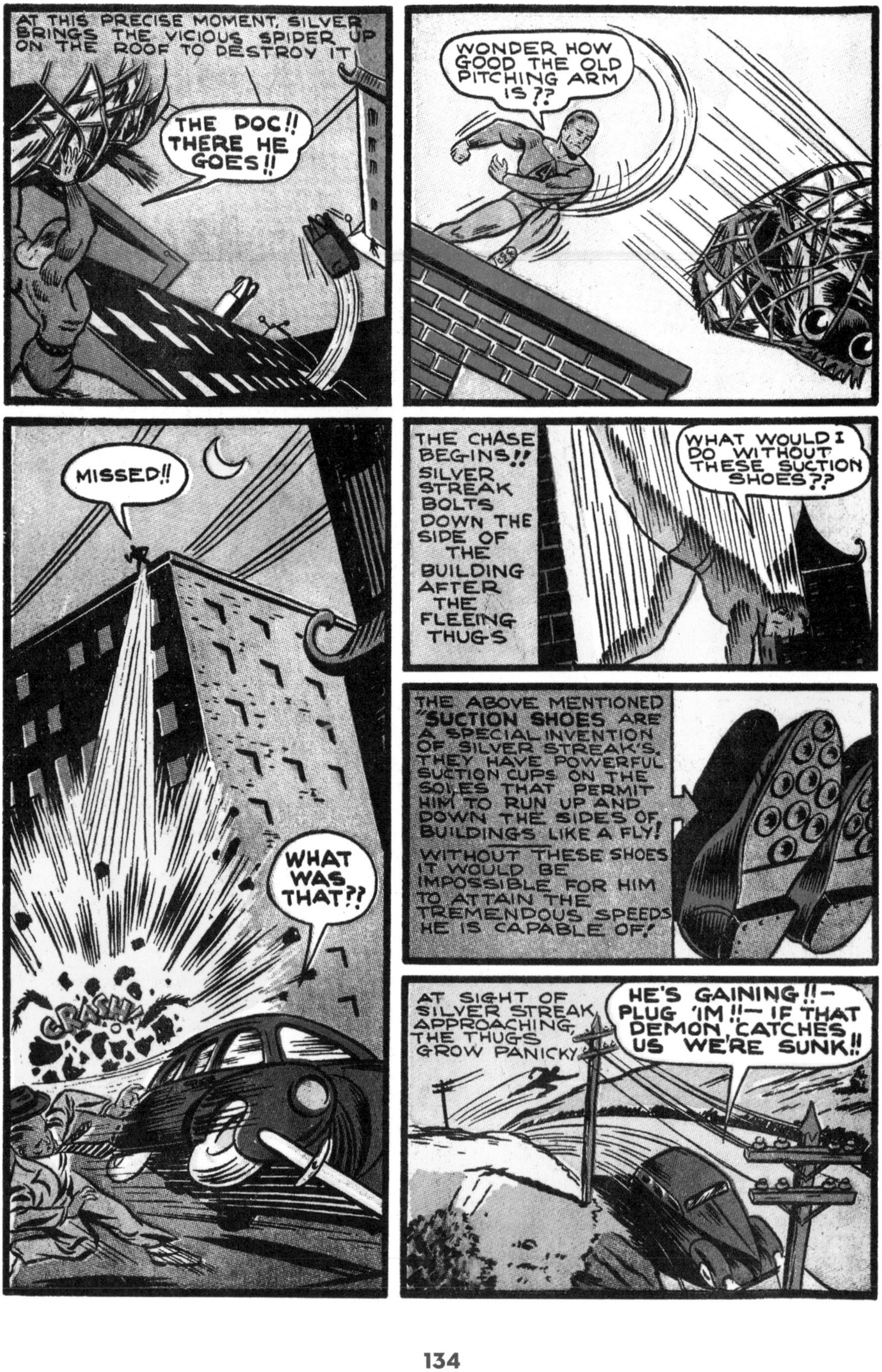
AT THIS PRECISE MOMENT, SILVER BRINGS THE VICIOUS SPIDER UP ON THE ROOF TO DESTROY IT
THE DOC!! THERE HE GOES!!
WONDER HOW GOOD THE OLD PITCHING ARM IS??
MISSED!!
WHAT WAS THAT??
CRASH
THE CHASE BEGINS!! SILVER STREAK BOLTS DOWN THE SIDE OF THE BUILDING AFTER THE FLEEING THUGS
WHAT WOULD I DO WITHOUT THESE SUCTION SHOES??
THE ABOVE MENTIONED "SUCTION SHOES ARE A SPECIAL INVENTION OF SILVER STREAK'S. THEY HAVE POWERFUL SUCTION CUPS ON THE SOLES THAT PERMIT HIM TO RUN UP AND DOWN THE SIDES OF BUILDINGS LIKE A FLY!
WITHOUT THESE SHOES IT WOULD BE IMPOSSIBLE FOR HIM TO ATTAIN THE TREMENDOUS SPEEDS HE IS CAPABLE OF!
AT SIGHT OF SILVER STREAK APPROACHING, THE THUGS GROW PANICKY
HE'S GAINING!!— PLUG 'IM!!— IF THAT DEMON CATCHES US WE'RE SUNK!!

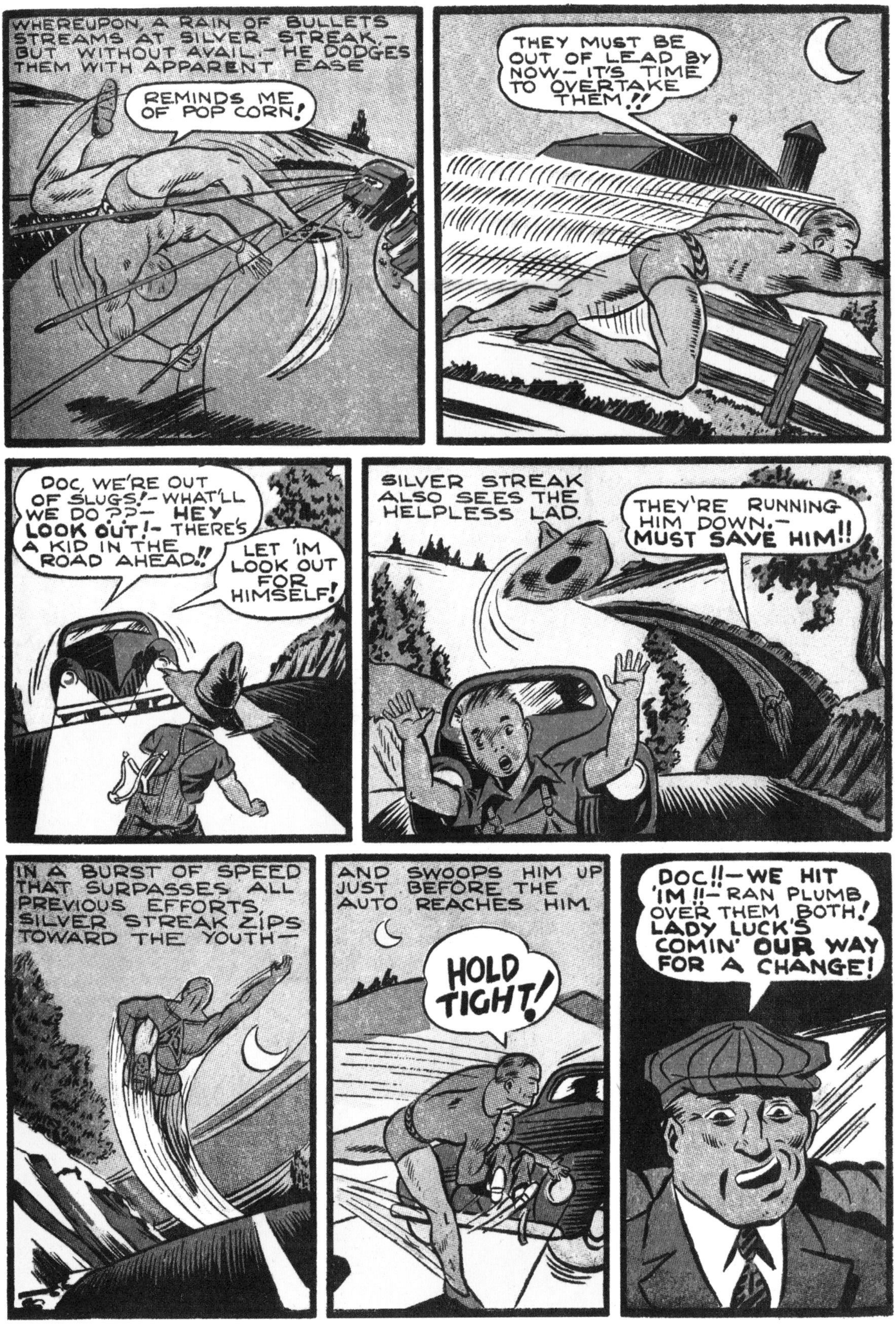
WHEREUPON, A RAIN OF BULLETS STREAMS AT SILVER STREAK,— BUT WITHOUT AVAIL,—HE DODGES THEM WITH APPARENT EASE
REMINDS ME OF POP CORN!
THEY MUST BE OUT OF LEAD BY NOW— IT'S TIME TO OVERTAKE THEM!!
DOC, WE'RE OUT OF SLUGS!—WHAT'LL WE DO??— HEY LOOK OUT!— THERE'S A KID IN THE ROAD AHEAD!!
LET 'IM LOOK OUT FOR HIMSELF!
SILVER STREAK ALSO SEES THE HELPLESS LAD.
THEY'RE RUNNING HIM DOWN.— MUST SAVE HIM!!
IN A BURST OF SPEED THAT SURPASSES ALL PREVIOUS EFFORTS, SILVER STREAK ZIPS TOWARD THE YOUTH—
AND SWOOPS HIM UP JUST BEFORE THE AUTO REACHES HIM.
HOLD TIGHT!
DOC!!—WE HIT 'IM!!—RAN PLUMB OVER THEM BOTH! LADY LUCK'S COMIN' OUR WAY FOR A CHANGE!

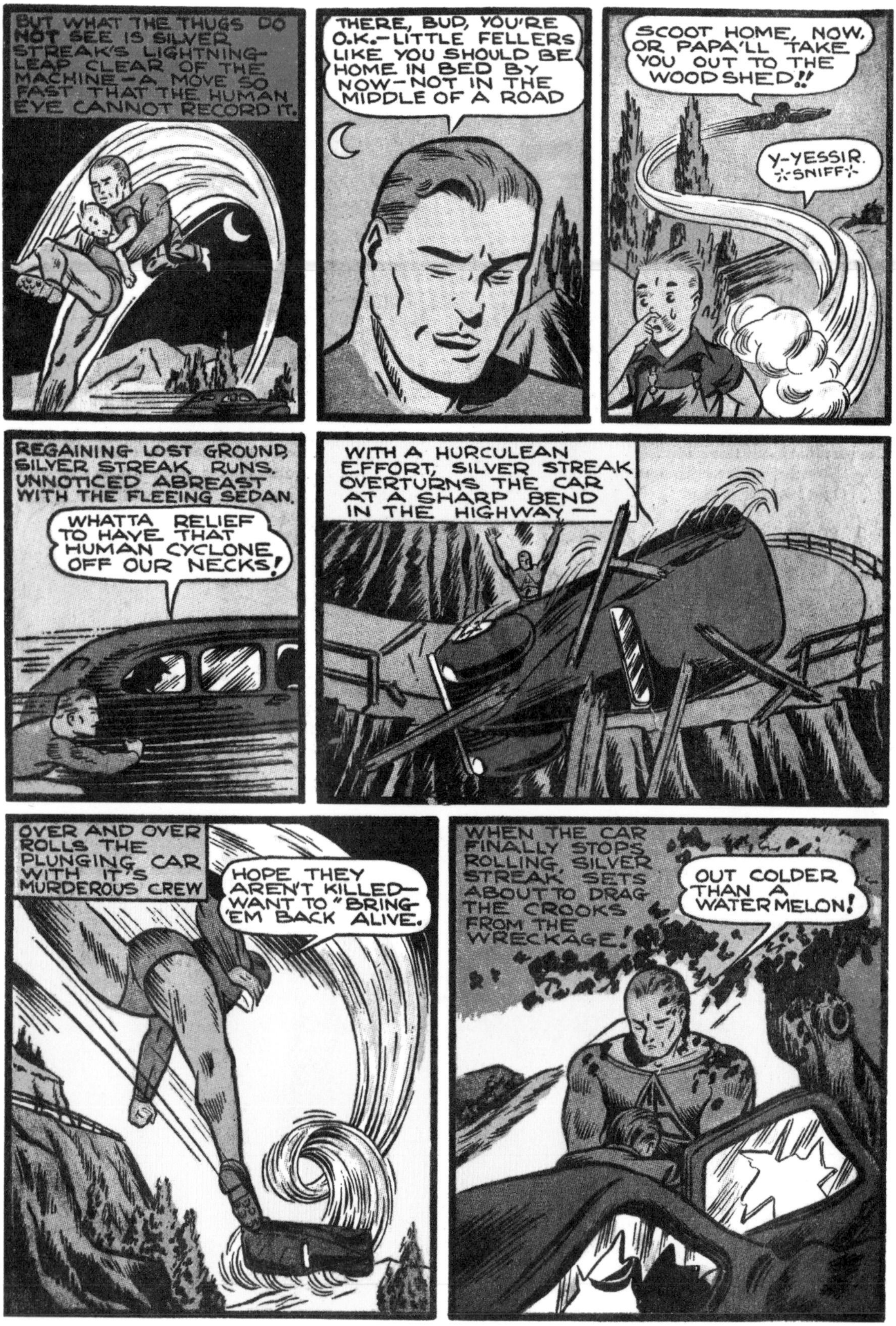
BUT WHAT THE THUGS DO NOT SEE IS SILVER STREAK'S LIGHTNING-LEAP CLEAR OF THE MACHINE—A MOVE SO FAST THAT THE HUMAN EYE CANNOT RECORD IT.
THERE, BUD, YOU'RE O.K.—LITTLE FELLERS LIKE YOU SHOULD BE HOME IN BED BY NOW—NOT IN THE MIDDLE OF A ROAD
SCOOT HOME, NOW, OR PAPA'LL TAKE YOU OUT TO THE WOODSHED!!
Y-YESSIR. *SNIFF*
REGAINING LOST GROUND, SILVER STREAK RUNS, UNNOTICED ABREAST WITH THE FLEEING SEDAN.
WHATTA RELIEF TO HAVE THAT HUMAN CYCLONE OFF OUR NECKS!
WITH A HURCULEAN EFFORT, SILVER STREAK OVERTURNS THE CAR AT A SHARP BEND IN THE HIGHWAY—
OVER AND OVER ROLLS THE PLUNGING CAR WITH IT'S MURDEROUS CREW
HOPE THEY AREN'T KILLED—WANT TO "BRING 'EM BACK ALIVE.
WHEN THE CAR FINALLY STOPS ROLLING, SILVER STREAK SETS ABOUT TO DRAG THE CROOKS FROM THE WRECKAGE!
OUT COLDER THAN A WATERMELON!

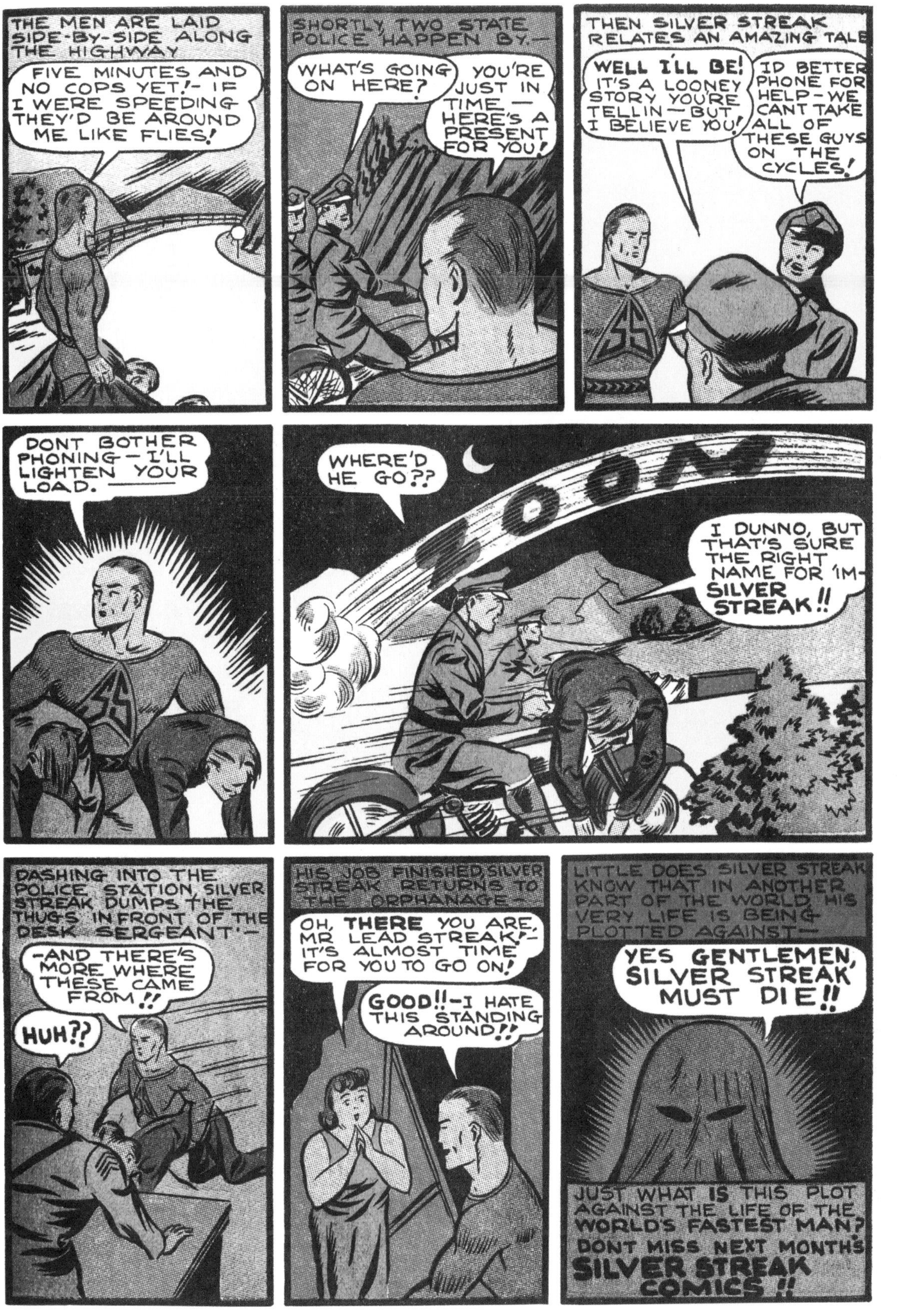
THE MEN ARE LAID SIDE-BY-SIDE ALONG THE HIGHWAY
FIVE MINUTES AND NO COPS YET!- IF I WERE SPEEDING THEY'D BE AROUND ME LIKE FLIES!
SHORTLY TWO STATE POLICE HAPPEN BY.-
WHAT'S GOING ON HERE?
YOU'RE JUST IN TIME — HERE'S A PRESENT FOR YOU!
THEN SILVER STREAK RELATES AN AMAZING TALE
WELL I'LL BE! IT'S A LOONEY STORY YOU'RE TELLIN — BUT, I BELIEVE YOU!
ID BETTER PHONE FOR HELP - WE CANT TAKE ALL OF THESE GUYS ON THE CYCLES!
DONT BOTHER PHONING - I'LL LIGHTEN YOUR LOAD.
WHERE'D HE GO??
ZOOM
I DUNNO, BUT THAT'S SURE THE RIGHT NAME FOR 'IM- SILVER STREAK!!
DASHING INTO THE POLICE STATION, SILVER STREAK DUMPS THE THUGS IN FRONT OF THE DESK SERGEANT'-
-AND THERE'S MORE WHERE THESE CAME FROM!!
HUH??
HIS JOB FINISHED SILVER STREAK RETURNS TO THE ORPHANAGE-
OH, THERE YOU ARE, MR LEAD STREAK!- IT'S ALMOST TIME FOR YOU TO GO ON!
GOOD!!-I HATE THIS STANDING AROUND!!
LITTLE DOES SILVER STREAK KNOW THAT IN ANOTHER PART OF THE WORLD HIS VERY LIFE IS BEING PLOTTED AGAINST—
YES GENTLEMEN, SILVER STREAK MUST DIE!!
JUST WHAT IS THIS PLOT AGAINST THE LIFE OF THE WORLD'S FASTEST MAN? DONT MISS NEXT MONTH'S SILVER STREAK COMICS!!

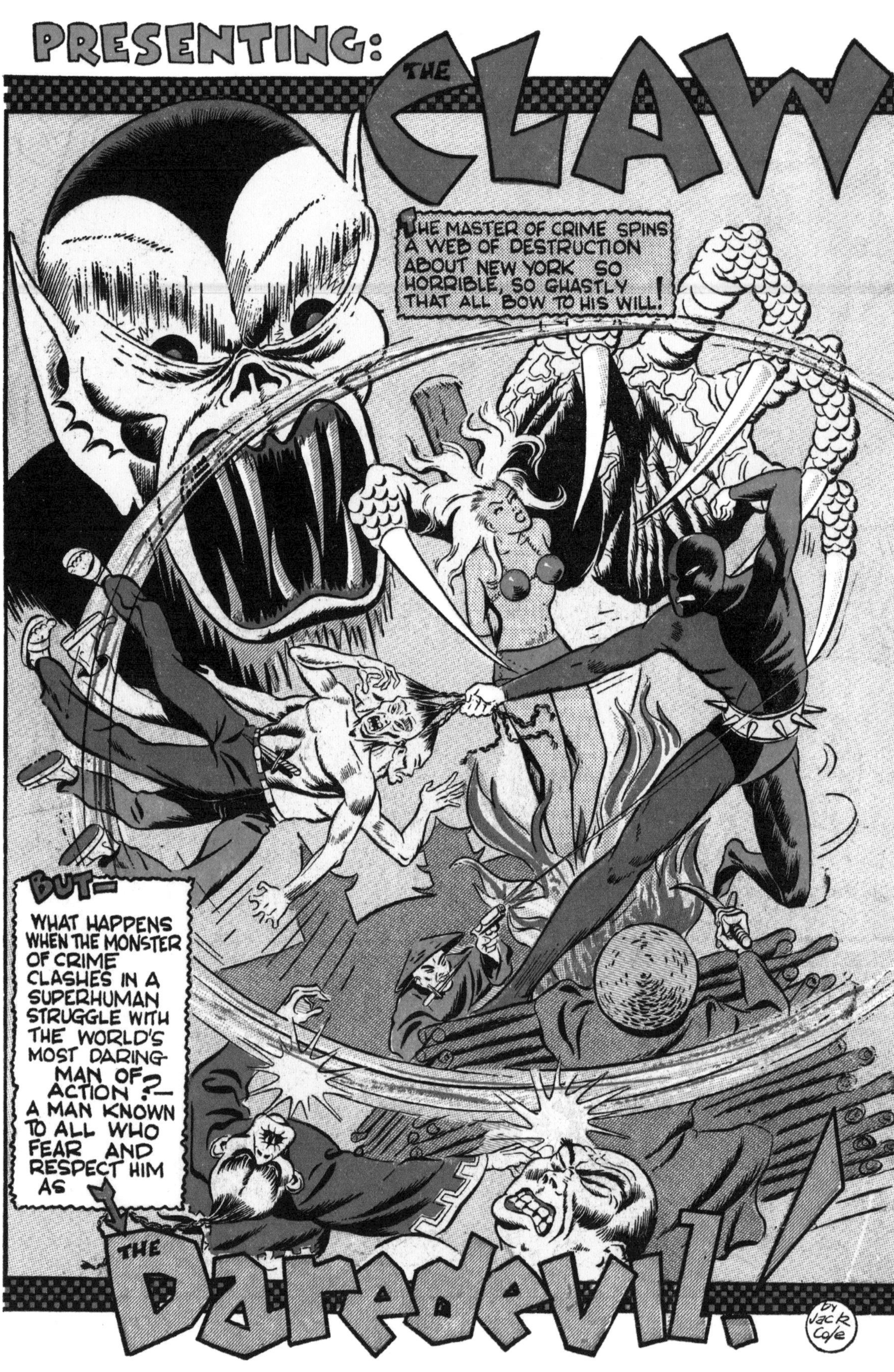
PRESENTING: THE CLAW
THE MASTER OF CRIME SPINS A WEB OF DESTRUCTION ABOUT NEW YORK SO HORRIBLE, SO GHASTLY THAT ALL BOW TO HIS WILL!
BUT— WHAT HAPPENS WHEN THE MONSTER OF CRIME CLASHES IN A SUPERHUMAN STRUGGLE WITH THE WORLD'S MOST DARING MAN OF ACTION?— A MAN KNOWN TO ALL WHO FEAR AND RESPECT HIM AS
THE DAREDEVIL!
BY JACK COLE

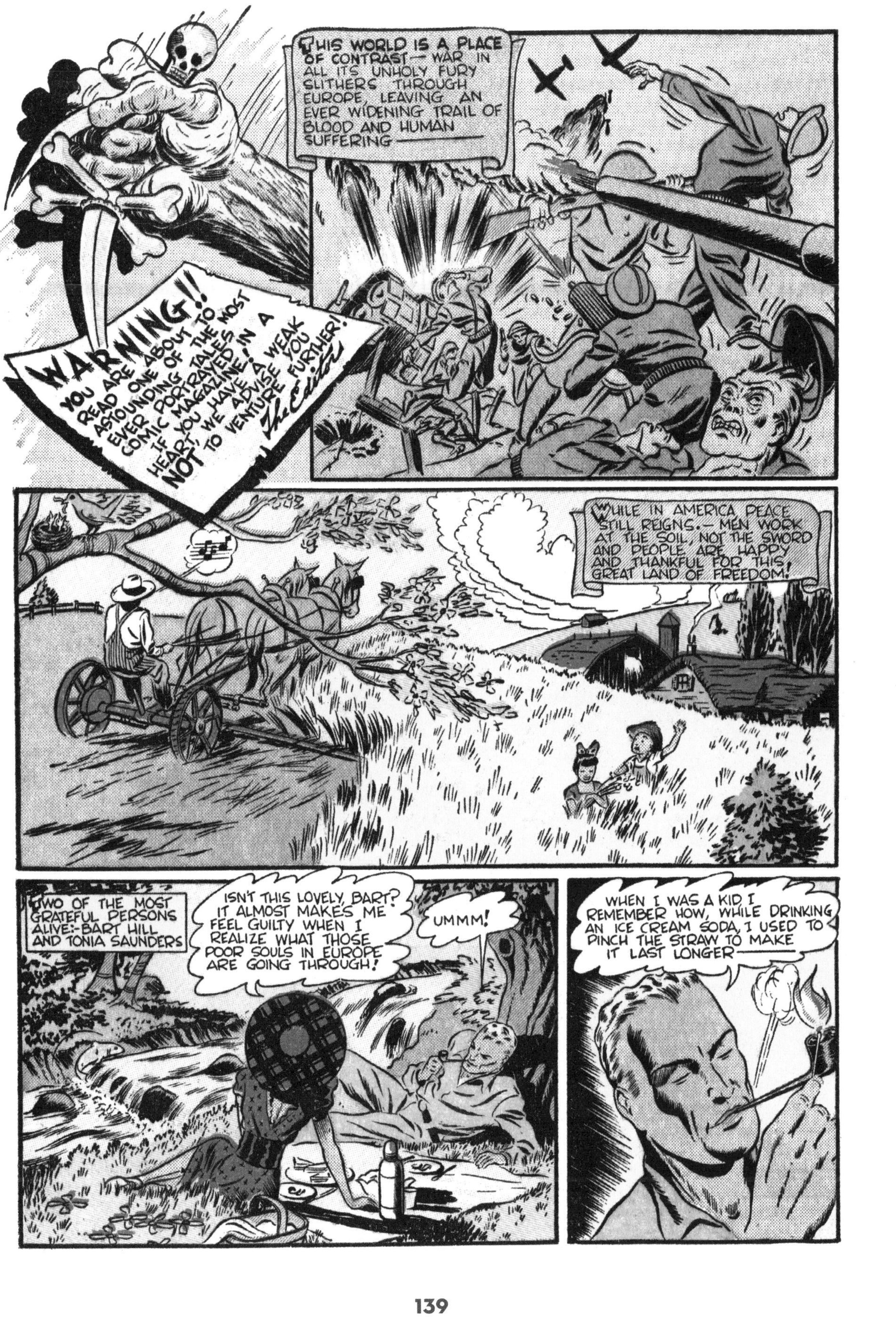
THIS WORLD IS A PLACE OF CONTRAST — WAR IN ALL ITS UNHOLY FURY SLITHERS THROUGH EUROPE, LEAVING AN EVER WIDENING TRAIL OF BLOOD AND HUMAN SUFFERING ——
WARNING!!
YOU ARE ABOUT TO READ ONE OF THE MOST ASTOUNDING TALES EVER PORTRAYED IN A COMIC MAGAZINE! IF YOU HAVE A WEAK HEART, WE ADVISE YOU NOT TO VENTURE FURTHER!
The Editor
WHILE IN AMERICA PEACE STILL REIGNS. — MEN WORK AT THE SOIL, NOT THE SWORD AND PEOPLE ARE HAPPY AND THANKFUL FOR THIS GREAT LAND OF FREEDOM!
TWO OF THE MOST GRATEFUL PERSONS ALIVE:- BART HILL AND TONIA SAUNDERS
ISN'T THIS LOVELY, BART? IT ALMOST MAKES ME FEEL GUILTY WHEN I REALIZE WHAT THOSE POOR SOULS IN EUROPE ARE GOING THROUGH!
UMMM!
WHEN I WAS A KID I REMEMBER HOW, WHILE DRINKING AN ICE CREAM SODA, I USED TO PINCH THE STRAW TO MAKE IT LAST LONGER ——

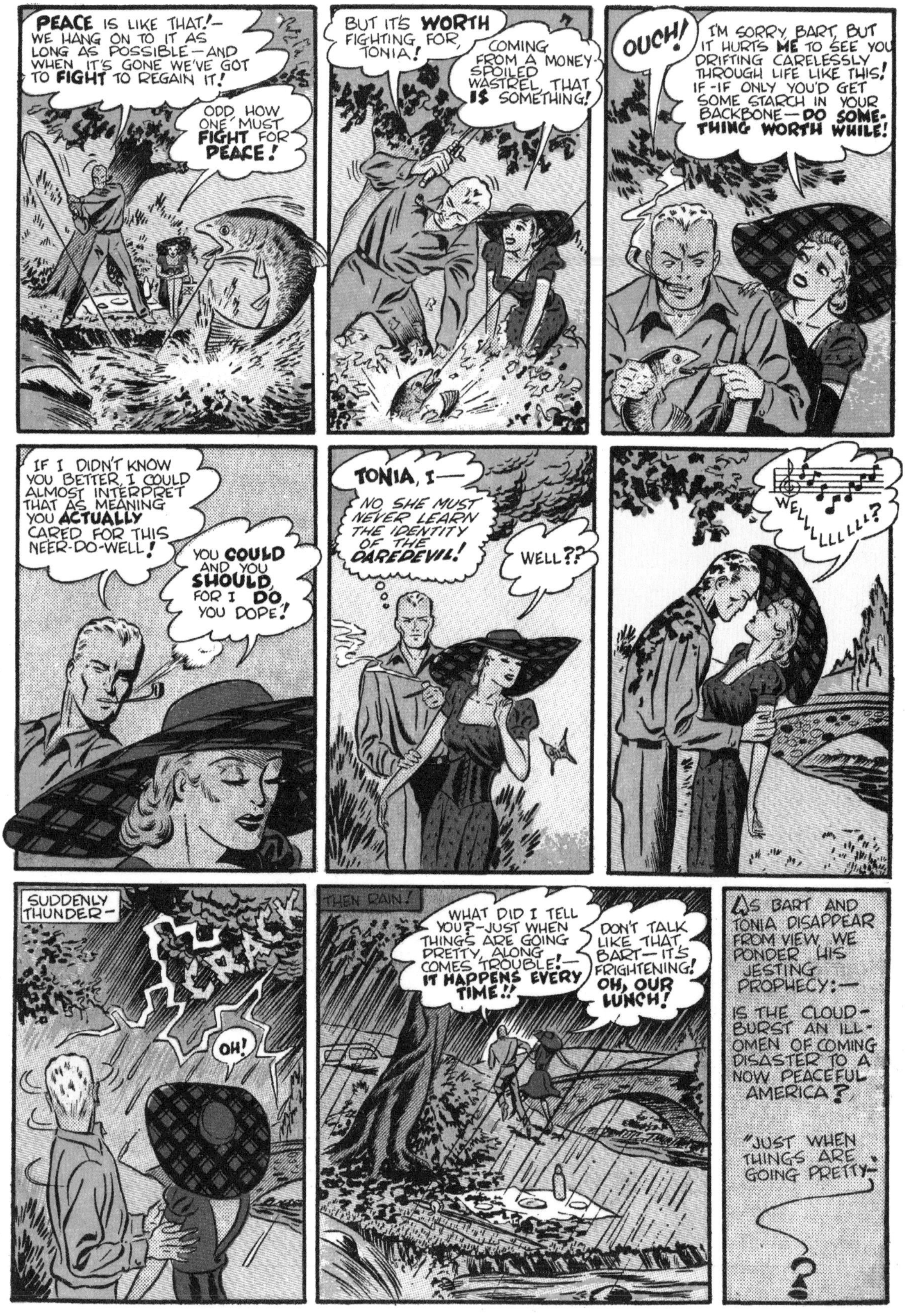
PEACE IS LIKE THAT!— WE HANG ON TO IT AS LONG AS POSSIBLE—AND WHEN IT'S GONE WE'VE GOT TO FIGHT TO REGAIN IT!
ODD HOW ONE MUST FIGHT FOR PEACE!
BUT IT'S WORTH FIGHTING FOR, TONIA!
COMING FROM A MONEY-SPOILED WASTREL, THAT IS SOMETHING!
OUCH!
I'M SORRY, BART, BUT IT HURTS ME TO SEE YOU DRIFTING CARELESSLY THROUGH LIFE LIKE THIS! IF-IF ONLY YOU'D GET SOME STARCH IN YOUR BACKBONE—DO SOMETHING WORTH WHILE!
IF I DIDN'T KNOW YOU BETTER, I COULD ALMOST INTERPRET THAT AS MEANING YOU ACTUALLY CARED FOR THIS NEER-DO-WELL!
YOU COULD AND YOU SHOULD, FOR I DO, YOU DOPE!
TONIA, I—
NO SHE MUST NEVER LEARN THE IDENTITY OF THE DAREDEVIL!
WELL??
WELLLLLLLLL?
SUDDENLY THUNDER—
CRACK
OH!
THEN RAIN!
WHAT DID I TELL YOU?—JUST WHEN THINGS ARE GOING PRETTY, ALONG COMES TROUBLE!— IT HAPPENS EVERY TIME!!
DON'T TALK LIKE THAT, BART—IT'S FRIGHTENING! OH, OUR LUNCH!
AS BART AND TONIA DISAPPEAR FROM VIEW WE PONDER HIS JESTING PROPHECY:—
IS THE CLOUDBURST AN ILL-OMEN OF COMING DISASTER TO A NOW PEACEFUL AMERICA?
"JUST WHEN THINGS ARE GOING PRETTY—"
?

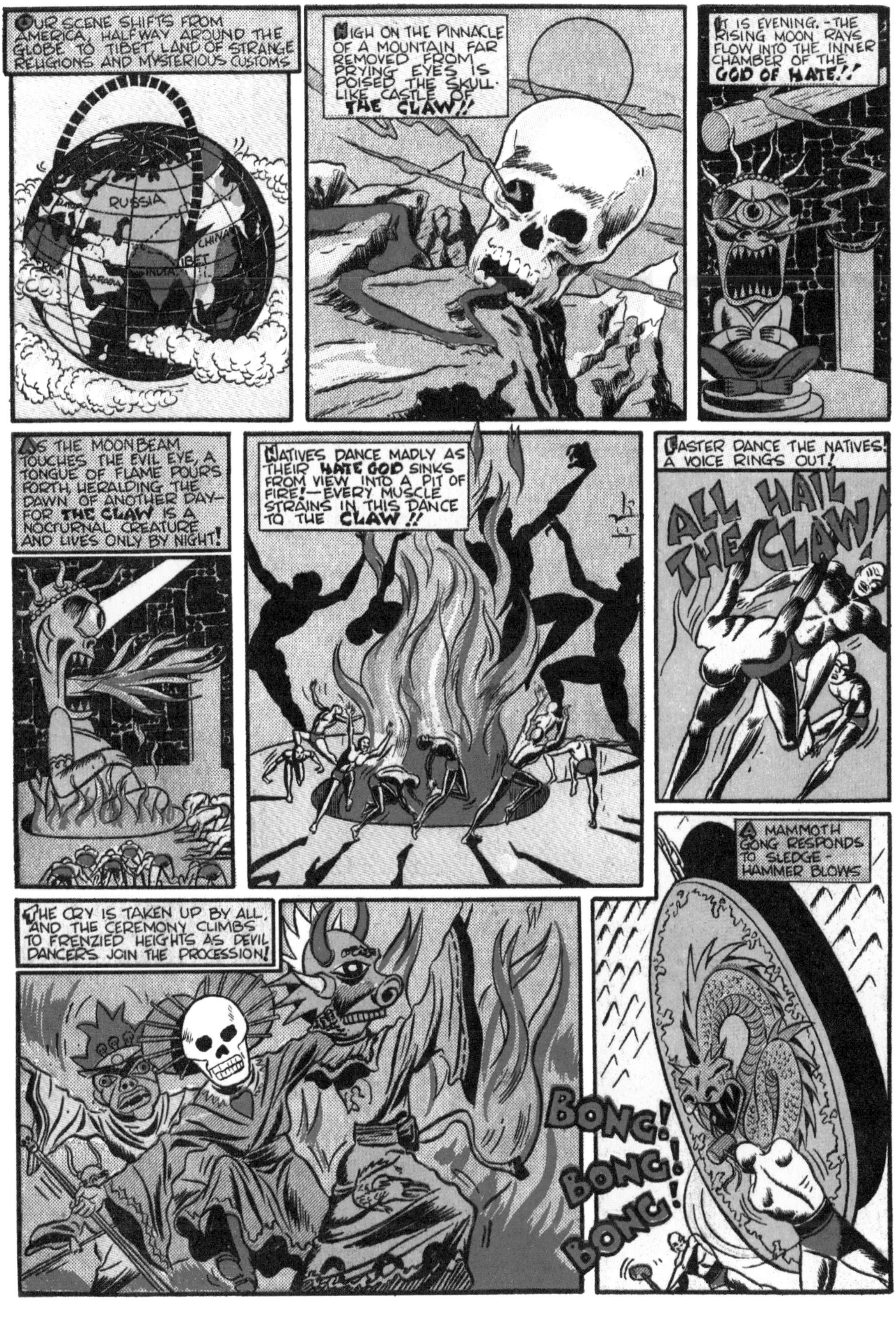
OUR SCENE SHIFTS FROM AMERICA, HALFWAY AROUND THE GLOBE TO TIBET, LAND OF STRANGE RELIGIONS AND MYSTERIOUS CUSTOMS
RUSSIA
CHINA
TIBET
INDIA
AFRICA
ARABIA
HIGH ON THE PINNACLE OF A MOUNTAIN FAR REMOVED FROM PRYING EYES IS POISED THE SKULL-LIKE CASTLE OF THE CLAW!!
IT IS EVENING. -THE RISING MOON RAYS FLOW INTO THE INNER CHAMBER OF THE GOD OF HATE!!
AS THE MOON BEAM TOUCHES THE EVIL EYE, A TONGUE OF FLAME POURS FORTH HERALDING THE DAWN OF ANOTHER DAY- FOR THE CLAW IS A NOCTURNAL CREATURE AND LIVES ONLY BY NIGHT!
NATIVES DANCE MADLY AS THEIR HATE GOD SINKS FROM VIEW INTO A PIT OF FIRE!—EVERY MUSCLE STRAINS IN THIS DANCE TO THE CLAW!!
FASTER DANCE THE NATIVES! A VOICE RINGS OUT!
ALL HAIL THE CLAW!
THE CRY IS TAKEN UP BY ALL, AND THE CEREMONY CLIMBS TO FRENZIED HEIGHTS AS DEVIL DANCERS JOIN THE PROCESSION!
A MAMMOTH GONG RESPONDS TO SLEDGE-HAMMER BLOWS
BONG! BONG! BONG!

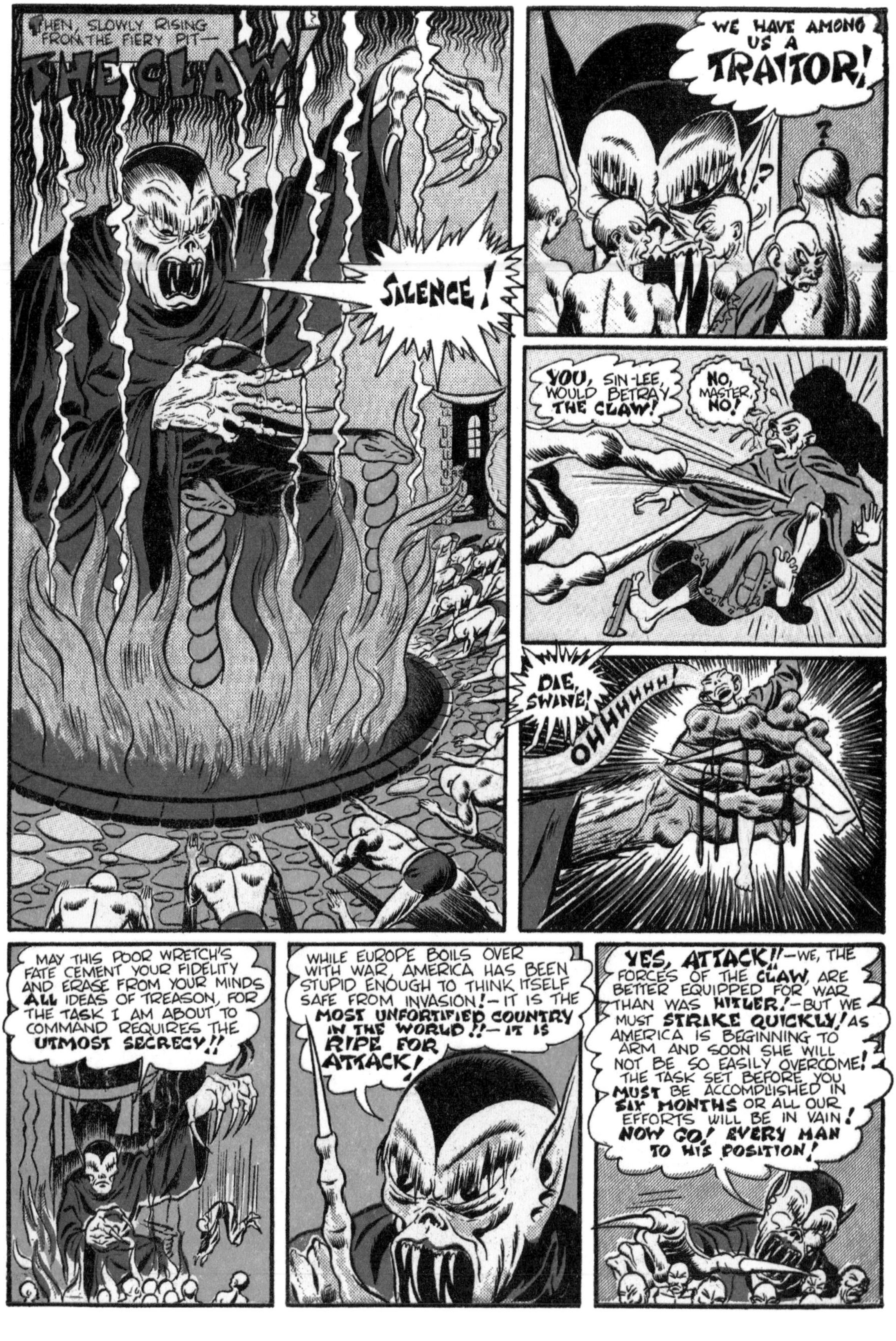
THEN, SLOWLY RISING FROM THE FIERY PIT—
THE CLAW
SILENCE!
WE HAVE AMONG US A TRAITOR!
YOU, SIN-LEE, WOULD BETRAY THE CLAW!
NO, MASTER, NO!
DIE, SWINE!
OHHHHHH!
MAY THIS POOR WRETCH'S FATE CEMENT YOUR FIDELITY AND ERASE FROM YOUR MINDS ALL IDEAS OF TREASON, FOR THE TASK I AM ABOUT TO COMMAND REQUIRES THE UTMOST SECRECY!!
WHILE EUROPE BOILS OVER WITH WAR, AMERICA HAS BEEN STUPID ENOUGH TO THINK ITSELF SAFE FROM INVASION!—IT IS THE MOST UNFORTIFIED COUNTRY IN THE WORLD!!—IT IS RIPE FOR ATTACK!
YES, ATTACK!!—WE, THE FORCES OF THE CLAW, ARE BETTER EQUIPPED FOR WAR THAN WAS HITLER!—BUT WE MUST STRIKE QUICKLY! AS AMERICA IS BEGINNING TO ARM AND SOON SHE WILL NOT BE SO EASILY OVERCOME! THE TASK SET BEFORE YOU MUST BE ACCOMPLISHED IN SIX MONTHS OR ALL OUR EFFORTS WILL BE IN VAIN! NOW GO! EVERY MAN TO HIS POSITION!

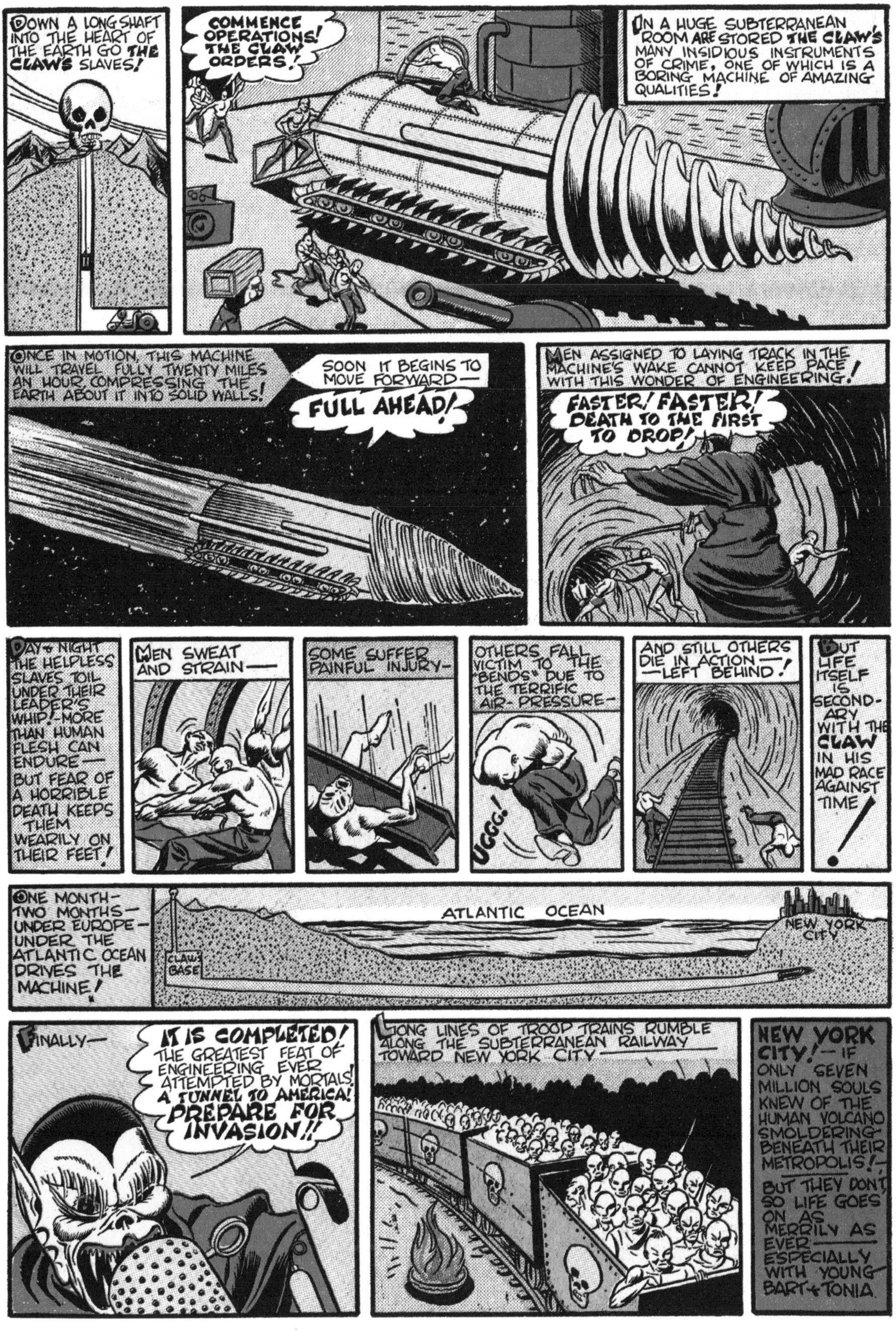
DOWN A LONG SHAFT INTO THE HEART OF THE EARTH GO THE CLAW'S SLAVES!
COMMENCE OPERATIONS! THE CLAW ORDERS!
IN A HUGE SUBTERRANEAN ROOM ARE STORED THE CLAW'S MANY INSIDIOUS INSTRUMENTS OF CRIME, ONE OF WHICH IS A BORING MACHINE OF AMAZING QUALITIES!
ONCE IN MOTION, THIS MACHINE WILL TRAVEL FULLY TWENTY MILES AN HOUR COMPRESSING THE EARTH ABOUT IT INTO SOLID WALLS!
SOON IT BEGINS TO MOVE FORWARD—
FULL AHEAD!
MEN ASSIGNED TO LAYING TRACK IN THE MACHINE'S WAKE CANNOT KEEP PACE WITH THIS WONDER OF ENGINEERING!
FASTER! FASTER! DEATH TO THE FIRST TO DROP!
DAY & NIGHT THE HELPLESS SLAVES TOIL UNDER THEIR LEADER'S WHIP!—MORE THAN HUMAN FLESH CAN ENDURE— BUT FEAR OF A HORRIBLE DEATH KEEPS THEM WEARILY ON THEIR FEET!
MEN SWEAT AND STRAIN—
SOME SUFFER PAINFUL INJURY—
OTHERS FALL VICTIM TO THE "BENDS" DUE TO THE TERRIFIC AIR-PRESSURE—
UGGG!
AND STILL OTHERS DIE IN ACTION— —LEFT BEHIND!
BUT LIFE ITSELF IS SECONDARY WITH THE CLAW IN HIS MAD RACE AGAINST TIME!
ONE MONTH— TWO MONTHS— UNDER EUROPE— UNDER THE ATLANTIC OCEAN DRIVES THE MACHINE!
ATLANTIC OCEAN
NEW YORK CITY
CLAW BASE
FINALLY—
IT IS COMPLETED! THE GREATEST FEAT OF ENGINEERING EVER ATTEMPTED BY MORTALS! A TUNNEL TO AMERICA! PREPARE FOR INVASION!!
LONG LINES OF TROOP TRAINS RUMBLE ALONG THE SUBTERRANEAN RAILWAY TOWARD NEW YORK CITY—
NEW YORK CITY!—IF ONLY SEVEN MILLION SOULS KNEW OF THE HUMAN VOLCANO SMOLDERING BENEATH THEIR METROPOLIS!— BUT THEY DON'T, SO LIFE GOES ON AS MERRILY AS EVER— ESPECIALLY WITH YOUNG BART & TONIA.

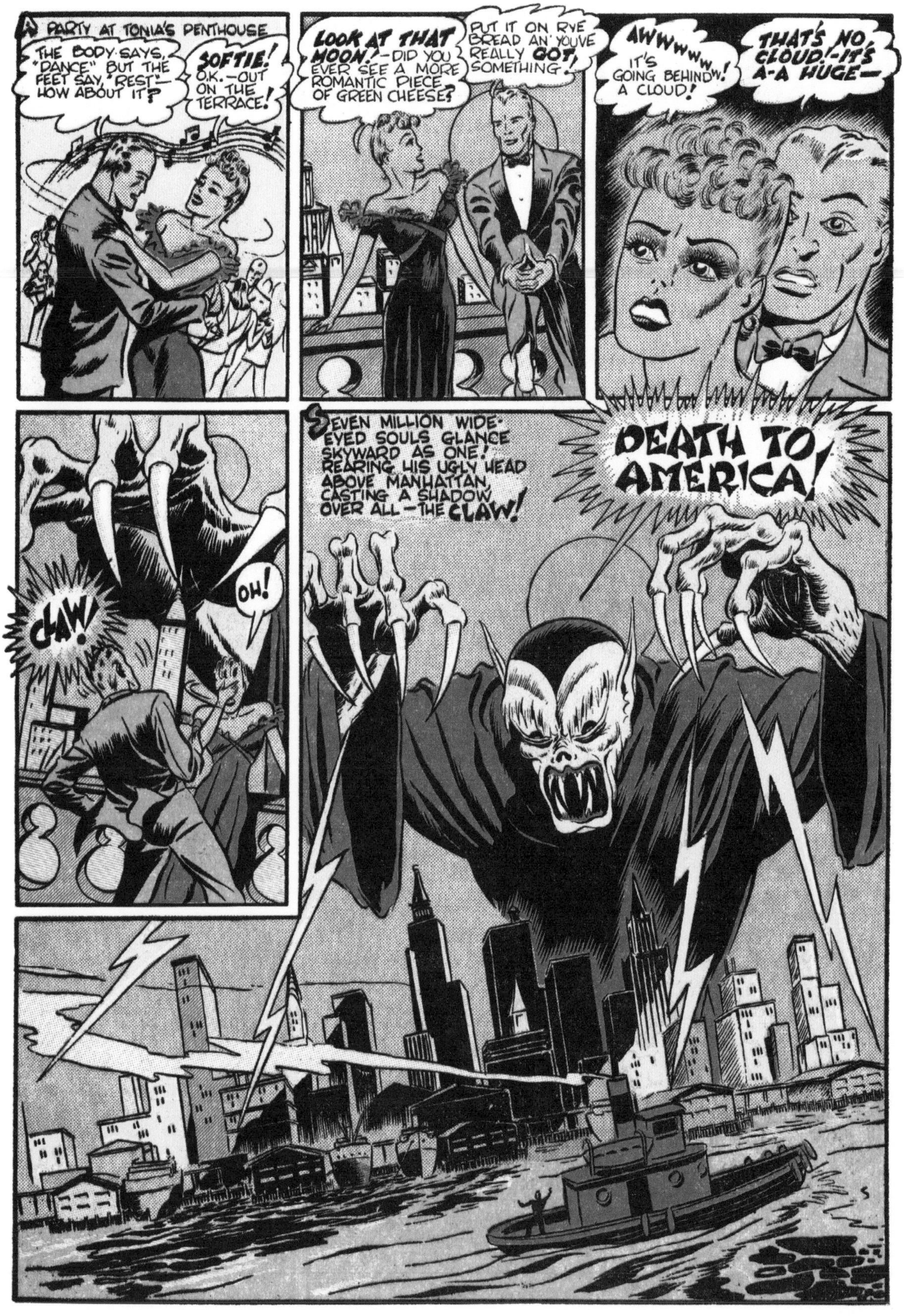
A PARTY AT TONIA'S PENTHOUSE
THE BODY SAYS, "DANCE" BUT THE FEET SAY, "REST"– HOW ABOUT IT?
SOFTIE! O.K.—OUT ON THE TERRACE!
LOOK AT THAT MOON!—DID YOU EVER SEE A MORE ROMANTIC PIECE OF GREEN CHEESE?
PUT IT ON RYE BREAD AN' YOU'VE REALLY GOT SOMETHING!
AWWWWWW! IT'S GOING BEHIND A CLOUD!
THAT'S NO CLOUD!–IT'S A-A HUGE—
CLAW!
OH!
SEVEN MILLION WIDE-EYED SOULS GLANCE SKYWARD AS ONE! REARING HIS UGLY HEAD ABOVE MANHATTAN, CASTING A SHADOW OVER ALL—THE CLAW!
DEATH TO AMERICA!

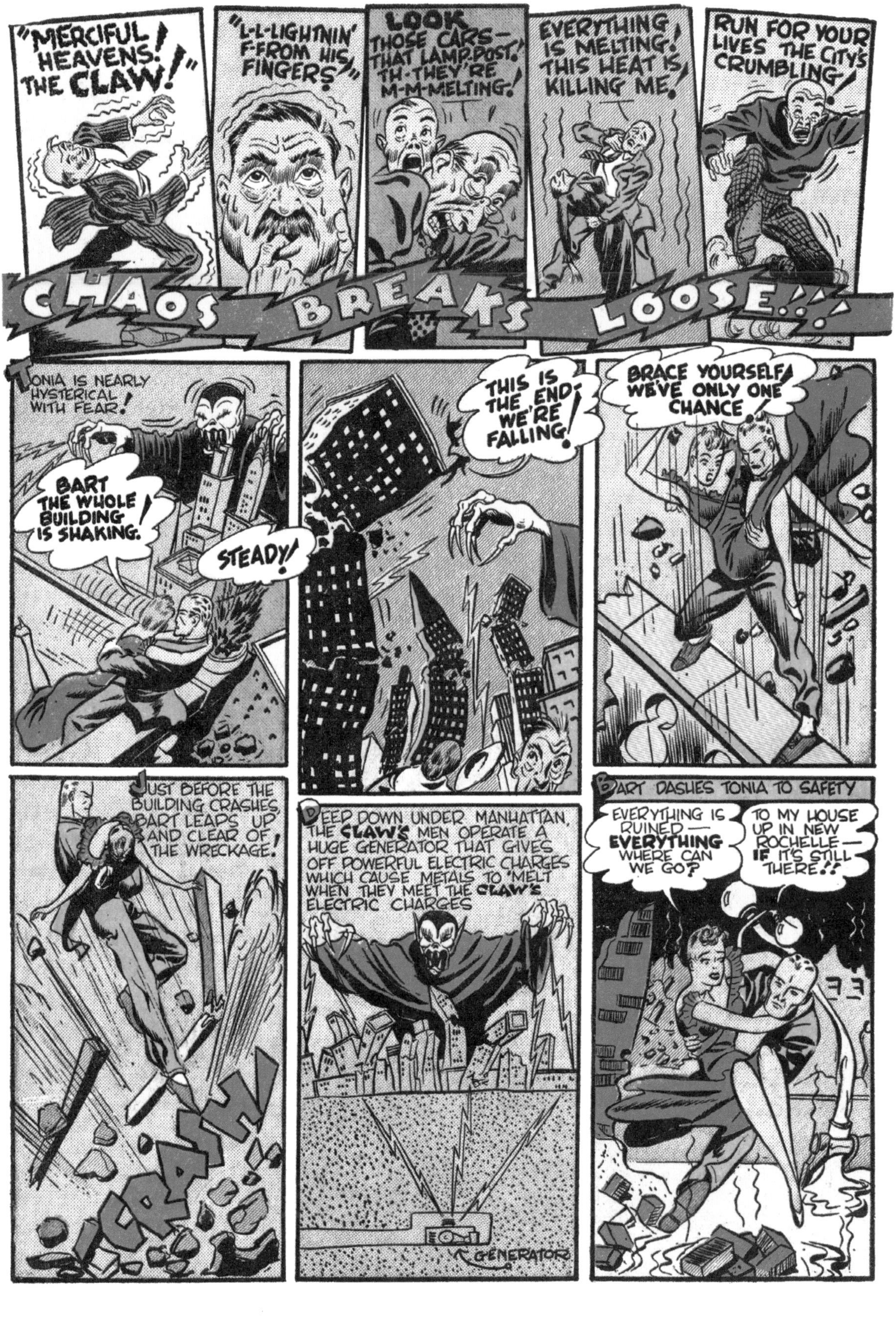
"MERCIFUL! HEAVENS! THE CLAW!"
"L-L-LIGHTNIN' F-FROM HIS FINGERS"
LOOK THOSE CARS— THAT LAMP POST! TH-THEY'RE M-M-MELTING!
EVERYTHING IS MELTING! THIS HEAT IS KILLING ME!
RUN FOR YOUR LIVES THE CITY'S CRUMBLING!
CHAOS BREAKS LOOSE!!!
TONIA IS NEARLY HYSTERICAL WITH FEAR!
BART THE WHOLE BUILDING IS SHAKING!
STEADY!
THIS IS THE END WE'RE FALLING!
BRACE YOURSELF! WE'VE ONLY ONE CHANCE
JUST BEFORE THE BUILDING CRASHES, BART LEAPS UP AND CLEAR OF THE WRECKAGE!
CRASH!
DEEP DOWN UNDER MANHATTAN, THE CLAW'S MEN OPERATE A HUGE GENERATOR THAT GIVES OFF POWERFUL ELECTRIC CHARGES WHICH CAUSE METALS TO 'MELT WHEN THEY MEET THE CLAW'S ELECTRIC CHARGES
GENERATOR
BART DASHES TONIA TO SAFETY
EVERYTHING IS RUINED — EVERYTHING WHERE CAN WE GO?
TO MY HOUSE UP IN NEW ROCHELLE— IF IT'S STILL THERE!!

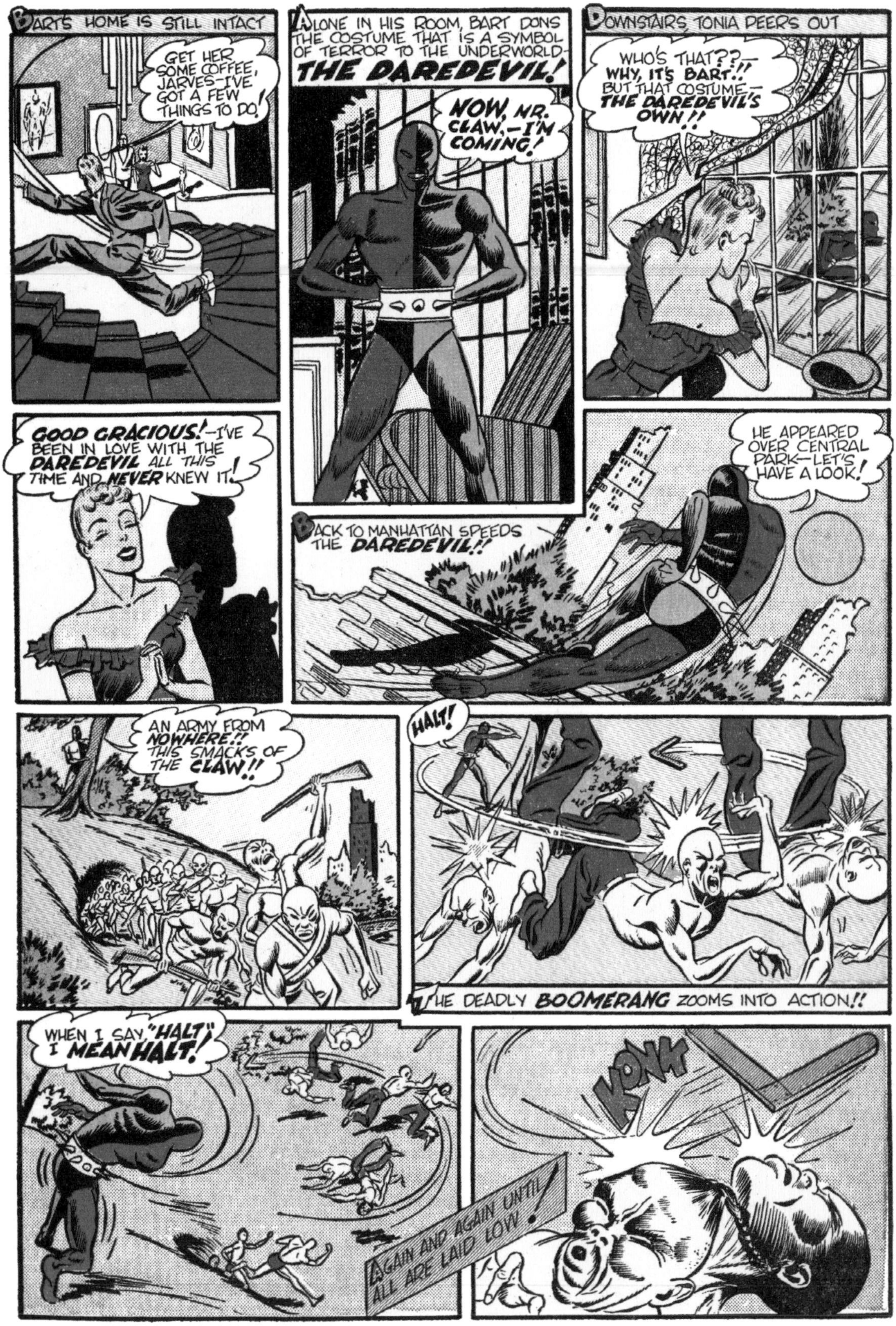
BART'S HOME IS STILL INTACT
GET HER SOME COFFEE, JARVES—I'VE GOT A FEW THINGS TO DO!
ALONE IN HIS ROOM, BART DONS THE COSTUME THAT IS A SYMBOL OF TERROR TO THE UNDERWORLD— THE DAREDEVIL!
NOW, MR. CLAW,—I'M COMING!
DOWNSTAIRS, TONIA PEERS OUT
WHO'S THAT??— WHY, IT'S BART.!! BUT THAT COSTUME— THE DAREDEVIL'S OWN!!
GOOD GRACIOUS!—I'VE BEEN IN LOVE WITH THE DAREDEVIL ALL THIS TIME AND NEVER KNEW IT!
BACK TO MANHATTAN SPEEDS THE DAREDEVIL!!
HE APPEARED OVER CENTRAL PARK—LET'S HAVE A LOOK!
AN ARMY FROM NOWHERE!! THIS SMACKS OF THE CLAW!!
HALT!
THE DEADLY BOOMERANG ZOOMS INTO ACTION!!
WHEN I SAY, "HALT" I MEAN HALT!
AGAIN AND AGAIN UNTIL ALL ARE LAID LOW!
KONK

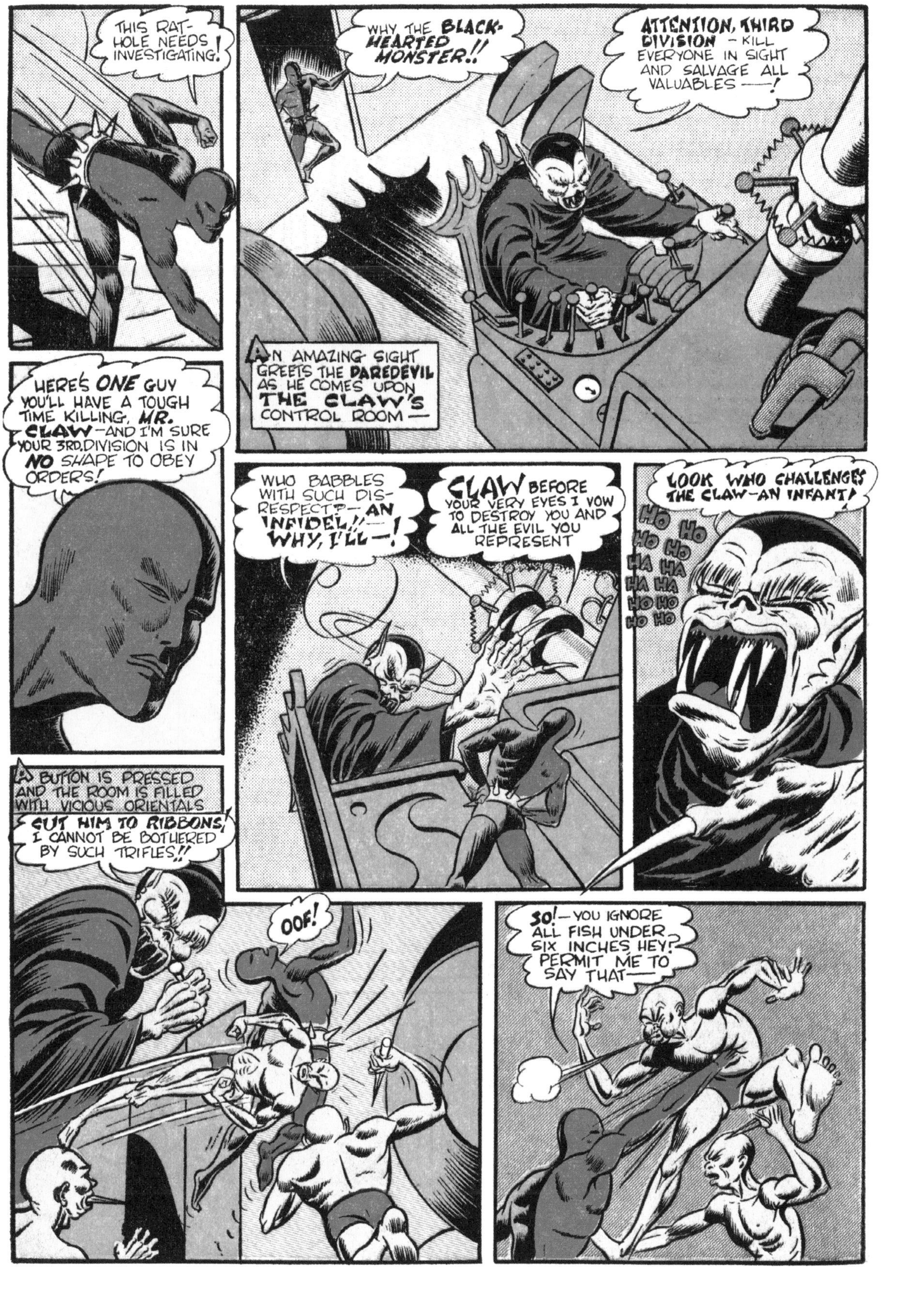
THIS RAT-HOLE NEEDS INVESTIGATING!
WHY THE BLACK-HEARTED MONSTER!!
ATTENTION, THIRD DIVISION - KILL EVERYONE IN SIGHT AND SALVAGE ALL VALUABLES ——!
AN AMAZING SIGHT GREETS THE DAREDEVIL AS HE COMES UPON THE CLAW'S CONTROL ROOM —
HERE'S ONE GUY YOU'LL HAVE A TOUGH TIME KILLING, MR. CLAW — AND I'M SURE YOUR 3RD. DIVISION IS IN NO SHAPE TO OBEY ORDERS!
WHO BABBLES WITH SUCH DISRESPECT? — AN INFIDEL!! — WHY, I'LL —!
CLAW BEFORE YOUR VERY EYES I VOW TO DESTROY YOU AND ALL THE EVIL YOU REPRESENT
LOOK WHO CHALLENGES THE CLAW — AN INFANT!
HO HO HO HO HA HA HA HA HO HO HO HO
A BUTTON IS PRESSED AND THE ROOM IS FILLED WITH VICIOUS ORIENTALS
CUT HIM TO RIBBONS, I CANNOT BE BOTHERED BY SUCH TRIFLES!!
OOF!
SO! — YOU IGNORE ALL FISH UNDER SIX INCHES HEY? PERMIT ME TO SAY THAT ——

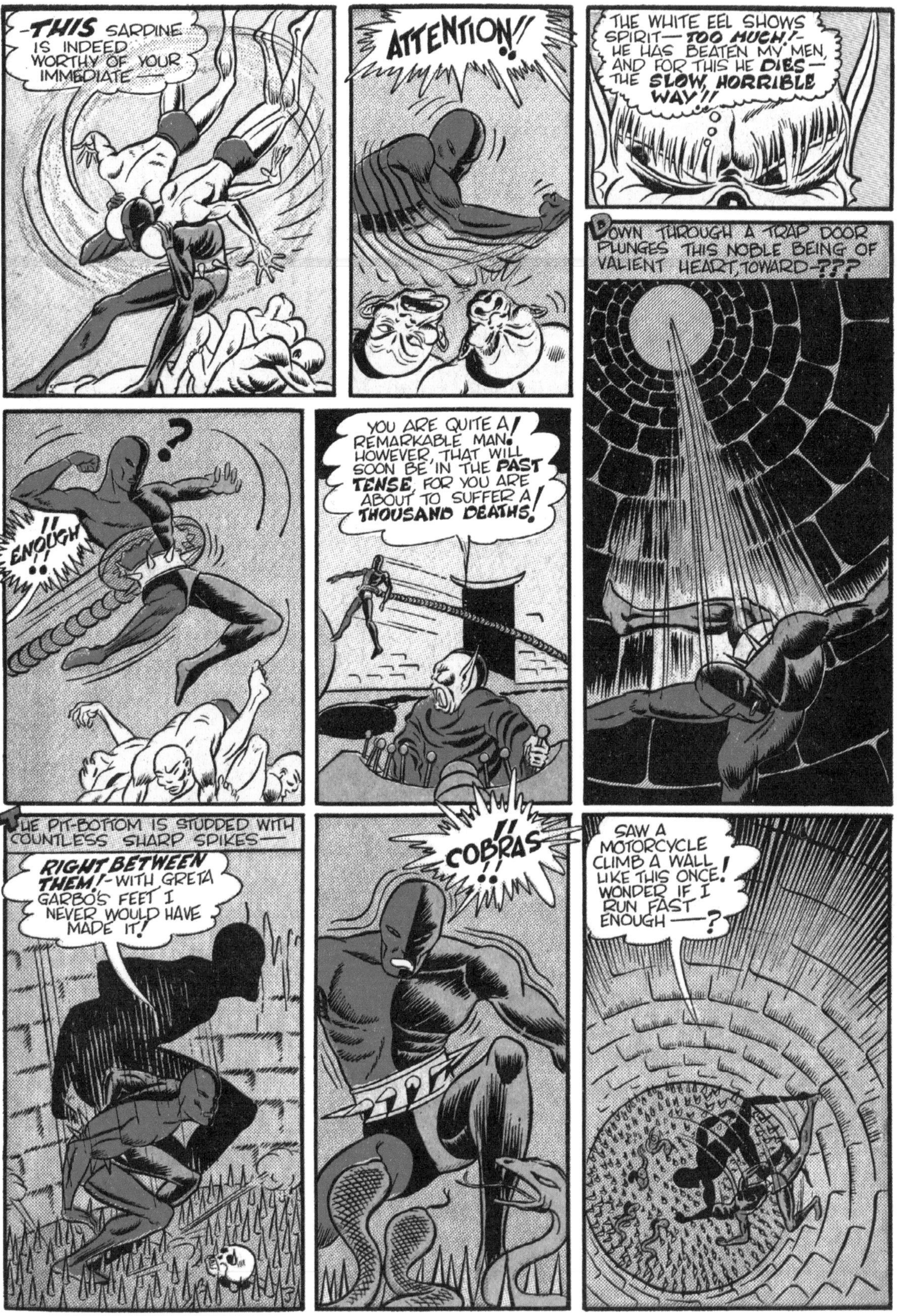
-THIS SARDINE IS INDEED WORTHY OF YOUR IMMEDIATE —
ATTENTION!!
THE WHITE EEL SHOWS SPIRIT— TOO MUCH!- HE HAS BEATEN MY MEN, AND FOR THIS HE DIES— THE SLOW, HORRIBLE WAY!!
DOWN THROUGH A TRAP DOOR PLUNGES THIS NOBLE BEING OF VALIENT HEART, TOWARD-???
?
!! ENOUGH !!
YOU ARE QUITE A REMARKABLE MAN! HOWEVER, THAT WILL SOON BE IN THE PAST TENSE, FOR YOU ARE ABOUT TO SUFFER A THOUSAND DEATHS!
THE PIT-BOTTOM IS STUDDED WITH COUNTLESS SHARP SPIKES—
RIGHT BETWEEN THEM!- WITH GRETA GARBO'S FEET I NEVER WOULD HAVE MADE IT!
!! COBRAS !!
SAW A MOTORCYCLE CLIMB A WALL LIKE THIS ONCE! WONDER IF I RUN FAST ENOUGH —?

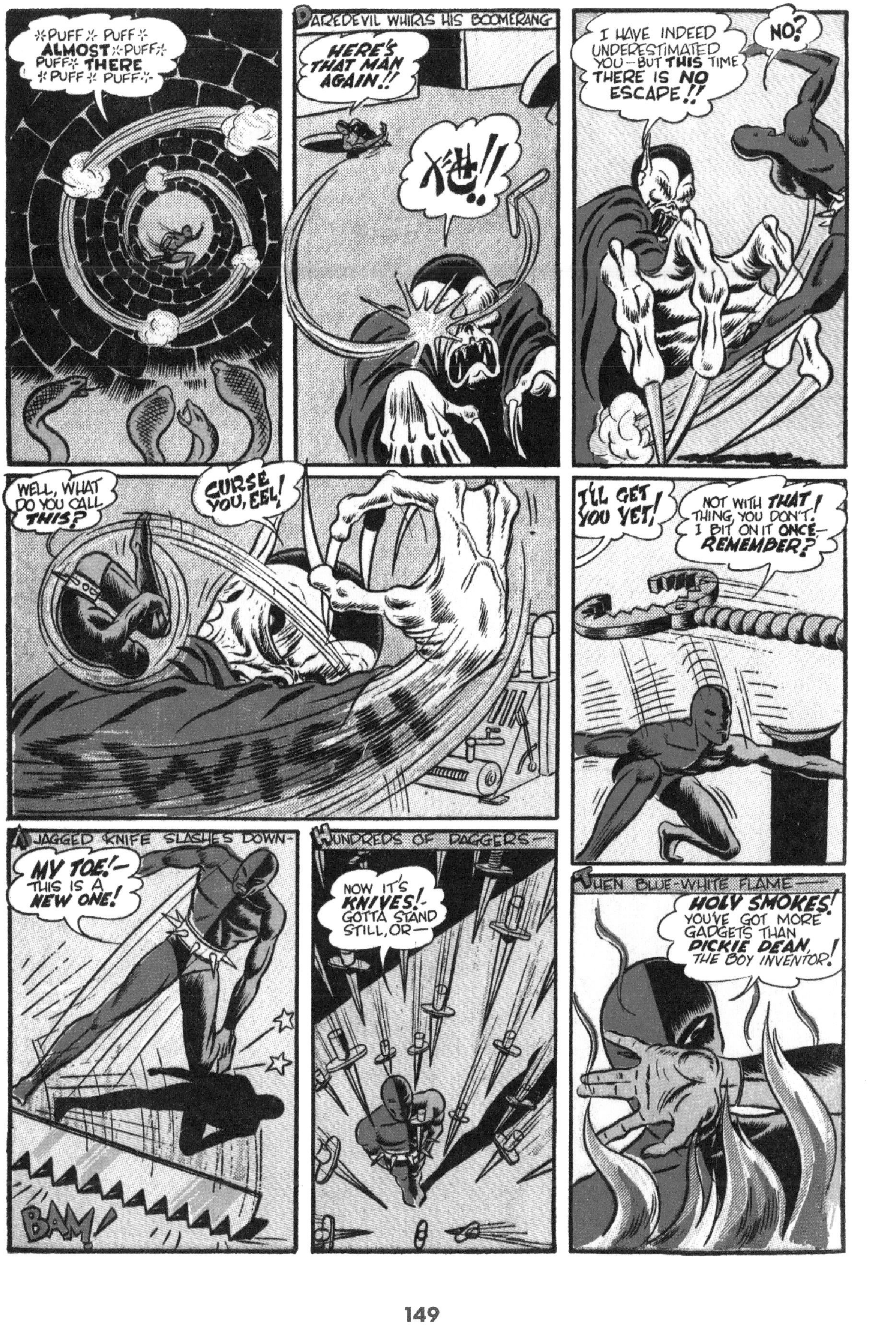
*PUFF* PUFF* ALMOST *PUFF* PUFF* THERE *PUFF* PUFF*
DAREDEVIL WHIRLS HIS BOOMERANG
HERE'S THAT MAN AGAIN!!
I HAVE INDEED UNDERESTIMATED YOU—BUT THIS TIME THERE IS NO ESCAPE!!
NO?
WELL, WHAT DO YOU CALL THIS?
CURSE YOU, EEL!
SWISH
I'LL GET YOU YET!
NOT WITH THAT THING, YOU DON'T! I BIT ON IT ONCE—REMEMBER?
A JAGGED KNIFE SLASHES DOWN—
MY TOE!— THIS IS A NEW ONE!
BAM!
HUNDREDS OF DAGGERS—
NOW IT'S KNIVES! GOTTA STAND STILL, OR—
THEN BLUE-WHITE FLAME—
HOLY SMOKES! YOU'VE GOT MORE GADGETS THAN DICKIE DEAN, THE BOY INVENTOR!

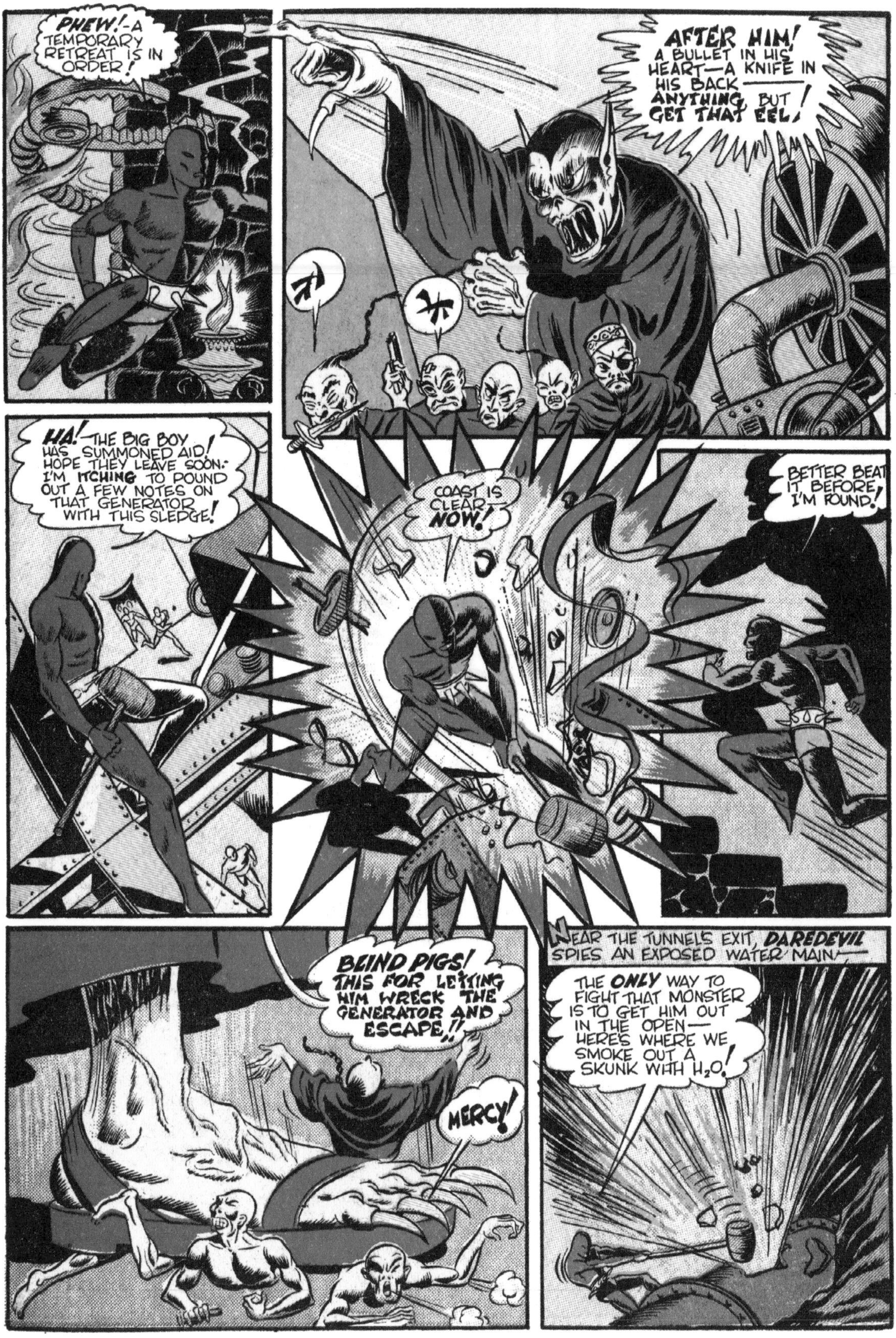
PHEW!—A TEMPORARY RETREAT IS IN ORDER!
AFTER HIM! A BULLET IN HIS HEART—A KNIFE IN HIS BACK— ANYTHING, BUT GET THAT EEL!
HA!—THE BIG BOY HAS SUMMONED AID! HOPE THEY LEAVE SOON. I'M ITCHING TO POUND OUT A FEW NOTES ON THAT GENERATOR WITH THIS SLEDGE!
COAST IS CLEAR NOW!
BETTER BEAT IT BEFORE I'M FOUND!
BLIND PIGS! THIS FOR LETTING HIM WRECK THE GENERATOR AND ESCAPE!!
MERCY!
NEAR THE TUNNEL'S EXIT, DAREDEVIL SPIES AN EXPOSED WATER MAIN—
THE ONLY WAY TO FIGHT THAT MONSTER IS TO GET HIM OUT IN THE OPEN— HERE'S WHERE WE SMOKE OUT A SKUNK WITH H2O!

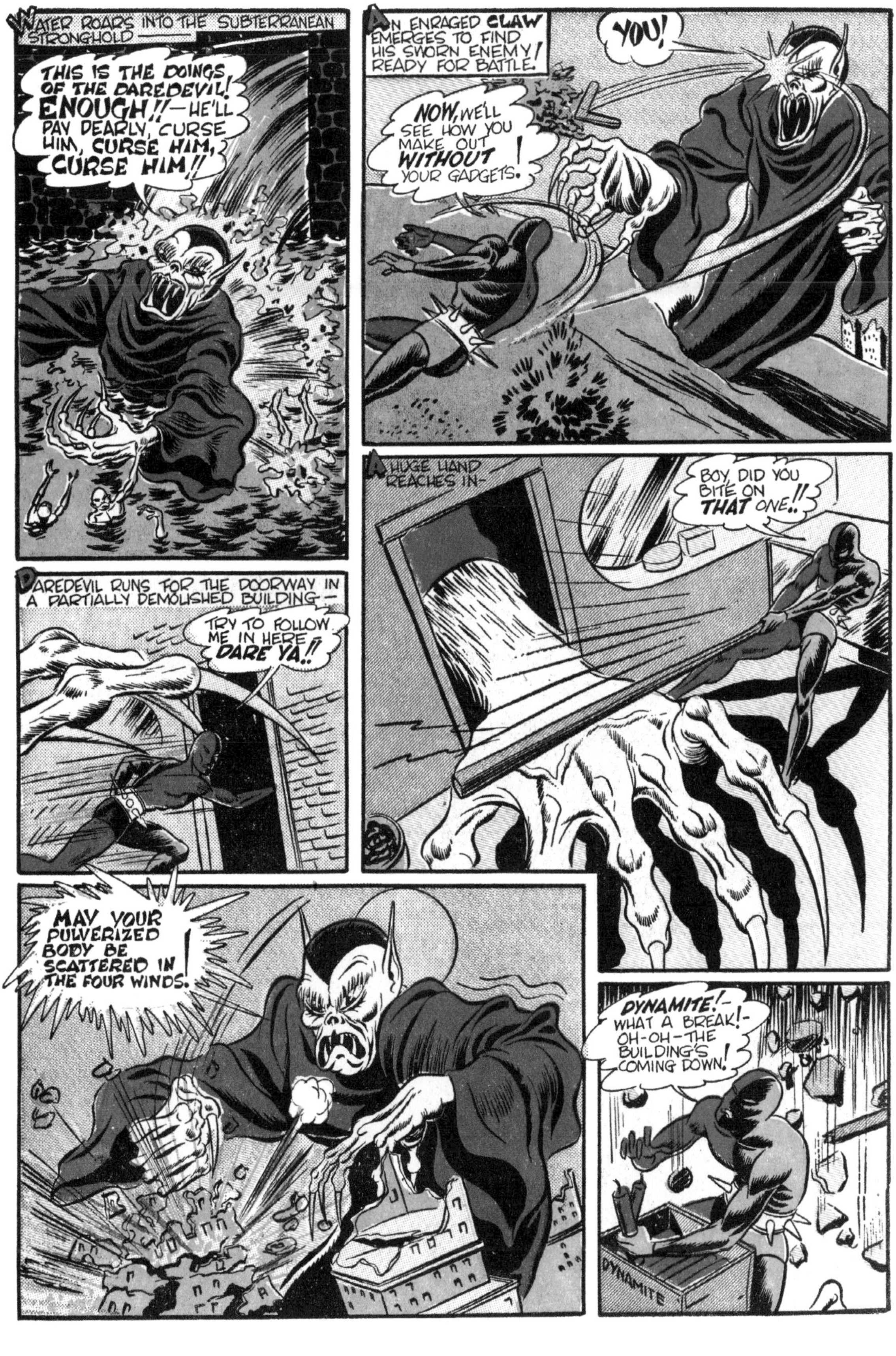
WATER ROARS INTO THE SUBTERRANEAN STRONGHOLD —
THIS IS THE DOINGS OF THE DAREDEVIL! ENOUGH!! — HE'LL PAY DEARLY, CURSE HIM, CURSE HIM, CURSE HIM!!
AN ENRAGED CLAW EMERGES TO FIND HIS SWORN ENEMY READY FOR BATTLE!
YOU!
NOW, WE'LL SEE HOW YOU MAKE OUT WITHOUT YOUR GADGETS!
A HUGE HAND REACHES IN—
BOY, DID YOU BITE ON THAT ONE!!
DAREDEVIL RUNS FOR THE DOORWAY IN A PARTIALLY DEMOLISHED BUILDING —
TRY TO FOLLOW ME IN HERE. DARE YA!!
MAY YOUR PULVERIZED BODY BE SCATTERED IN THE FOUR WINDS!
DYNAMITE! — WHAT A BREAK! — OH-OH — THE BUILDING'S COMING DOWN!
DYNAMITE

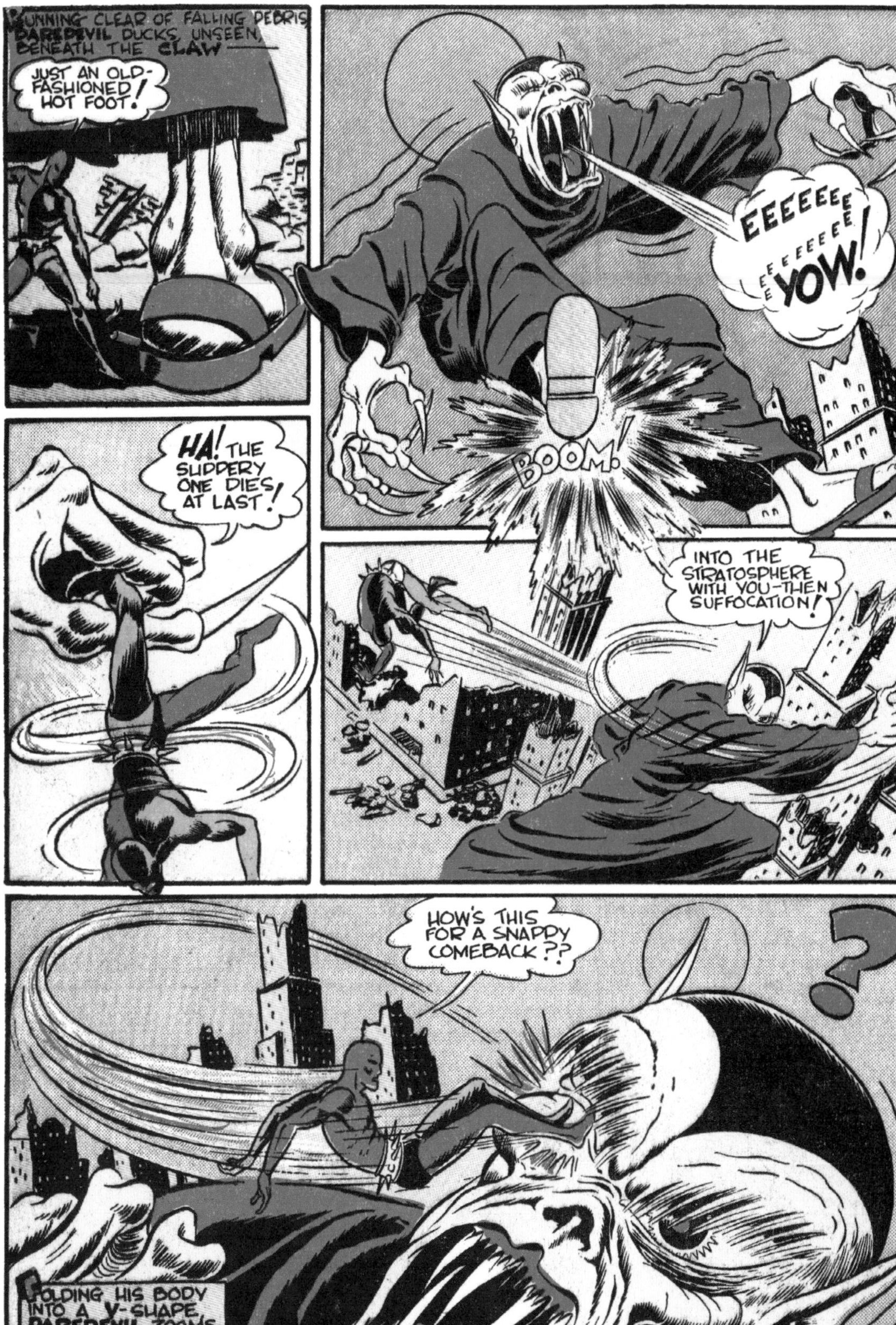
RUNNING CLEAR OF FALLING DEBRIS, DAREDEVIL DUCKS, UNSEEN, BENEATH THE CLAW
JUST AN OLD-FASHIONED HOT FOOT!
EEEEEEE EEEEEEEEYOW!
BOOM!
HA! THE SLIPPERY ONE DIES AT LAST!
INTO THE STRATOSPHERE WITH YOU-THEN SUFFOCATION!
HOW'S THIS FOR A SNAPPY COMEBACK??
?
FOLDING HIS BODY INTO A V-SHAPE, DAREDEVIL ZOOMS AROUND AND BACK AT THE CLAW LIKE A GIANT BOOMERANG!

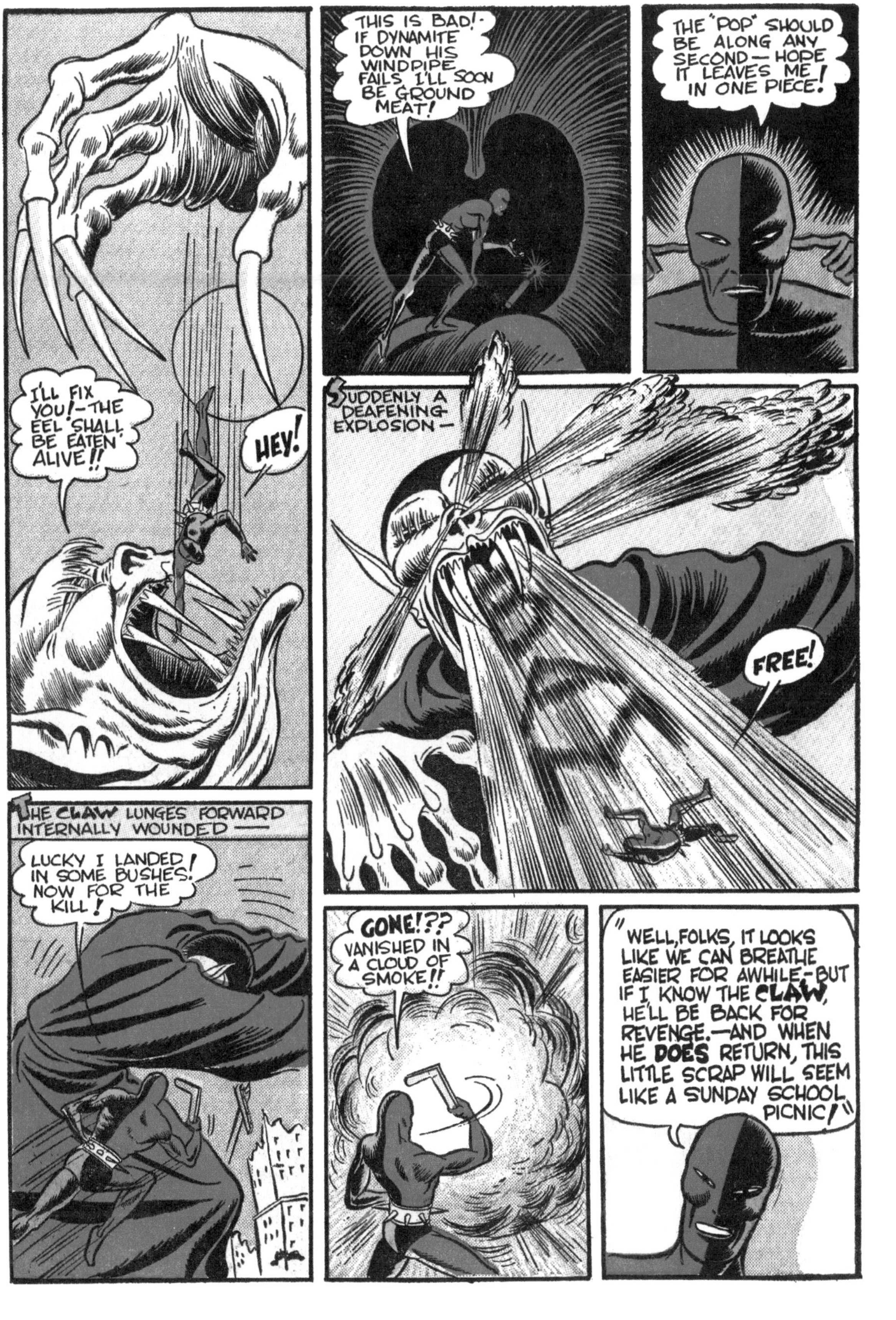
THIS IS BAD! - IF DYNAMITE DOWN HIS WINDPIPE FAILS I'LL SOON BE GROUND MEAT!
THE "POP" SHOULD BE ALONG ANY SECOND— HOPE IT LEAVES ME IN ONE PIECE!
I'LL FIX YOU!—THE EEL SHALL BE EATEN ALIVE!!
HEY!
SUDDENLY A DEAFENING EXPLOSION—
FREE!
THE CLAW LUNGES FORWARD INTERNALLY WOUNDED—
LUCKY I LANDED IN SOME BUSHES! NOW FOR THE KILL!
GONE!?? VANISHED IN A CLOUD OF SMOKE!!
"WELL, FOLKS, IT LOOKS LIKE WE CAN BREATHE EASIER FOR AWHILE - BUT IF I KNOW THE CLAW, HE'LL BE BACK FOR REVENGE.—AND WHEN HE DOES RETURN, THIS LITTLE SCRAP WILL SEEM LIKE A SUNDAY SCHOOL PICNIC!"

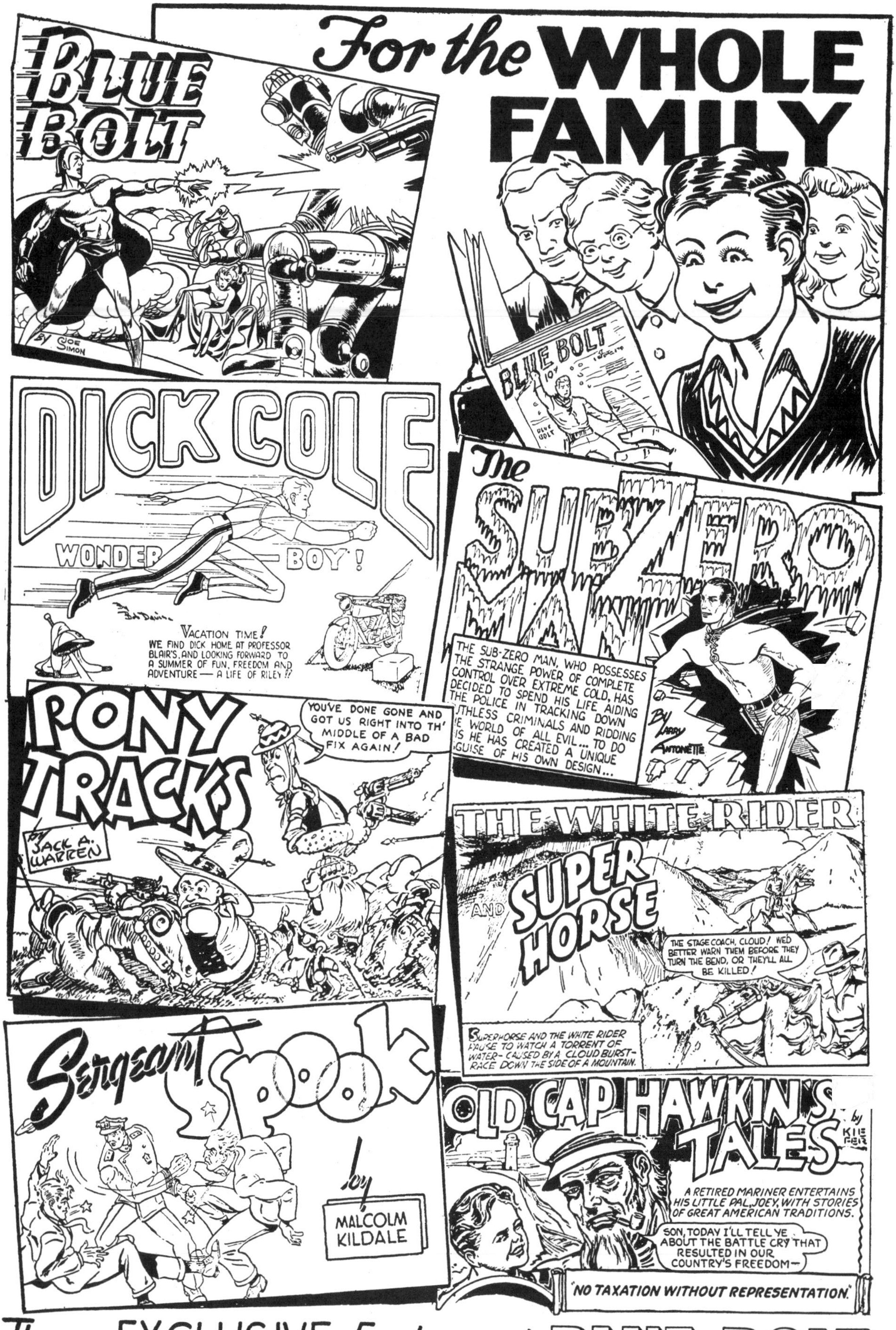
For the WHOLE FAMILY
BLUE BOLT
BY JOE SIMON
BLUE BOLT 10¢
DICK COLE
WONDER BOY!
VACATION TIME! WE FIND DICK HOME AT PROFESSOR BLAIR'S, AND LOOKING FORWARD TO A SUMMER OF FUN, FREEDOM AND ADVENTURE — A LIFE OF RILEY!!
The SUB-ZERO MAN
THE SUB-ZERO MAN, WHO POSSESSES THE STRANGE POWER OF COMPLETE CONTROL OVER EXTREME COLD, HAS DECIDED TO SPEND HIS LIFE AIDING THE POLICE IN TRACKING DOWN
UTHLESS CRIMINALS AND RIDDING
E WORLD OF ALL EVIL... TO DO
IS HE HAS CREATED A UNIQUE
GUISE OF HIS OWN DESIGN...
BY LARRY ANTONETTE
PONY TRACKS
BY JACK A. WARREN
YOU'VE DONE GONE AND GOT US RIGHT INTO TH' MIDDLE OF A BAD FIX AGAIN!
THE WHITE RIDER AND SUPER HORSE
THE STAGE COACH, CLOUD! WE'D BETTER WARN THEM BEFORE THEY TURN THE BEND, OR THEY'LL ALL BE KILLED!
SUPERHORSE AND THE WHITE RIDER PAUSE TO WATCH A TORRENT OF WATER- CAUSED BY A CLOUD BURST- RACE DOWN THE SIDE OF A MOUNTAIN.
Sergeant Spook
by MALCOLM KILDALE
OLD CAP HAWKIN'S TALES
by KIEFER
A RETIRED MARINER ENTERTAINS HIS LITTLE PAL, JOEY, WITH STORIES OF GREAT AMERICAN TRADITIONS.
SON, TODAY I'LL TELL YE ABOUT THE BATTLE CRY THAT RESULTED IN OUR COUNTRY'S FREEDOM—
"NO TAXATION WITHOUT REPRESENTATION."

These EXCLUSIVE Features in BLUE BOLT

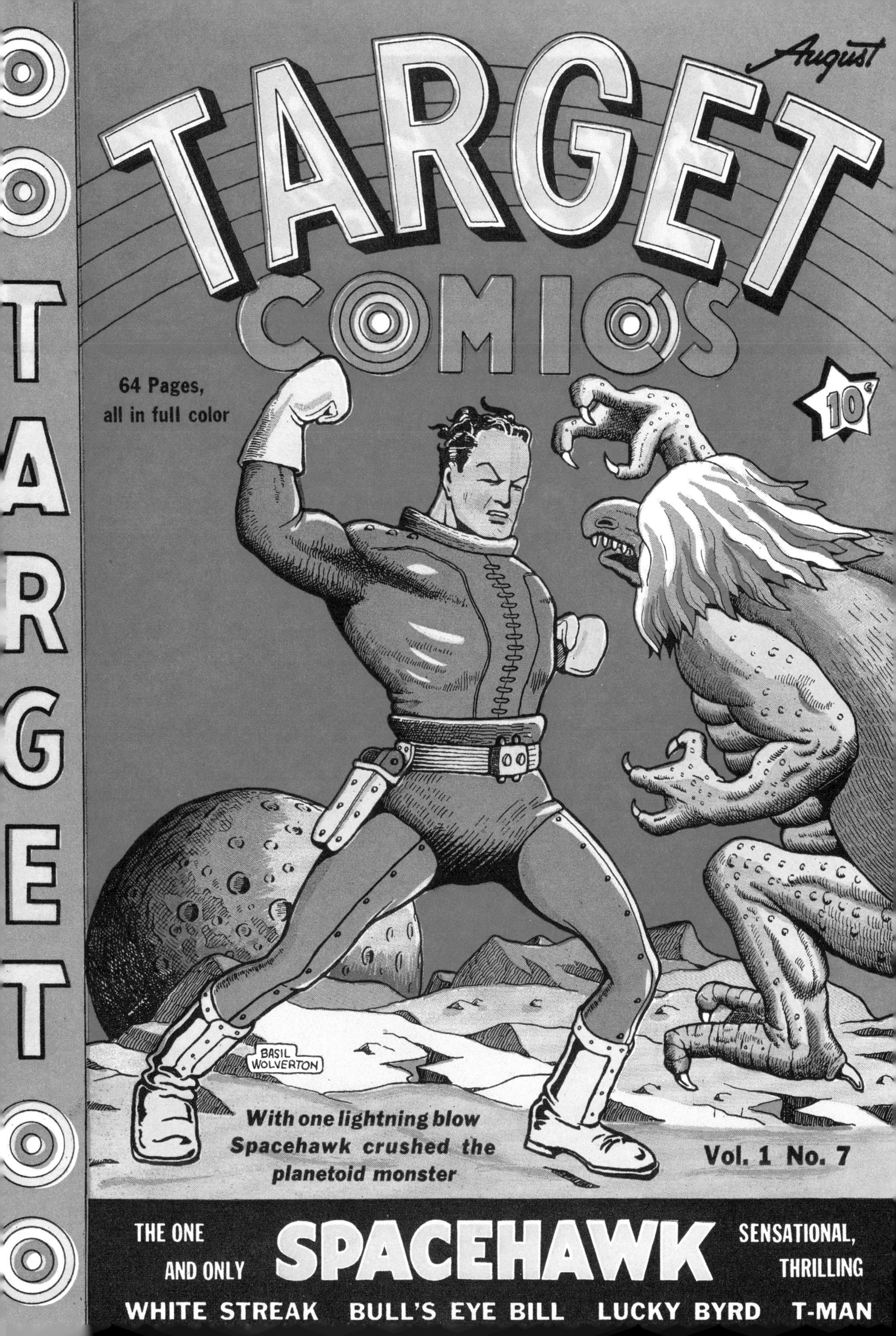
TARGET
August
TARGET COMICS
64 Pages, all in full color
10¢
BASIL WOLVERTON
With one lightning blow Spacehawk crushed the planetoid monster
Vol. 1 No. 7
THE ONE AND ONLY
SPACEHAWK
SENSATIONAL, THRILLING
WHITE STREAK BULL'S EYE BILL LUCKY BYRD T-MAN

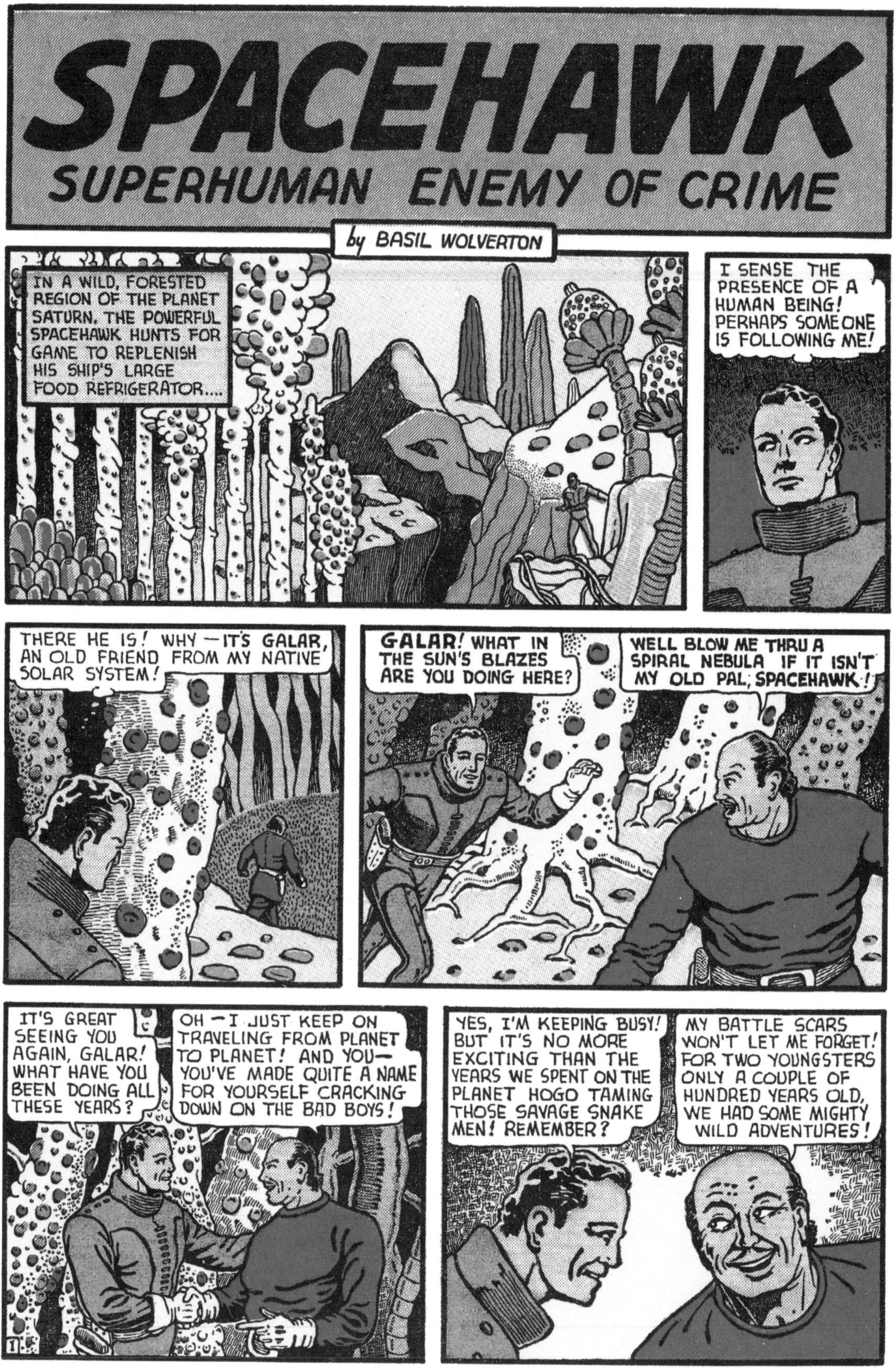
SPACEHAWK
SUPERHUMAN ENEMY OF CRIME
by BASIL WOLVERTON
IN A WILD, FORESTED REGION OF THE PLANET SATURN, THE POWERFUL SPACEHAWK HUNTS FOR GAME TO REPLENISH HIS SHIP'S LARGE FOOD REFRIGERATOR....
I SENSE THE PRESENCE OF A HUMAN BEING! PERHAPS SOME ONE IS FOLLOWING ME!
THERE HE IS! WHY — IT'S GALAR, AN OLD FRIEND FROM MY NATIVE SOLAR SYSTEM!
GALAR! WHAT IN THE SUN'S BLAZES ARE YOU DOING HERE?
WELL BLOW ME THRU A SPIRAL NEBULA IF IT ISN'T MY OLD PAL, SPACEHAWK!
IT'S GREAT SEEING YOU AGAIN, GALAR! WHAT HAVE YOU BEEN DOING ALL THESE YEARS?
OH — I JUST KEEP ON TRAVELING FROM PLANET TO PLANET! AND YOU — YOU'VE MADE QUITE A NAME FOR YOURSELF CRACKING DOWN ON THE BAD BOYS!
YES, I'M KEEPING BUSY! BUT IT'S NO MORE EXCITING THAN THE YEARS WE SPENT ON THE PLANET HOGO TAMING THOSE SAVAGE SNAKE MEN! REMEMBER?
MY BATTLE SCARS WON'T LET ME FORGET! FOR TWO YOUNGSTERS ONLY A COUPLE OF HUNDRED YEARS OLD, WE HAD SOME MIGHTY WILD ADVENTURES!

TELL ME, GALAR — IF YOU DO NOTHING BUT TRAVEL, HOW HAVE YOU MANAGED TO EXIST FOR THE PAST SIX HUNDRED YEARS?

I — WELL, I MANAGE TO SCARE UP ENOUGH RAW SUPPLIES TO KEEP ME GOING!

GALAR, OUR KIND TALKS WITH THE MIND AS WELL AS WITH THE TONGUE, BUT YOU HAVE THROWN UP A MENTAL BARRICADE AGAINST ME! WHAT ARE YOU TRYING TO HIDE?

ALL RIGHT, SPACEHAWK! I MAY AS WELL ADMIT I ROB SPACE SHIPS FOR MY LIVING! BUT BELIEVE ME, I'VE NEVER KILLED OR CRIPPLED SO MUCH AS A SINGLE PERSON IN MY CAREER!

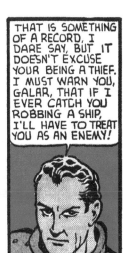

THAT IS SOMETHING OF A RECORD, I DARE SAY, BUT IT DOESN'T EXCUSE YOUR BEING A THIEF. I MUST WARN YOU, GALAR, THAT IF I EVER CATCH YOU ROBBING A SHIP, I'LL HAVE TO TREAT YOU AS AN ENEMY!

OH-HO! BUT I AM NOT ONE TO BE CAUGHT — EVEN BY YOU, SPACEHAWK! IF YOU SHOULD EVER MANAGE TO DO IT, I GIVE YOU MY WORD I'LL WILLINGLY GIVE UP MY PROFESSION!

I'D LIKE TO SEE THAT HAPPEN! I CAN'T UNDERSTAND WHY A MAN OF YOUR MENTAL AND PHYSICAL STRENGTH SHOULD CHOOSE TO LIVE SO DISHONORABLY!

WELL, — SO LONG, SPACEHAWK! UNDER THE CIRCUMSTANCES, I SUPPOSE I'D BETTER SHOVE OFF!

GOOD-BYE, GALAR!

GALAR STRIDES TO HIS SHIP, AND A MOMENT LATER IT ROARS INTO THE SATURNIAN SKY......

SPACEHAWK HURRIES TO HIS OWN SHIP, AND TRAINS THE ELECTROSCOPE ON GALAR'S CRAFT....

I CAN'T LET HIM GO ON LIKE THAT! HE'S BOUND TO END UP AT THE BUSINESS END OF SOMEONE'S ATOM PISTOL!

HOURS LATER.

HERE I AM MILLIONS OF MILES OUT IN SPACE, AND NOT ANOTHER SHIP IN SIGHT — EXCEPT THAT APPROACHING PASSENGER LINER! THIS JOB WILL BE A CINCH!

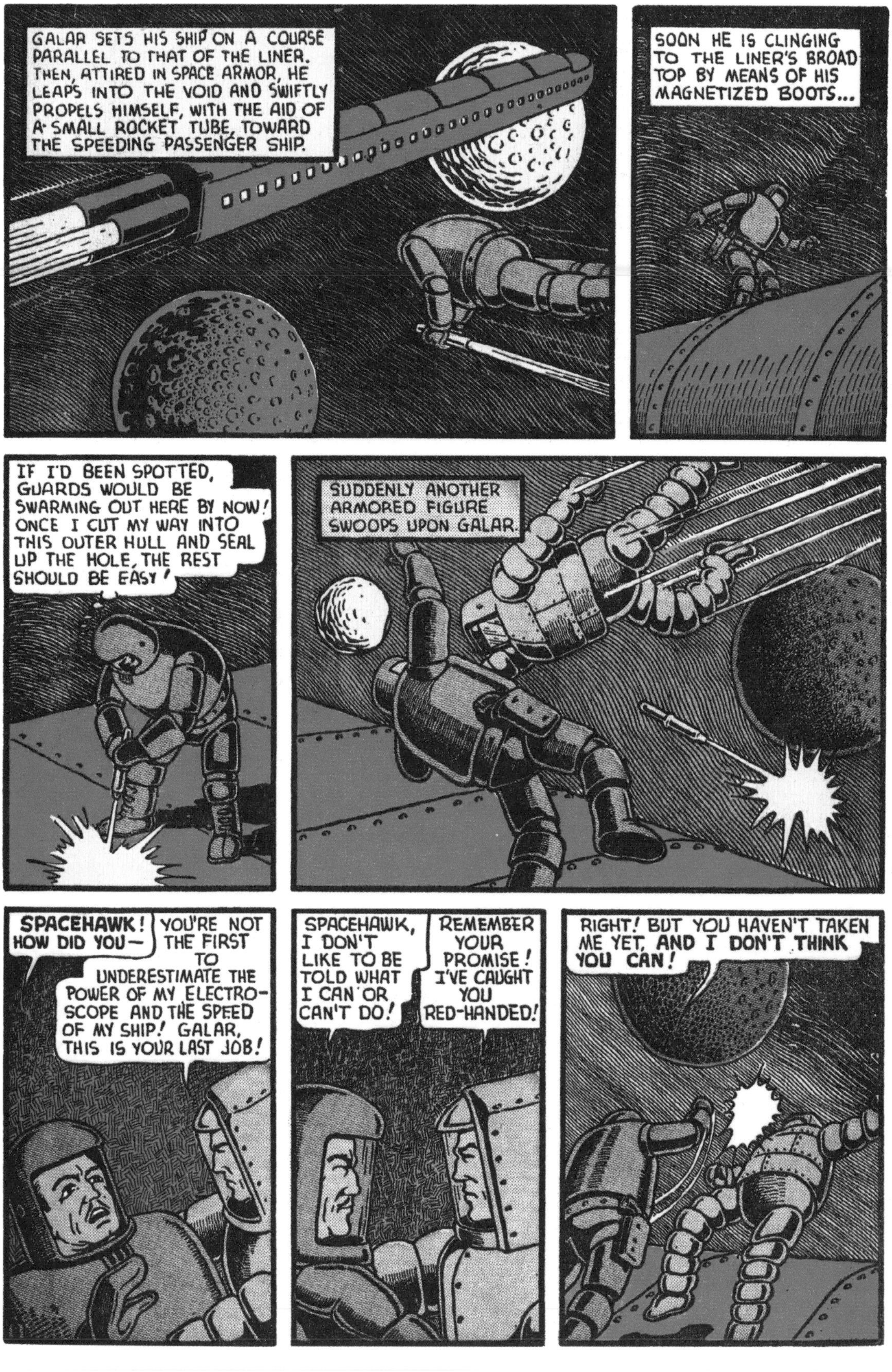
GALAR SETS HIS SHIP ON A COURSE PARALLEL TO THAT OF THE LINER. THEN, ATTIRED IN SPACE ARMOR, HE LEAPS INTO THE VOID AND SWIFTLY PROPELS HIMSELF, WITH THE AID OF A SMALL ROCKET TUBE, TOWARD THE SPEEDING PASSENGER SHIP.
SOON HE IS CLINGING TO THE LINER'S BROAD TOP BY MEANS OF HIS MAGNETIZED BOOTS...
IF I'D BEEN SPOTTED, GUARDS WOULD BE SWARMING OUT HERE BY NOW! ONCE I CUT MY WAY INTO THIS OUTER HULL AND SEAL UP THE HOLE, THE REST SHOULD BE EASY!
SUDDENLY ANOTHER ARMORED FIGURE SWOOPS UPON GALAR.
SPACEHAWK! HOW DID YOU—
YOU'RE NOT THE FIRST TO UNDERESTIMATE THE POWER OF MY ELECTROSCOPE AND THE SPEED OF MY SHIP! GALAR, THIS IS YOUR LAST JOB!
SPACEHAWK, I DON'T LIKE TO BE TOLD WHAT I CAN OR CAN'T DO!
REMEMBER YOUR PROMISE! I'VE CAUGHT YOU RED-HANDED!
RIGHT! BUT YOU HAVEN'T TAKEN ME YET, AND I DON'T THINK YOU CAN!

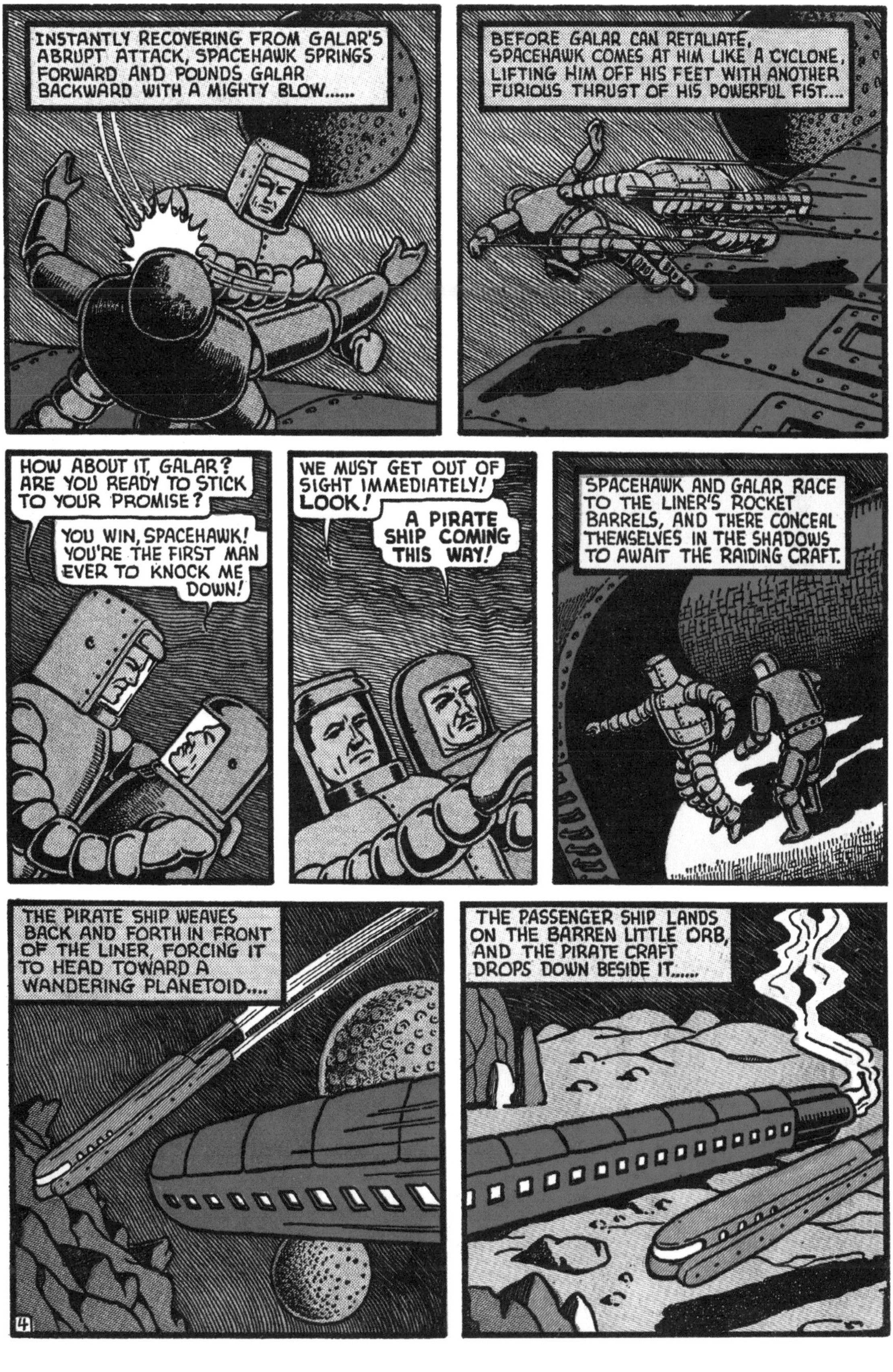

INSTANTLY RECOVERING FROM GALAR'S ABRUPT ATTACK, SPACEHAWK SPRINGS FORWARD AND POUNDS GALAR BACKWARD WITH A MIGHTY BLOW.....
BEFORE GALAR CAN RETALIATE, SPACEHAWK COMES AT HIM LIKE A CYCLONE, LIFTING HIM OFF HIS FEET WITH ANOTHER FURIOUS THRUST OF HIS POWERFUL FIST....
HOW ABOUT IT, GALAR? ARE YOU READY TO STICK TO YOUR PROMISE?
YOU WIN, SPACEHAWK! YOU'RE THE FIRST MAN EVER TO KNOCK ME DOWN!
WE MUST GET OUT OF SIGHT IMMEDIATELY! LOOK!
A PIRATE SHIP COMING THIS WAY!
SPACEHAWK AND GALAR RACE TO THE LINER'S ROCKET BARRELS, AND THERE CONCEAL THEMSELVES IN THE SHADOWS TO AWAIT THE RAIDING CRAFT.
THE PIRATE SHIP WEAVES BACK AND FORTH IN FRONT OF THE LINER, FORCING IT TO HEAD TOWARD A WANDERING PLANETOID....
4
THE PASSENGER SHIP LANDS ON THE BARREN LITTLE ORB, AND THE PIRATE CRAFT DROPS DOWN BESIDE IT.....

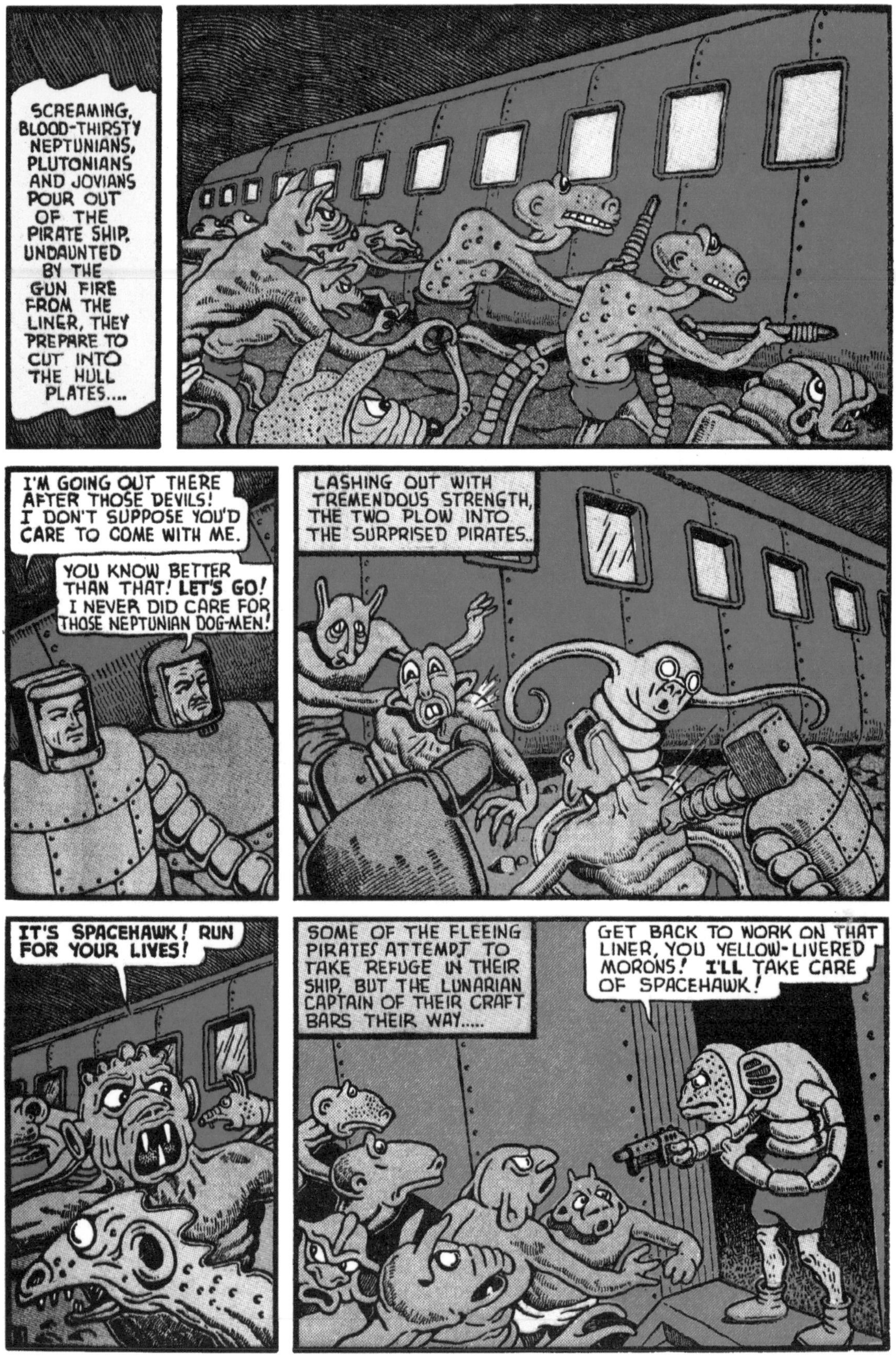
SCREAMING, BLOOD-THIRSTY NEPTUNIANS, PLUTONIANS AND JOVIANS POUR OUT OF THE PIRATE SHIP, UNDAUNTED BY THE GUN FIRE FROM THE LINER, THEY PREPARE TO CUT INTO THE HULL PLATES....
I'M GOING OUT THERE AFTER THOSE DEVILS! I DON'T SUPPOSE YOU'D CARE TO COME WITH ME.
YOU KNOW BETTER THAN THAT! LET'S GO! I NEVER DID CARE FOR THOSE NEPTUNIAN DOG-MEN!
LASHING OUT WITH TREMENDOUS STRENGTH, THE TWO PLOW INTO THE SURPRISED PIRATES..
IT'S SPACEHAWK! RUN FOR YOUR LIVES!
SOME OF THE FLEEING PIRATES ATTEMPT TO TAKE REFUGE IN THEIR SHIP, BUT THE LUNARIAN CAPTAIN OF THEIR CRAFT BARS THEIR WAY.....
GET BACK TO WORK ON THAT LINER, YOU YELLOW-LIVERED MORONS! I'LL TAKE CARE OF SPACEHAWK!

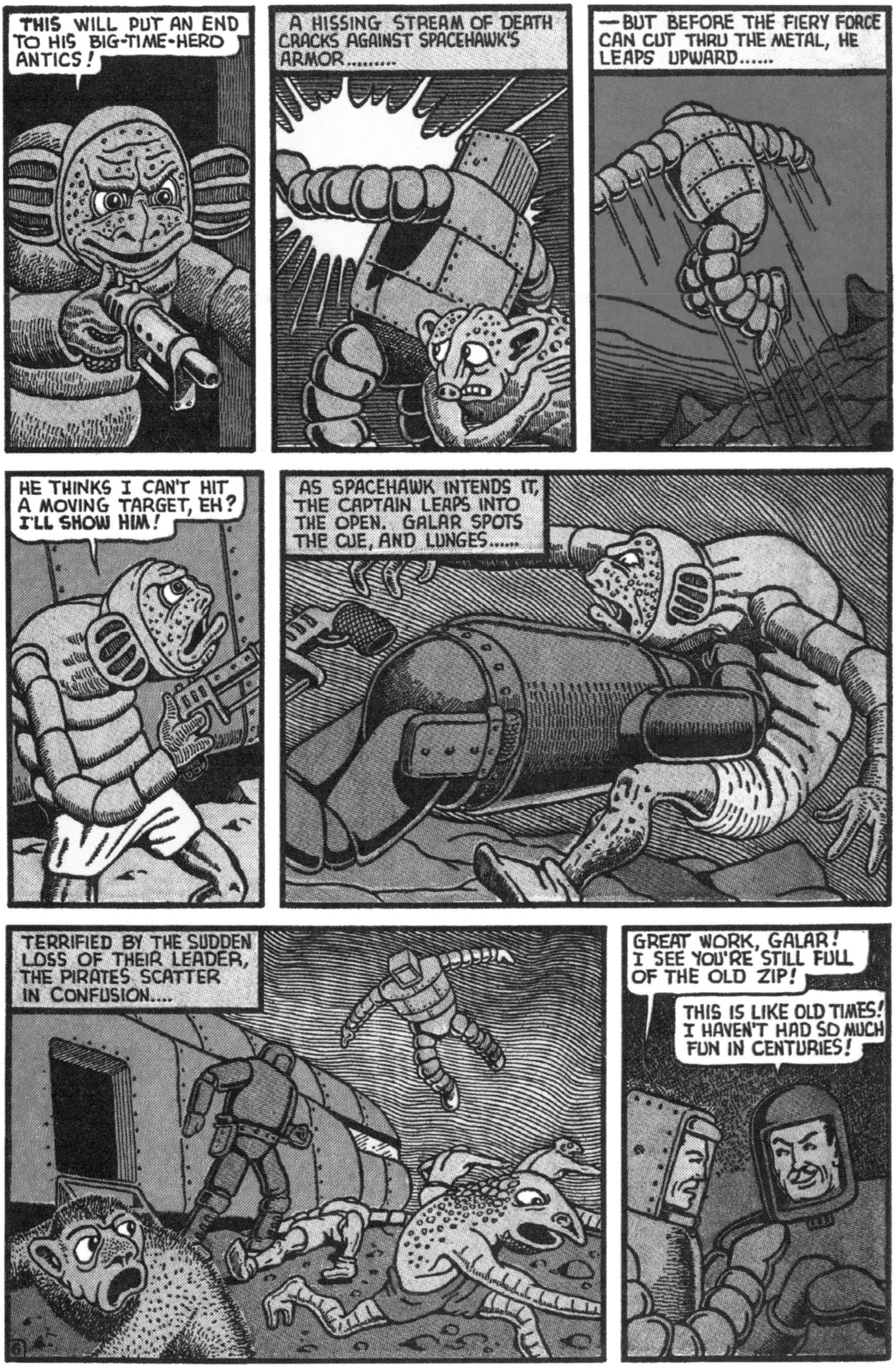
THIS WILL PUT AN END TO HIS BIG-TIME-HERO ANTICS!
A HISSING STREAM OF DEATH CRACKS AGAINST SPACEHAWK'S ARMOR.........
—BUT BEFORE THE FIERY FORCE CAN CUT THRU THE METAL, HE LEAPS UPWARD......
HE THINKS I CAN'T HIT A MOVING TARGET, EH? I'LL SHOW HIM!
AS SPACEHAWK INTENDS IT, THE CAPTAIN LEAPS INTO THE OPEN. GALAR SPOTS THE CUE, AND LUNGES......
TERRIFIED BY THE SUDDEN LOSS OF THEIR LEADER, THE PIRATES SCATTER IN CONFUSION....
GREAT WORK, GALAR! I SEE YOU'RE STILL FULL OF THE OLD ZIP!
THIS IS LIKE OLD TIMES! I HAVEN'T HAD SO MUCH FUN IN CENTURIES!

THE MARTIAN COMMANDER OF THE LINER WAVES HIS THANKS—

—AND THE SHIP ROARS AWAY.....

WELL, SPACEHAWK, BOTH OUR SHIPS HAVE FLOWN OFF INTO SPACE, AND WE'LL NEVER SEE THEM AGAIN! WE'LL HAVE TO USE THE PIRATE CRATE TO ESCAPE FROM HERE!

I'M SURE WE'LL MAKE OUT ALL RIGHT, GALAR. FIRST, I WANT TO MAKE CERTAIN THAT NONE OF THE PIRATES CAN ESCAPE FROM HERE. I'LL BE BACK RIGHT AWAY!

SPACEHAWK TAKES OFF IN THE PIRATE SHIP.....

WONDER WHY HE'S CLIMBING SO HIGH INTO THE SKY ——?

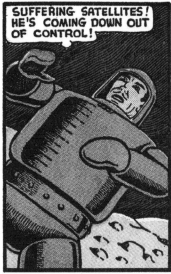

SUFFERING SATELLITES! HE'S COMING DOWN OUT OF CONTROL!

TO GALAR'S HORROR, THE SHIP PLOWS INTO THE ASTEROID!

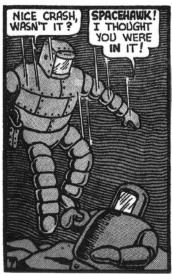

NICE CRASH, WASN'T IT?

SPACEHAWK! I THOUGHT YOU WERE IN IT!

NOT MUCH! I JUMPED OUT AND LET IT CRASH! NOW THE PIRATES WILL BE BOTTLED UP HERE!

BUT HOW ARE WE GOING TO ESCAPE?

SPACEHAWK'S POWERFUL MIND SENDS OUT A MENTAL SIGNAL. THOUSANDS OF MILES AWAY, HIS ROBOT PILOT RECEIVES THE MESSAGE, AND TURNS THE CRAFT BACK TOWARD THE PLANETOID.

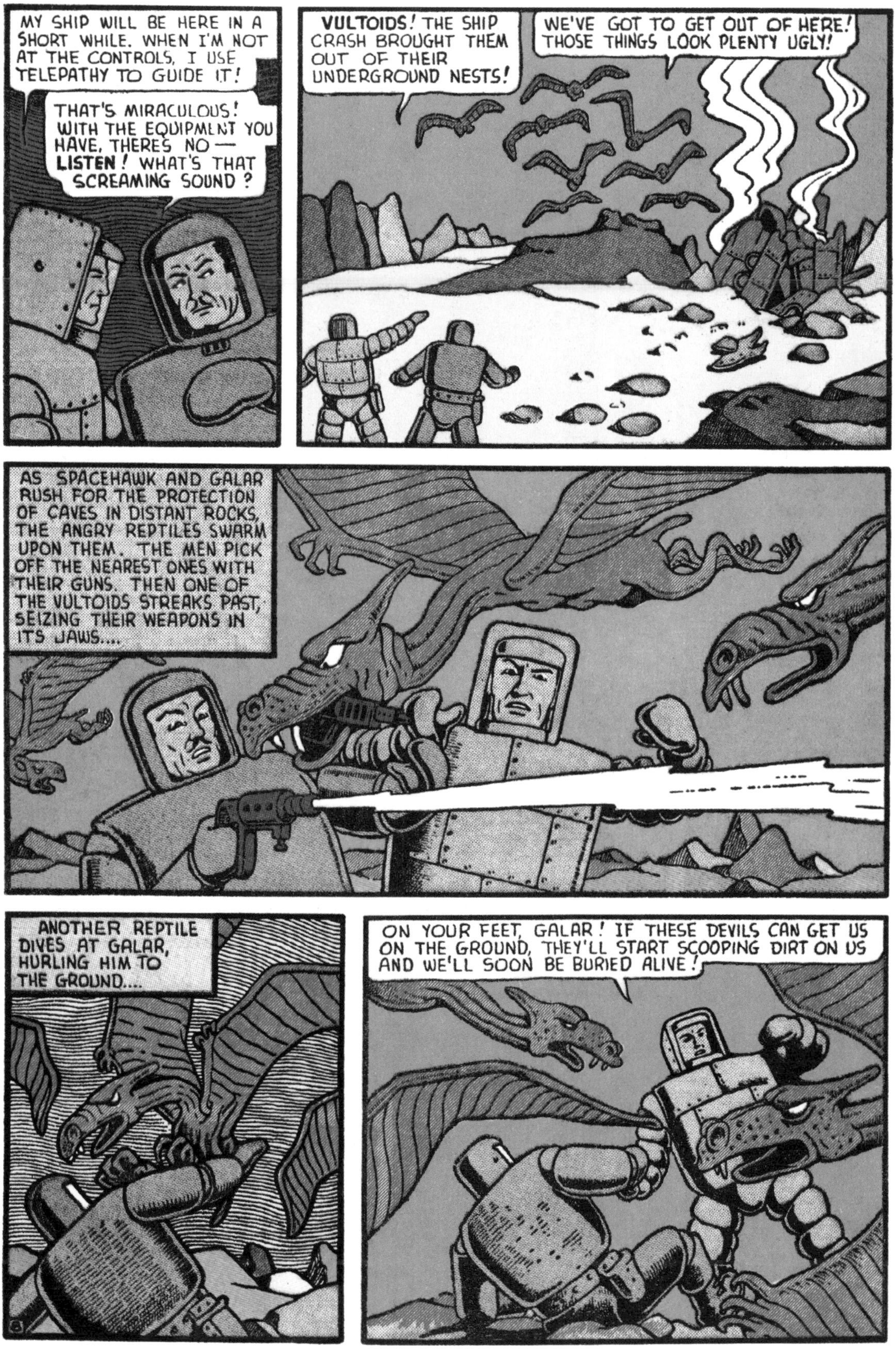
MY SHIP WILL BE HERE IN A SHORT WHILE. WHEN I'M NOT AT THE CONTROLS, I USE TELEPATHY TO GUIDE IT!
THAT'S MIRACULOUS! WITH THE EQUIPMENT YOU HAVE, THERES NO— LISTEN! WHAT'S THAT SCREAMING SOUND?
VULTOIDS! THE SHIP CRASH BROUGHT THEM OUT OF THEIR UNDERGROUND NESTS!
WE'VE GOT TO GET OUT OF HERE! THOSE THINGS LOOK PLENTY UGLY!
AS SPACEHAWK AND GALAR RUSH FOR THE PROTECTION OF CAVES IN DISTANT ROCKS, THE ANGRY REPTILES SWARM UPON THEM. THE MEN PICK OFF THE NEAREST ONES WITH THEIR GUNS. THEN ONE OF THE VULTOIDS STREAKS PAST, SEIZING THEIR WEAPONS IN ITS JAWS....
ANOTHER REPTILE DIVES AT GALAR, HURLING HIM TO THE GROUND....
ON YOUR FEET, GALAR! IF THESE DEVILS CAN GET US ON THE GROUND, THEY'LL START SCOOPING DIRT ON US AND WE'LL SOON BE BURIED ALIVE!

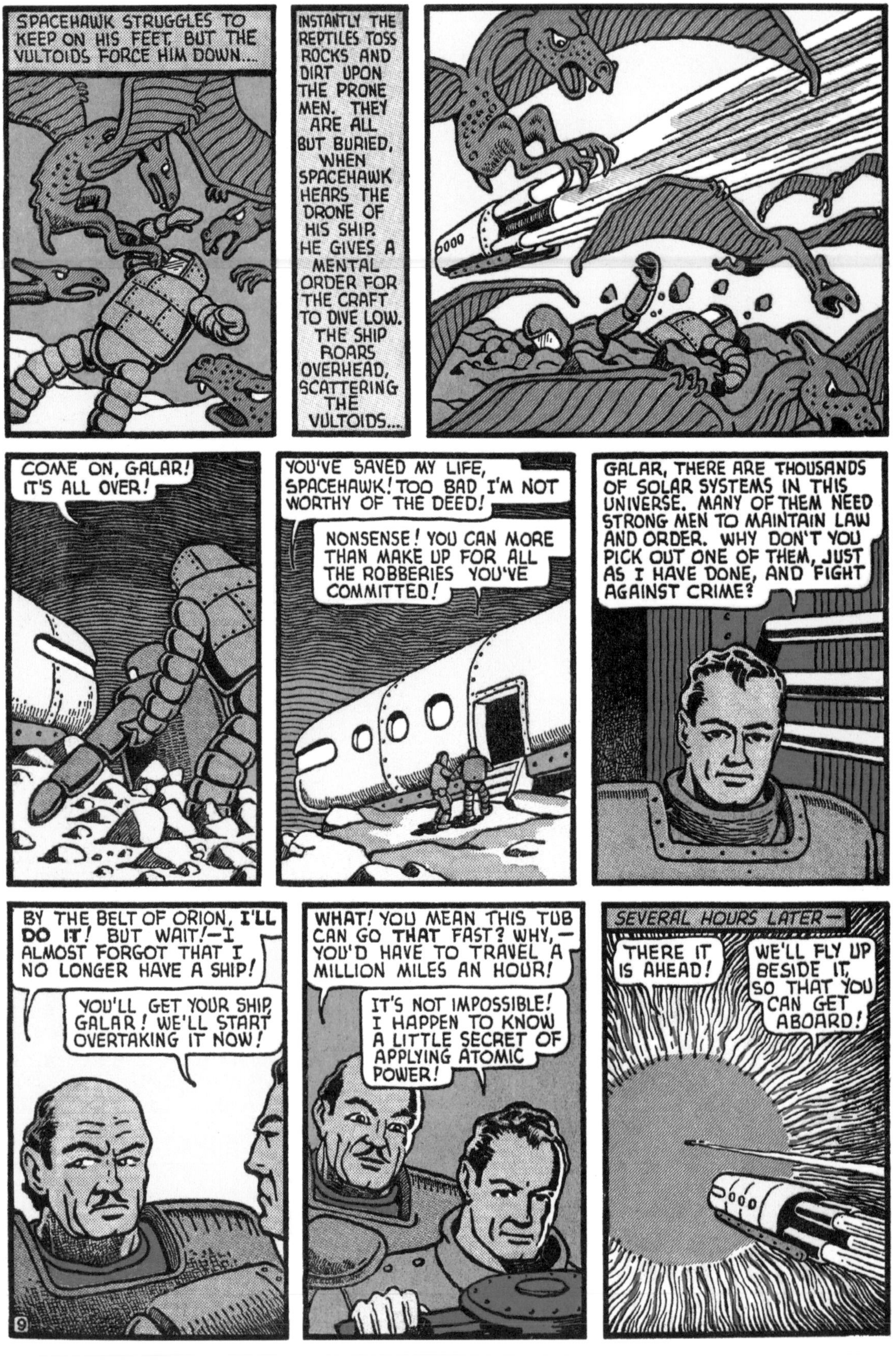
SPACEHAWK STRUGGLES TO KEEP ON HIS FEET, BUT THE VULTOIDS FORCE HIM DOWN...
INSTANTLY THE REPTILES TOSS ROCKS AND DIRT UPON THE PRONE MEN. THEY ARE ALL BUT BURIED, WHEN SPACEHAWK HEARS THE DRONE OF HIS SHIP. HE GIVES A MENTAL ORDER FOR THE CRAFT TO DIVE LOW. THE SHIP ROARS OVERHEAD, SCATTERING THE VULTOIDS...
COME ON, GALAR! IT'S ALL OVER!
YOU'VE SAVED MY LIFE, SPACEHAWK! TOO BAD I'M NOT WORTHY OF THE DEED!
NONSENSE! YOU CAN MORE THAN MAKE UP FOR ALL THE ROBBERIES YOU'VE COMMITTED!
GALAR, THERE ARE THOUSANDS OF SOLAR SYSTEMS IN THIS UNIVERSE. MANY OF THEM NEED STRONG MEN TO MAINTAIN LAW AND ORDER. WHY DON'T YOU PICK OUT ONE OF THEM, JUST AS I HAVE DONE, AND FIGHT AGAINST CRIME?
BY THE BELT OF ORION, I'LL DO IT! BUT WAIT!—I ALMOST FORGOT THAT I NO LONGER HAVE A SHIP!
YOU'LL GET YOUR SHIP, GALAR! WE'LL START OVERTAKING IT NOW!
9
WHAT! YOU MEAN THIS TUB CAN GO THAT FAST? WHY,—YOU'D HAVE TO TRAVEL A MILLION MILES AN HOUR!
IT'S NOT IMPOSSIBLE! I HAPPEN TO KNOW A LITTLE SECRET OF APPLYING ATOMIC POWER!
SEVERAL HOURS LATER—
THERE IT IS AHEAD!
WE'LL FLY UP BESIDE IT, SO THAT YOU CAN GET ABOARD!

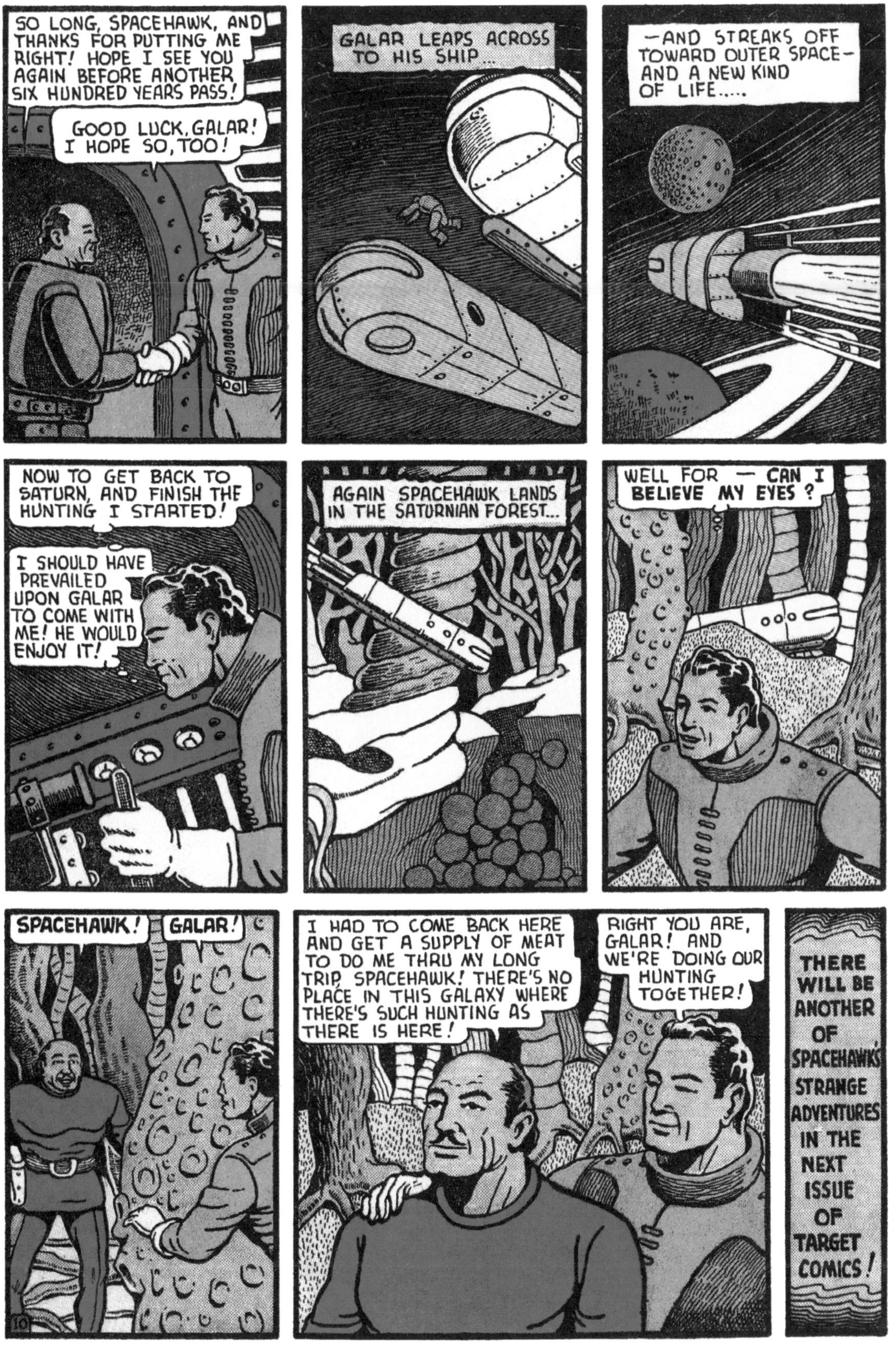
SO LONG, SPACEHAWK, AND THANKS FOR PUTTING ME RIGHT! HOPE I SEE YOU AGAIN BEFORE ANOTHER SIX HUNDRED YEARS PASS!
GOOD LUCK, GALAR! I HOPE SO, TOO!
GALAR LEAPS ACROSS TO HIS SHIP...
—AND STREAKS OFF TOWARD OUTER SPACE— AND A NEW KIND OF LIFE.....
NOW TO GET BACK TO SATURN, AND FINISH THE HUNTING I STARTED!
I SHOULD HAVE PREVAILED UPON GALAR TO COME WITH ME! HE WOULD ENJOY IT!
AGAIN SPACEHAWK LANDS IN THE SATURNIAN FOREST...
WELL FOR — CAN I BELIEVE MY EYES?
SPACEHAWK!
GALAR!
10
I HAD TO COME BACK HERE AND GET A SUPPLY OF MEAT TO DO ME THRU MY LONG TRIP, SPACEHAWK! THERE'S NO PLACE IN THIS GALAXY WHERE THERE'S SUCH HUNTING AS THERE IS HERE!
RIGHT YOU ARE, GALAR! AND WE'RE DOING OUR HUNTING TOGETHER!
THERE WILL BE ANOTHER OF SPACEHAWK'S STRANGE ADVENTURES IN THE NEXT ISSUE OF TARGET COMICS!

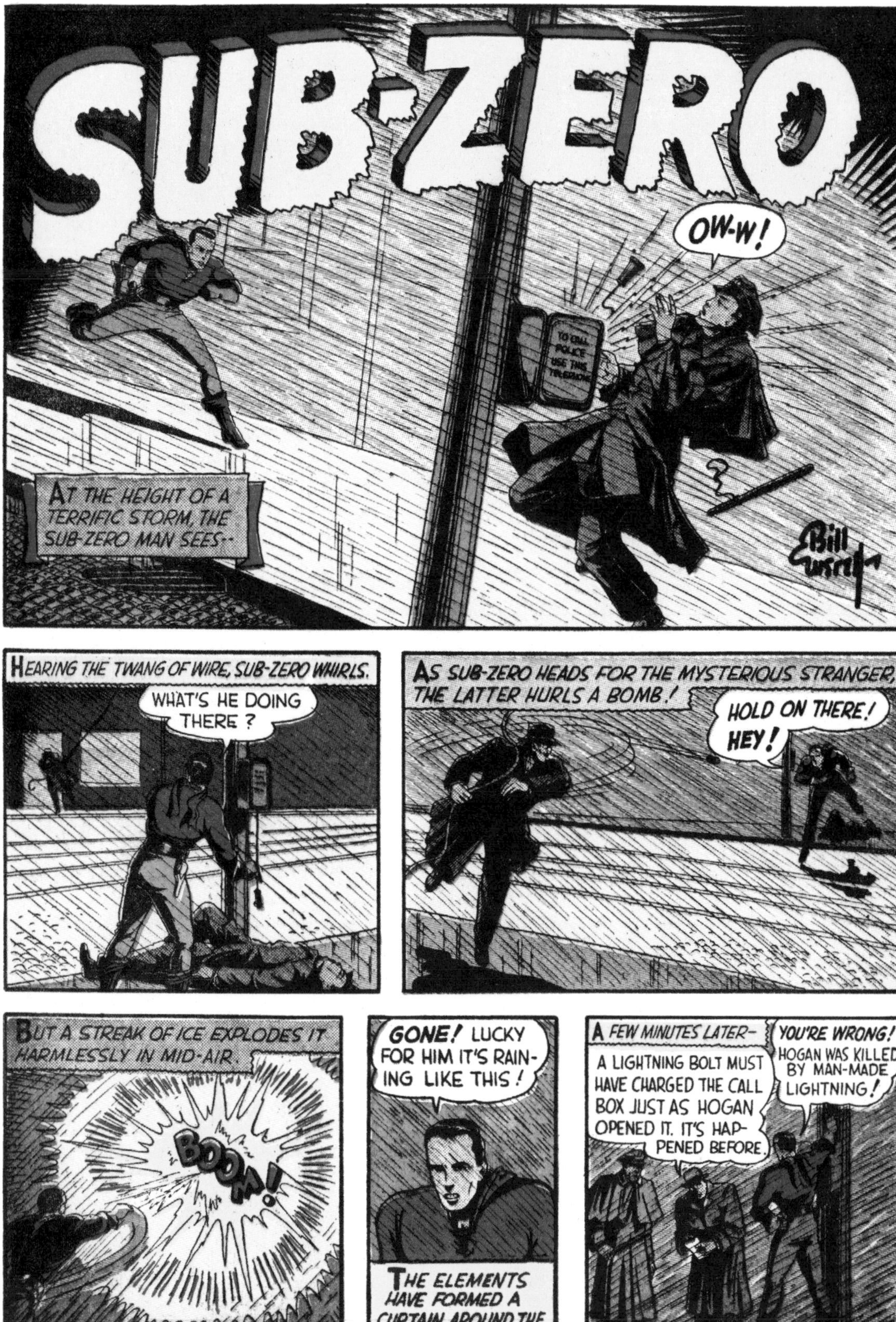
SUB-ZERO
OW-W!
TO CALL POLICE USE THIS TELEPHONE
AT THE HEIGHT OF A TERRIFIC STORM, THE SUB-ZERO MAN SEES--
Bill Everett
HEARING THE TWANG OF WIRE, SUB-ZERO WHIRLS.
WHAT'S HE DOING THERE ?
AS SUB-ZERO HEADS FOR THE MYSTERIOUS STRANGER, THE LATTER HURLS A BOMB !
HOLD ON THERE! HEY!
BUT A STREAK OF ICE EXPLODES IT HARMLESSLY IN MID-AIR.
BOOM!
GONE! LUCKY FOR HIM IT'S RAINING LIKE THIS !
THE ELEMENTS HAVE FORMED A CURTAIN AROUND THE FLEEING FUGITIVE.
A FEW MINUTES LATER--
A LIGHTNING BOLT MUST HAVE CHARGED THE CALL BOX JUST AS HOGAN OPENED IT. IT'S HAPPENED BEFORE.
YOU'RE WRONG! HOGAN WAS KILLED BY MAN-MADE LIGHTNING!

SOMEONE RAN A WIRE FROM THOSE HIGH-TENSION TROLLEY CAR LINES TO THE CALL BOX. I SAW HIM, BUT HE GOT AWAY!

*THE FOLLOWING NIGHT, THE SUB-ZERO MAN IS SUMMONED TO THE HOME OF DISTRICT ATTORNEY JOHNSON...*

I WANT YOU TO HELP ME FIND THE SLAYER OF PATROLMAN HOGAN. IF ANYONE CAN DO IT, IT'S **YOU!**

ANY IDEA WHO IT MIGHT BE?

I HAVEN'T ANY PROOF YET, BUT I'LL STAKE MY REPUTATION ON ITS BEING "PROFESSOR X" —ONE OF THE MOST DIABOLICAL CRIMINALS I'VE EVER KNOWN. I FIRST RAN ACROSS HIM.....

"... BACK IN THE BOOTLEGGING ERA, HE WAS EMPLOYED TO MANUFACTURE INGENIOUS WEAPONS OF DEATH FOR GANGSTERS."

BULKY LITTLE MACHINE, BUT, *AH-* SO SENSITIVE!

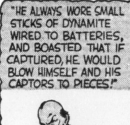

"HE ALWAYS WORE SMALL STICKS OF DYNAMITE WIRED TO BATTERIES, AND BOASTED THAT IF CAPTURED, HE WOULD BLOW HIMSELF AND HIS CAPTORS TO PIECES!"

"BUT ONE DAY HOGAN KNOCKED THE PROFESSOR INTO THE RIVER. THE WATER RENDERED THE DYNAMITE USELESS, AND HOGAN HAULED HIM TO SHORE."

*TAKE THAT, SMART GUY!*

"I HAD THE PLEASURE OF PROSECUTING THE CASE."

I HEREBY SENTENCE YOU TO TWENTY YEARS PENAL SERVITUDE IN STATE'S PRISON!

*WHAT!?!*

"PROFESSOR X SWORE HE'D GET REVENGE. HE SAID NO JAIL COULD EVER HOLD HIM. LAST WEEK—

*HA! THE FOOLS!*

—HE MADE GOOD HIS BOAST."

I GOT IN JUST A FEW MINUTES AGO AND FOUND A MESSAGE. IT WAS SIGNED,"PROFESSOR X", AND SAID,"I GOT HOGAN— YOU'RE NEXT!"

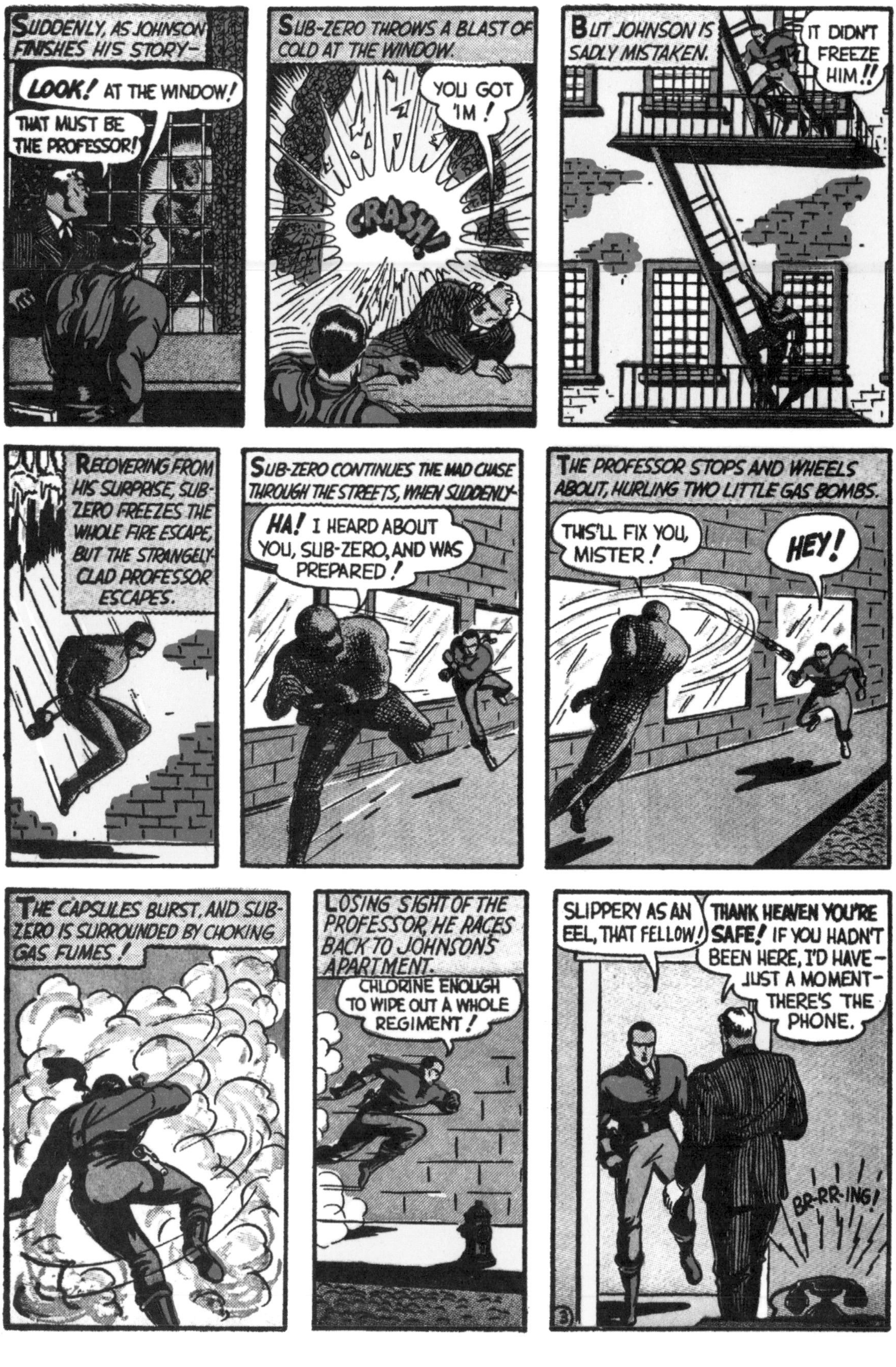
SUDDENLY, AS JOHNSON FINISHES HIS STORY—
LOOK! AT THE WINDOW!
THAT MUST BE THE PROFESSOR!
SUB-ZERO THROWS A BLAST OF COLD AT THE WINDOW.
YOU GOT 'IM!
CRASH!
BUT JOHNSON IS SADLY MISTAKEN.
IT DIDN'T FREEZE HIM!!
RECOVERING FROM HIS SURPRISE, SUB-ZERO FREEZES THE WHOLE FIRE ESCAPE, BUT THE STRANGELY-CLAD PROFESSOR ESCAPES.
SUB-ZERO CONTINUES THE MAD CHASE THROUGH THE STREETS, WHEN SUDDENLY—
HA! I HEARD ABOUT YOU, SUB-ZERO, AND WAS PREPARED!
THE PROFESSOR STOPS AND WHEELS ABOUT, HURLING TWO LITTLE GAS BOMBS.
THIS'LL FIX YOU, MISTER!
HEY!
THE CAPSULES BURST, AND SUB-ZERO IS SURROUNDED BY CHOKING GAS FUMES!
LOSING SIGHT OF THE PROFESSOR, HE RACES BACK TO JOHNSON'S APARTMENT.
CHLORINE ENOUGH TO WIPE OUT A WHOLE REGIMENT!
SLIPPERY AS AN EEL, THAT FELLOW!
THANK HEAVEN YOU'RE SAFE! IF YOU HADN'T BEEN HERE, I'D HAVE— JUST A MOMENT— THERE'S THE PHONE.
BR-RR-ING!
3

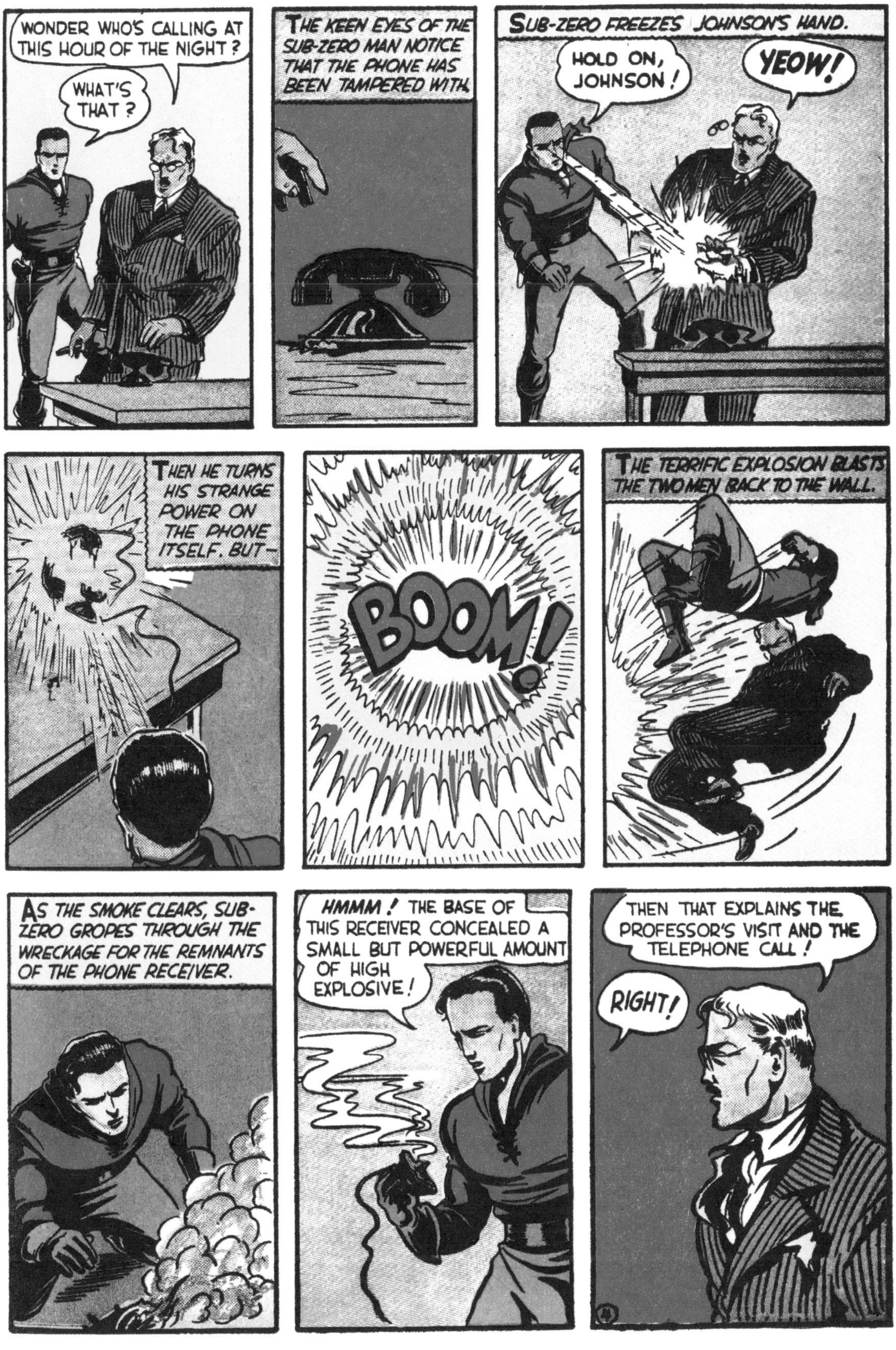
WONDER WHO'S CALLING AT THIS HOUR OF THE NIGHT?
WHAT'S THAT?
THE KEEN EYES OF THE SUB-ZERO MAN NOTICE THAT THE PHONE HAS BEEN TAMPERED WITH.
SUB-ZERO FREEZES JOHNSON'S HAND.
HOLD ON, JOHNSON!
YEOW!
THEN HE TURNS HIS STRANGE POWER ON THE PHONE ITSELF. BUT–
BOOM!
THE TERRIFIC EXPLOSION BLASTS THE TWO MEN BACK TO THE WALL.
AS THE SMOKE CLEARS, SUB-ZERO GROPES THROUGH THE WRECKAGE FOR THE REMNANTS OF THE PHONE RECEIVER.
HMMM! THE BASE OF THIS RECEIVER CONCEALED A SMALL BUT POWERFUL AMOUNT OF HIGH EXPLOSIVE!
THEN THAT EXPLAINS THE PROFESSOR'S VISIT AND THE TELEPHONE CALL!
RIGHT!

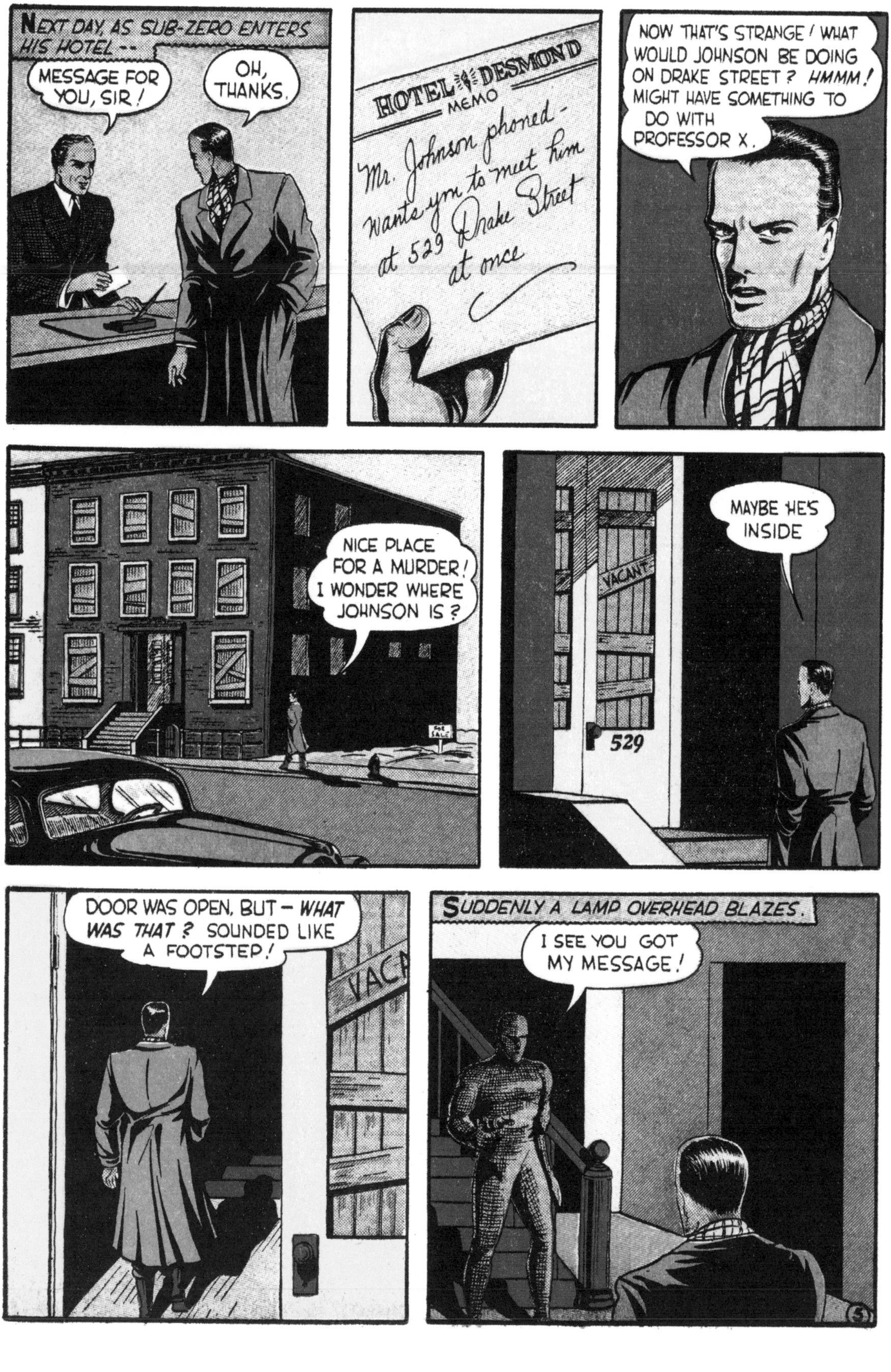
NEXT DAY, AS SUB-ZERO ENTERS HIS HOTEL --
MESSAGE FOR YOU, SIR!
OH, THANKS.
HOTEL DESMOND
MEMO
Mr. Johnson phoned - wants you to meet him at 529 Drake Street at once
NOW THAT'S STRANGE! WHAT WOULD JOHNSON BE DOING ON DRAKE STREET? HMMM! MIGHT HAVE SOMETHING TO DO WITH PROFESSOR X.
NICE PLACE FOR A MURDER! I WONDER WHERE JOHNSON IS?
VACANT
529
MAYBE HE'S INSIDE
DOOR WAS OPEN, BUT - WHAT WAS THAT? SOUNDED LIKE A FOOTSTEP!
SUDDENLY A LAMP OVERHEAD BLAZES.
I SEE YOU GOT MY MESSAGE!

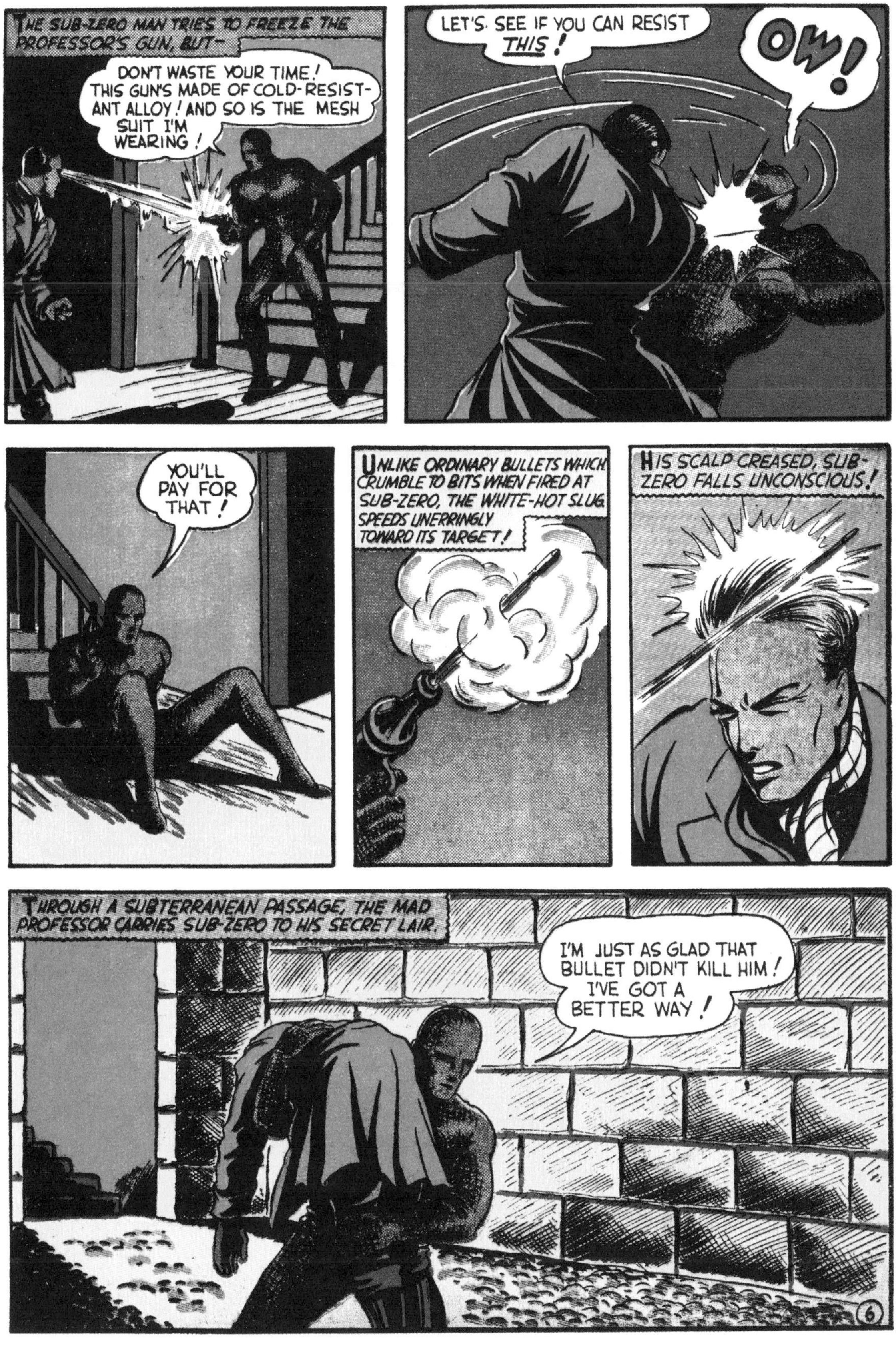
THE SUB-ZERO MAN TRIES TO FREEZE THE PROFESSOR'S GUN, BUT—
DON'T WASTE YOUR TIME! THIS GUN'S MADE OF COLD-RESISTANT ALLOY! AND SO IS THE MESH SUIT I'M WEARING!
LET'S SEE IF YOU CAN RESIST THIS!
OW!
YOU'LL PAY FOR THAT!
UNLIKE ORDINARY BULLETS WHICH CRUMBLE TO BITS WHEN FIRED AT SUB-ZERO, THE WHITE-HOT SLUG SPEEDS UNERRINGLY TOWARD ITS TARGET!
HIS SCALP CREASED, SUB-ZERO FALLS UNCONSCIOUS!
THROUGH A SUBTERRANEAN PASSAGE, THE MAD PROFESSOR CARRIES SUB-ZERO TO HIS SECRET LAIR.
I'M JUST AS GLAD THAT BULLET DIDN'T KILL HIM! I'VE GOT A BETTER WAY!
6

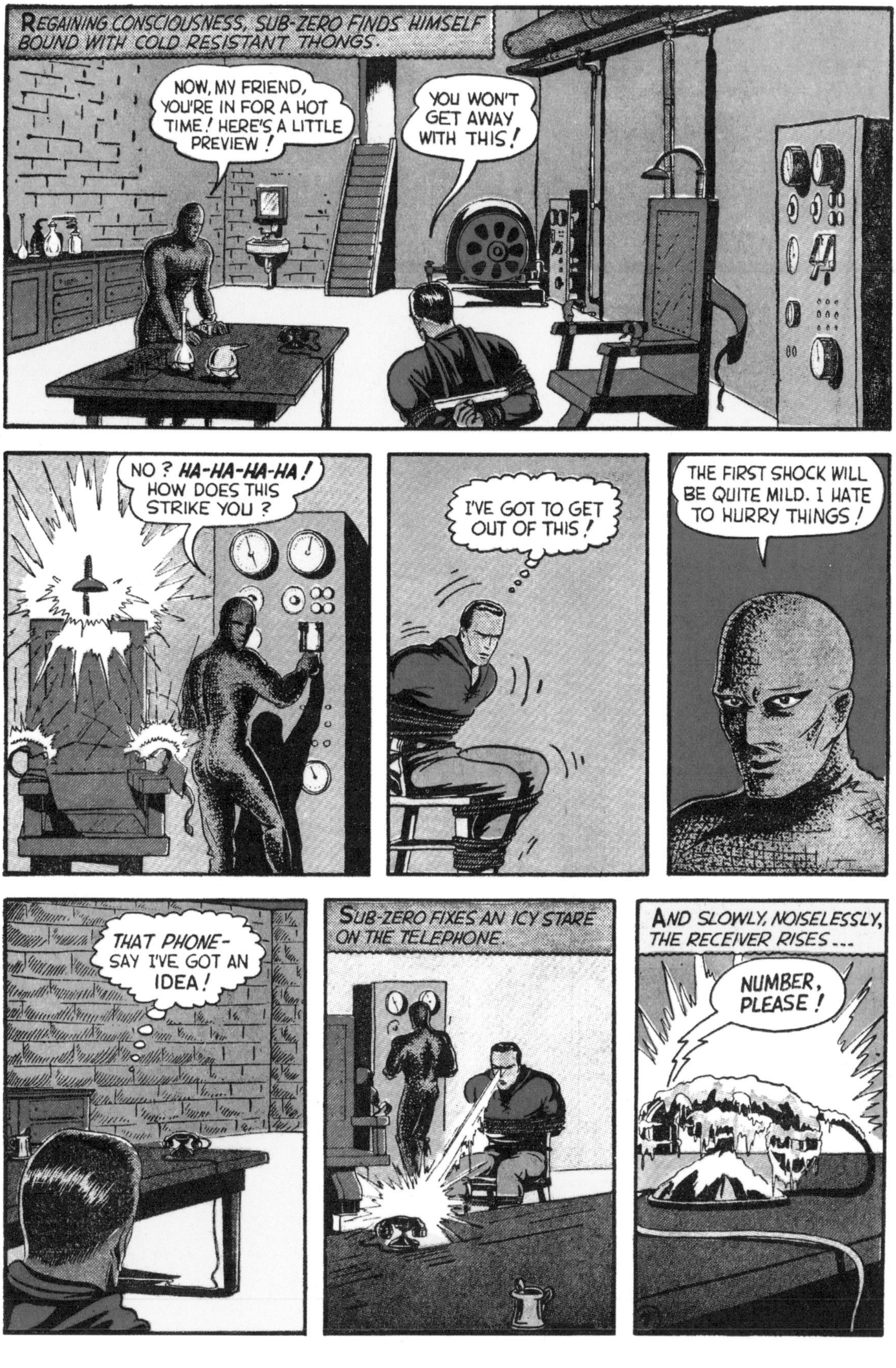
REGAINING CONSCIOUSNESS, SUB-ZERO FINDS HIMSELF BOUND WITH COLD RESISTANT THONGS.
NOW, MY FRIEND, YOU'RE IN FOR A HOT TIME! HERE'S A LITTLE PREVIEW!
YOU WON'T GET AWAY WITH THIS!
NO? HA-HA-HA-HA! HOW DOES THIS STRIKE YOU?
I'VE GOT TO GET OUT OF THIS!
THE FIRST SHOCK WILL BE QUITE MILD. I HATE TO HURRY THINGS!
THAT PHONE- SAY I'VE GOT AN IDEA!
SUB-ZERO FIXES AN ICY STARE ON THE TELEPHONE.
AND SLOWLY, NOISELESSLY, THE RECEIVER RISES...
NUMBER, PLEASE!

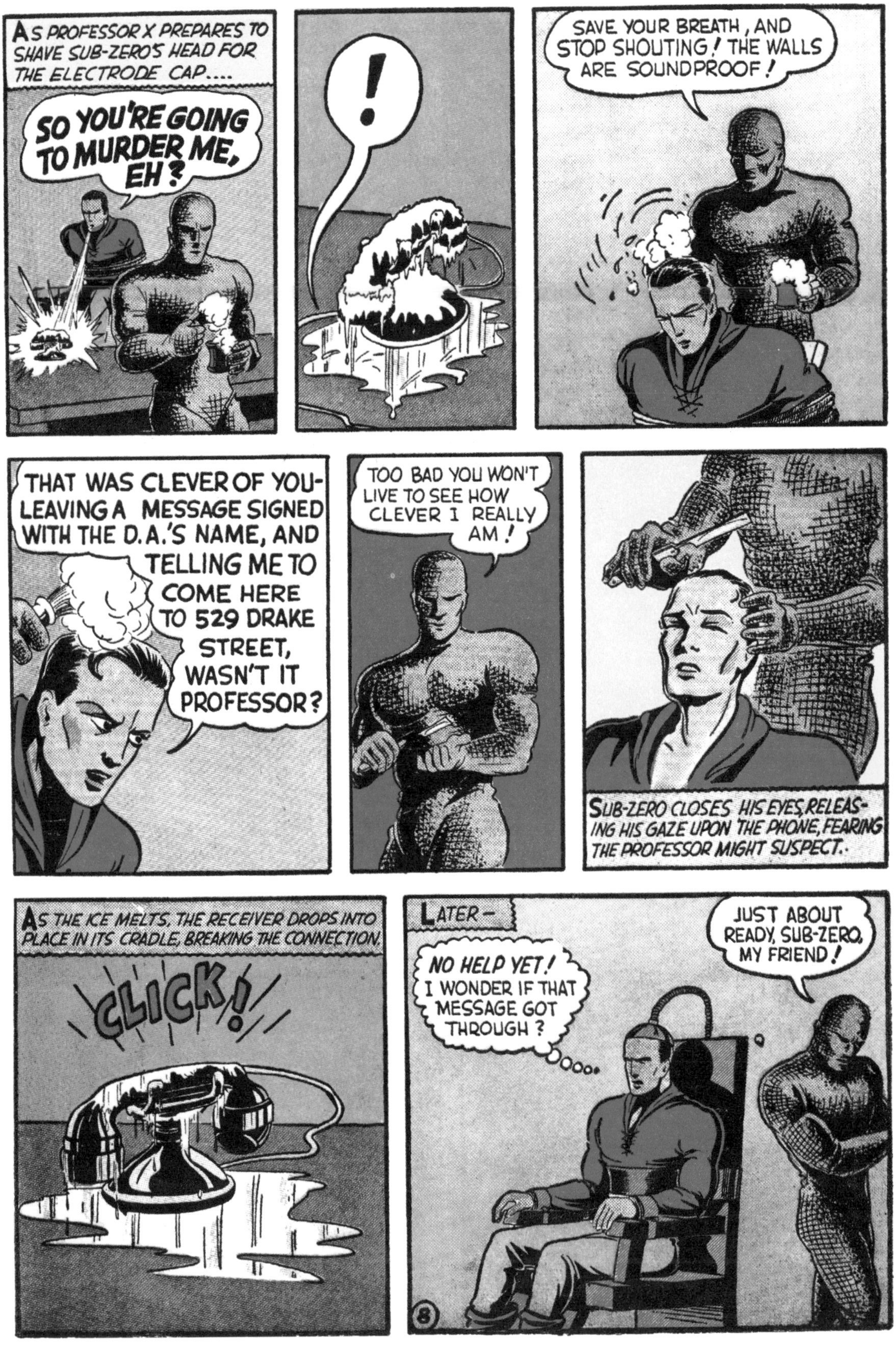
AS PROFESSOR X PREPARES TO SHAVE SUB-ZERO'S HEAD FOR THE ELECTRODE CAP....
SO YOU'RE GOING TO MURDER ME, EH?
!
SAVE YOUR BREATH, AND STOP SHOUTING! THE WALLS ARE SOUNDPROOF!
THAT WAS CLEVER OF YOU-LEAVING A MESSAGE SIGNED WITH THE D.A.'S NAME, AND TELLING ME TO COME HERE TO 529 DRAKE STREET, WASN'T IT PROFESSOR?
TOO BAD YOU WON'T LIVE TO SEE HOW CLEVER I REALLY AM!
SUB-ZERO CLOSES HIS EYES, RELEASING HIS GAZE UPON THE PHONE, FEARING THE PROFESSOR MIGHT SUSPECT.
AS THE ICE MELTS, THE RECEIVER DROPS INTO PLACE IN ITS CRADLE, BREAKING THE CONNECTION.
CLICK!
LATER-
JUST ABOUT READY, SUB-ZERO, MY FRIEND!
NO HELP YET! I WONDER IF THAT MESSAGE GOT THROUGH?
8

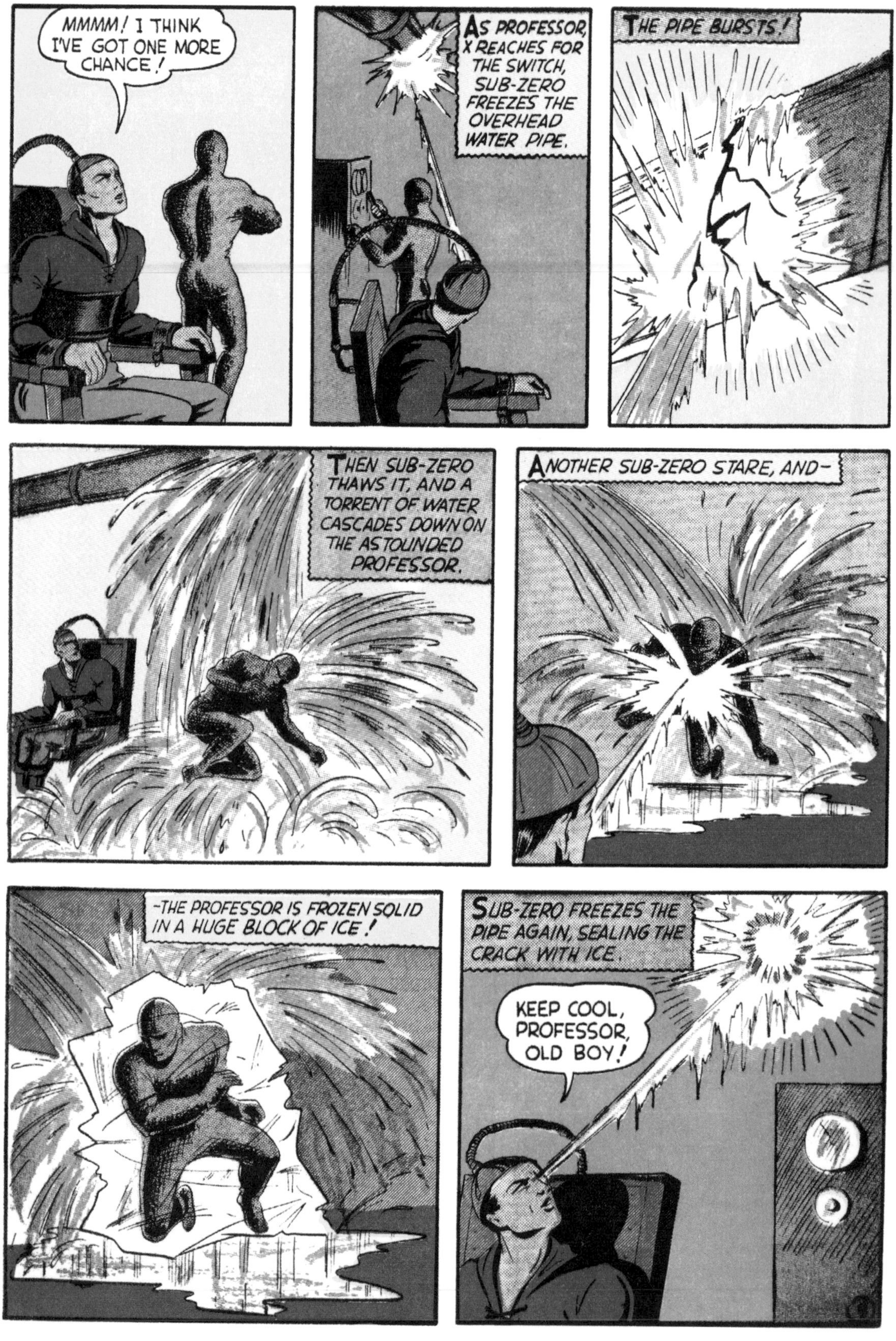
MMMM! I THINK I'VE GOT ONE MORE CHANCE!
AS PROFESSOR X REACHES FOR THE SWITCH, SUB-ZERO FREEZES THE OVERHEAD WATER PIPE.
THE PIPE BURSTS!
THEN SUB-ZERO THAWS IT, AND A TORRENT OF WATER CASCADES DOWN ON THE ASTOUNDED PROFESSOR.
ANOTHER SUB-ZERO STARE, AND-
-THE PROFESSOR IS FROZEN SOLID IN A HUGE BLOCK OF ICE!
SUB-ZERO FREEZES THE PIPE AGAIN, SEALING THE CRACK WITH ICE.
KEEP COOL, PROFESSOR, OLD BOY!

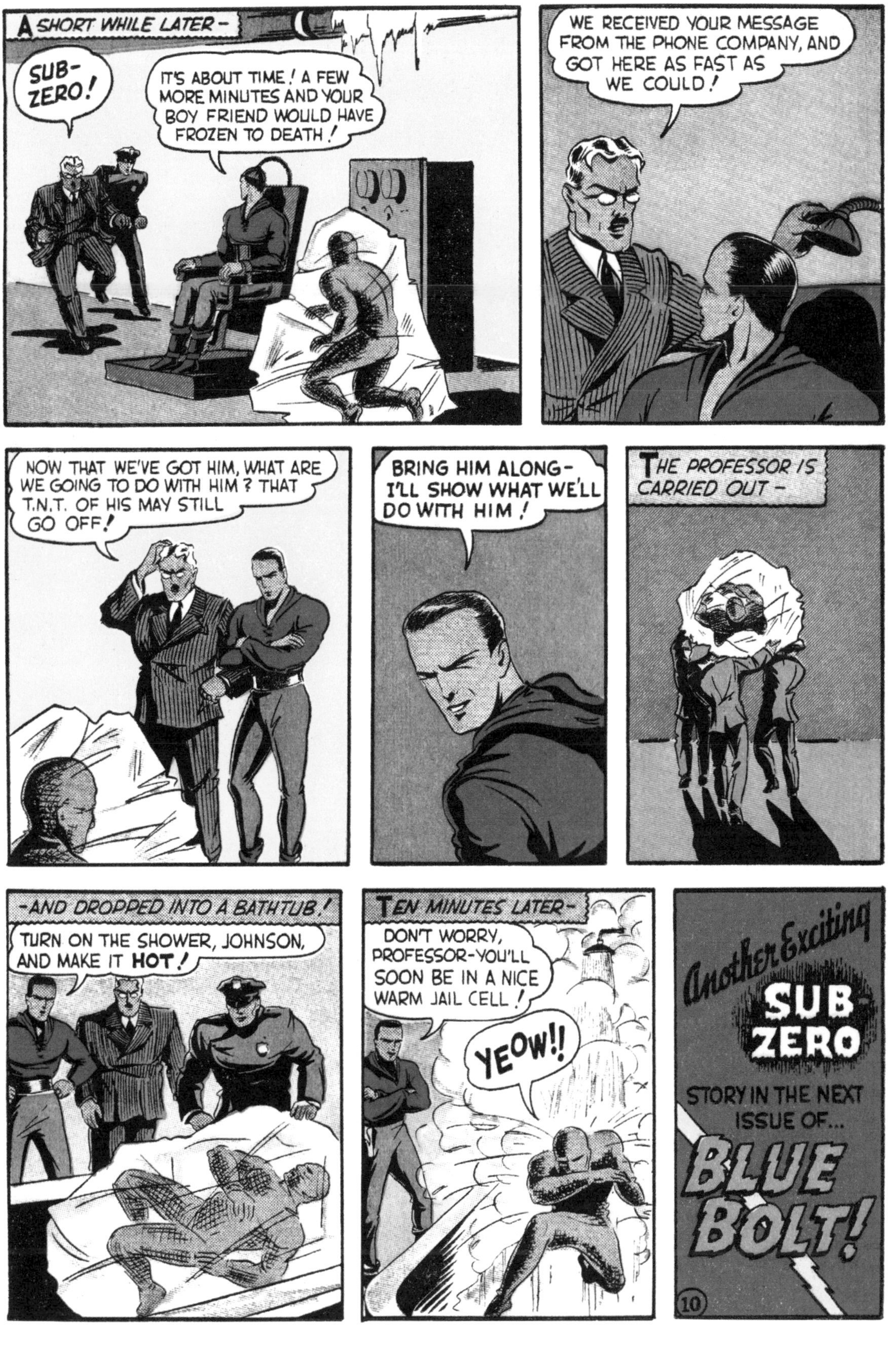
A SHORT WHILE LATER -
SUB-ZERO!
IT'S ABOUT TIME! A FEW MORE MINUTES AND YOUR BOY FRIEND WOULD HAVE FROZEN TO DEATH!
WE RECEIVED YOUR MESSAGE FROM THE PHONE COMPANY, AND GOT HERE AS FAST AS WE COULD!
NOW THAT WE'VE GOT HIM, WHAT ARE WE GOING TO DO WITH HIM? THAT T.N.T. OF HIS MAY STILL GO OFF!
BRING HIM ALONG- I'LL SHOW WHAT WE'LL DO WITH HIM!
THE PROFESSOR IS CARRIED OUT -
-AND DROPPED INTO A BATHTUB!
TURN ON THE SHOWER, JOHNSON, AND MAKE IT HOT!
TEN MINUTES LATER -
DON'T WORRY, PROFESSOR-YOU'LL SOON BE IN A NICE WARM JAIL CELL!
YEOW!!
Another Exciting
SUB-ZERO
STORY IN THE NEXT ISSUE OF...
BLUE BOLT!
10

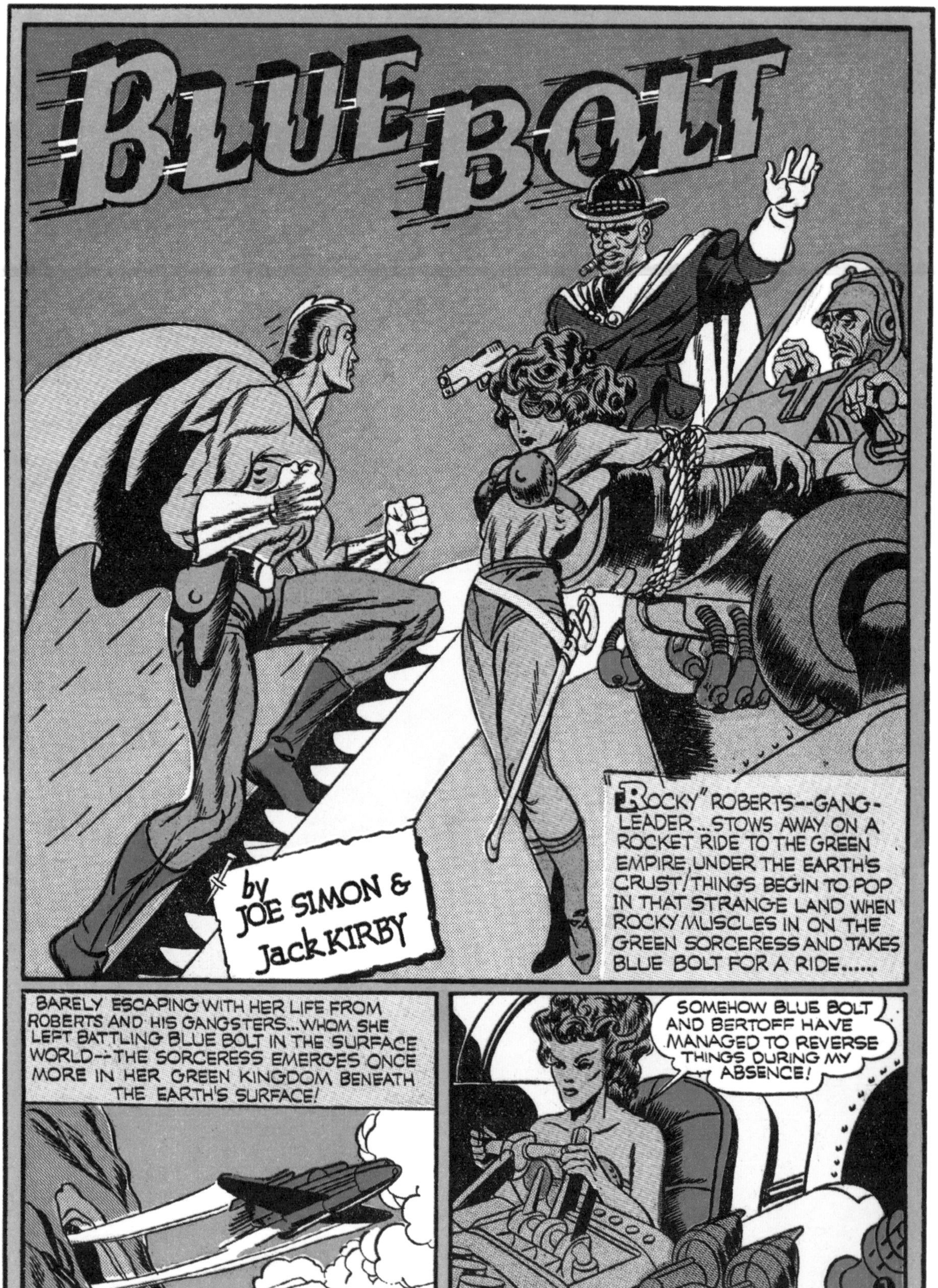
BLUE BOLT
by JOE SIMON & Jack KIRBY
"ROCKY" ROBERTS--GANG-LEADER...STOWS AWAY ON A ROCKET RIDE TO THE GREEN EMPIRE UNDER THE EARTH'S CRUST! THINGS BEGIN TO POP IN THAT STRANGE LAND WHEN ROCKY MUSCLES IN ON THE GREEN SORCERESS AND TAKES BLUE BOLT FOR A RIDE......
BARELY ESCAPING WITH HER LIFE FROM ROBERTS AND HIS GANGSTERS...WHOM SHE LEFT BATTLING BLUE BOLT IN THE SURFACE WORLD--THE SORCERESS EMERGES ONCE MORE IN HER GREEN KINGDOM BENEATH THE EARTH'S SURFACE!
SOMEHOW BLUE BOLT AND BERTOFF HAVE MANAGED TO REVERSE THINGS DURING MY ABSENCE!
1

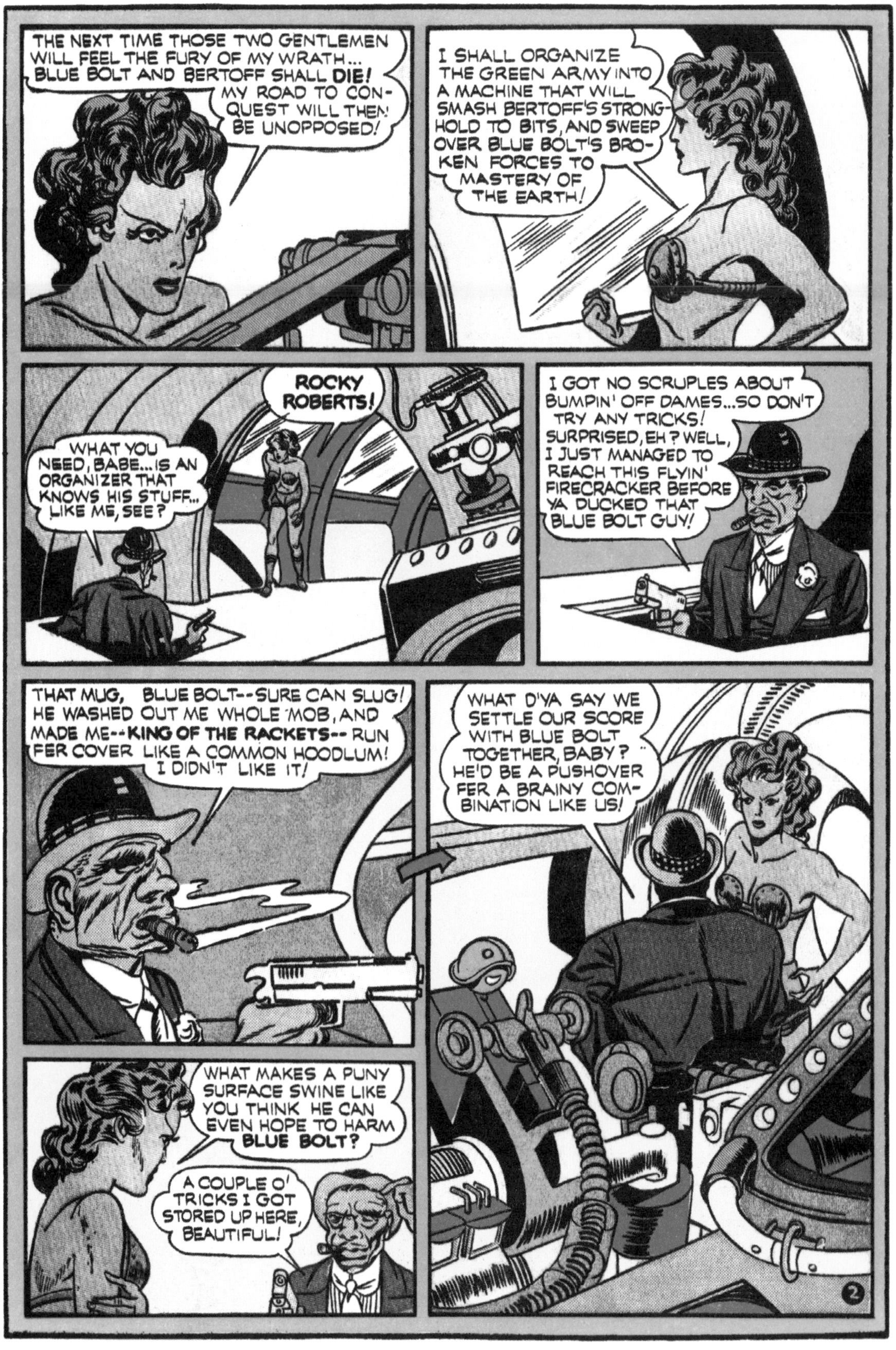
THE NEXT TIME THOSE TWO GENTLEMEN WILL FEEL THE FURY OF MY WRATH... BLUE BOLT AND BERTOFF SHALL DIE!
MY ROAD TO CONQUEST WILL THEN BE UNOPPOSED!
I SHALL ORGANIZE THE GREEN ARMY INTO A MACHINE THAT WILL SMASH BERTOFF'S STRONGHOLD TO BITS, AND SWEEP OVER BLUE BOLT'S BROKEN FORCES TO MASTERY OF THE EARTH!
WHAT YOU NEED, BABE...IS AN ORGANIZER THAT KNOWS HIS STUFF.. LIKE ME, SEE?
ROCKY ROBERTS!
I GOT NO SCRUPLES ABOUT BUMPIN' OFF DAMES...SO DON'T TRY ANY TRICKS! SURPRISED, EH? WELL, I JUST MANAGED TO REACH THIS FLYIN' FIRECRACKER BEFORE YA DUCKED THAT BLUE BOLT GUY!
THAT MUG, BLUE BOLT--SURE CAN SLUG! HE WASHED OUT ME WHOLE MOB, AND MADE ME--KING OF THE RACKETS-- RUN FER COVER LIKE A COMMON HOODLUM! I DIDN'T LIKE IT!
WHAT MAKES A PUNY SURFACE SWINE LIKE YOU THINK HE CAN EVEN HOPE TO HARM BLUE BOLT?
A COUPLE O' TRICKS I GOT STORED UP HERE, BEAUTIFUL!
WHAT D'YA SAY WE SETTLE OUR SCORE WITH BLUE BOLT TOGETHER, BABY? HE'D BE A PUSHOVER FER A BRAINY COMBINATION LIKE US!
2

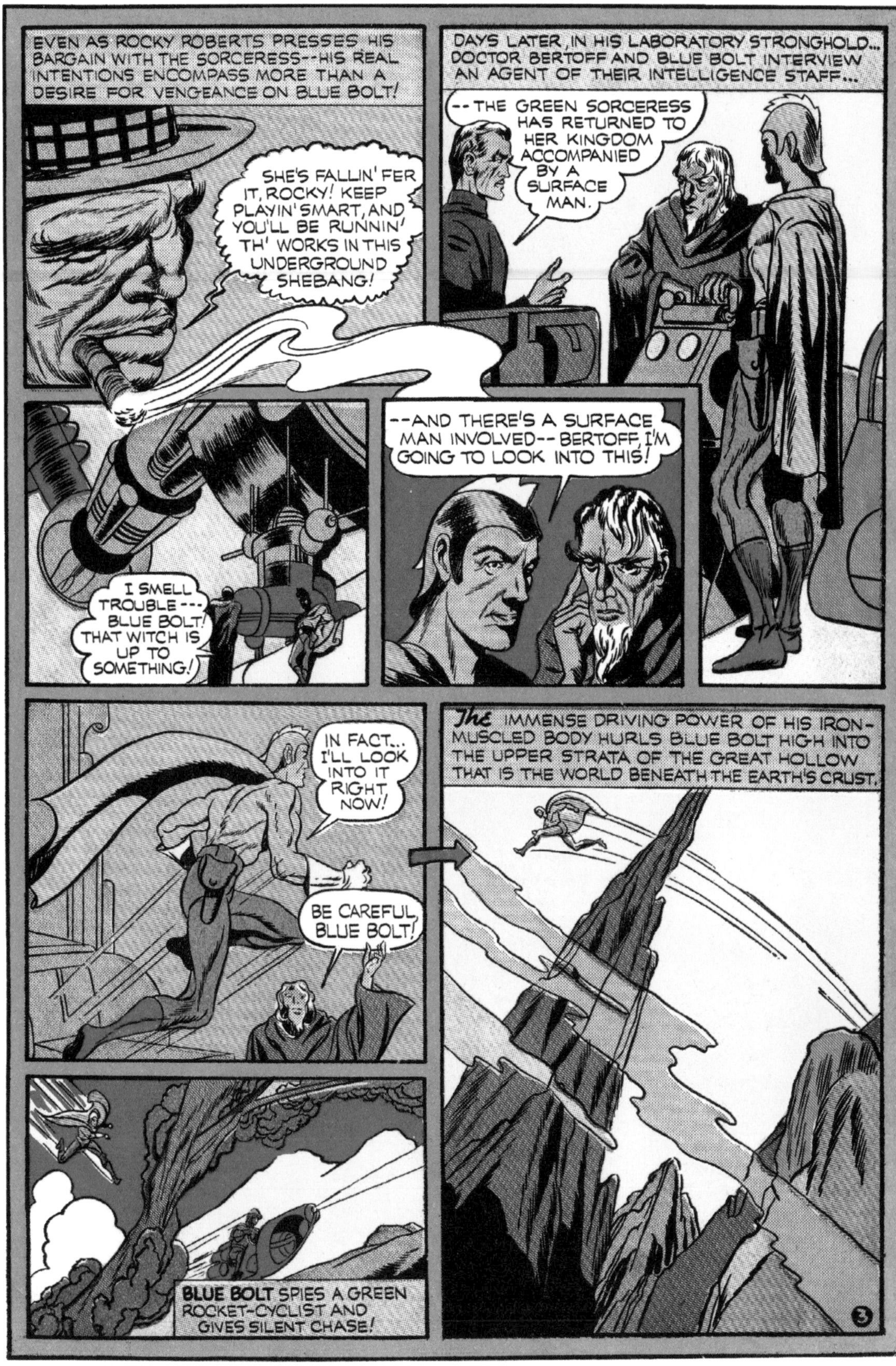
EVEN AS ROCKY ROBERTS PRESSES HIS BARGAIN WITH THE SORCERESS--HIS REAL INTENTIONS ENCOMPASS MORE THAN A DESIRE FOR VENGEANCE ON BLUE BOLT!
SHE'S FALLIN' FER IT, ROCKY! KEEP PLAYIN' SMART, AND YOU'LL BE RUNNIN' TH' WORKS IN THIS UNDERGROUND SHEBANG!
DAYS LATER, IN HIS LABORATORY STRONGHOLD... DOCTOR BERTOFF AND BLUE BOLT INTERVIEW AN AGENT OF THEIR INTELLIGENCE STAFF...
--THE GREEN SORCERESS HAS RETURNED TO HER KINGDOM ACCOMPANIED BY A SURFACE MAN.
I SMELL TROUBLE--- BLUE BOLT! THAT WITCH IS UP TO SOMETHING!
--AND THERE'S A SURFACE MAN INVOLVED-- BERTOFF, I'M GOING TO LOOK INTO THIS!
IN FACT... I'LL LOOK INTO IT RIGHT NOW!
BE CAREFUL, BLUE BOLT!
THE IMMENSE DRIVING POWER OF HIS IRON-MUSCLED BODY HURLS BLUE BOLT HIGH INTO THE UPPER STRATA OF THE GREAT HOLLOW THAT IS THE WORLD BENEATH THE EARTH'S CRUST.
BLUE BOLT SPIES A GREEN ROCKET-CYCLIST AND GIVES SILENT CHASE!
3

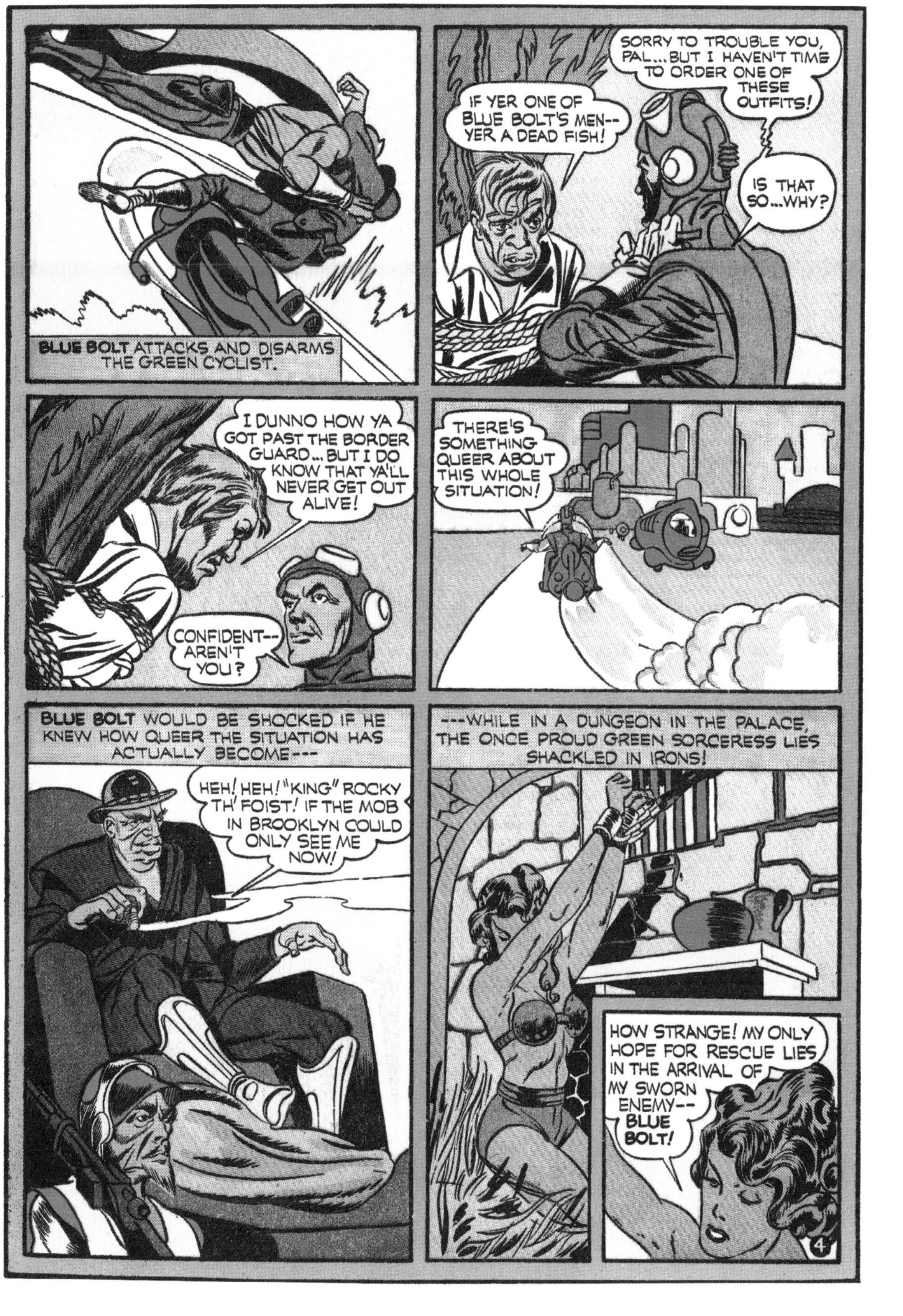
BLUE BOLT ATTACKS AND DISARMS THE GREEN CYCLIST.
SORRY TO TROUBLE YOU, PAL... BUT I HAVEN'T TIME TO ORDER ONE OF THESE OUTFITS!
IF YER ONE OF BLUE BOLT'S MEN-- YER A DEAD FISH!
IS THAT SO...WHY?
I DUNNO HOW YA GOT PAST THE BORDER GUARD... BUT I DO KNOW THAT YA'LL NEVER GET OUT ALIVE!
CONFIDENT-- AREN'T YOU?
THERE'S SOMETHING QUEER ABOUT THIS WHOLE SITUATION!
BLUE BOLT WOULD BE SHOCKED IF HE KNEW HOW QUEER THE SITUATION HAS ACTUALLY BECOME---
HEH! HEH! "KING" ROCKY TH' FOIST! IF THE MOB IN BROOKLYN COULD ONLY SEE ME NOW!
---WHILE IN A DUNGEON IN THE PALACE, THE ONCE PROUD GREEN SORCERESS LIES SHACKLED IN IRONS!
HOW STRANGE! MY ONLY HOPE FOR RESCUE LIES IN THE ARRIVAL OF MY SWORN ENEMY-- BLUE BOLT!
4

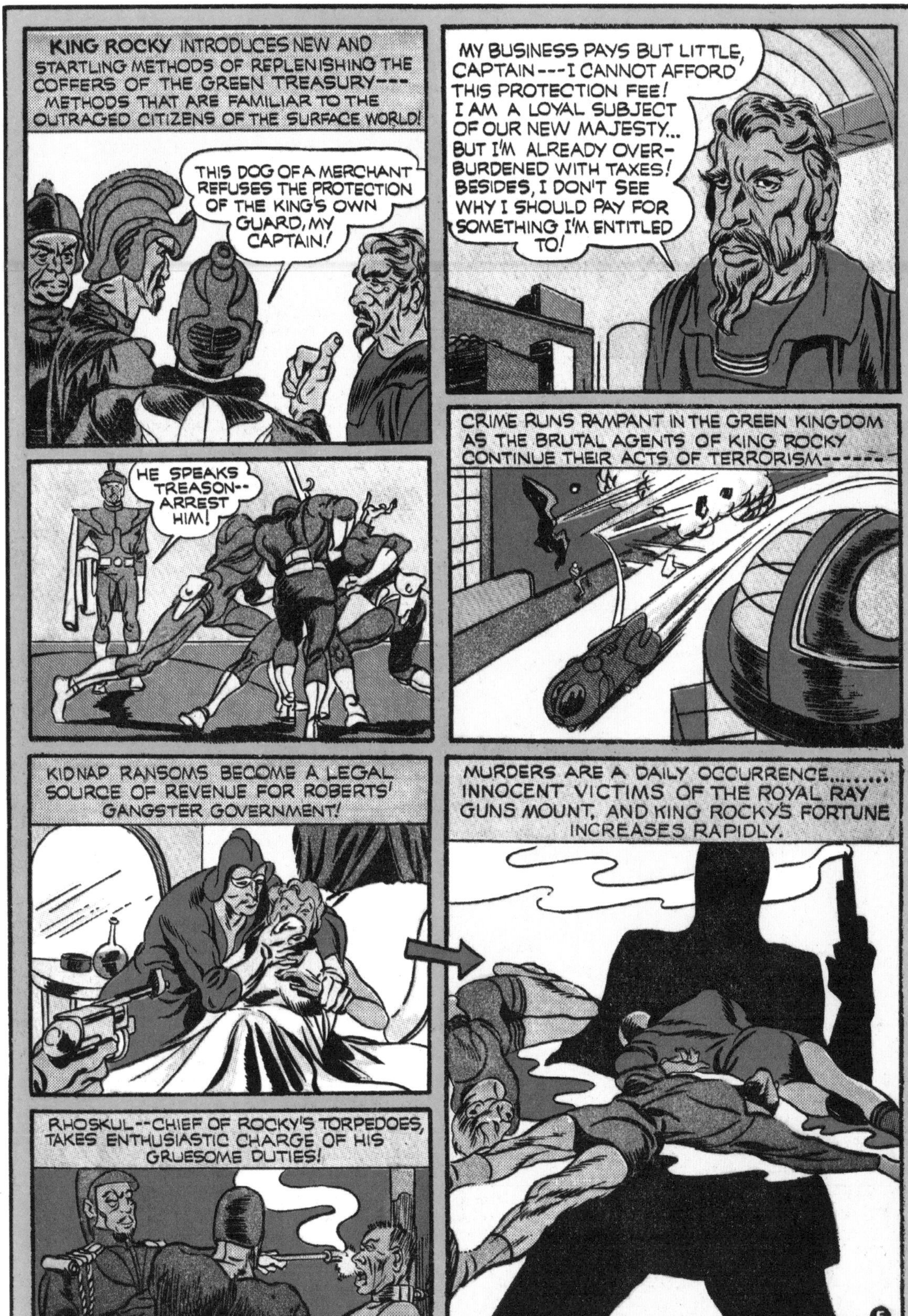
KING ROCKY INTRODUCES NEW AND STARTLING METHODS OF REPLENISHING THE COFFERS OF THE GREEN TREASURY--- METHODS THAT ARE FAMILIAR TO THE OUTRAGED CITIZENS OF THE SURFACE WORLD!
THIS DOG OF A MERCHANT REFUSES THE PROTECTION OF THE KING'S OWN GUARD, MY CAPTAIN!
MY BUSINESS PAYS BUT LITTLE, CAPTAIN ---I CANNOT AFFORD THIS PROTECTION FEE! I AM A LOYAL SUBJECT OF OUR NEW MAJESTY... BUT I'M ALREADY OVER-BURDENED WITH TAXES! BESIDES, I DON'T SEE WHY I SHOULD PAY FOR SOMETHING I'M ENTITLED TO!
HE SPEAKS TREASON-- ARREST HIM!
CRIME RUNS RAMPANT IN THE GREEN KINGDOM AS THE BRUTAL AGENTS OF KING ROCKY CONTINUE THEIR ACTS OF TERRORISM------
KIDNAP RANSOMS BECOME A LEGAL SOURCE OF REVENUE FOR ROBERTS' GANGSTER GOVERNMENT!
MURDERS ARE A DAILY OCCURRENCE........ INNOCENT VICTIMS OF THE ROYAL RAY GUNS MOUNT, AND KING ROCKY'S FORTUNE INCREASES RAPIDLY.
RHOSKUL--CHIEF OF ROCKY'S TORPEDOES, TAKES ENTHUSIASTIC CHARGE OF HIS GRUESOME DUTIES!
5

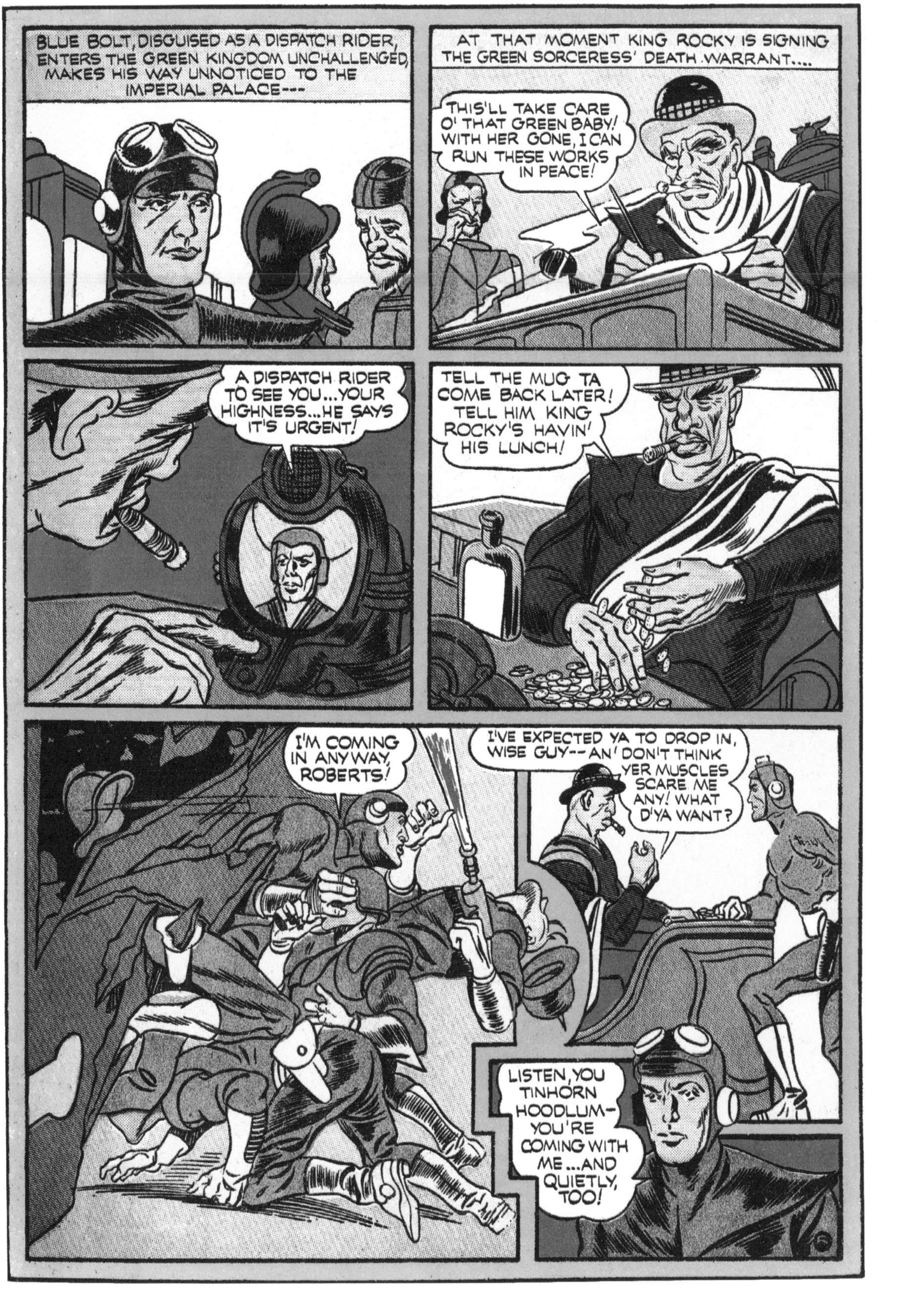
BLUE BOLT, DISGUISED AS A DISPATCH RIDER, ENTERS THE GREEN KINGDOM UNCHALLENGED, MAKES HIS WAY UNNOTICED TO THE IMPERIAL PALACE---
AT THAT MOMENT KING ROCKY IS SIGNING THE GREEN SORCERESS' DEATH WARRANT....
THIS'LL TAKE CARE O' THAT GREEN BABY! WITH HER GONE, I CAN RUN THESE WORKS IN PEACE!
A DISPATCH RIDER TO SEE YOU...YOUR HIGHNESS...HE SAYS IT'S URGENT!
TELL THE MUG TA COME BACK LATER! TELL HIM KING ROCKY'S HAVIN' HIS LUNCH!
I'M COMING IN ANYWAY, ROBERTS!
I'VE EXPECTED YA TO DROP IN, WISE GUY-- AN' DON'T THINK YER MUSCLES SCARE ME ANY! WHAT D'YA WANT?
LISTEN, YOU TINHORN HOODLUM- YOU'RE COMING WITH ME ...AND QUIETLY, TOO!

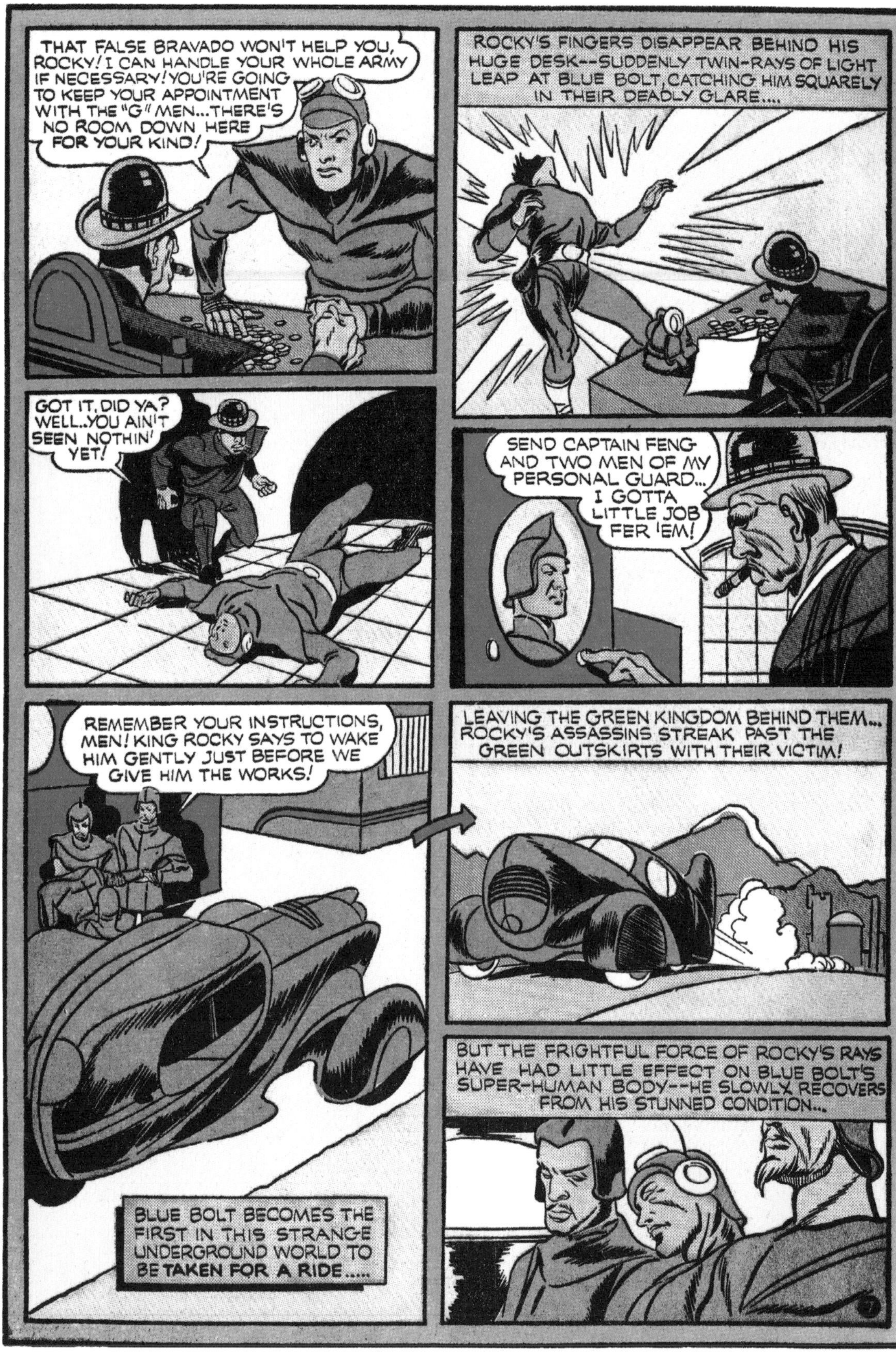
THAT FALSE BRAVADO WON'T HELP YOU, ROCKY! I CAN HANDLE YOUR WHOLE ARMY IF NECESSARY! YOU'RE GOING TO KEEP YOUR APPOINTMENT WITH THE "G" MEN...THERE'S NO ROOM DOWN HERE FOR YOUR KIND!
ROCKY'S FINGERS DISAPPEAR BEHIND HIS HUGE DESK--SUDDENLY TWIN-RAYS OF LIGHT LEAP AT BLUE BOLT, CATCHING HIM SQUARELY IN THEIR DEADLY GLARE....
GOT IT, DID YA? WELL..YOU AIN'T SEEN NOTHIN' YET!
SEND CAPTAIN FENG AND TWO MEN OF MY PERSONAL GUARD... I GOTTA LITTLE JOB FER 'EM!
REMEMBER YOUR INSTRUCTIONS, MEN! KING ROCKY SAYS TO WAKE HIM GENTLY JUST BEFORE WE GIVE HIM THE WORKS!
BLUE BOLT BECOMES THE FIRST IN THIS STRANGE UNDERGROUND WORLD TO BE TAKEN FOR A RIDE.....
LEAVING THE GREEN KINGDOM BEHIND THEM... ROCKY'S ASSASSINS STREAK PAST THE GREEN OUTSKIRTS WITH THEIR VICTIM!
BUT THE FRIGHTFUL FORCE OF ROCKY'S RAYS HAVE HAD LITTLE EFFECT ON BLUE BOLT'S SUPER-HUMAN BODY--HE SLOWLY RECOVERS FROM HIS STUNNED CONDITION...
7

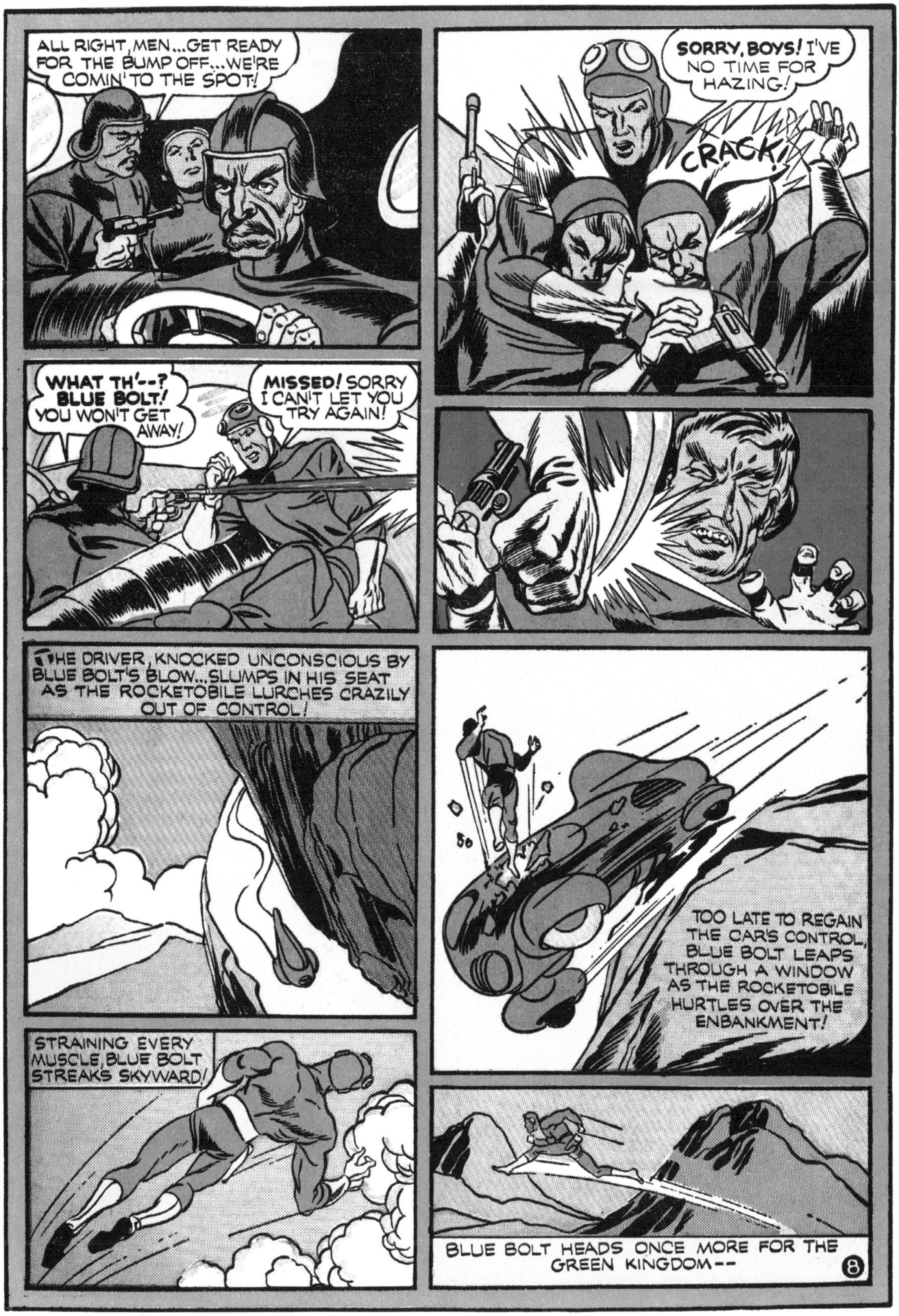
ALL RIGHT, MEN...GET READY FOR THE BUMP OFF...WE'RE COMIN' TO THE SPOT!
SORRY, BOYS! I'VE NO TIME FOR HAZING!
CRACK!
WHAT TH'--? BLUE BOLT! YOU WON'T GET AWAY!
MISSED! SORRY I CAN'T LET YOU TRY AGAIN!
THE DRIVER, KNOCKED UNCONSCIOUS BY BLUE BOLT'S BLOW...SLUMPS IN HIS SEAT AS THE ROCKETOBILE LURCHES CRAZILY OUT OF CONTROL!
TOO LATE TO REGAIN THE CAR'S CONTROL, BLUE BOLT LEAPS THROUGH A WINDOW AS THE ROCKETOBILE HURTLES OVER THE ENBANKMENT!
STRAINING EVERY MUSCLE, BLUE BOLT STREAKS SKYWARD!
BLUE BOLT HEADS ONCE MORE FOR THE GREEN KINGDOM--
8

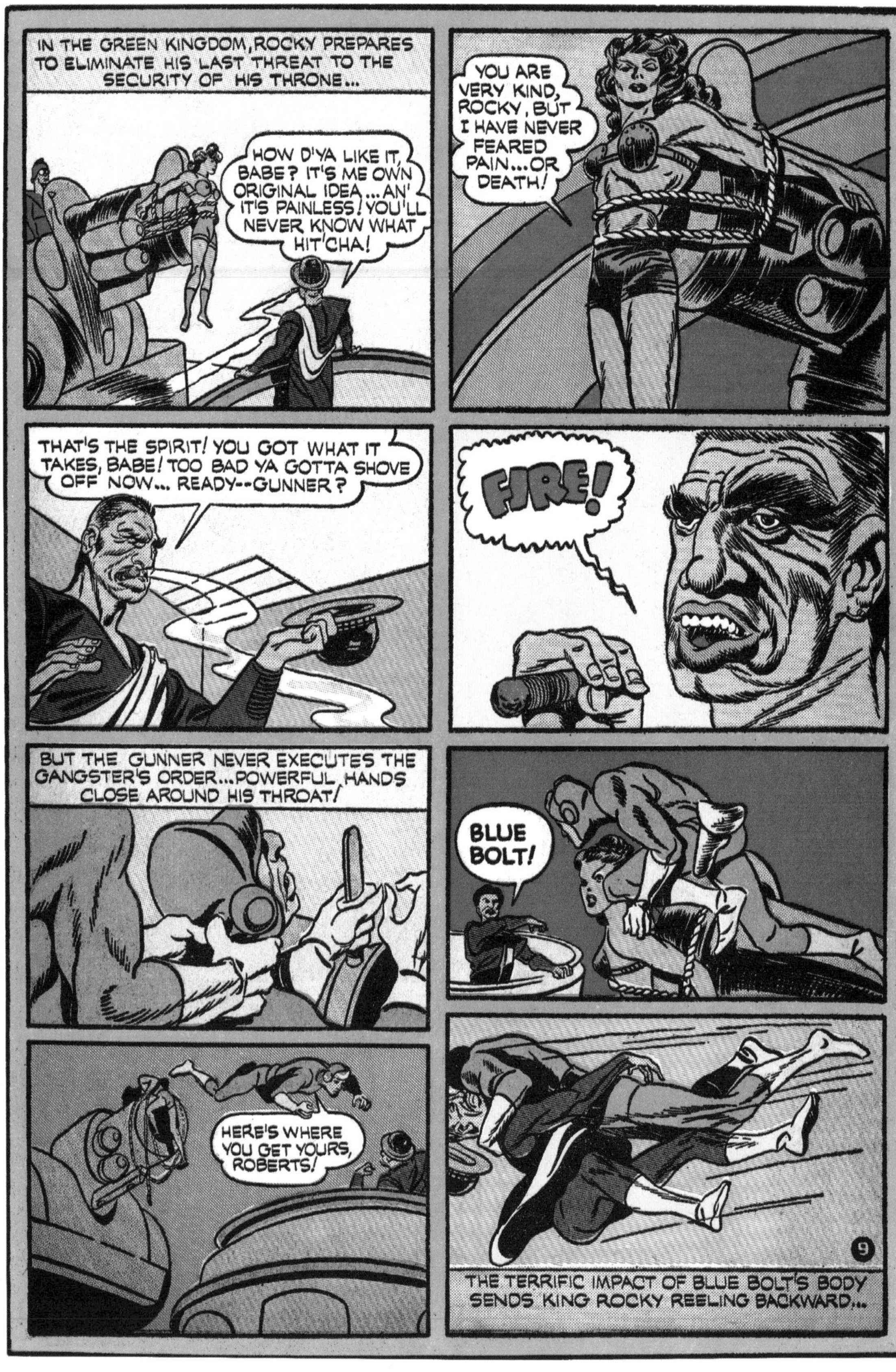
IN THE GREEN KINGDOM, ROCKY PREPARES TO ELIMINATE HIS LAST THREAT TO THE SECURITY OF HIS THRONE...
HOW D'YA LIKE IT, BABE? IT'S ME OWN ORIGINAL IDEA...AN' IT'S PAINLESS! YOU'LL NEVER KNOW WHAT HIT'CHA!
YOU ARE VERY KIND, ROCKY, BUT I HAVE NEVER FEARED PAIN...OR DEATH!
THAT'S THE SPIRIT! YOU GOT WHAT IT TAKES, BABE! TOO BAD YA GOTTA SHOVE OFF NOW... READY--GUNNER?
FIRE!
BUT THE GUNNER NEVER EXECUTES THE GANGSTER'S ORDER...POWERFUL HANDS CLOSE AROUND HIS THROAT!
BLUE BOLT!
HERE'S WHERE YOU GET YOURS, ROBERTS!
9
THE TERRIFIC IMPACT OF BLUE BOLT'S BODY SENDS KING ROCKY REELING BACKWARD...

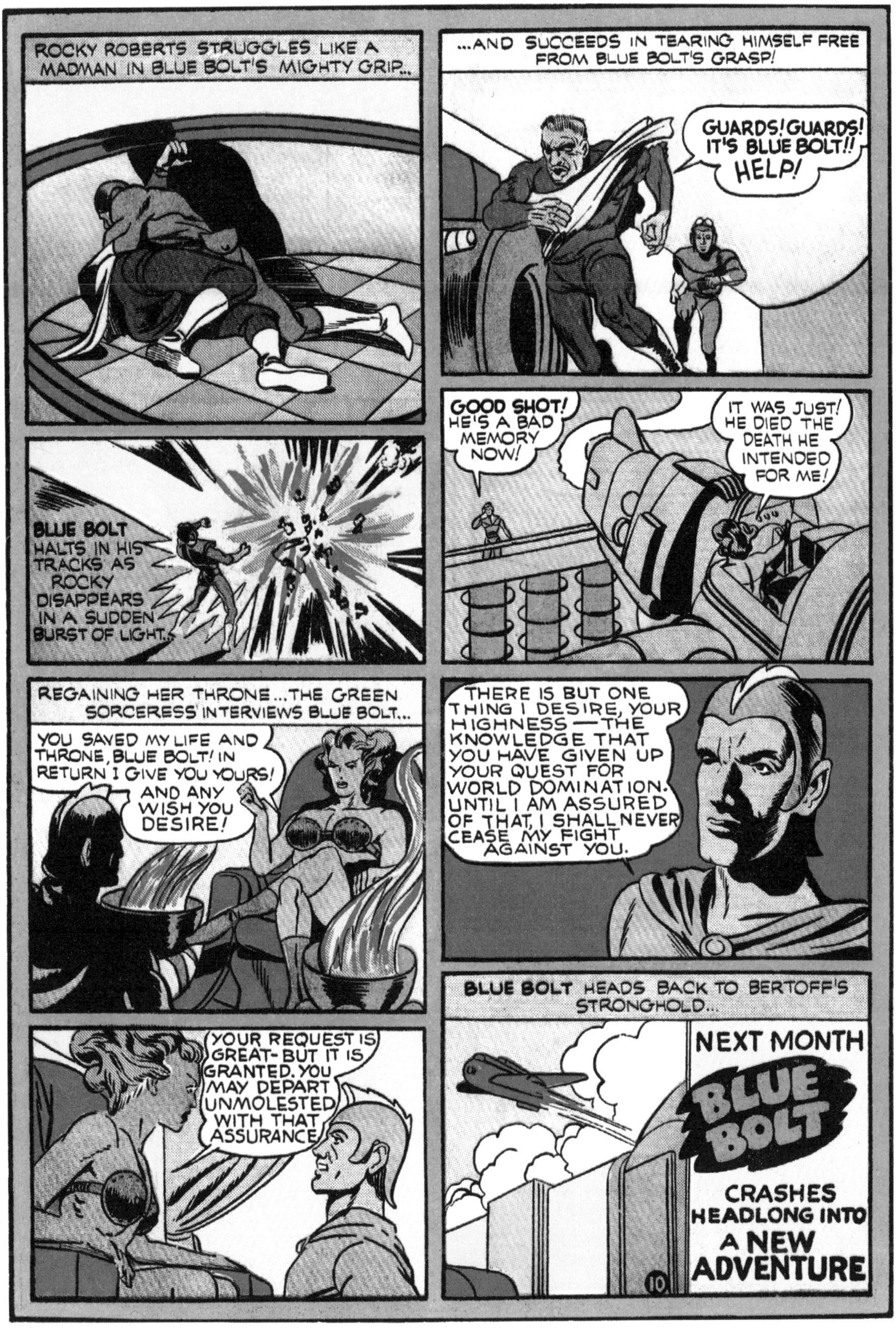
ROCKY ROBERTS STRUGGLES LIKE A MADMAN IN BLUE BOLT'S MIGHTY GRIP...
...AND SUCCEEDS IN TEARING HIMSELF FREE FROM BLUE BOLT'S GRASP!
GUARDS! GUARDS! IT'S BLUE BOLT!! HELP!
BLUE BOLT HALTS IN HIS TRACKS AS ROCKY DISAPPEARS IN A SUDDEN BURST OF LIGHT...
GOOD SHOT! HE'S A BAD MEMORY NOW!
IT WAS JUST! HE DIED THE DEATH HE INTENDED FOR ME!
REGAINING HER THRONE...THE GREEN SORCERESS INTERVIEWS BLUE BOLT...
YOU SAVED MY LIFE AND THRONE, BLUE BOLT! IN RETURN I GIVE YOU YOURS!
AND ANY WISH YOU DESIRE!
THERE IS BUT ONE THING I DESIRE, YOUR HIGHNESS — THE KNOWLEDGE THAT YOU HAVE GIVEN UP YOUR QUEST FOR WORLD DOMINATION. UNTIL I AM ASSURED OF THAT, I SHALL NEVER CEASE MY FIGHT AGAINST YOU.
YOUR REQUEST IS GREAT- BUT IT IS GRANTED. YOU MAY DEPART UNMOLESTED WITH THAT ASSURANCE
BLUE BOLT HEADS BACK TO BERTOFF'S STRONGHOLD...
NEXT MONTH
BLUE BOLT
CRASHES HEADLONG INTO A NEW ADVENTURE
10

BOOKS OF COMICS have been around since the first color newspaper comic strip, Richard Outcault's *Hogan's Alley*, which introduced the Yellow Kid in 1897. The following year the Kid appeared in the first ever book of comic strip reprints, *The Yellow Kid in McFadden's Flats*, and for the next thirty-five years hundreds of books of all shapes and sizes collected reprinted comic strips. One of the newspaper strip printers, Eastern Color Printing, discovered in 1933 that by shrinking a full-page tabloid strip fifty precent and by binding together tabloid-sized sheets folded in half, they could create a 7 ½ × 10-inch book containing a full reduced strip on each page. By such means Eastern created *Funnies on Parade*, the first "standard"-sized comic book. Eastern salesman Max C. "Charlie" Gaines sold the books to soap manufacturer Procter and Gamble, who disposed of the entire print-run of 10,000 within weeks by offering it as a coupon premium to its customers.

Another revolution occurred that autumn, when Gaines slapped ten-cent stickers on a few dozen of Eastern's second promotional giveaway comic book, the thirty-six-page *Famous Funnies: A Carnival of Comics*. As the story goes, he dropped them off on a Friday at several newsstands, and when he returned that Monday every issue had been sold, proving that there were dimes to be had. Several months later, Eastern convinced George Delacorte to publish the first ten-cent comic book, *Famous Funnies* no. 1, which repackaged fifty-two pages from *Funnies on Parade* and *Famous Funnies: A Carnival of Comics*, plus sixteen new pages of reprints. Earlier in the decade Delacorte had lost money on the first oversized tabloid-type comic book of all-original material, *The Funnies* (also printed by Eastern), and refused to commit to a new periodical, despite *Famous Funnies* selling out its 35,000 copies. Eastern Printing decided to take over the publishing itself, and with a cover date of July 1934 created the first standard-sized monthly newsstand ten-cent comic book.

Noticing that *Famous Funnies* was showing a profit by its third issue, Delacorte reconsidered in late 1935 and began publishing *Popular Comics*, leasing strips from the Chicago Tribune-New York News Syndicate, owners of *Dick Tracy*, *Gasoline Alley*, *Little Orphan Annie*, *Moon Mullins*, and *Terry and the Pirates*. With Delacorte now invested, others followed. Within months, the David McKay Company began its reprint book of King Features strips, *King Comics*, and United Feature Syndicate eliminated the middleman by publishing its own *Tip Top Comics*.

In late 1934, pulp writer and retired World War I cavalry officer Major Malcolm Wheeler-Nicholson created a new publishing enterprise, National Allied Publications, hiring pulp colleagues John Mahon as business manager and William Cook as managing editor. National published the second newsstand comic book with all-new original material, *New Fun Comics* (February 1935). Inspired heavily by Delacorte's unsuccessful *The Funnies*, *New Fun*'s 10 × 15-inch size and single-page stories insured its affinity with a Sunday tabloid section, which was precisely what the Major was after. He conceived the title as a way to pitch his strips to newspapers – not that any were ever interested. Unable to pay his mounting bill, the Major lost his distributor after six issues and cancelled *New Fun*.

Alarmed by *New Fun*'s demise and the Major's endless string of debts – which included their back salaries – Cook and Mahon decided to start their own comic book company, and settled up with Wheeler-Nicholson by agreeing

to take (some say swiping) half the art inventory. A few months later, Wheeler-Nicholson found a new distributor to be indebted to, Independent News, owned by soft-porn magazine magnate Harry Donenfeld (his most infamous titles were the *Spicy* line of pulps) and silent partner Paul Sampliner, with management handled by accountant Jack Liebowitz. A month before restarting the title as *More Fun Comics* no. 7 (January 1936), the Major published the third newsstand comic book, *New Comics*, this time complying with Donenfeld's demands that its format share the half-tabloid size of the profitable *Famous Funnies*. With its ninth issue, *More Fun* also adopted these dimensions, now the standard for comic books. Story page-counts inched up to four pages, taking another evolutionary step away from the single-page newspaper comic strip.

1. "Dr. Mystic," story by Jerry Siegel; art by Joe Shuster
*Comics Magazine* no. 1, May 1936

In late 1935, Wheeler-Nicholson's former associates Cook and Mahon formed the sixth comic book company, Comics Magazine Company, Inc. Its first book, *Comics Magazine* no. 1 (five issues later renamed *Funny Pages*) was art directed by the Major's former editor, Lloyd Jacquet, and consisted entirely of the pages Cook and Mahon claimed from National Allied's inventory.

The most historically significant of this material was the first and only appearance of Dr. Mystic, the Occult Detective, a two-page uncolored story by Cleveland's Jerry Siegel (1914–96) and Joe Shuster (1914–92). Notable for showing comic books' first flying caped figure (Mystic's ally, Zator), it is the earliest published precursor to Siegel and Shuster's "Superman," versions of which they had been pitching to newspapers since 1933. Dr. Mystic had appeared earlier as Dr. Occult in the final issue of *New Fun* (October 1935), and the plot line of Dr. Mystic, the Occult Detective picks up later in the year as Dr. Occult, the Mystic Detective in *More Fun* no. 14 (October 1936).

2. "Murder by Proxy," story and art by George E. Brenner
*Detective Picture Stories* no. 5, April 1937

Despite its title, Comics Magazine's *Funny Picture Stories* was the first comic book dedicated to non-humor themes: "Mystery, Thriller, Ace, Adventure, Western." The cover of no. 1 (a blown-up story panel) introduced the first masked comic book hero, The Clock, created by artist/writer George Brenner (c. 1913–1952). The Clock appeared simultaneously in CMC's *Funny Pages* no. 6 (November 1936), continuing for five issues in a two- or three-page serial (his two appearances in *Funny Picture Stories* were in self-contained seven-page stories). A month later Cook and Mahon published a third title, *Detective Picture Stories*, the first anthology comic book to focus on a single theme (its December 1936 cover date beat out Malcolm-Wheeler's *Detective Comics* by three months). This Clock story, "Murder by Proxy," appeared in *Detective Picture Stories* no. 5, its final issue. Note that each panel is numbered, as if the artist wasn't sure if readers, used to newspaper strips, could decipher a comic book.

In February 1937 CMC's fourth book, *Western Picture Stories*, tied Harry "A" Chesler's *Star Ranger Comics* as the first all-Western comic. Unfortunately, the demand for original material had not yet taken hold (the all-newspaper-reprint *Famous Funnies* was the only title showing a consistent profit) and, despite having pioneered several durable genres, in mid-1937 Cook and Mahon sold their interests in Comics Magazine Co. to I.W. Ullman and Frank Temerson, who continued the line as Ultem Publications until January 1938, when they in turn were taken over by Joe Hardie's new venture, Centaur Publications. As for the Clock, in late 1937 Brenner moved to Everett "Busy" Arnold's Quality Comics, bringing his creation with him.

3. "Dan Hastings"
story by Ken Fitch; art by Fred Guardineer
*Star Comics* no. 5, July 1937

Harry "A" Chesler started the first Manhattan comic book packaging service in early 1936, providing new material for the Cook/Mahon titles, as well as National Allied's. Chesler himself tried publishing in mid-1936, introducing the oversized (8 1/4 × 11 3/8 in.) *Star Comics* and *Star Ranger*, but turned the titles over to Ultem about six months later, and stayed on as editor (Ultem reduced the dimensions of both titles to standard format). As comic book historian Hames Ware has noted, "Ultem was probably a holding-company proposition that both the Cook/Mahon and Chesler titles fell into, as I don't think much if any original material appeared during Ultem's short reign."

Many early comic book artists got their start at Chesler's dingy shop on the fourth floor of an old 23rd Street warehouse with a temperamental elevator (seasoned artists climbed the stairs). Chesler artists from the first generation included William Allison, Rafael Astarita, Jack Binder, Charles Biro, Jack Cole, Fred Guardineer, Creig Flessel, Gill Fox, Paul Gustavson, Irwin Hasen, Mort Meskin, and Irv Novick, as many others came and went.

The first continuing comic book science fiction strip, "Dan Hastings" (written by staffer Ken Fitch), was initially shopped around by Chesler to the newspapers; early episodes by artist Clem Gretter in the first two issues of *Star* were reformatted to the classic six-panels-per-page comic book layout. In *Star* no. 3 (May 1937), Fine Arts graduate Fred Guardineer took over the feature, and his modern well-delineated style seemed tailor-made for the new medium.

4. "Dirk the Demon," story and art by Bill Everett
*Amazing Mystery Funnies* vol. 2, no. 3, March 1939

With books dated March 1938, Centaur's Joe Hardie ("Uncle Joe" to his readers) began publishing the titles he bought from Ultem, *Funny Pages* and *Funny Picture Stories*, and Chesler, *Star Comics* and *Star Ranger*. That summer Centaur began forging its own identity, first by revamping *Detective Picture Stories* (which hadn't seen print for over a year) as *Keen Detective Funnies*, then by publishing the first science-fiction-themed anthology, *Amazing Mystery Funnies*, cover dated August 1938.

*Amazing Mystery Funnies* introduced the work of artist/writer Bill Everett (1917–73), who spent two years at Boston's Vesper George School of Art before dropping out in 1935 to attempt a career in illustration. Looking for freelance work in 1938, Everett found out about comic books from a friend who had just broken into the field. "I wasn't actually interested in it at all; I was talked into it," Everett told interviewer Roy Thomas. "I sold my first page for two dollars – writing, penciling, inking, and all." He was hired by Centaur editor/art director Lloyd Jacquet and immediately tossed into the arena.

Everett's dashing art (including heroes in capes) and imaginative writing quickly made him one of the busiest creators in a brand new industry. "This was a beautiful part of the beginning of the field; we had nobody to imitate. All of us had idols in the daily comics, our Alex Raymonds, Milton Caniffs, and so forth, but we couldn't very well imitate them because our field was another expression of what they were doing." In mid-1939, Everett and Jacquet introduced the first superhero launched in his own title, *Amazing Man Comics*.

Everett's first work, for early issues of *AMF*, featured his creations Skyrocket Steele and Dirk the Demon. The artist himself makes a cameo in the opening panel of this Dirk episode, with the young hero leaping from his drawing board. While an adolescent hero was a sound idea, it became more commercially viable when paired with an adult mentor.

5. "The Flame," story by Will Eisner;
art by Lou Fine ("Basil Berold")
*Wonderworld Comics* no. 7, November 1939

Encouraged by the sales of *Detective Comics*, and heeding Jack Liebowitz's advice to get out of the smut business, Harry Donenfeld sat back while Wheeler-Nicholson's unpaid account continued to escalate. By late 1937, the Major was forced to default on his debt and, taking Donenfeld's advice, surrendered his company (now called "Detective Comics, Inc.," or "DC") into receivership; soon it became the property of Donenfeld and Sampliner, with day-to-day activity supervised by Liebowitz. *Detective Comics* editor Vin Sullivan remained, working on a new title, *Action Comics.*

In the summer of 1936, out-of-work nineteen-year-old artist Will Eisner opened up a comic book packaging shop with partner Samuel Maxwell ("Jerry") Iger. Eisner had met Iger that spring by answering a newspaper ad Iger placed soliciting artists for *Wow Comics*, a short-lived (four issues) comic book he was editing. As Eisner explained to R.C. Harvey, "...the only comic books being started were all reprinting newspaper comic strips...and it suddenly hit me, out of the blue, that they would run out of a supply of these strips very soon, and then there'll be an opportunity to sell original material, drawn especially for these comic books."

With Iger as salesman and Eisner as production manager and main artist, Eisner & Iger, Inc. got off the ground with Eisner's fifteen-dollar investment; enough to give him top billing and afford a month's rent for an office on 41st Street and Madison Avenue. To get around the problem that there were as yet hardly any comic book publishers, Iger struck a deal with Editors Press, an outfit that sold comics to foreign countries, and Eisner & Iger's earliest packaging appeared in the British magazines *Wags* and *Okay Comics Weekly*. Early Eisner art also appeared in a few 1937 issues of CMC's *Funny Pages* and *Western Picture Stories*.

Eisner & Iger finally hit domestic pay dirt in mid-1938 when pulp magazine publisher Fiction House decided to break into comics. Eisner came up with its first title, the oversized *Jumbo Comics*. To create a staff he placed an ad in the *New York Times*, and the next day found a line of artists out the door. Those first *Jumbo*s contain some of the earliest work by Eisner, Lou Fine, Bob Kane, Jack Kirby, and Mort Meskin. In late 1939, influenced by the success of Superman, Fiction House changed *Jumbo* to standard size, and ordered three new Eisner & Iger titles: *Fight Comics*, *Jungle Comics*, and *Planet Comics*.

Pasted up from various rejected strip submissions, Siegel and Shuster's first Superman story awkwardly lifted off in *Action Comics* no. 1 (June 1938). Though the kids loved it right off, it took DC almost a year to realize what it had stepped in. Donenfeld was said to have been so embarrassed by the character that he allowed Superman to appear only occasionally on *Action* covers until no. 19 (November 1939), by which time there was no question that comic books had at last found its cash cow and defining genre.

In early 1939, entrepreneur Victor Fox started a new comic book company, Fox Publications, in the same Lexington Avenue building as DC, only with a bigger office. In no uncertain terms, Fox told packagers Eisner & Iger to invent him another Superman. Eisner whipped up Wonder Man, giving him more or less identical powers. The hero appeared that March as the cover story of Fox's inaugural title, *Wonder Comics* (May 1939), but DC started copyright infringement proceedings as soon as it hit the stands, and on April 16 the courts awarded a permanent injunction that prevented any further appearances.

Undaunted, Fox changed the title to *Wonderworld* with issue no. 3 (July 1939) and quickly unveiled four other Eisner anthology titles: *Mystery Men Comics* (August 1939), *Fantastic Comics* (December 1939), *Science Comics* (February 1940), and *Weird Comics* (April 1940).

Artist Lou Fine joined the Eisner & Iger shop on *Jumbo* no. 4, taking over Jack Kirby's "The Count of Monte Cristo." Fine's figure-drawing skills and polished inking made him a natural for supermen, and Eisner assigned him *Wonderworld*'s flagship hero, the Flame. This example was written and probably laid out by Eisner (compare the similarity of these breakdowns with Eisner's "Yarko" story). Eisner and Fine also collaborated on celebrated covers for Fox and Quality. Eisner's usual method was to rough out the cover composition, then hand it off to Fine to tighten the pencils and ink the drawing – all under Eisner's watchful eye. He had come up with a way of getting good work out of his artists, as he explained to R.C. Harvey:

"It was the tail end of the Depression, and the most important thing that people wanted was a salary, a regular income. So I offered to pay weekly salaries instead of paying by the page. What that did for me was to give me total control of the quality of the art. If you have a freelancer who's getting paid so much a page and you ask him to change the page, he's going to resent that or demand more money. But if he's working on salary, he's going to say, 'I don't give a damn; I get my salary no matter what.' The only potential problem was getting production, getting the necessary quantity of pages completed. But strangely enough, it worked out fine. They were quite honest. I was gambling on their pride. And I was walking around like a German schoolmaster all day long, with my hands behind my back; exhorting them to do this, change that."

6. "Yarko the Great," story and art by Will Eisner
*Wonderworld Comics* no. 8, December 1939
Eisner originally planned to follow in the footsteps of his father, an off-Broadway set designer, and these ambitions can be felt in the impressive settings of this Yarko tale, done shortly before Eisner turned the character over to Bob Powell (née Stanley Robert Pawlowski). Eisner's method was to design a character and then let a staff member take the reins. He described the studio to R.C. Harvey in 2002:

"Imagine a big room. In the front of the big room was a little office, and that's where Iger's desk was. So when you came in the door, you came upon a desk normally occupied by a receptionist except that, in our case, Iger's desk was

there. Then you would go into the main room, and to the left as you entered was my desk. I had a roll-top desk and a drawing board. My drawing board was against the wall, and my desk was in front of me, facing the staff. Before me, all the way up to the window at the back, was the staff of people – very much like a classroom.

"Each one had a desk and a taboret [a stand for holding supplies]. Very early on, I organized it in a way that would give me an opportunity to direct production. When you're dealing with a five-dollars-per-page income, you have to watch your nickels pretty closely. Down the right-hand wall facing me were the pencilers – although penciling and inking were done by the same people. If you penciled it, you inked it. We eventually got some background people; and lettering was done by somebody else. And erasing and clean-up was done by young kids. Then I hit on the idea of using non-photo blue pencils, which eliminated the need to erase the artwork. Down the right-hand side was Jacob Kurtzberg – Jack Kirby – then a writer and then Mort Meskin. And down the center were Bob Powell, Lou Fine, George Tuska, and so on.

"We had to hire people from other fields. Lou Fine and Bob Powell had just gotten out of school; they came from Pratt. Lou Fine wanted to be an illustrator, Bob Powell too. They all wanted to be illustrators; nobody wanted to be a cartoonist. There was no background for comics. Nobody saw any future in this thing. It was just a quick buck, a steady way to make money."

The Eisner & Iger partnership lasted until late 1939, when Eisner sold his interest to Iger to start a smaller studio anchored by Fine and Powell. He formed a partnership with Everett "Busy" Arnold to produce the sixteen-page *Spirit* newspaper supplement and provide art for Quality titles. Iger continued as S.M. Iger Studios, supplying material for over a dozen publishers for the next twenty years. During the seventies Iger could be found at New York comic book conventions peddling his stockpile of original pages.

7. "Rex Dexter of Mars," story and art by Dick Briefer
*Mystery Men* no. 4, November 1939
A New Yorker born and bred, Dick Briefer (1915–82) had been with Eisner & Iger since the beginning, doing work for *Wow Comics* and a "Hunchback of Notre Dame" adaptation for *Jumbo* no. 1. He was never a part of the studio group, however. He always worked at home doing the whole ball of wax: scripting, penciling, inking, and lettering. Briefer's first continuing feature, Rex Dexter of Mars, was briefly tested in a Fox solo title, *Rex Dexter of Mars* no. 1 (Fall 1940), but unlike more popular *Mystery Men* offshoots *The Green Mask* (seventeen issues) and *The Blue Beetle* (sixty issues), Rex never caught on as a standalone feature.

When asked about the character in 1975, Briefer offered only, "Rex Dexter…I had absolutely no interest in, and the art was terrible…" His greatest comic book success came in adapting "Frankenstein" for *Prize Comics* beginning in 1940, and then in its own title from 1945 to 1949. Briefer revived the monster in 1952 to cash in on the horror craze, then left the field in 1954 and went into advertising.

8. "Cosmic Carson"
story and art by Jack Kirby (Michael Griffith)
*Science Comics* no. 4, May 1940
A child of New York's rough-and-tumble Lower East Side, Jack Kirby (1917–94) said he began teaching himself

how to draw at about the age of eleven. In a 1989 interview with the *Comics Journal*'s Gary Groth he explained, "I wanted to [draw]. I felt that I could. I'd been drawing all along because I felt anybody could do that. All human beings have the capability of doing what they want, what they're attracted to." Kirby was accepted to Pratt Institute when he was just fourteen, but he didn't last long. "I went to Pratt for a week. I wasn't the kind of student that Pratt was looking for. They wanted patient people who would work on something forever. I intended to get things done fast." He loved the medium from the start, one of the few who didn't view comic books as a stepping-stone. To Kirby, this was *it*. "Storytelling was my style. I was an artist, but not a self-proclaimed 'great' artist, just a common man who was working in a form of art which is now universal."

Kirby first joined Eisner & Iger in 1937, turning in three installments of the tabloid-inspired "Count of Monte Cristo" for the oversized *Jumbo Comics*. After working for a time at Lincoln News doing syndicated editorial work, he returned to Eisner & Iger in 1939 as they began their Fox account. Kirby told Groth, "Victor Fox was a character. He'd look up at the ceiling with a big cigar, this little fellow, very broad, going back and forth with his hands behind him saying, 'I'm the king of comics! I'm the king of comics!' And we would watch him. And of course we would smile because he was a genuine type. You'd see his type in a movie, and you'd recognize him."

This Cosmic Carson eight-pager is one of two Kirby stories from May 1940, his earliest solo work done in "comic book" style. Though signed "Michael Griffith" (another shop pseudonym), there is no mistaking Kirby's powerful drawings, action, and storytelling.

Though effective in spots, the story's arbitrary coloring can be distracting. On pages six and seven, for instance, Carson alternates from bare-chested to blue-chested, and his entire head turns red on page seven, panel one. But color gaffes of this kind rarely occur in these early stories (the task was handled by the printer), a tribute to the skill of these anonymous colorists.

9. "Stardust," story and art by Fletcher Hanks
*Fantastic Comics* no. 12, November 1940

Virtually everything we know about Fletcher Hanks (1887–1976) we owe to artist/writer/editor Paul Karasik, whose collection, *I Shall Destroy All the Civilized Planets!*, rescued this unique creator from a sixty-year sojourn on the comic book scrap heap – aside from the 1983 appearance of a Stardust story in *Raw* no. 5, where many contemporary Hanks fans enjoyed their first intoxicating taste of his work (including Karasik, *Raw*'s associate editor).

An abusive husband and father and an alcoholic, Hanks had been estranged from his family for almost a decade and he was in his fifties when he embarked on his brief career in comics, more or less exclusively through the Eisner & Iger shop (though always as a freelancer, never as part of the "bullpen"). Hanks' singular, obsessive – and at times unintentionally hilarious – approach found a fortuitous opening in comics' formative period; his work would have been unthinkable only a year or two later.

10. "The Comet," story and art by Jack Cole
*Pep Comics* no. 3, April 1940

M.L.J. Comics (which stood for the first names of its owners: Morris Coyne, Louis Silberkleit, and company head John Goldwater) entered the field with *Blue Ribbon Comics* no. 1 (November 1939), an anthology starring Rang-A-Tang the Wonder Dog. The book relied heavily on the Chesler shop, as did the superhero titles that closely followed: *Top Notch Comics* (December 1939), *Pep Comics* (January 1940), and *Zip Comics* (February 1940). M.L.J.'s greatest success came in 1941 with the debut of Bob Montana's "Archie," who has kept them in the black to this day.

Jack Cole (1914–58) got his start at Chesler's studio in early 1938, doing big-foot cartoons for *Funny Picture Stories, Star Comics* and *Funny Pages*. When comic books began to shift toward serious material, Cole did his first adventure story, "Little Dynamite," for Centaur's *Keen Detective Funnies* vol. 2, no. 6 (February 1939). In late 1939 Cole made his initial attempt at a superhero, inventing The Comet for *Pep Comics* no. 1. But Cole had painted himself into a corner with this very limited hero, and after four tries abandoned the character for others to wrestle with.

The Comet's power, a disintegrating ray that shot out of his eyes, was more often than not directed at his adversary's head. After evaporating four criminals in his debut, the Comet sends several more to fiery deaths by burning a hole in their dirigible in *Pep* no. 2 (February 1940). By the Comet's sixth appearance, his reputation preceding him, criminals would often just shout, "I give up! Don't kill me!" thereby eliminating any tension in the storyline. Finally, in *Pep* no. 17 (July 1941), the Comet becomes the first superhero to die in action, bequeathing not only his girl friend Thel but also his slot in *Pep* to his kid brother Bob as the avenging Hangman – who turned out to be every bit as brutal as his predecessor.

In this example, the Comet's third appearance, Cole's storytelling reaches new levels of sophistication. His amusing banter between the two villains establishes their mutual contempt, the flaw in their relationship that hastens their demise. Fluid breakdowns build to a climax on page five, with the Comet's murderous rampage too spectacular to be contained in a typical comic book grid.

11. "Fero, Planet Detective"
story and art by Al Bryant ("Allison Brant")
*Planet Comics* no. 5, May 1940

Though hardly representative of the *Planet* imprint, which specialized in pulpish science fiction and *Flash Gordon*-inspired space operas, this bizarre little horror tale was hard to resist. It seems to be the first published work of artist Al Bryant (c. 1917–93), who would have been still attending New York's Pratt Institute when he sold it to Eisner. After graduating in the summer of 1940, Bryant joined Iger's studio and became a fixture at Quality Comics.

12. "Fantomah, Mystery Queen of the Jungle"
story and art by Fletcher Hanks
*Jungle Comics* no. 4, April 1940

Not to be outdone by Stardust, "the most remarkable man that ever lived," Fletcher Hanks offers bipolar jungle heroine Fantomah, "the most remarkable woman ever known." Hanks never gets around to actually describing her powers other than "strange," providing him the latitude to add to them as the plot warrants. It's still enough to qualify Fantomah as the medium's first female superhero. In this story Hanks combines two common motifs of the medium's postwar years, hypodermic syringes and gorillas, thus reinforcing his status as a comic book visionary.

Hanks worked in comic books for about sixteen months, beginning with Stardust and Space Smith stories in the first issue of *Fantastic* (December 1939), ending with Fantomah in *Jungle* no. 15 (March 1941). In that short span he left behind forty-nine stories before vanishing into the ether.

You'll see a lot more of Fantomah in the eagerly awaited *You Shall Die by Your Own Creation!*, Paul Karasik's follow-up to *I Shall Destroy All the Civilized Planets!* that neatly wraps up Hanks' complete comic book work.

13. "Marvelo, Monarch of Magicians"
story by Gardner Fox; art by Fred Guardineer
*Big Shot Comics* no. 1, May 1940

McNaught Newspaper Syndicate entered comic book publishing in 1940 with its Columbia Comics Corporation, and lured Vin Sullivan away from DC to edit. Columbia concentrated on a single regular title, *Big Shot Comics*, mixing reprints of McNaught features (*Charlie Chan*, *Dixie Dugan*, *Joe Palooka*, et al.) with Sullivan's new heroes, the Skyman, the Face, and Marvelo. Though *Big Shot* would last until the late forties, McNaught always seemed a bit uncomfortable with this superhero business, and gradually eased them out completely from its covers in favor of Joe Palooka. This lack of support for original material would drive Sullivan to leave Columbia in 1943 and form his own company, Magazine Enterprises (ME).

DC alumni Mart Bailey, Fred Guardineer, Ogden Whitney, and writer Gardner Fox liked Sullivan and followed him to *Big Shot*. Guardineer was the logical choice for Marvelo, having done DC's Zatara the Master Magician, and later taking over Mr. Mystic on Eisner's *Spirit* section when Bob Powell entered the military. In his *Great Comic Book Artists*, Ron Goulart writes:

"[Guardineer's] style was almost fully formed from the start. He seems always to have thought in terms of the entire page, never the individual panel. Each of his pages is a thoughtfully designed whole, giving the impression sometimes that Guardineer is arranging a series of similar snapshots into an attractive overall pattern, a personal design that will both tell the story clearly and be pleasing to the eye. He was another artist who very early understood that a comic book page is not a newspaper page."

Marvelo was cancelled in *Big Shot* no. 20 (Dec. 1941), but Guardineer had already left a year earlier, moving on to Quality and then joining Sullivan at ME. After twenty years in comics with little to show for it, Guardineer left the field in 1955 and spent the rest of his career working as a mail carrier at his Long Island post office. He kept up his art skills by doing occasional promos for local organizations, such as the fishing school of the Babylon Tuna Club.

14. "The Face," story by Gardner Fox; art by Mart Bailey ("Michael Blake")
*Big Shot Comics* no. 1, May 1940

Artist Mart Bailey broke into comic books in the late thirties, teaming up with Jerry Siegel on a string of back-up features (including "Bart Regan, Spy") in 1939 issues of *Detective Comics* before leaving DC for Columbia in 1940. He was assigned the Face, based on an offbeat idea by Sullivan. Though the character had remarkable staying power (undoubtedly due to Bailey's fine artwork), by 1947 its shock value had worn off completely. Bailey continued the Face sans mask as detective Tony Trent until *Big Shot*'s final issue, no. 104 (August 1949).

15. "The Skyman," story by Gardner Fox;
art by Ogden Whitney ("Paul Dean")
*Big Shot Comics* no. 2, June 1940

The Skyman, a cross-pollinating of the aviator and superhero genres, was one of the most durable heroes of the 1940s, appearing in 101 issues of *Big Shot*. Though not technically "super," he usually got the upper hand with his "Stagmatic" gun ("a weapon that can paralyze or kill"), and while he may not have used it to kill anyone in this story, he does toss a crook out a window to his death for pulling a gun on him. Drawn by the capable Ogden Whitney, the Skyman seems to have been conceived as the most indefatigable hero in comics, finishing out this eleven-page endurance test thoroughly worn out and with a gaping gunshot wound. But he accepts it all good-naturedly. After all, he muses, "What's a wound and tiredness – compared with the safety of a hundred million U.S. citizens?"

16. "Silver Streak," story and art by Jack Cole ("Ralph Johns")
*Silver Streak Comics* no. 4, May 1940

Publisher Arthur Bernhard had been involved in publishing at least since the mid-twenties; in 1924 he became (with future DC partner Paul Sampliner) one of the partners of Eastern Distributing until it went bankrupt in 1931. After a string of unsuccessful magazines, Bernhard turned to comic books in 1939 with *Silver Streak Comics,* naming it after his new Pontiac. Early issues contain artists and writers from both the Chesler shop (Jack Cole, Will Harr, John Hampton) and Funnies, Inc. (Larry Antonette, Malcolm Kildale, Arthur Pinajian, Joe Simon). Cole is listed as editor in issue no. 7, and he may have had the role from the start.

*Silver Streak* was unique in that its original cover character was a villain, Cole's monolithic creation the Claw, ruler of the tiny fictional island of Ricca, "A mammoth creature of supernatural powers who keeps a constant reign of terror over the island's 10,000 inhabitants!" In issue two Cole calls him, "A monster of miraculous powers who is out to dominate the universe!" and just to make sure you know this guy is not to be trusted, he pairs him up with Hitler. Eventually somebody must have caught on that a megalomaniacal murderous monster wasn't the best choice to wrap a title around, for the Claw disappears by the third issue (though he would return) and is replaced with a brand new hero called...Silver Streak!

Silver Streak's origin by Joe Simon (*Silver Streak* no. 3, March 1940) is one of the most contrived and convoluted stories of the early golden age, and that's saying something. In his next appearance, this story, Cole takes over the character and smoothes out the rough edges, giving Silver Streak a proper long-underwear costume (Simon dressed him as a civilian) and the ability to fly and run amazingly fast. By the way, those big insects are a holdover from Simon's opus, and mercifully vanish from future episodes.

17. "The Claw Battles the Daredevil"
story and art by Jack Cole
*Silver Streak Comics* no. 7, January 1941

Jack Cole turns in a whopping thirty-eight pages for *Silver Streak*'s seventh issue, commencing with this sixteen-page epic based on the novel idea of pitting a superhero (the Daredevil, in his second appearance) against a super villain (the Claw returns!). Here we find Jack Cole at last having unabashed fun with his characters, setting the stage for his most famous and enduring creation, Plastic

Man, later that year in Quality's *Police Comics*. (By the way, Daredevil's aside in page twelve's last panel refers to Cole's back-up feature, "Dickie Dare, Boy Inventor.")

## 18. "Spacehawk," story and art by Basil Wolverton
*Target Comics* vol. 1, no. 11, December 1940

In mid-1939, Lloyd Jacquet left Centaur and (with former Comics Magazine owner John Mahon and Centaur sales director Frank Torpey) formed a new independent packaging service, Funnies, Inc. Bill Everett was the first onboard, followed by other Centaur artists Carl Burgos, Paul Gustavson, and Ben Thompson. The first Funnies, Inc. package was *Marvel Comics* no. 1 (November 1939), a landmark title published by Martin Goodman's new Timely Comics that introduced the first Marvel superheroes, Burgos' Human Torch and Everett's Sub-Mariner. (Seventy years later the company is still going strong as a subsidiary of media powerhouse Marvel Entertainment, Inc.)

In late 1939, magazine titan Curtis Publishing, whose titles included *Ladies' Home Journal* and the *Saturday Evening Post*, launched a comic book imprint, Novelty Press, and hired Funnies, Inc. to package its two titles, *Target Comics* and *Blue Bolt Comics*.

A long-distance member of the Funnies, Inc. team was the inimitable Basil Wolverton (1909–1978), whose first comic book work appeared in Globe Syndicate's shortlived *Circus the Comic Riot* no. 1 (June 1938). Residing in Vancouver, Washington, Wolverton was one of the few artists outside of New York City; he had to mail his art crosscountry. During a 1939 trip to Manhattan to pitch his science fiction strips, Wolverton approached Jacquet, who accepted "Space Patrol" for Centaur's *Amazing Mystery Funnies*. After securing the Novelty account, Jacquet asked Wolverton for a new space hero. The result was Spacehawk, "Lone Wolf of the Void," who began in the fifth issue of *Target Comics* (June 1940). Wolverton had a day job as foreman at the local cannery, and he often had to draw through the night to meet his deadlines.

Though Spacehawk lasted until *Target*'s thirty-fourth issue (December 1942), by his tenth episode he was fighting Nazis on Earth instead of vulture men in space, to comply with Novelty's wish that the character contribute to anti-fascist propaganda. By the May 1941 issue of *Target*, Spacehawk's subtitle was no longer "Superhuman Enemy of Crime" but "Defender of America." Wolverton complained to Dick Voll in 1971 that this ruined his creation. "It took the zip from the strip to relegate the character to ordinary Earth backgrounds, and so he lasted only a short while thereafter. Within a few months the strip had lost its appeal and was shoved out." This story, Spacehawk's sixth appearance, represents Wolverton at the height of his engagement.

## 19. "Sub-Zero," story and art by Bill Everett
*Blue Bolt Comics*, vol. 1, no. 5, October 1940

Bill Everett's output at Novelty began in the first four issues of *Target* with the Western hero Bulls-Eye Bill, followed by five installments of The Chameleon. Larry Antonette introduced "The Sub-Zero Man" in *Target Comics* no. 1 (February 1939), and Everett picked up the character four issues later, streamlining its sobriquet in the process. Everett had an affinity for water in his work, so the iceman would have been a natural for him. But he seems to have had his hands full with covers and stories for two other "wet" features, Timely's Sub-Mariner and Hydroman

for Eastern Color's new title, *Heroic Comics*, and this deliciously creepy episode was Everett's only stab at Sub-Zero.

## 20. "Blue Bolt"
story by Joe Simon; art by Joe Simon and Jack Kirby
*Blue Bolt Comics*, vol. 1, no. 10, March 1941

*Blue Bolt Comics* was based on a strip Joe Simon (b. 1913) had submitted to Jacquet, who used it months later as part of the package to cement the deal with Novelty. The publisher not only liked the character but decided to name one of its books after it (though Simon complained they never paid him for the title). Simon's submission strip kicked off *Blue Bolt* no. 1, with succeeding issues containing his earliest collaborations with future partner Jack Kirby.

Simon and Kirby met when their respective tenures at Fox overlapped. After parting ways with Eisner & Iger in late 1939, Victor Fox started an in-house studio, and hired Simon to run it as his new editor in chief. Kirby (still known as Jacob Kurtzberg) was one of the artists slaving away at fifteen dollars a week, and he became enamored of Simon. "I had never met a guy like Joe. I'd never met a guy who wasn't a New Yorker. Joe looked like a politician. I said, 'Gee, isn't that wonderful?' Joe was an impressive guy." Eventually Kirby asked his editor if he had any extra work he could do at home. Simon had plenty, but not for Fox: "I had taken on more assignments than I could handle so the announcement that Jacob was ready to moonlight with me was good news." Unbeknownst to the king of comics, they opened a one-room office on West 45th Street and, beginning with Blue Bolt, got to work. Simon recalls the young Kirby in his book, *The Comic Book Makers*:

"Jacob had a great flair for comics. He could take an ordinary script and make it come alive with his dramatic interpretations. I would write the script on the boards as we went along, sketch in rough layouts and notations, and Jacob would follow up by doing more exact penciling. I did the inking with a brush to make it go faster (brush work dried faster than the pen).

"Jacob would cringe when the phone rang. Once I was in the middle of a particularly involved scene and snapped, 'Answer it, will you, Jake, for Christ's sake.'

"'I can't,' he said. 'Maybe it's Victor Fox!'"

"I couldn't blame Jacob for fearing to give up a steady job, but for fifteen bucks a week?"

Simon left Fox after his contract expired, and Kirby got up the nerve to follow him three months later. Simon struck a deal with Timely's Martin Goodman to invent new characters, and he hit the bulls-eye with Captain America, an idea lifted from M.L.J.'s patriotic hero, the Shield. Convinced he had a hit, Goodman introduced the feature in its own title, *Captain America* no. 1 (May 1941). Sure enough, it sold out, and the next issue's print-run topped a million. Anointed as Timely's new editor and art director respectively, Simon and Kirby were promised fifteen percent of the profits.

But ten best-selling issues of *Captain America* yielded not a dime of profit-sharing for the team, so they left Timely for DC, with their vacuum filled by nineteen-year-old office boy (and Goodman's second cousin) Stan Lee.

Comic book heroes would never be the same after Captain America. As the country braced for war, superhuman enemies of crime turned into shills for the American cause, enlisted to safeguard the homeland and battle the Axis villains. Their freewheeling days were over.

G.S.

Thanks: Jim Amash, Thomas Andre, John Benson, Paul Baresh, Robert Beerbohm, Lee Boyett, Glenn Bray, Sean Burns, Craig Carlson, Howard Leroy Davis, Al Dellinges, the Will Eisner estate, Ray Funk, Michael T. Gilbert, Ron Goulart, William Paul Huey, Paul Karasik, Denis Kitchen, John Lind, Bruce Mason, John Morrow, Ken Quattro, Bill Schelly, Bhob Stewart, Kristy Valenti, Hames Ware, Dylan Williams, Monte Wolverton, Lena Zwalve
Shoutout: Paige Burns; Special thanks: Jim Vadeboncoeur, Jr.; Impossible without: Jon Berk, Bud Plant

References: Jerry Bails, "Who's Who of American Comics" (www.bailsproject.com); Mike Benton, *The Comic Book in America* and *Masters of Imagination*; Jon Berk, various writings; Ron Goulart, *The Great Comic Book Artists* and *Ron Goulart's Great History of Comic Books*; Gary Groth, Michael Dean, et al., editors, *The Comics Journal*, various issues; R.C. Harvey, *The Art of the Comic Book*; Gerard Jones, *Men of Tomorrow*; Don Markstein's Toonopedia (www.toonopedia.com); Joe Simon, *The Comic Book Makers*; Jim Steranko, *The Steranko History of Comics* (vol. 2); Roy Thomas, editor, *Alter Ego*, various issues; *Illustrator Biographies* (www.bpib.com); Monte Wolverton, *Basil Wolverton in Space*

Misc. credits: page 2: *Green Mask* no. 3 (Winter 1940-41), cover by Edd Ashe; page 3: *Mystery Men* no. 2 (September 1939), cover by Will Eisner and Lou Fine; page 14: Comics Magazine ad (December 1936); page 32: Fox ad (August 1939); page 42: Fox ad (September 1939); page 66: Fox ad (Winter 1940-41); page 83: M.L.J. ad (April 1941); page 84: Fiction House ad (June 1940); page 98: *Big Shot* no. 2, back cover by Ogden Whitney (June 1940); page 126: *Silver Streak* no. 5, back cover by Jack Cole (July 1940); page 154: Novelty Press ad (December 1940)

FANTAGRAPHICS BOOKS
7563 Lake City Way NE
Seattle, WA 98115

Editor, Design and Production: Greg Sadowski
Cover design: Jacob Covey
Production assistance: Jon Berk, Craig Carlson, Jim Vadeboncoeur, Jr.
Promotion: Eric Reynolds
Publishers: Gary Groth and Kim Thompson



To receive a free catalog of comics call 1-800-657-1100 or write us at the address above or visit the Fantagraphics website at www.fantagraphics.com.

Distributed in the U.S. by W.W. Norton and Company, Inc. (212-354-5500)
Distributed in Canada by Canadian Manda Group (416-516-0911)
Distributed in the United Kingdom by Turnaround Distribution (208-829-3009)

Set in Jovica Veljović's Esprit and Christian Schwartz's Neutraface

First Fantagraphics Books edition: February 2009
ISBN 978-1-56097-971-5
Printed in Malaysia

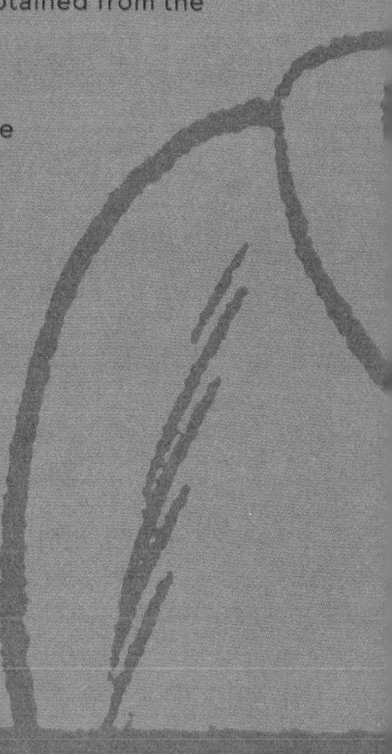